"RECONOMICS should be mandatory reading for Mayors, Chief Executives & Directors of Planning in cities and regions."
—- RICK FINC, PRINCIPAL, RFA DEVELOPMENT PLANNING.

"RECONOMICS is a must-read for every mayor, resilience activist, planning commissioner and urban redevelopment professional who has been frustrated in their attempts to revitalize a place. It succinctly describes why most revitalization plans fail, analyzes what's missing, and provides a simple, easy-to-follow strategic process for success."
—- KEVIN L. MAEVERS, D.MGMT., AICP; PRESIDENT, ARIVITAS STRATEGIES, VICE DIRECTOR OF POLICY, IES, CA CHAPTER, AMERICAN PLANNING ASSOCIATION.

"Storm Cunningham is so far ahead of the community revitalization game, I'm in awe."
—- SARAH SIELOFF, EXECUTIVE DIRECTOR, CCLR (2019).

"Storm Cunningham's RECONOMICS transformed our latest project, which uses his 3Re strategy."
—DUMAS F. LAFONTANT, DIRECTOR, LOWER ROXBURY COALITION, BOSTON, MASSACHUSETTS

"RECONOMICS hits the nail on the head!"
—NALIN SENEVIRATNE, DIRECTOR OF CITY CENTRE DEVELOPMENT, SHEFFIELD, ENGLAND

"Storm's RECONOMICS Process raises the bar for community and regional revitalization. It's a powerful package, succinctly capturing the process that we have doggedly tried to identify over time, not always knowing the next step. The RECONOMICS Process brings a holistic dimension to redevelopment, inextricably linking vision and task."
— ERIC BONHAM, P.ENG, PARTNERSHIP FOR WATER SUSTAINABILITY IN BC, FORMER DIRECTOR, BC MINISTRIES OF ENVIRONMENT & MUNICIPAL AFFAIRS

RECONOMICS

The Path To Resilient Prosperity

Storm Cunningham

RECONOMICS Copyright © 2020 by Storm Cunningham. All Rights Reserved.

All rights reserved. No part of this book may be reproduced in any form or by any electronic or mechanical means including information storage and retrieval systems, without permission in writing from the author. The only exception is by a reviewer, who may quote short excerpts in a review.

Cover designed by Brijmohan Chourasiya.

Storm Cunningham, RE
Visit my website at StormCunningham.com

Printed in the United States of America

First Printing: January 2020
RECONOMICS Institute

ISBN-9781657011724

CONTENTS

PREFACE - Holy Grail: Fixing Economy, Society, Nature & Climate Together...4
INTRODUCTION - Why Your Next Small Renewal Project Could Trigger Massive Ongoing Revitalization. 14
PART A - CONTEXT: The Challenges of Creating Resilient Prosperity..............30
Chapter 1 - TRENDS & TERMINOLOGY: OUR Shift from Adaptive Conquest to Adaptive Renewal..........32

    The Adaptive Renewal Megatrend 32
    Adaptive Management..........35
    Surprise! 44
    Terminology and Concepts..........45
    The Rise of Fixers..........51
    Restorative Sprawl..........55

Chapter 2 - THE CRISIS RESTORATION ECONOMY: ReCOVERY, REvitalization & Resilience SHOULD BE ACHIEVED TOGETHER. 56

    RE: A Prefix-Based Strategy for Global Revitalization via Policymaking. 61
    Regarding Demolition 62
    Wabi-Sabi: Some decrepit structures need neither renewal nor demolition to revitalize a place...just promotion..........63
    Finance & Tax Policies for Resilient Prosperity..........77
    Revitalizing Taxation Strategies 80
    Tax Increment Financing (TIF)..........83
    GreenTIF..........86
    Adaptive Funding 89
    A Climate Restoration Economy Based on Numbers, Assets and People 91
    Regenerative Capitalism 93

Chapter 3 - THE PROBLEM: Much Activity and Planning; Not Much Strategy, Process or Progress. 95

    The Devitalizing Power of Silos 98

Boosting Your Strategic Awareness...102
Planning Without a Strategy is Planning to Fail...107
The Problems With Plans: Most are just a formality, and over 95% have neither a strategy nor AN implementation process..107
From Perpetual Planning to Resilient Prosperity..114
What Triggers Devitalization?...121
The Zero-Sum Approach to Revitalization..122
Revitalization is Messy...124
Fragmented Renewal 127

Chapter 4 - EQUITY & INCLUSION: Revitalizing Our Institutions to Create Resilient Prosperity For All. 129

The Strategic Importance of Equity AND Inclusion 134
Revitalizing Our Institutions to Revitalize Our World....................................137
Land Banks + Community Land Trusts: An inclusive, equitable, revitalizing marriage?..142
Motivating, Recognizing & Tracking Revitalization..143
Recivilizing 147
Fixing our broken future 150

PART B - STRATEGY: Mastering the Missing Key to Success, to Fix Your Present and Future Together. 152

Chapter 5 - REVELATION: Seeing Strategies that Are Invisible to Others.........155

Strategic Thinking on Main Street...156
Strategic Thinking in South Africa..158
Strategic Thinking in Special Forces...159
Strategic Thinking on Gentrification 162
Good Strategies are so Succinct, They Look Like No-Brainers........................169
Strategy Failures at the National Level 171
Fixing the Present and Future Together..172
Community Leaders Awaken to their Strategic Vacuum................................178

Chapter 6 - THE PARTIAL SOLUTION: How to Create a Vision and a Strategy...and Who Should Do It. 181

The Right Vision and Map Directs Us to the Right Goals. The Right Strategy Drives Us to Success..183
How Are the Right Strategies Created? 187
Who Should Create Your Strategy?...188
How Qualified Are You to Create a Strategy for Your City? Maybe More Than You Think. 191

Tactics versus Strategies 192
Timing, Scope, and Starting Point 194
Reframing Assumptions..196
The Role of Governments in Advancing Resilient Prosperity 197
The Role of Foundations in Advancing Resilient Prosperity 201
Partnering with a Community Foundation for Resilient Prosperity..........206
The Role of Higher Education in Advancing Resilient Prosperity.............209
Partnering with a Business for Resilient Prosperity 214

Chapter 7 - THE 3Re STRATEGY: Repurpose. Renew. Reconnect......................219

Can a 3-Word Strategy Really be Effective?..222
3Re: Revitalization Strategies for Nature, Neighborhoods, and Nations..........224
Reconnecting Strategically 227
Competitive vs. Cooperative: The 3Re Strategy Can be Either. 228
Lessons from Tampa, Florida 229
Lessons from Ryerson University...231
Lessons from Denver, Colorado..233
Want to See a List of Good Strategies? 235

Chapter 8 - REGENERATIVE STRATEGIES: Examples, Thoughts & Insights ..237

Socioeconomic Revitalization Factors 242
Transition Management: A Key to Resilience..245
Strategic Recap 249
Measuring Progress Toward Resilient Prosperity for All 252
60 Insights for Creating Prosperous, Green, Equitable, Resilient Places 257

PART C - PROCESS: Mastering the Other Missing Key to Success...................263
Chapter 9 - PROJECTS vs. PROGRAMS: from Sporadic Renewal to Real Momentum. 266

Project Management vs. Program Management 272
THE Universal GOAL of RECOVERY, Revitalization AND Resilience EFFORTS: Increasing Confidence in the Future..273
Inspiring Confidence in Your Local Future: The Calgary Example 283
We Can't Create an Effective Revitalization Program if We Don't Understand Revitalization 287
Designing Resilient Prosperity 294

Chapter 10 - THE COMPLETE SOLUTION: Creating a Strategic Renewal Process. 296

From Strategy to Strategic Process...300
Understanding Policymaking...310

The Revitalizing (and Devitalizing) Power of Policies 313
Regenerative policies 315
Where Should Your Local RECONOMICS Process be Based? 317
A Starting Point for Creating Your RECONOMICS Process 320
A Better Way to Create Local Partnerships 324
Hard Projects vs. Soft Services 326

Chapter 11 - RECONOMICS: Fusing RECOVERY, REVITALIZATION & ReSILIENCE. 328

Sequencing and Public Engagement 329
Who Really Revitalizes Downtowns? 330
From Economic Development to Resilient Prosperity 332
A Better Way to Produce Better Jobs 336
A Feedback Loop to Create the Revitalization Tipping Point 338
Transient Chaos, Pulsing, and False Alarms 340
Where can the RECONOMICS Process 343
be applied? 343
Mixed-Agenda Redevelopment 344
Creating Resilient Prosperity is a Natural Process 348
Enhancing Public & Private Resources for Public Gain 351
The Subjective Economics of Resilient Prosperity 353
One Last Note on Design 355
Can Places with Corrupt Governments Revitalize? 356

Chapter 12 - The Rise of Revitalization & Resilience Facilitators 358

Stasis is Not an Option: If a place isn't revitalizing, it's devitalizing. 359
But First, One Last Review of the Challenges 361
Glimmers of Brilliance in the Darkness of Revitalization Ignorance 365
So, Who Should Lead a Resilient Prosperity Initiative? 369
You Can be Part of the Solution to All of Those Challenges 373
Certified Revitalization & Resilience Facilitators ("RE Facilitators") 374
How Could a Revitalization & Resilience Facilitator Earn a Living? 381
Creating an Agency and/or Team to Implement Resilient Prosperity 384
The World's Most Resilient Organizational Model: The Green Beret A-Team 388
Revitalizing "Retirements" 391
A Few Final Thoughts 393
INDEX 397

PREFACE – HOLY GRAIL: FIXING ECONOMY, SOCIETY, NATURE & CLIMATE TOGETHER.

On the last day of 2019, exactly 3 weeks before this book was published, the lights went out and ferry service stopped in the town of Little Bay Islands, Nova Scotia. Permanently.

This picturesque array of brightly-painted fishing houses on narrow streets on Canada's North Atlantic coast is now dead: purposely abandoned, as all 51 residents left at the same time.

Once a thriving fishing village, it was killed by the decline of the local fishery. This led to the loss of job opportunities, which led to the loss of young people, which led to the loss of confidence in the community's future. In 2019, residents voted in favor of resettlement elsewhere.

They once had prosperity, but it wasn't resilient prosperity. If the fishery had been restored, that would have restored jobs, young people and confidence in the future in one fell swoop. That's how a restoration economy works.

Thousands of communities around the world have, for decades, been on a "Holy Grail" quest without knowing it. All of them want two things: 1) resilient prosperity and 2) an efficient, reliable process to produce it.

Resilient Prosperity: No matter whether a place is thriving or distressed, all want a higher quality of life and a more vibrant, inclusive economy: in other words, revitalization. And they want it to last in the face of national economic cycles, political turmoil and the climate crisis. In other words, resilience. Thus, the universal goal is "resilient prosperity" (though few have clarified their thinking enough to use that phrase).

Strategic Process: Every public leader knows that the reliable production of anything requires a process, whether it's a factory producing air conditioners, a tailor producing clothing or a tree producing nuts, wood and oxygen. They also know, deep down, that they have no real strategy or reliable process for producing either revitalization or resilience in their community (though few would acknowledge it).

I've spent the past 20 years leading workshops, keynoting summits and consulting in planning sessions at urban and rural places worldwide. All of these events were focused on some aspect of creating revitalization or resilience.

Most of those events had other speakers who recounted their on-the-ground efforts and lessons learned. I've thus spent the past two decades researching commonalities: what's usually present in the successes, and what's usually missing in the failures?

I've boiled it down to six elements. Each of them individually increases the likelihood of success. The more of them you have, the more likely you are to succeed. All of them together creates a process that's far more dynamic than the sum of its parts. If you're a community leader, you can thus start assembling the locally-missing pieces of the process in whatever order makes sense—and is least disruptive—for your situation.

Many mayors, governors and presidents have intuitively tried to form such a process. Most had two or three of the six elements. Some had four or five: none had all. Even in those few places that came close, the elements didn't form a process. They were disjointed—usually spread over a long period of time—and had no logical order. In other words, they had the body parts, but no fully-functional body. Thus, they often went nowhere...or not very far. No process = no progress.

> *"If you want to truly understand something, try to change it."* – Kurt Lewin, psychologist.

I have encountered a few effective renewal processes, but they only address very limited scopes—such as revitalizing downtowns, redeveloping old industrial sites or restoring wetlands—and for very specific kinds of assets, such as brownfields, infrastructure or heritage. Processes for regenerating entire communities or regions seem to be entirely missing.

The goal of creating resilient prosperity for all is obviously of vital importance. So why are efforts to create a process for revitalization or resilience so haphazard?

Two reasons: 1) They didn't consciously know that creating a process was what they were trying to do; and 2) They didn't have an ideal process template to shoot for. It's been like trying to assemble a jigsaw puzzle without knowing what it was supposed to look like when finished.

That's the focus of this book: to present that ideal process for producing resilient prosperity. Like all good processes, it can be adapted to local goals and constraints: it's the basic flow that's of crucial importance, not the specific activities that ensue. Most newly-established processes of any kind will accrue elements as they mature. The key is to put the right bones in place initially: the flesh can develop over time. Thus, the process recommended here is a "minimum viable process": you can add to it if necessary, but deleting even a single element will drastically reduce its effectiveness.

Without a process to connect to, projects tend to wither on the vine from lack of support. Or, projects die because they expend too many resources reinventing functions that should have been provided by a local renewal process. Or, lacking a local "flywheel," projects don't add momentum, so confidence in a better future doesn't increase; residents and employers leave and new ones aren't attracted as a result.

Of course, it isn't just lack of process that stymies renewal efforts. The list of potential roadblocks is endless: defeatist public attitudes; empty public coffers; unenlightened leadership, etc. But there's one obstacle that's as universal as the lack of process: the "assumptions trap".

People assume that their fellow stakeholders share their definition of "revitalization" or "resilience"...that they're all heading in the same direction. They assume that their leadership has had some training in the art of renewal: that they know how to make it happen. They assume that someone is in charge of creating a better future. In most places, none of those assumptions is correct. We'll dive into those problems—and their solutions—later: this is just the Preface.

Why am I the one who's writing this book, as opposed to someone famous, powerful...or at least good-looking? Because, as a lifelong world traveler, nature lover, and fan of cities with unique cultures and beautiful heritage, I'm frequently horrified when returning to my favorite places, only to find them degraded or destroyed. I seldom SCUBA or snorkel any more: the barren, lifeless sea floors found all around the planet are just too depressing. I'm old enough to remember the vibrant beauty and rich diversity of just four decades ago.

Badly planned (or unplanned) urban growth and poorly-regulated (or unregulated) natural resource extraction—plus the climate crisis—are the usual culprits. But in the 90s, I started perceiving a glimmer of hope. I increasingly encountered places where governments, businesses, and non-profits were restoring nature, restoring heritage, restoring health and beauty, and revitalizing economies.

I decided to champion this nascent trend, starting out with great enthusiasm and confidence when my first book, *The Restoration Economy* (Berrett Koehler), was published in 2002. It was the first book to document the rise of a vast global trend I dubbed "restorative development". It described eight huge, fast-growing industries and disciplines that are renewing various aspects of our natural, built and socioeconomic environments.

> *"The question is not*
> *'how do we become the best in the world?' but*
> *"how do we become the best for the world?"*
> *– Uffe Albaek, Founder, The Kaos Pilots.*

Some were new industries, like brownfields remediation/redevelopment, which now accounts for some $7 billion in annual activity in the U.S. alone. Some were new sciences, like restoration ecology. Others, such as restoring/reusing historic buildings—or renewing/replacing aging infrastructure—have been around for as long as humankind has been building cities. But even those older forms of renewal have expanded dramatically over the past 20 years, with far more growth to come as a tipping point from degeneration to regeneration nears.

I had found my niche. I'm earning a living I love, being paid well—sometimes over $12,000 for a 60-minute talk—to travel the world as an author, speaker and consultant. I'm not getting rich, but life is good.

One of my more-recent clients, the Partnership for Water Sustainability in British Columbia (PWSBC) recently showed itself to be on the leading edge of watershed restoration. How? By focusing a significant portion of their April 2-4, 2019 conference in Parksville (Vancouver Island) on the subject of regional revitalization.

I was asked to deliver most of that content to an audience that largely comprised Streamkeepers and other technical experts who do the on-the-ground work of restoring watersheds. One might wonder what someone who spends their days moving dirt, reducing pollution, removing invasive species and restoring native species might have in learning how places revitalize themselves socially and economically.

The short answer is that such understanding is the key to attracting more funding and more support (citizen and political) for their watershed projects. If they better-understand how their work contributes to economic renewal and quality of life, they will be far more persuasive when it comes time to justify their budgets. And if they better-understand the process of revitalization, they will know where best to insert themselves into local decision-making.

The major flaw in that last statement is that most places don't actually have a renewal process. So experts, asset owners and other stakeholders have no efficient way to insert themselves into local regeneration. As a result, they just tend to do a lot of isolated projects, hoping that larger-scale revitalization (or resilience) magically appears as a reward for their hard work. But hope is not a strategy.

Most people who are traditionally seen as being responsible for creating community revitalization—mayors, economic developers, private developers, planners, etc.—don't actually know how to think about revitalization. Most of them tend to think of it as a goal, rather than as a process. As a result, they have "magical" expectations: they assume that revitalization will automatically emerge if they just keep doing more of whatever it is they know how to do:

- If they're a mayor, they try to lead the way to revitalization via vision and deal-making;
- If they're developers, they try to build their way to revitalization;
- If they're architects or engineers, they try to design their way to revitalization;
- If they're planners, they write plans as a way to revitalization;
- If they 're economics developers, they try to incentivize their way to revitalization;
- If they're activists, they try to organize or sue their way to revitalization; and
- If they're ecologists or watershed managers, they try to restore their way to revitalization.

All are doing their best with what they have, but is it enough? Only rarely... when stars align and the right things happen in the right order in the right place at the right time. But we're talking about the future of the place, and everyone in it. Is hoping for the best the best we can do?

This lack of process is a wonderful career growth opportunity for those involved in reviving almost anything...whether watersheds, brownfields, heritage, infrastructure, workforce, housing, etc. Being the one at the table who actually understands how to structure local activities to increase the ROI (revitalization on investment) positions you for a real leadership role in your community or region.

The folks who attended any of the three talks and workshops I did for those watershed leaders in British Columbia in April of 2019 now have a greater appreciation of process. If you weren't there—or at any of my other presentations around the world in recent years—here's a quick recap of what I told them about creating regional revitalization and resilience.

The first step is to create an ongoing revitalization (or resilience) program, which constantly initiates, perpetuates, evaluates and adjusts local renewal efforts. Without an ongoing program, you have little chance of building momentum, which—as mentioned earlier—is essential to increasing confidence in the future of the place, in order to attract and retain residents, employers and funding.

The first job of that program (which could be housed by a foundation or non-profit organization) is to facilitate a regenerative vision for the future, along with a "renewable asset" map that reveals opportunities to achieve that vision. The second step is to create a regenerative strategy to overcomes obstacles to achieving that vision. Next, it's best to do some regenerative policymaking, adding support for that strategy (via zoning, codes, ordinances, etc.) while removing policies that undermine it.

Once all of that is done, it's time to move into action. Recruiting public and private partners into your program is the next step. This provides the human, financial and physical (such as properties) resources needed to do regenerative projects, which are the "final" step of the process. I put "final" in quotes because regeneration is a never-ending activity, so the process is circular, not linear. A place that is no longer revitalizing is devitalizing. Stasis is usually an illusion that masks decline.

Armed with an understanding of the above, those BC Streamkeepers and other watershed heroes are no longer operating in a silo, totally dependent on others to champion, fund and support their work. They are far more capable of being their own champions when face-to-face with funders, politicians and stakeholders.

And, they are better able to identify where in the revitalization / resilience process they or their organization should be engaged, in order to be most effective: the program, the vision, the strategy, the policymaking, the partnering or the projects. But let's back up a bit, for context.

I started writing that first book, *The Restoration Economy* way back in 1996. Many now-huge regenerative disciplines and industries were just emerging then.

I've been enormously gratified to hear from regenerative leaders worldwide, who credit their reading of that 2002 book with the genesis of their career and/or organization.

It apparently helped advance many of today's regenerative trends, such as resilience, regenerative agriculture (it had a whole chapter on this now-hot trend), circular economies, carbon-negative (climate restoration), heritage renewal, integrated disaster reconstruction, etc.

As a result, many leaders who normally would have defaulted to the failed paradigms of "green" and "sustainable"—which helped create today's global crises by not yielding effective solutions—are now defaulting to restoration. For example, in the November 2019 issue of *Fast Company* magazine, Kat Taylor, CEO of Beneficial State Bank in Oakland, California said that we need a *"new economy that's fully inclusive, racially and gender just, and environmentally restorative."*

RECONOMICS

In 2008, my second book, *Rewealth*, was published by McGraw-Hill.

Whereas *The Restoration Economy* documented—and created an eight-sector taxonomy for—the broad variety of regenerative projects, Rewealth documented the best practices for turning those projects into the desired outcome of local revitalization: economic growth coupled with enhanced quality of life. You'll find a brief overview of both books' key concepts in Chapter 2.

Here in RECONOMICS, I reveal the most important and useful insights I've gained in the 23 years I've spent researching, writing about and teaching this subject.

The title of this book derives from reconomics: a new framework and process for revitalizing economies and making them more resilient. Resilient prosperity, in other words. "Economies", in this case, includes every scale: national, regional, community, organizational, and even personal.

Communities all around the planet are suffering from economic, social and/or environmental decline. Some due to technological shifts, and others to economic shifts. Some due to local disturbance like war, and others due to global factors like changing weather patterns and sea level rise. In other words, tens of thousands of communities need to produce some form of revitalization. And they don't just want a brief burst of revitalization: they want resilience as well. The speed of their renewal cycle will be determined locally, depending on a combination of urgency of need, size of the community/region, and management capacity.

Adding a reliable, replicable process for community and regional improvement is the first truly fundamental change in local governance in decades. I specified "public" leaders above because successful corporate leaders are all about process. They know that production and process are virtually synonymous: one simply cannot get the former with the latter. It doesn't matter whether they are producing vacuum cleaners or marmalade: without a process, there's no production.

In retrospect, it seems I've always been process-oriented. Here's a truly mundane example. When the personal computer industry was just getting started (yes: I'm that old), I was hired as Director of Marketing for a company selling hardware and software for auto body shops. Nationwide, they were in last place out of about a dozen competitors. Their major marketing mechanism was exhibiting at trade shows, where they tried to sell business owners a $20,000 system straight from their show booth, with little success.

I replaced that single-step sales pitch with a three-step sales process. I figured out what decision they could reasonably expect a person to make at each step. In the few minutes they had a prospect's attention at the booth, I changed the sale of a $20,000 to getting the person to sign up for a group presentation at the conference. At the group presentation, the goal was to get them to sign up for an individual consultation at the conference. Only at the individual consultation did we try to sell the $20,000 system.

Each of those three steps had an extremely high success rate. Instead of selling the usual single sale at the conference, they sold over 40. They used this process at every trade show after that, and within two years they were the #1 firm in the industry. A year after that, the company was purchased by a Fortune 500 firm. The only thing that had changed was the addition of a simple process.

> *"You may be disappointed if you fail, but you are doomed if you don't try." – Beverly Sills.*

In the two decades I've spent on regenerating places worldwide, I've seen many fail. I've seen many move towards an uncertain outcome. And I've seen many succeed. But what I've never seen is a properly-funded Director of Revitalization whose remit covered all necessary environments: natural, built and socioeconomic. In other words, the whole community or region.

It's time to get serious about renewing our world. The destruction of our planet has been normalized: we've been programmed to expect it as the price of progress. We now need to normalize the recovery of our world. We—and our children—need to expect things to get better. Revitalization could be called "Place Medicine"; restoring wellness to communities, regions, and nations. But where are this medicine's scientists, doctors and schools?

Many places try to revitalize. Few succeed. Few of the successes last. Resilient prosperity should thus be a primary goal of public management. An ongoing process of fixing the present and the future together is how places revitalize in a resilient manner. Few places aim for resilient prosperity, so devitalization is in the cards for most.

If resilient prosperity is what we want, government should focus on it. And the starting point has to be the revitalization process, along with the myriad "re" activities that comprise it: regeneration, redevelopment, brownfields remediation, historic restoration/reuse, infrastructure renewal, etc. Why? For the same reason that Willy Sutton robbed banks: that's where the money is.

Of the three components of the adaptive renewal megatrend (which you'll learn about in Chapter 1)—revitalization, resilience, and adaptive management—understanding the first, revitalization, is the most important. Resilience and adaptive management are of somewhat lesser importance for two reasons: 1) they are both relatively new to the public dialogue, so people are more open to learning about them (whereas most leaders erroneously assume they already understand revitalization); and 2) fewer resources are devoted to resilience and adaptive management in most cities and regions, so there's not as much to work with.

On the other hand, well over $3 trillion is already spent annually worldwide on urban revitalization and natural resource restoration. Integrating resilience and adaptive management with those existing budgets is thus the quickest way for them to get traction. There's nothing forced about this 3-way wedding; they reinforce each other quite naturally. Together, they can solve both today's persistent problems and tomorrow's unknown—but potentially calamitous—problems.

If you ask a city council to define "revitalization", how many different answers will you receive? Hint: take the number of council members, and divide by one. Contrary to current practice, revitalization shouldn't just be a reaction to devitalization: it should be a constant process of breathing new life into a place, regardless of current condition.

In Vietnam, America won most battles, but lost the war. It's similar in cities: many successful projects, but a failure to revitalize. Part of the problem is ignorance: few communities have anyone who understands the dynamics of revitalization well enough to create a strategy. The other problem is that—even with such a person—they don't have a Revitalization (or Resilience) Director position in their governance structure. We'll address this in more detail in the final chapter.

In Chapter 12, you'll also discover a new, practical way for you to turn this knowledge into a career that helps revitalize your community, or helps regenerate our planet. A vitally-important new type of professional is emerging: the certified Revitalization & Resilience Facilitator (RE Facilitators). These folks put "RE" after their name, often in addition to certifications from related professions such as planning, architecture, economic development, project management, etc.

We're capable of tapping deep wellsprings of strength, courage and creativity when family members are in danger. Our economic, ecological, and social future now depends on our extending such concern and compassion to our communities and planet. Our survival—or at least our quality of life—depend on it. Humans and wildlife worldwide are suffering as never before, and both are in greater peril than ever before.

What we destroy, destroys us. Since strategies are our path to success, they become our primary interface with our world, and thus determine in large part how the world responds to us. Thus, what we restore, restores us. What we revitalize, revitalizes us.

INTRODUCTION - WHY YOUR NEXT SMALL RENEWAL PROJECT COULD TRIGGER MASSIVE ONGOING REVITALIZATION.

> *"We spent hundreds of billions of dollars that occasionally dealt with very real problems. In most cases, however, the money was wasted changing the physical layout... when that was not the cause of the economic and social problems facing that particular city."* –
> Alexander Garvin,
> The Heart of the City (Island Press, 2019).

In Woodbridge, New Jersey---less than 40 miles from where I was born---a slow-motion evacuation is taking place. Since 2013, the state has purchased and demolished 145 residences. They are then ecologically restoring the land to the wetlands they used to be, in the hope of making the rest of their township more resilient to sea level rise.

We often hear about the towns, tribes and entire islands---from Louisiana to the South Pacific---whose populations are being relocated *en masse*. But the thousands of coastal and estuarine places that are being nibbled to death by the climate crisis seldom get much press.

Some cities are economically devitalized in one fell swoop by the loss of a major employer, while others degrade incrementally, with their residents trickling away over decades. Some cities revitalize in a sudden burst of investment and renewal, while others regenerate in bits and pieces over many years. So too are we presented today with a broad spectrum of resilience challenges; not just differing in type of damage, but in rate of damage. This has always been the case, of course: what's new is the explosive increase in the volume of these challenges, and their thoroughly global distribution.

In October of 2019, the International City/County Management Association (ICMA) conducted their 2019 Disaster Resilience and Recovery Survey, which asked municipal and county administrators about their level of preparation for natural disasters. Most of the 901 respondents had experienced a federally-declared disaster within the past five years: winter storms (60%), floods (54%), hurricanes (27%), tornadoes (19%), drought (17%) and wildfires (14%).

But, despite the increasing frequency and severity of such disasters, not even a third (31%) of them had a long-term sustainability or resilience plan, and only 16% were in the process of creating one. Over half hadn't even considered doing so.

In ICMA's 2019 Prediction on Disaster Recovery and Resilience, Abena Ojetayo—Tallahassee, Florida's chief resilience officer—said *"For cities that keep their heads in the sand, the impacts of these shocks and stresses will ripple throughout the entire community in profound ways. For those that plan ahead and invest upstream, their efforts will be greeted with enthusiastic new partners from unlikely sectors and innovative financial resources."*

Those survey numbers are bad enough, but keep in mind that the research only addressed the type of resilience that's simplest to comprehend and easiest to sell to taxpayers as necessary: natural disasters. More-subtle forms of resilience—such as social and economic—weren't considered, despite the fact that far more communities have experienced socioeconomic disaster than natural.

The ICMA survey also only focused on disaster training, recovery funding and resilience plans. No mention was made of a process for turning those resources and plans into actual resilience. Had that question been included, it's likely the response would have been near 0%.

Resilience to social disasters (civil unrest, riots, war, etc.), economic disasters (sudden and gradual) and natural disasters (normal and climate change-related) is real resilience...what might be called holistic resilience. This book is an attempt to help places create holistic resilience by remedying that "process deficit". It is NOT about designing resilience: there are literally thousands of books on the technical aspects of resilient design by civil engineers, architects, landscape architects, planners, ecologists, etc. RECONOMICS is about actually succeeding in your efforts to create resilient prosperity. That takes a lot more than good design.

Psychologists sometimes divide people's mindsets into two groups: prove and improve. The former spend much of their energy trying to prove to others that what they believe is right. They fear and are closed to feedback, and are usually on a path to failure. As that failure becomes more apparent, they tend to become even more vociferous in defending their assumptions and justifying their actions. The latter group spends their energy improving their knowledge, so they can improve their beliefs. This tends to improve the effectiveness of their actions, putting them on a path to success.

Local government leaders, being people (for the most part), can be similarly parsed. Most will tell you they know what they're doing, and are already performing all the right actions to improve their community. And they can prove it, because it's what almost everyone else in their situation is doing.

A much smaller group constantly works to improve their knowledge and practices, with progress towards resilient prosperity the likely result. Are you a prover or an improver? Are you open to improving the process of improving your place? If so, you're about to learn how to at least double your local ROI (revitalization on investment) with minimal disruption to your existing systems, minimal stress from the change and almost no cost whatsoever.

It's called the RECONOMICS Process, and your community probably has several of its elements in place already. As a result, you can use a "plug the gaps" approach to implementing the process that reduces or eliminates disruption. And, you can do it at whatever pace suits your situation, which reduces the stress of change. What's more, other than some personnel time, there are no costs involved. What's crucially-important to remember is that it's a minimum viable process: adding to it might be necessary, but removing any elements from it is never a good idea.

My research for this book often made leaders of community redevelopment, revitalization and resilience efforts uncomfortable. Here's a typical conversation:

ME: *"What's your strategy?"*

THEM: *"It's over 400 pages: I'll send you a link to it."*

ME: *"No, that's a plan. A strategy can usually be stated in a sentence or two."*

THEM: *"Oh, well in that case, our strategy is to grow jobs, enhance the quality of life and increase affordable housing."*

ME: *"No, those are goals. What's your strategy for overcoming the obstacles to achieving those goals?"*

It's at this point that the conversation usually becomes uncomfortable. Someone who is seen locally as a competent and knowledgeable leader is realizing that he/she doesn't know what a strategy is. Which, in leadership circles, is akin to a farmer not knowing what soil is. I try hard not to come across as threatening or obnoxious, but such questions have to be asked when writing a book on revitalization and resilience strategies and processes.

I have the same problem when I get to the "process" portion of the interview. When I ask local leaders if they have a process for revitalizing their city or region, they say "yes". But when I ask for details about the elements of their process, the reality seldom matches the perception.

I ask them if they did a visioning session, and they say "yes". I ask for details, and it turns out that it was actually a design charrette.

I ask them to state their strategy in a sentence or two, and they're still expounding 15 minutes later.

I ask them if they have an ongoing revitalization program, and they say "yes". I ask for details and they point to organizations that have committed long-term funding. I ask who's in charge of their program and where it's based, and they draw a blank.

Vision, strategy and program are just three of the six elements of the basic renewal process, and already the interview is in trouble. Such answers indicate that they don't actually know the meaning of "process" or "strategy" (even though every one of them would swear that they do). So it's hardly surprising that most places have neither a strategy nor a process for their renewal. That absence is usually the primary factor retarding their revitalization, even though every one of them would swear that what's really holding them back is insufficient federal funding, foreign competition for jobs, the national economy, etc.

Other times, when asked about having a proven process or strategy, they say *"no such thing exists; each place is unique, so its method of renewal will also be unique."* The part about each place's being unique is true enough, but the rest is pure caca de toro. They usually believe there's no reliable path to revitalization (or resilience) for two reasons: 1) They are focusing on what makes their place different from other places, rather than on the far greater number of characteristics they share; and 2) It gives them an excuse to continue in their favorite mode...winging it. If there's no rigorous approach to regenerating their economy, society and quality of life, then no one can accuse them of using the wrong approach.

Leaders of cities, planning departments and redevelopment agencies often do most of the right things when trying to bring a place back to life, but fail to produce revitalization or resilience for two reasons:
- they missed one or more key elements; and/or
- they did them in the wrong order.

Why are such two very fundamental mistakes so common? Because few of those folks ever received any training in how to create those mysterious qualities we call revitalization and resilience (AKA: "resilient prosperity"). This book is a guide for social, economic, and environmental change agents, public and private, who wish to be truly effective.

It describes how to strengthen what works in your community or region, and how to eliminate or bypass obstacles places put in the way of their own success. Places everywhere want resilient prosperity: they want health, wealth, and happiness if they don't have it. They want to keep or increase it if they do have it.

This book will show you how to help bring that about. But, even armed with this knowledge, revitalizing a city or region—not to mention our planet—is hard. Revitalizing a place you don't care about is harder. Revitalizing a place when you don't understand the dynamics of regeneration is harder still. So, if you don't have a real passion for such work, stop right here.

The good news is that what you'll learn in this book will make this inherently-difficult job much easier. Once you understand the 6-part process described here, you'll be able to plug in whichever parts your community is missing. And you'll be able to do this in a locally-appropriate manner and pace that avoids most of the usual resistance to change.

Virtually all communities want to attract new residents, employers and real estate investors...and keep the ones they have. To succeed, they must do One Thing above all others: inspire confidence in a better local future, both short-term and long-term. Not hope. Not optimism. Confidence.

I differentiate "optimism" from "confidence in the future" because the former is generally based on a person's (or society's) general attitude towards life, whereas confidence is normally evidence-based. Don't get me wrong: optimism is a good thing, and will help boost your success. But too much optimism can be deleterious, as can false (non-evidence-based) confidence.

For example, here's an excerpt from an article titled "Time to wake up: Days of abundant resources and falling prices are over forever" by Jeremy Grantham—Chief Investment Officer of GMO Capital (over $106 billion in managed assets) and former economist with Royal Dutch Shell—published April 29, 2011 in The Oil Drum: "*...we are in the midst of one of the giant inflection points in economic history. This is likely the beginning of the end for the heroic growth spurt in population and wealth caused by what I think of as the Hydrocarbon Revolution rather than the Industrial Revolution. ...We (are) an optimistic and overconfident species. ...Fortunately, optimism appears to be a real indicator of future success. A famous Harvard study in the 1930s found that optimistic students had more success in all aspects of their early life and, eventually, they even lived longer.*"

He continued: "*...But optimism has a downside. No one likes to hear bad news, but in my experience, no one hates it as passionately as the U.S. and Australia. Less optimistic Europeans and others are more open to gloomy talk. Tell a Brit you think they're in a housing bubble, and you'll have a discussion. Tell an Australian, and you'll have World War III. ....if we mean to avoid increased starvation and international instability, we will need global ingenuity and generosity on a scale hitherto unheard of.*"

Creating confidence in the future of a place requires a flow of credible progress. That, in turn, requires a regenerative strategy—and a proven process to generate, sustain and accelerate momentum—so you'll constantly produce the evidence needed to create ever more confidence. A strategic renewal process can double your initiative's results and make it (almost) failure-proof, at almost zero additional cost.

Good leaders help communities obey the reverse law of gravity: what goes down must come up. Unfortunately, few mayors have a clue when it comes to that process of reversing a place's downward socioeconomic trajectory. In such places, normal Newtonian physics applies: a community at rest tends to stay at rest. But stasis equates to deterioration in living systems, such as cities. So, while taking a rest after a community improvement effort is restorative, remaining at rest leads to urban decay.

Community and regional revitalization / resilience efforts are widespread these days, thanks to global economic shifts and the global climate crisis. But most of them achieve little, for the same reason that the "smart growth" movement in the U.S. never achieved its potential: most are a collection of worthwhile activities that lack an effective strategy and a cohesive implementation process.

Over the past decade, that situation has been improving, with more places adding the missing pieces to their local renewal process. The problem is that they don't have an ideal process to shoot for: it's all trial and error. They need someone with a deep understanding of the kinds of strategic processes that reliably produce economic, social and environmental regeneration. That's the knowledge you'll soon have, if you keep reading this until the end.

Most community leaders know intuitively that a process is needed, but aren't consciously aware that this is the goal they are working towards. Here's what Eric Bonham, P. Eng. (Board member of the Partnership for Water Sustainability in British Columbia, and Former Director, BC Ministry of Environment & BC Ministry of Municipal Affairs) said after reading an early excerpt from this book: "(the) *RECONOMICS Process raises the bar for community and regional revitalization. It's a powerful package, succinctly capturing the process that we have doggedly tried to identify over time, not always knowing the next step. The RECONOMICS Process brings a holistic dimension to redevelopment, inextricably linking vision and task.*"

Sometimes, cities have a spectacular revitalization success, and thus assume they know what they're doing. But they then find that they can't replicate that success in other parts of their community. That's usually because they had no process to replicate.

The initial success might have derived from good timing, or good instincts, or charismatic leadership. It's even possible that they accidentally created a complete renewal process by instinct the first time around. But, since no one was actually thinking in terms of process, it wasn't documented as such. Thus, they had to start from scratch with the next initiative. They probably replicating most of the previous elements of success, but left out a key part of the process because they had no ideal process template to follow.

But we'll return to the full process later. For now, let's focus on the crucial missing element in most partial processes: strategy. Two polar-opposite strategies are currently popular among revitalizers: critical mass and incremental.

The capital-intensive critical mass strategy says you should throw all your investments into an area at the same time, so that each amenity help attracts customers to the other amenities, and so that people will be drawn from a much larger area by the "critical mass" of offerings. This strategy also tends to gain far more free publicity, and does a faster job of changing peoples' perceptions of the area.

The incremental redevelopment strategy says that slow, steady, small improvements are better, and the agenda is more likely to be driven by the needs of the residents, and less likely to be dominated by big developers. The incremental strategy requires little or no up-front investment: projects simply happen when they can. Boston's Back Bay and New York City's Brooklyn Heights are two examples of successful incremental neighborhood redevelopment. On a citywide scale, New Orleans, Charleston and Savannah come to mind.

Both can work, and both can fail. When the critical mass strategy fails, it fails big: hundreds of millions of dollars can be lost. When the incremental strategy fails, people often don't realize it: it usually has no timeline or deadlines, and there's often no one tracking and reporting on it.

If your community has the potential to assemble the public and private resources needed to try the critical mass approach, and you decide it's the right way to go, then the question shifts from "which strategy" to "How do we make it succeed?" But you shouldn't forget that "critical mass" and "incremental" are only two of the most popular approaches: other—often better—strategies are available, as you'll see in later chapters.

If your community has no significant resources available and wants to try the incremental approach, the question becomes: "How do we avoid the heartbreak of having stores and restaurants open, only to see them fail a year or two later because there weren't enough other new businesses, and the downtown remained largely abandoned?" The incremental approach's biggest weakness is often timing: insufficient synergies among component projects.

Often, when I congratulate people who are working on affordable housing, transit, walkability, green infrastructure, historic preservation, infrastructure renewal, regenerative agriculture, ecological restoration, climate resilience, etc.

for their revitalization efforts, they say *"What do you mean? This isn't a revitalization project."*

That's a signal that their work is taking place in a strategic vacuum.

That, in turn, means the local economy is likely getting a low ROI (revitalization on investment) on their community improvement expenditures.

Visionaries, designers, planners, policymakers, and project managers abound. Strategists are rare.

As a result, resilience and revitalization efforts often fail due to 1) bad strategy, and 2) no strategy. If they have a good strategy and still fail, it's usually because of a missing or incomplete implementation process.

So, this book is as much about strategy and process as it is about revitalization and resilience. I call this strategic renewal process the RECONOMICS Process, and its intended output is resilient prosperity.

Most people assume that expertise in their discipline automatically conveys the ability to create a relevant strategy within that discipline. That assumption might be the world's single greatest source of failure. A thorough grasp of one's subject is, of course, essential. But just as essential to success in any field is an understanding of strategy. Implementation skills are key too, but they're easier to find, since there's an entire profession dedicated to that skill set: project management.

How does one revitalize a place, or make it more resilient?
- Planners say it's all about having a plan.
- Engineers say it's all about efficient infrastructure.
- Sociologists say it's all about community pride and harmony.
- Marketers say it's all about branding, beautification and street banners.
- Environmentalists say it's all about health and greenspace.
- Developers say it's all about housing, office space, and retail.
- Law enforcement says it's all about public safety.
- Underserved citizens (low income, minority, etc.) say it's all about economic mobility, transparency and justice.
- Economic developers say it's all about jobs and incentives.
- Architects say it's all about design.
- Politicians say it's all about vision and leadership.
- Consultants say it's all about _____ (fill in the fad of the moment).

Successful community leaders know the key is having the right strategy, and an effective process to integrate ALL of the above activities and disciplines.

Every one of the professionals in the above list are partially right: their activity (probably) contributes to revitalization. But few acknowledge that theirs is only a small part of the overall process. That's not surprising, since they seldom what the process is. They're like assembly line workers making fuel pumps, without understanding how an automobile works.

That division of labor works fine when there's a functioning assembly line to bring all those specialties together. But few places actually have such a process to "manufacture" revitalization or resilience. Nor do they have anyone who knows how to create one.

Don't let that mechanistic metaphor mislead you, though. Revitalization is an emergent quality of a complex adaptive system; whether a body, a swamp or an economy. It can't be engineered or summoned on command. But an appropriate strategic process can greatly increase the likelihood of success, the speed of success, and the quality of success. That's what this book is about.

In the right place at the right time—and with a lot of luck—any of those above-listed, narrowly-focused activities can trigger revitalization. But what reliably triggers it—and keeps it going—is a process that aligns all of those activities toward a common goal. And that process must be driven by an regenerative strategy. The above list mostly comprises tactics, and tactics without strategies have very limited outcomes. True success—such as resilient economic growth—derives from a strategic process (or luck). A strategic process creates capacity that's far greater than the sum of all those parts listed above.

We all dream of reducing complex problems to a simple, single factor, like Jack Palance telling Billy Crystal in *City Slickers* that *"the secret to life is just one thing."*

But trying to reduce community revitalization to just one—or even a few—of the factors listed above is like reducing personal happiness to just health, just money, or just relationships. The key to success when dealing with such complexity isn't one factor: it's an adaptive, strategic, ongoing cycle of acting, learning and adjusting that enables all of the relevant local factors to come into play at the appropriate time.

Over the past two decades, dozens of people with visionary sprawl projects has asked for my endorsement, and I've turned them all down. Some were truly brilliant designs, but we're on a finite planet with a growing population. Sprawling onto arable land or wildlife habitat is just dumb, no matter how intelligently we do it. It's as if someone were to ask me *"Is it OK if I shoot some people? I promise to only use a .38, not a .44 magnum."*

Some sprawl is less damaging than other sprawl, but sprawl is sprawl, and less damage is not regeneration. That's not to say that no sprawl is needed: there's a limit to how dense we can make our cities to handle our metastasizing population. So some sprawl will eventually be needed, and it should be intelligent sprawl.

"Eventually" is the key word above: few, if any, cities have reached that "maximum densification" point. If they think they have, they probably need more innovative thinking, not more sprawl.

Revitalization ignorance results in many myths regarding economic justice, such as "gentrification." This is a word that's often mistakenly used in place of "revitalization". Studying the past 20 years, researchers recently found that the displacement of long-term, low-income, minority residents from revitalized neighborhoods (gentrification) is not as common as believed, though it can be quite severe in the places—such as Washington, DC—where it is happening.

In fact, those researchers discovered that the opposite is far more common: lower-income residents tend to move from revitalized places less frequently than they move from non-revitalized neighborhoods. The reason is common sense: revitalized places offer a better quality of life for all, regardless of income: nicer parks, better shopping, prettier and safer streetscapes, more job opportunities, better transit, etc.

The major problem with most revitalization efforts is that they comprise mostly tactics, with little or no strategy. Short-term benefits sometimes result, but seldom long-term gains. Lots of activity, but not much insight or shared purpose. They are busy redeveloping, renewing, regenerating, renovating, reimagining, redesigning, replacing, reusing, reconnecting, and repurposing. Nothing wrong with that: it's the stuff of revitalization.

But they are mostly isolated packages of stuff. Even when unified visually by a plan, they lack a process for building momentum and actually achieving that mysterious emergent quality we call revitalization. So, much of that good stuff often goes to waste. Truth be told, we often don't even agree on what revitalization is. We fire CEOs who use such grope-in-the-dark approaches to growing a company, but we seem to tolerate it—even expect it—in public leaders.

Another major reason places devitalize is because they think revitalization is something one only does when in crisis...a reaction to decline. But ALL places—no matter how healthy, wealthy, and beautiful—should be striving for more strength and vibrance, if only to avoid going backwards.

> *"You can't do all the good the world needs,*
> *but the world needs all the good you can do."*
> *– from "All the Good," by singer Jana Stanfield.*

Places are like people. It's said that all anyone needs to be happy is something to look forward to. Having an inspiring, shared vision, a map of your opportunities, a credible strategy, and trusted leaders does this for a community. The best way for individuals to break out of depressing doldrums is via action: it's no different for communities. Many places recede because they treat revitalization as a remedy, rather than as a mode of existence. They forget to continue revitalizing. That lack of action leads to fear and loss of confidence, which creates additional barriers to action.

Places exist in 3 basic states: degeneration, equilibrium, and regeneration. But what seems to be healthy equilibrium on paper (such as "state of the economy" reports) is often an illusory, brittle, stagnating form of stasis in disguise. Resilience is a far better goal than stability. As with all complex adaptive systems, cities and nations can shift states seemingly overnight. The triggers for these shifts are often tiny; far out of proportion to the magnitude of the ensuing change. In today's technology-driven, internet-connected world, economies and societies are more tightly coupled than ever, so minor local disturbances to the system more frequently have major national—or even global—effects.

Strategies are a technology. Technology is the manufacture, use, and/or understanding of tools, machines, techniques, or systems designed to solve problems or perform functions. In the case of strategies, that function is to produce success. That's it: all strategies have that single purpose.

After Boeing lost several big military contracts to competitors, its recently-hired CEO, Leanne Caret, adopted a new strategy in 2016. When a Bloomberg reporter asked her how she would know if her strategy was working, she said *"When we start winning."* She knows that this is the sole metric of a strategy's value. In November of 2018, Boeing won a $13 billion Pentagon contract.

Technologies aren't just hardware, or even software: they are also wetware (us). Our bodies are technologies, as are our thought constructs (techniques) that help us achieve an end.

Strategies (and tactics) are thus very simple technologies. A strategy is a technique that increases the likelihood of success for an action, project, or program.

Like DNA (which responds to the environment and guides a body's decisions), a strategy must be concise: usually just a sentence or three. Any longer, and it can't be remembered. That renders it useless, since it can't then guide moment-to-moment decision-making. The previously-mentioned strategic vacuums in leadership can even happen when a strategy is present...if it's too wordy to be useful.

But the situation gets worse. Most places enjoy a surfeit of public and private leaders with expertise in creating buildings, infrastructure, and critical services. But they suffer ignorance of the principles, frameworks, and theory related to revitalization: the process of boosting strength and vibrance.

As mentioned earlier, all places need regeneration of some sort, whether after a long decline, a brief catastrophe, an excessive period of comfortable stagnation. Or, they might need revitalization in order to build environmental, economic and/or social resilience. Whatever the causes and goals, the necessary regenerative expertise is similar...and similarly lacking.

Also as mentioned earlier, lack of a strategy—or lack of the right strategy—is the primary reason so many excellent renewal projects fail to reverse a community's downward trajectory. In many cases, those projects should have revitalized the place, but there was nothing to capture, leverage, and perpetuate their momentum.

But a strategy by itself can't do that, of course. The right strategy makes needed changes less painful and less expensive, which lubricates the desired shift. But the shift itself comes from process. The RECONOMICS Process in this book can—if properly applied—leverage your next expensive redevelopment or restoration project into resilient prosperity for all. The irony is that adding the RECONOMICS Process costs almost nothing. The costs are mostly in the projects, but the revitalization is mostly in the process.

Processes drive all life on Earth. Plants have a process for turning water, carbon and solar energy into biomass. Animals have a survival process for finding shelter, food and mates.

When the first human learned how to build a fire, it wasn't because he/she observed that certain things burn. It wasn't because he/she had discovered how to create a spark or harvest an ember from friction or a lightning strike. It was because they developed a process for applying a spark or ember to tinder, which ignited kindling, which ignited firewood. Skip one of those, and no warmth is forthcoming.

So, process is the real key to success. But not just any management process will do when the desired result is resilient prosperity. It must be the right program. The right vision. The right strategy. The right policies. The right partners. And the right projects. This book defines all of those "rights."

But not in a prescriptive manner. In construction, one can have prescriptive specifications or performance specifications. The former says "build this bridge with heat-treated carbon steel girders." The latter says "build this bridge to last for 100 years, handle 50,000 cars and trucks daily, and withstand 140 mile per hour winds."

Performance specifications allow you to use the latest knowledge and the most up-to-date materials and technologies to achieve your goals. And so it is with the resilient prosperity process we call reconomics.

Reconomics is not an economic theory, although it contains one. Neither is it an economic policy framework, although it makes use of policy. Reconomics can be seen as an adaptive, circular flow of regenerative program, vision, strategy, policy, partnership, and projects for the purpose of creating resilient prosperity.

This book will explain—and give examples of—that process in action. It will also describe each of the components: regenerative programs, regenerative visions (with a map of local renewable assets), regenerative strategies, regenerative policies, regenerative partnerships and regenerative projects.

The word "regenerative" is used repeatedly because it's not enough for you to simply have those six elements in your community: each of them needs to actually contribute to creating revitalization and/or resilience.

For instance, it's not uncommon for a place to have many environmental restoration projects in their area, while their policies are still incentivizing environmental destruction.

There are two aspects to each element: structural and functional. Having a community visioning group is structural. Whether they produce intelligent, revitalizing visions or devitalizing visions based on obsolete assumptions is the functional aspect. So, it's possible for a community to have all six elements of the strategic process, but it won't be a strategic renewal process unless the function of each of those elements is regenerative.

By "regenerative vision", I mean that it must be centered on equitable improvement of the economy and quality of life. The 2019 Fall Meeting of the Urban Land Institute in Washington, DC had media briefing on real estate trends. Every member of the panel was a national redevelopment leader, presenting many sophisticated ways of slicing and dicing the numbers to get a better feel for trends. During the Q&A, I asked them if any non-numerical indicators had emerged, on which they based their decisions as to which cities were investment-worthy. All of them agreed that the key indicator was quality of life.

This doesn't mean other kinds of visions and goals are never appropriate, of course. If you were in Rwanda in July of 1994, you would probably choose a vision centered on stopping citizens from hacking each other to death. That could be seen as a prerequisite of revitalization. But it still relates to quality of life. (The word "vision" is ubiquitous in this book: we must focus on outcomes, not obstacles.)

By "regenerative strategy", I mean that accomplishing your vision should accomplished primarily by repurposing, renewing and reconnecting your existing natural, built and socioeconomic assets. This is as opposed to basing it on acquiring new assets, such as sprawl in the context of cities, or on M&A (mergers and acquisitions) in the context of corporations.

> *"Inspiration usually comes during work,*
> *rather than before it."*
> *– Madeleine L'Engle, American writer.*

This book will make specific recommendations as to the kinds of programs, visions, strategies, policies, partnerships and projects that will help you revitalize your career, your organization, your community or your nation. But turning that advice into the revitalization of what you care about is going to be a uniquely personal—and probably very enjoyable—exercise.

Yet another reason most community revitalization efforts fail is because people confuse the parts with the whole. Here's a list of activities that are often confused with revitalization:

- Adaptively reusing a vacant building;
- Restoring a historic building;
- Remediating and building on a brownfield;
- Beautifying streetscapes and storefronts;
- Enhancing public spaces;
- Creating and improving green infrastructure;
- Redesigning transportation infrastructure;
- Erecting iconic structures; and
- Branding and improving the image/awareness of the place.

Revitalization is an ongoing process. The above list comprises one-time projects. Most of them are very good projects that can contribute to revitalization, but that doesn't mean they are revitalization, any more than mixing pigments is the same as painting a masterpiece. One can mix pigments all day long—and do it absolutely perfectly—but never produce a piece of art.

> *"But maybe everything that dies someday comes*
> *back. Maybe Asbury Park is back?"*
> *– Bruce Springsteen (2015)*

Strategic processes make all the difference in the world...and to the world. Do we love our children enough to not be satisfied with our current "save the world" efforts, most of which "merely" slow the rate of new degradation? Are we ready to focus more seriously on restoring already-damaged and depleted natural resources and on revitalizing already-damaged and depleted communities? If so, that's a worthy vision, but it will go nowhere without a strategic process to fund and implement it.

Let's stop ignoring the elephant in the room: Is revitalization even real? Real world evidence proves that it is, but you'd never know it based on the state of the revitalization profession. Or lack thereof. Devitalization happens to all places at some time, and revitalization is desired by most places at all times. So, why don't community leaders take revitalization more seriously? Why do most treat it like some unmanageable form of magic?

Most public leaders will say they're seriously working towards it, but when was the last time you met a public Director of Revitalization? Or a Ph.D. in Community Revitalization? Or saw a substantial, ongoing public budget item with "revitalization" in its name? In recent years, we've begun to see Chief Resilience Officers (CRO) appointed, but true resilience is based in regeneration, not on writing plans (which seems to be 90% of what most CROs do).

Revitalization's causes, effects, and flows tend to manifest in four ways:
- Top-Down (planned): Often characterized by large "magic-bullet" projects;
- Extemporaneous: (middle-out) Miscellaneous "fixers" doing their thing on an opportunistic basis;
- Bottom-up (self-organized): Neighborhood-by-neighborhood, incremental, resident-led revitalization; and
- Process-driven: With a strategic renewal process, revitalization is reliably and constantly produced, often harnessing all three of the above modes.

As a result of this multitude of ways revitalization can manifest, most places don't give anyone the responsibility for advancing local revitalization, thinking everyone will just do their part. But when everyone is in charge, no one is in charge, and chaos often ensues.

So, is revitalization a Grand Delusion with no substance, or an industry in need of a profession? When we look at a place transformed from dirty, hopeless, sickly, divided, and poor to clean, healthy, optimistic, harmonious, and prosperous, are we looking at something real? Yes. Is it an activity that should be taken more seriously? Yes. Is in need of a strategic process to deliver it more reliably? Absolutely.

But, in our pursuit of resilient prosperity, we must remember that all the strategy and process in the world won't do us much good if it's not regenerative. We must be careful not to let comfortable-but-failed old paradigms like sustainability sneak in. Nowhere is this dynamic more crucial than as regards carob emissions. The climate crisis is an existential threat, and the time is long past for "reassuring incrementalism".

For instance, low-carbon and zero-carbon solutions—like sustainability—are what we should have been doing for the past half-century. We failed at that, so carbon-negative must now be a basic goal of everything we do. Slowing down the rate at which we exacerbate the climate crisis is just a different path to failure: climate restoration is the only sane goal, and extreme urgency is the only sane level of priority. Fortunately, creating a carbon-negative city or region requires the same tactics and strategies that contribute to resilient prosperity: restoring urban tree canopies and other green infrastructure, turning old landfills into renewable energy facilities (methane, solar, wind), etc.

But eliminating new emissions is obviously crucial, too, and infrastructure renewal is the most important of the restoration economy sectors in this regard. For instance, wastewater treatment plants consume at least a third of the entire energy budget of most cities. Renovating existing plants to derive 100% of their energy from anaerobic digestion of their own biosolids needs to happen worldwide, and now. This is proven technology: Los Angeles already has a wastewater plant that's completely off the grid. So, while this technology obviously helps the climate, it's not restorative in terms of being carbon-negative. On the other hand, it counts as a regenerative activity in general, since such conversions renovate our built environment.

In the final chapter of this book, you'll discover the newest, fastest and easiest way to obtain the knowledge and credentials needed to become a resilient prosperity professional, and how to find one if that's what your community needs (and what place doesn't?) But don't skip ahead: it will make much more sense if you've read what comes before that chapter.

On February 28, 2016---after reading an early draft of this manuscript---Mikkel Schønning Sørensen, Senior Project Manager, at the Danish Architecture Centre (Dansk Arkitektur Center) said this in an email to me: *"I read (it) with great joy. Public officials in Danish municipalities often seem to confuse strategies, plans and projects...or mix them all up into one."*

Mikkel shouldn't fret too much about the Danish situation: what he describes is the norm worldwide. I hope RECONOMICS helps clear the confusion, since the future of communities, regions, nations---and maybe civilization itself---depends on our ability to create appropriate strategies and implement them successfully.

PART A - CONTEXT: THE CHALLENGES OF CREATING RESILIENT PROSPERITY.

Revitalizing, restoring, regenerating, and boosting resilience are all modes of making a place healthier, wealthier, stronger, and more beautiful. Those "re" words are all interrelated, and not just by a shared prefix. Both physical and economic resilience, for example, come in large part from a constant process of regenerating (repurposing, renewing, reconnecting) one's natural, built and socioeconomic assets...which also happens to lead to revitalization.

It also leads to climate restoration. In my first book, The Restoration Economy, I pointed out that sustainable development is what we should have been doing since the Industrial Revolution started. But we didn't, so our world is now so depleted, degraded, fragmented and polluted that only restorative development is capable of creating a healthier, wealthier future for all.

That same dynamic has been playing out as regards the global climate crisis. For the past two decades or so, the focus has mostly been on mitigating climate change and adapting to it. The latter is appropriate, since we might well fail to arrest the syndrome before it passes the tipping point (if it hasn't already) and enters an unstoppable feedback loop.

But saving us from that fate won't happen as the result of climate mitigation efforts: only climate restoration efforts can do that. Carbon negative, not low-carbon or carbon-neutral. By all means, continue any climate mitigation efforts that are working, but the path forward must be climate restoration.

The good news is that it's doable, but not just by cleaning-up industry and switching to renewable energy. Those are essential, of course, but there's a more-oblique path to climate restoration that has vast potential because it's what everyone wants (even climate crisis deniers): resilient prosperity.

This book is about a path to creating resilient prosperity for communities, regions and nations that simultaneously:
- Grows their economy while boosting environmental health and quality of life;
- Adapts the place to the effects of the climate crisis to make them more resilient; and
- Helps restore the global climate as a side effect, because the regenerative process I describe here—when properly applied—automatically creates carbon-negative economic growth.

In other words, we can revitalize our way to climate restoration.

Every place needs revitalization. City leaders often say "oh, WE don't need revitalization", as if it's something only poor, dirty, post-industrial places do. If I mention a struggling (often ethnic) neighborhood of their city, the reaction is often "well, of course THEY need revitalization." Any community that thinks it doesn't need to work on this is probably on its way down. We tend to lose what we take for granted.

They're also wrong because revitalization isn't just about the economy. Can any city say that their quality of life and environmental health can't possibly be any better? Even if a place doesn't have many assets (like vacant buildings) that need to be repurposed or renewed, their cit almost certainly needs to reconnection. Concentrated wealth and concentrated poverty fragment places, and disguises their overall decline. So, investing in the reconnection and revitalization of distressed neighborhoods is also an investment in social resilience.

Revitalization isn't defined by current conditions: it's defined by past conditions, trajectories and trendlines. It doesn't have to start from a state of distress; just a lower level of whatever you want more of (or a higher level of what you want less of, such as pollution, crime, etc.) Revitalization is defined by the gap between a previous baseline condition—good or bad—and an improved present or future condition.

So revitalization isn't just for post-industrial economies: it's for post-bad-planning, post-austerity, post-excessive-economic growth, post-laissez-faire, and post-resting-on-laurels situations as well.

In these days of more and worse disasters fueled by the climate crisis, even places ruled by conservative politicians are realizing they need more resilience.

To avoid repeatedly saying "revitalization and resilience" as if they were separate, unrelated goals, let's conflate those two universal desires into "resilient prosperity" for the rest of this book to keep things simple.

So, if resilient prosperity is what everyone wants, why do so few enjoy it? Why do so few public leaders know how to create it? That's what this first section of the book is about.

CHAPTER 1 - TRENDS & TERMINOLOGY: OUR SHIFT FROM ADAPTIVE CONQUEST TO ADAPTIVE RENEWAL.

In today's increasingly broken, dialog-deprived, disaster-fatigued world, we often dive into remedies without understanding the problem, without really talking about the problem, and without even perceiving our level of ignorance.

So let's explore some of the underlying terms, trends and concepts before discussing solutions.

THE ADAPTIVE RENEWAL MEGATREND

Once upon a time, we humans grew our economies—and accommodated growing populations—by sprawling, and by extracting irreplaceable virgin resources. In other words, we were adapting the planet to our needs, a mode I call adaptive conquest. In most cases, those adaptations were solely for our needs: wildlife be damned.

Many indigenous cultures had ways of limiting their population growth, and used resources in a more sustainable manner. But they usually went the way of wildlife (towards extinction) when the sprawl and extraction machine of adaptive conquest cultures discovered their lands.

That adaptive conquest model has had many unintended consequences—and it has obvious limits on a planet of finite size with a growing population—but it worked fine for about 12,000 years. This was the period that scientists refer to as the Holocene: the epoch during which human activity started to affect the planet.

We're now in the Anthropocene—which "officially" began in 1950—the epoch during which human activity dominates the planet's life-supporting processes.

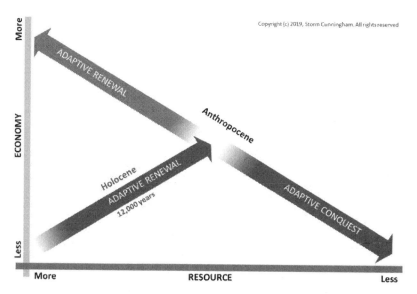

How can we survive and even thrive on our tiny planet, despite exploding populations in Africa, Latin America and most of the Muslim world? The only viable alternate mode is to base our economies on restoring our depleted natural resources (and climate), on remediating our vast inventory of contaminated land (and water), and on revitalizing and boosting the capacity of the cities we've already created. In other words, we must adapt to our adaptations, a mode I call adaptive renewal.

Economic growth based on adaptive conquest comes in a variety of flavors—capitalism, socialism, communism, etc.—but all are adaptive conquest nonetheless.

> *"He that will not apply new remedies must expect new evils; for time is the greatest innovator."* — Francis Bacon.

In the Balearic archipelago of Spain is a paradise called Cabrera Island. It's part of a sub-archipelago called Archipiélago de Cabrera, which has been a natural reserve since 1991. Here, wildlife flourishes, and human visitors bliss-out on beauty, surrounded by the Mediterranean's turquoise waters. It wasn't always so. Between 1973 to 1986, it was a base for the Spanish Armed Forces, although military usage actually goes back to 1916.

Between 1808 and 1814, Isla de Cabrera was a hellhole of suffering for humans and wildlife alike. 9000 of Napoleon's soldiers were imprisoned there after their defeat in the Peninsular War (when the allied forces of Spain, the United Kingdom, and Portugal repelled Napoleon's invasion of the Iberian Peninsula). Only 3600 made it out alive, due to starvation, disease, neglect, and abuse.

But the island's history of adaptive reuse goes even further back. During the 13th and 14th Century, the island was a base of pirate operations, due to its well-concealed harbor. That ended when Cabrera's castle was built, with its cannons guarding the entrance to the harbor.

Pirate base. Death camp. Armed garrison. Nature reserve. The way humans have constantly adapted the island to their changing needs serves as a microcosmic metaphor for our entire history—and future—on this planet. With the rise of the adaptive renewal megatrend, there's hope that the entire planet can follow a similar trajectory...similarly ending in paradise. But first we need to know how to manage adaptively—and how to institutionalize the practice—because it's a very different animal from the old plan-execute-plan-execute model.

> *"I work in whatever medium likes me at the moment." – Marc Chagall, artist.*

The global adaptive renewal megatrend has arisen from the convergence of three trends, each of which is huge and of vital importance in its own right: regeneration (of natural, built and socioeconomic assets); resilience (physical, economic and social); and adaptive management (which boosts the success of regeneration and resilience efforts by combining learning with action).

Revitalization makes poor places wealthier. It makes wealthy places healthier. It makes healthy, wealthy places healthier, wealthier, and happier. Combining revitalization with resilience makes the good times last. Managing revitalization and resilience efforts in an adaptive manner enables us to take action before we fully understand the problem, and keeps our remedies responsive to new knowledge, challenges and opportunities.

You can recognize the adaptive renewal megatrend at work in places that are constantly repurposing, renewing and reconnecting their natural, built, and socioeconomic environments in an integrated manner, that are monitoring their results and that are improving their methods as they go along.

Resilience efforts are mostly long-term, with few short-term benefits. That makes them a hard sell to both politicians and citizens, and thus difficult to fund. Revitalization, on the other hand, is an easy sell. It's been the most common political promise for millennia. Combining the two is thus logical. But both revitalization and resilience efforts usually have the same problem: lack of adaptive management.

ADAPTIVE MANAGEMENT

"You have to be fast on your feet and adaptive or else a strategy is useless."
— General Charles de Gaulle, President of France

Under today's incessant bombardment of change, plans tend to produce great stress for those charged with writing or executing them. Each day, the assumptions on which the plans are based diverge further from reality, yet professional managers are usually required to "stick to the plan". Adaptive management is a healthy recent trend that allows places and organizations to implement and evolve plans simultaneously. Such a plan is sometimes called a "living document".

Adaptive management is formally defined as "a structured, iterative process of robust decision making in the face of uncertainty, with an aim to reducing uncertainty over time via system monitoring." My informal definition is "a flexible management style that learns from—and quickly responds to—reality."

There are six key steps in adaptive management: 1) assess the problem; 2) design the solution; 3) implement the solution; 4) monitor the results; 5) evaluate the results; 6) adjust the solution. For practical purposes, I normally condense them into three pairs of related steps: 1) assess/design; 2) implement/monitor; 3) evaluate/adjust.

Adaptive management is a global trend in natural resource management that has yet to be widely adopted in urban applications. This is because natural resource managers and restoration ecologists are very aware of the deficiencies in their knowledge. As a result, they wisely developed adaptive management, in which plans are just starting points.

The business world is also catching on. Entrepreneurship professor Steve Blank (UC Berkeley) captured the spirit of adaptive management when he defined a startup as a "temporary organization searching for a repeatable business model."

Adaptive management arose primarily from two relatively recent realms of scientific research: 1) restoration ecology (the corresponding practice of which is known as ecological restoration), and 2) complexity science (the study of how complex adaptive systems arise, grow, die and are reborn.

Many insights—both useful and profound—have derived from complexity science, and you use technologies every day that are based on those insights.

Here are two of those insights that apply directly to the process of bringing places back to life: (1) Qualitatively new behaviors tend to emerge in dissipative (complex) systems that are out of equilibrium; and (2) Healthy complex systems tend to lie at the border of phase transitions and bifurcation points. The bottom line? Managing change effectively requires a tremendously open and adaptive mindset...one that doesn't panic when surrounded by uncertainty...one that welcomes and embraces surprise.

I was one of the first 250 members of the Society for Ecological Restoration, and was peripherally involved with the Santa Fe Institute, where I met complexity economist W. Brian Arthur in the late 90's. I've thus been privileged to witness the evolution of both of those new disciplines, and how they have benefited our lives.

Adaptive management arose because the rise of ecological restoration quickly revealed our vast ignorance as to how ecosystems form, how they build and maintain resilience, how they collapse and how they recover.

For centuries, we've deluded ourselves into thinking we understood nature, so we simply threw fences around large wildlands, assumed we had conserved them, and developed all around them. In many—maybe most—cases, such "protection" contributed to their devitalization. This was not a learning-intensive process.

Few activities reveal our lack of understanding of natural processes faster than the process of trying to recreate a damaged or destroyed ecosystem. The science of restoration ecology has probably revealed more useful insights into the dynamics of natural systems in the past two decades than we learned in the previous two millennia.

So, our search for better ways of managing urban revitalization—and the discovery of underlying principles, taxonomies, and frameworks—started with those scientists who bring complex systems back to life for a living: restoration ecologists. Scientists experiment on revitalizing ecosystems in ways that can't be done on human communities. This can lead to useful insights and metaphors for thinking about cities. One of the most important lessons emerging from the restoration of natural systems is the need for adaptive management.

Urban managers seem to be less aware of their ignorance than ecosystem managers, so comprehensive plans adopted by cities are expected to function unchanged for 5, 10, or even 15 years. But few such plans are ever implemented, and few that are implemented succeed to any significant degree. One thing that's common to both the failures and the successes is a paucity of monitoring: the process is seldom measured in any rigorous manner, so whatever lessons we learn are usually anecdotal.

Urban leaders seeking socioeconomic revitalization have much to learn from restoration ecology. The results of both their tactics and their strategies are monitored scientifically, and the lessons published in scientific journals such as *Restoration Ecology*, and in practitioner journals such as *Ecological Restoration*.

The starting point for this transition to adaptive management in urban environments will likely begin where the city and nature meet.

Here's a quote from the 2013 Healthy Waterways Strategy report from Melbourne, Queensland, Australia: "*Melbourne Water uses adaptive management to ensure that decision making is based on sound and current knowledge. This increases our ability to carry out activities that will result in the greatest gains for waterway health. Adaptive management relies on focused monitoring, investigations and research to build our knowledge of waterways and understand changing environmental conditions, outcomes of management approaches and the effect of external drivers such as climate change. We evaluate these programs to inform our planning and implementation and report outcomes to ensure knowledge is shared.*"

New York City's *PlaNYC 2030* plan for adapting to climate change—while accommodating 9 million new residents—is well-designed (the jury is still out on whether it's well-implemented) because it focuses on three key areas: 1) infrastructure renewal (especially green infrastructure); 2) retrofitting existing buildings; and 3) updating old building codes to current needs. Adapting the natural, built, socioeconomic, and policy/regulatory environments together is where the real magic will be found.

The best plans are not only adaptive, but are based on adapting (repurposing, renewing and/or reconnecting) existing assets. How did Chicago adapt its planning to fix its urban heat island problem, which killed 750 people in 1995? By repurposing roofs. Unlike in many traditional cultures—with their sod, moss or even crop-covered roofs—"modern" roofs are single-purpose: shield occupants from weather. But that design actually changes the local weather. With extremely hot days on the increase (July 2019 was officially the hottest month in recorded history), Chicago has transformed 4 million square feet of roofs into "green roofs". Besides cooling the city, they:

- reduce flooding from storms;
- help restore Lake Michigan by reducing combined sewer overflow; and

- help restore the climate by absorbing carbon.

Buildings and businesses aren't the only things that can outlive their form and function. Unchanging building codes, zoning, development incentives, and most other aspects of governance almost inevitably shift from contributing to community progress to retarding it. Keep your policies—not just your plans—adaptive, if you wish to improve your community's resilience.

But having adaptive policies is one thing. Having the courage to change them when you're making a lot of money from current bad policies is another. Bad policies can be incredibly destructive, especially those based in the Holocene's ancient sprawl-based model.

When I was doing some work in Belize back in the 80s, a local environmentalist was bemoaning the fact that the only way he could take ownership of the land he loved was by destroying it. The country's policy then (hopefully no longer) was that any citizen was entitled to land free of charge, provided they clear it first. This "destroy it and it's yours" policy resulted in widespread devastation of a place whose economy is strongly tourism-based. And most of those tourists come to see nature.

Throughout the 20th century, water engineers seemed to be on a quest to pollute the maximum amount of clean water with any given amount of raw sewage or industrial discharge.

They were driven by a poetic-but-brainless maxim: "the solution to pollution is dilution." But diluting 1 gallon of sewage with 100 gallons of clean water simply yields 101 gallons of polluted water. Diluting 1 gallon of sewage with 100,000 gallons of clean water yields 100,001 gallons of polluted water.

Combined sewer and stormwater systems made sense a century ago, when urban populations were relatively small, sewage treatment technologies were not in wide use, and cities still had significant amounts of permeable surfaces to absorb rainwater.

Flushing sewers with stormwater could be forgiven then, but what shouldn't be forgiven is how long it took communities to stop specifying them, and how long it took civil engineers to stop recommending them...decades after combined sewer overflows (CSO) were recognized as a crisis.

The need for adaptive management isn't the only lesson in managing urban areas that we can derive from the science of restoring ecosystems, of course. Three examples of other potential crossover lessons:

Restoration ecologists speak of "reparative restoration" (fixing damage, such as by reintroducing native species) versus "replacement restoration" (providing functional equivalents, such as hunters replacing wolves as top predators).

Lesson: Cities suffering industrial flight to lower-wage countries could choose between recruiting functionally equivalent employers versus restoring jobs by "repurposing" citizens via education, training, and entrepreneurial support.

Restoration ecologists can't restore nature 100%, so they aim for resilience. They use "foundational" species—such as corals, seagrasses, and oysters—that form the structural basis of ecosystems and contribute most to community stability. Nature then takes over, repairing itself and diversifying without further intervention.

Lesson: With limited funding, public leaders must focus on reaching the revitalization tipping point, where the free market takes over. This often involves renewing foundational assets; infrastructure, water, heritage, public services, etc.

Here's a quote from the paper "The Rapid Riparian Revegetation (R3) Approach" in Ecological Restoration (June 2014): *"With hundreds of thousands of kilometers of riparian corridors in need of restoration, and limited public funds for implementation, practitioners need to identify strategies that lower the unit cost and accelerate the pace of reestablishment of native riparian forests in sustainable ways. The R3 approach is grounded in ecological principles and geared towards producing outcomes consistent with restoration programming and the human desire to see "progress" for the investments made."*

Lesson: Replace "riparian corridors" with "cities", have R3 stand for "rapid resilient renewal", and this passage describes good urban strategies.

The constant arrival and territorial expansion of invasive species is just one of myriad factors creating a need for adaptive management of landscapes. In the U.S. alone, there are over 5000 invasive plant and animal species. A very conservative estimate by the U.S. Fish and Wildlife Service puts their annual national economic damage at about $120 billion.

Those charged with managing the problem have to juggle removing well-established invasive species, reducing the introduction of new invasive species, and reestablishing native species...all while the climate is changing and human activities are altering the air, soil and water.

Creating an effective, static long-term plan for such a mission under such circumstances is quite literally impossible. The only static situations are those devoid of life. Strategies and tactics must adapt not only to the changing situation, but to the changes they themselves cause, resulting in a constant—and often accelerating—loop of cause and effect, feedback and evolution.

> *"Life is not about waiting for the storms to pass......it's about learning to dance in the rain."*
> *— Vivian Greene*

This ignorance of complex adaptive systems dynamics is rife among managers of systems other than nature, such as human societies and economies. As a result, adaptive management is appearing everywhere, though often not by that name. Business people, for instance, have probably encountered the Minimum Viable Product strategy used by many technology start-ups. That's an example of adaptive management.

The "adaptive" in adaptive renewal might best be defined in terms of flow. Want a specific example of using adaptive management to revitalize a downtown? Look at parking policies and traffic flow.

Some say free or cheap parking causes traffic jams and undermines efforts to improve public transit. Others say traffic jams are a good problem to have: the goal is more shoppers, so the more free parking, the better. Still others say expensive parking is best: it encourages pedestrian-friendly, transit-oriented development, and the increased revenue funds downtown improvements. Who's right? All of them are.

Downtowns evolve and devolve like all living systems, so parking policies must adapt to current problems, needs and goals. If a downtown has a dearth of retail, then scaring people away with expensive, strongly-enforced parking isn't a good idea. It only takes one downtown parking ticket to convince a shopper that the sprawl mall is the better place to go. In that case, a switch to free parking might stimulate more visitors. This will encourage more retailers, which will stimulate more visitors, and so on in a positive feedback loop of revitalization.

But if that loop continues long enough, it will eventually result in traffic jams. That will make the downtown noisy, polluted, and dangerous for pedestrians, and they'll start coming less often. Parking fees can then be reintroduced, starting with cheap parking. If that doesn't bring traffic down to levels that restore the quality of downtown life, they can be hiked again, until the right balance is achieved.

But then someone is bound to say "Ah: we've found the right balance. Let's engrave this parking price in stone." Now they're heading for trouble again, because, again, cities are complex, living systems, and healthy systems never stay the same.

Parking policies are deceptively simple, but they are just one of myriad factors affecting the health and survival of your community that can be managed via policies. So, parking is a good place to start your journey into adaptive public management. Taking an adaptive approach to policymaking is a core element of resilience planning, but it's rarely practiced. I've seen many recent resilience plans for cities: few even mention adaptive management, much less were based on it.

When Manhattan's Times Square was pedestrianized, cars were completely banned. The rate of visitors quadrupled (delighting the merchants) and the crime rate dropped by half. So to many cars degrade a city center, as can a paucity of cars. The "right" number can revitalize it, and that number might be zero.

What revitalizes a dying place might devitalize a vibrant place. And what revitalizes a place now can kill the same place later. Such complexities are anathema to most public leaders, who like simple, easy "solutions." Adaptive management is a lot easier to write about than it is to practice, but fear not: technology is coming to the rescue.

We now have systems enabling real-time adaptability, as with demand-price parking meters, similar to Uber's surge pricing. So, revisions to parking policies might not be needed as frequently as before, as algorithms take over. Maybe we will one day have an Internet of Renewal (IoR) to go along with our Internet of Things (IoT): verb-based, rather than noun-based software.

Here's a recent example of this adaptive traffic flow dynamic at work. In April 2018, Buffalo, New York was on the verge of wasting a hoped-for TIGER Grant. This was a vestige of the late-and-lamented Transportation Investment Generating Economic Recovery program that helped revitalize many cities during the Obama administration, and which has been reincarnated by the Trump administration in a lobotomized form (it ignores most of what we've learned about cities in the past 30 years) rebranded as BUILD Grants.

Over 30 years ago, Buffalo city leaders were ahead of their time in banning cars from their Main Street. This greatly improved the quality of life downtown, but the desired economic revitalization never manifested.

The problem is that they never followed-through on the logical next step after eliminating the traffic problem: taking advantage of that increased quality of life to add what the downtown (and its businesses) desperately needed: more residents. One would think that the relationship of housing to residents to customers would be fairly easy to perceive. Not so at that time in Buffalo, apparently.

How did they plan to revitalize Main Street? By spending that precious TIGER Grant on restoring automobile traffic! Cars don't buy goods. Pedestrians do. This is the kind of wasteful, self-destructive decision that cities make when they don't think strategically. A good strategy affects the underlying cause to create the desired effect.

Adaptive management is the key to dealing with evolving challenges and evolving tools (like surge pricing and smart meters) in an evolving environment that we are changing as a result of our adaptive management…and doing so when we don't fully understand the dynamics of the system we wish to revitalize.

Pittsburgh's Mayor Bill Peduto is one public leader who "gets it": he's taking an adaptive management approach to the city's multi-decade, multi-river restoration challenge. Other city, county, state, national and multinational leaders are now doing likewise, as we'll see in a moment.

With all this constant, self-referential adaptation, we need to be especially careful that we don't lose sight of our goal. Any changes made to strategies, plans, and projects should reference the vision, to prevent "mission drift". As Steven Covey says, *"The main thing is to keep the main thing the main thing."* That's the importance of basing your resilient prosperity efforts on a shared vision, as we'll describe later.

Oscar Wilde described the importance of having an inspiring vision when he said *"We are all in the gutter, but some of us are looking at the stars."* The function of a clear vision is to keep an iterative (adaptive) strategy or iterative plan from iterating itself into a hole.

> *"Everybody has a plan until they get punched in the mouth." – Mike Tyson*

There are several ways of interpreting Mike Tyson's well-known above quote. It might mean that most people panic in the face of adversity, and lose track of their purpose. It might mean that having a plan is useless. Or, it might mean that having a fixed plan is useless: when it's reality that's punching us in the mouth, the plan must be adapted to reality. But in the rapidly-changing circumstances of a boxing match, it wouldn't a plan that's being adapted: it would be the strategy. (Referees frown on fighters consulting documents while they're in the ring.)

Large institutions seldom announce that they are switching from a "follow the plan at all costs" approach to an adaptive management approach.

This is partly because once it's understood, it makes their previous leadership look less than brilliant, and some of those previous leaders might now be on the board. But it's mainly because the process of adopting an adaptive approach should itself be adaptive. (Say that three times rapidly!)

For instance, the United States Agency for International Development (USAID) is the federal agency responsible for administering civilian (i.e. non-defense-related) foreign aid. USAID's annual budget is about $36 billion.

USAID has recently been embedding adaptive management into its funding mechanisms, but you'd hardly know it if you weren't directly involved in the process. They refer to it as the CLA Framework (Collaborating, Learning, Adapting).

In their new Program Cycle Operational Policy, they state that one of the three key requirements of funding applications from their international partners is "*Learning from performance monitoring, evaluations, and other relevant sources of information to make course corrections as needed and inform future programming.*"

For those involved in modern disaster-response and/or climate crisis adaptation initiatives, no such cultural change is needed: any true professional working in those areas knows that adaptive management is not optional.

A recent example of this can be found in the draft Adaptive Management Plan, published in October of 2016 by Louisiana's Coastal Protection and Restoration Authority.

The switch to adaptive management need not be disruptive. After all, all one is really doing is injecting common sense into the previously rigid, blind-faith-in-the-plan culture. Or, as Divyesh Mistry of the Toronto Transit Commission says: "Cities change. Get over it."

Due to the rapid rise in vacant commercial properties—malls, big box stores, office buildings, etc.—some architects are finally starting to think about designing buildings in a way that facilitates eventual adaptive reuse.

The architecture firm Gensler invented the term "hackable" buildings back in 2014 to capture the idea. They feel we should be constructing—and renovating—in a way that accommodates the desired immediate use, but that responds to changing market demands or preferences by making it easy for the structure to be reworked for a productive new life. It's basically a proactive approach to the concepts Stewart Brand laid out in his classic book, *How Buildings Learn*.

In today's climate of constant crisis and heightened uncertainty, planning for success means assuming the plan will probably fail, but not the project or program. Projects, plans, and programs for improving our built, natural, socioeconomic, and geopolitical environments must adapt not just to rapid change, but to an accelerating rate of change in each of these intrinsically-connected arenas.

Such conditions are highly corrosive to 5-year plans, which now decompose and putrefy at an accelerated rate. Longer-term plans are best suited to fundraising pitches, political posturing, and other fiction-rich endeavors. That said, the process of planning is often of great value, even when the relevance of the resulting plan is decaying even while it's still being written. An evolutionary ethos is the key to success in such an environment.

> *"Adapt what is useful, reject what is useless,*
> *and add what is specifically your own."*
> *– Bruce Lee (on creating a style of martial art).*

The only preservative we can add to our rust-prone plans is adaptability. Once implementation begins, we must be ready to defenestrate our highly-perishable plans at a moment's notice, lest they become toxic to our future. These days, only our shared visions of our desired future should be long-term, not the strategies, policies or plans we devise for achieving them. Adaptive management provides the flexibility (and reflects the humility) needed to deal with today's social, economic, political, and environmental precariousness.

While some manifestations of the adaptive renewal megatrend are well-established, many others are more recent or are still emerging. The latter include adaptive strategies related to climate change, sea level rise, and natural disasters, such as for cities, agriculture, and natural resources (including the creation of novel ecosystems).

Experts sometimes refer to "passive" vs. "active" adaptive management. Passive adaptive management is normal planning plus the monitoring and evaluation of results. Common sense, in other words. The passive form was invented to allow traditional managers to say they use adaptive management when they don't have the courage for it. The active form is what we've been discussing here.

SURPRISE!

As mentioned earlier, one characteristic that defines all living systems is the capacity to surprise. Adaptive management could thus be called "surprise management". It's the polar opposite of the engineering-based approach that dominates public management today.

In addition to maximizing efficiency, the primary purpose of an engineer is to eliminate surprises. This is wonderful skill when dealing with structures: no one likes driving over a bridge that behaves in an unpredictable manner. But it's a disaster when dealing with ecosystems or cities. Removing surprises from a living system is synonymous with killing it.

But even their efficiency goal can be problematic. Again: it's desirable for mechanical and structural engineering work, but is often inappropriate when applied by civil engineers working on complex systems.

Nature does many things that are inefficient in the microcosm, but highly efficient in the macrocosm. Plants create thousands of seeds—and fish lay thousands of eggs—since maybe 1/10th of 1% will reach reproductive age. The rest become food for other species. Forest fires are another example of (apparent) waste, and we've now seen the vast damage done to our ecosystems (and towns) when we try to engineer fires out of existence.

These are two of the major reasons the U.S. Army Corps of Engineers—in controlling the life out of our estuaries and waterways—has done more economic damage to America than all foreign armies combined. It's also why China might eventually be headed towards another national meltdown: they have far more engineers in local and national government than any other country.

Manhattan's magnificent High Line Park (which we'll return to later) is emblematic of the adaptive renewal megatrend. It created jobs, boosted real estate values, and increased quality of life. It revitalized, in other words.

The High Line was initially a bottom-up flow, a resident-led effort that led to a top-down flow of support by the city. It accomplished all of this through reuse of existing assets (an elevated railroad track), which reconnected neighborhoods and reestablished flows. These are the trends and models you'll see throughout this book.

Single-use places are a form of disconnection and isolation, whether urban or agricultural. Civil engineering has traditionally been oriented toward isolating functions, separating asset types and preventing flows.

So, it's not just that adaptive conquest must shift to adaptive renewal: the nature of our adaptations must shift from our traditional mode of fragmenting systems, blocking flows and eradicating surprises to a mode of reconnecting systems, restoring flows and encouraging surprises.

TERMINOLOGY AND CONCEPTS

"The problem with investing in resilience is where is the cash flow? What we're doing is protecting against future damage, but there's not a new positive cash flow. You're not creating new value. You're protecting against loss of existing value." – David Levy, UMass – Boston.

Revitalization is the process of regaining lost vitality.
Resilience is the process of retaining vitality.
Resilient prosperity is the process of regaining and retaining vitality.

Terminology is important, and becomes even more important when huge sums of money—and the future of communities—are involved. In the 50s and 60s, the U.S. federal government offered cities hundreds of millions of dollars to revitalize any area they labeled "blighted." White politicians and urban planners usually decided that the word meant any place with large numbers of darker-skinned, lower-income people and/or immigrants. Hundreds of vibrant neighborhoods were demolished as a result, all in the name of "urban renewal." A more-rigorous definition of blight embedded in policy might have prevented a lot of unnecessary suffering.

While most articles about the horrors of urban renewal focus (rightly) on the human cost, it should be noted that vast numbers of manufacturers and retail businesses fled the downtowns for the suburbs while all of the physical devastation was taking place. This was an example of destructive federal policymaking: the catalytic funding initially came from the Housing Act of 1949, and was accelerated by the National Interstate Defense and Highways Act of 1956. It was called "urban renewal", but it was just demolition and new infrastructure. A more-rigorous definition of revitalization might have prevented a lot of unnecessary devitalization.

My current working definition of revitalization: *"Revitalization is a cycle of rising optimism, equitable prosperity, quality of life, and environmental health—usually triggered by renewing, reconnecting, and/ or repurposing distressed natural, built, socioeconomic, and human assets—and often preceded by a cycle of devitalization."*

The 2008 movie, *Slum Dog Millionaire* was praised outside India, but largely reviled within India. Why? Because it perpetuated the faulty perceptions of slum life that help Westerners feel superior. It ignored the positive aspects of slum communities, which can often make American suburbs look dysfunctional—even sociopathic—by comparison. These days, many socially-rich slums are being bulldozed In India, to be replaced with the isolated, anonymous life of apartment and condo towers.

In his December 19, 2014 article in Global Site Plans, "Why Some Mumbai, India Slum Dwellers Prefer Slums to Condos", writer Adwitya Das Gupta quoted his slum-dwelling maid as *"If I am late from work, my neighbours bring my children dinner and make sure they are taken care of without me needing to ask... I have friends there and people I can rely on. Why would I want to move? I think the communities we have there are much stronger than you would even have here."*

Maybe we need to redefine "slum". Those examples are just a tiny sampling of the suffering that can arise from imprecise terminology. Sometimes, a perfectly good word takes on a negative meaning as a result of bad practices. In Milton Keynes, England several public housing projects are being demolished and replaced with better housing. But it's apparently being done in a way that results in unnecessarily-high levels of displacement and social trauma.

A February 28, 2019 article in the Milton Keynes Citizen reported that Former Milton Keynes Council leader Kevin Wilson said *"I want the word regeneration replaced with something more community-inclusive. The word 'regeneration' has become synonymous with the word 'demolition'. The moment that you raise the spectre of 'regeneration', residents think that you are hiding something. The word itself has become toxic."*

In February of 2019, the Colorado Springs City Council was asked to declare 40 acres of virgin greenfields in the foothills to be an "urban renewal" zone. Some city leaders wanted to boost their tourism revenue by letting the U.S. Air Force Academy build a new 57-acre visitors' center in this sprawl area.

The visitors center may or may not be a good idea, but calling it "urban renewal" is most definitely a bad idea. Doing so will undermine the city's credibility in any future attempts to attract state or federal revitalization funding. This behavior certainly isn't limited to Colorado: any time national governments create a pot of money with a given label, local politicians will call their project whatever's necessary to get their hands on it.

That abuse of terminology in the scramble for money isn't always totally misguided. In Michigan, for instance, any vacant property (usually residential) that's accepted into a local land bank's inventory is automatically designated a brownfield, whether or not there's any suspected or actual contamination. This gives the land bank access to state brownfields funding.

That's terminological misuse in a good cause, but it could undermine "real" brownfields reuse efforts. On the other hand, every plot of land on the planet is contaminated by something—old lead-based paint, oil leaks from vehicles, brake pad dust, etc.—so it's a relative term. Most homes and lawns in the U.S. could be considered brownfields, given the heavy applications of toxins to kill weeds, mosquitoes, termites, fleas, rats, etc.

And so it is with resilience, where terminological fuzziness abounds. Part of the problem is that people often say they seek community resilience without specifying the type of resilience: social, natural disaster, climate, economic, etc. Or, they aren't aware that all of those types of resilience must be addressed to create real community resilience.

> *"Revitalization goes beyond the achievement of bouncing forward...As a community revitalizes, it increases its capacity to reap the resilience dividend."* – Dr. Judith Rodin, former President of The Rockefeller Foundation (2014)

If you're new to the study of resilience, let me explain the "bouncing forward" reference in Dr. Rodin's above quote about revitalization and resilience. Traditionally, cities hit by catastrophe (whether sudden and natural, or gradual and socioeconomic) have rather mindlessly gone about rebuilding in a way that merely reconstructed what had been lost. Their goal was to "bounce back."

If resilience is your goal, you want to "bounce forward"...rebuilding better than you were before, in a way that makes you less vulnerable to future disasters. One might call this "preemptive planning". Leadership of ANY kind can be actually defined as "acting before one has to," which fits a resilience agenda perfectly.

I described this concept in my 2002 book, *The Restoration Economy*, showing how Lisbon, Portugal rebuilt the entire city on higher ground after a massive earthquake and tsunami in 1755.

They were also smart enough to take advantage of the opportunity to correct a number of urban planning mistakes (actually, lack of planning). That redesign was led by the Marquês de Pombal, who is sometimes called the world's first urban planner. He was probably Robert Moses' inspiration, as his style of planning has been called "despotic." Nonetheless, the present-day result is one of the world's most beautiful cities.

"Bouncing forward" is, in fact, a pretty good example of a strategy: it's succinct, memorable, an effective guide in decision-making, and reliably successful when well-implemented in the right place at the right time.

Unfortunately, government bureaucracies are often stuck in "bounce-back" mode, as FEMA has often demonstrated. Even worse are maladaptive recovery efforts that actually compound problems (usually due to short-term, palliative thinking and/or budget constraints from tax cuts).

> *"There really is this claustrophobic pressure to innovate instead of to adapt."*
> – Chelsea Clinton, Clinton Foundation.

Again: resilience is revitalization plus adaptability. Revitalization makes poor (or damaged) places wealthier, and wealthy places healthier. It makes healthy, wealthy places healthier, wealthier, and happier. Adaptability helps make the good times last. Resilient prosperity, in other words.

We should keep in mind that health and wealth (both in their holistic senses) are emergent qualities of doing the right things in the right way for the right amount of time. So, they should not be goals in themselves. Their nature is too ephemeral, and their emergence is too unpredictable to serve as deliverables. As Eleanor Roosevelt wisely said of another ephemeral goal: "*Happiness is not a goal...it's a by-product.*"

Most folks define resilience along the lines of "the ability to bounce back from adversity or trauma, or adjust to change". Traditionally applied primarily to materials and individuals, it has now become a goal of institutions and communities (as well as restored ecosystems). [Note: I use "resilience" in this book, rather than "resiliency." Their meanings are identical, and both are real words. But "resiliency" is mostly used in casual American conversation. This guide uses the shorter, more elegant form preferred by scientists and educators, and by most English-speakers worldwide.]

A systems-oriented definition of resilience is: "the capacity of a system to absorb disturbance and re-organize while undergoing change so as to still retain essentially the same function, structure, identity, and feedbacks."

In their 2012 book *Resilience: Why Things Bounce Back*, authors Zolli and Healy offer an institutionally-oriented definition: "*the capacity of a system, enterprise, or a person to maintain its core purpose and integrity in the face of dramatically changed circumstances.*"

Resilient solutions are normally 1) redundant (to endure loss or damage); 2) flexible/scalable (to endure growth, contraction, and change); and 3) integrative/strategic (to endure time and heal fragmentation).

The desire for revitalization can be triggered by a long, slow decline, a sudden disaster, or simply dissatisfaction with the current quality of life. The desire for resilience is often triggered by recent or impending disaster: a fishery on the edge of collapse, a fragile economy, climate-related agricultural challenges, etc. So, revitalization is motivated by present-day pain, whereas resilience is motivated by a desire to avoid future pain. The two goals have obvious overlaps.

This book is not about resilience in the traditional sense. There are many excellent books on that subject. One of the more recent is *The Resilience Dividend*, by the Rockefeller Foundation's former CEO, Dr. Judith Rodin, published in November of 2014. Her 384-page work on resilience was especially insightful because it included a chapter on revitalization.

This book, RECONOMICS, has the opposite emphasis: it focuses more heavily on revitalization, and its role in resilience. That's because resilience is the poorly-funded newcomer, whereas revitalization, regeneration, and redevelopment agencies and budgets have been around for decades, if not centuries. Refocusing these established community and regional assets on resilient prosperity is thus the low-hanging fruit. An obvious and frequent connection between resilience and regeneration is in post-disaster situations.

This book thus comes at resilience from an oblique angle. Rather than focusing on traditional resilience strategies, it shows how the parallel trends/activities of community revitalization and natural resource restoration are ideal paths to a resilience effort. This is as opposed to launching yet another silo, this one called "resilience."

Zolli and Healy state in their book, "*preserving adaptive capacity—the ability to adapt to changed circumstances while fulfilling one's core purpose—[is] an essential skill in an age of unforeseeable disruption and volatility.*" This is where most resilience efforts falter. They know that one of the most important principles of resilience is flexibility, yet they try to use their old, inflexible planning and management systems to implement it. It's like removing tumors with a shotgun: simply not the right tool.

A related area in which resilience efforts get into trouble is in making safety their primary (or even sole) goal. Safety sounds like a reasonable objective, but it can become a rigid, fear-based ethos, preventing us from taking the risks needed to innovate and become more flexible and, ironically, safer. There is no safety: there is only safer. In excessive fear lies vulnerability.

As Will Rogers said, "*You've got to go out on a limb sometimes, because that's where the fruit is.*" He also said "A vision, without a plan, is just a hallucination." But he said that back in the days before planning became a formal discipline and industry, and before plans became a product and a formality...an end unto themselves.

Redundant, flexible/scalable, and integrative/strategic are the key (not only) factors in creating resilience. But again: resilience by itself won't produce prosperity: revitalization does that. Resilience makes revitalization durable, and adaptive management keeps it relevant via flexible implementation.

Together, these three trends form the conceptual basis of a path to resilient prosperity. This book will turn those broad concepts into a specific process you can put to use immediately in your community or organization. Adaptive management constantly reorients actions towards what actually works. It's the key to making resilience initiatives resilient (many aren't, as we saw with the failed 100 Resilient Cities program).

Resilience and adaptation most often converge when places prepare for climate change-related sea level rise and storms. Not surprisingly, Florida has a great deal of activity in this regard. Their Department of Economic Opportunity (DEO) offers many web resources on community resilience and adaptation planning.

It describes three basic strategies for coastal communities in response to sea level rise: protection (armoring the shore with hard and/or green infrastructure), accommodation (elevating structures to minimize flood damage), and retreat (turning at-risk areas into parks, and moving structures to safer locations). They list dozens of potential funding sources for such projects.

In 2012, the Florida DEO launched a 5-year project called "Community Resiliency Initiative: Planning for Adaptation." It integrated adaptation to potential sea level rise into all three local planning mechanisms: the comprehensive plan, the hazard mitigation plan, and the post-disaster redevelopment plan.

> *"It is good to have an end to journey towards,*
> *but it is the journey that matters, in the end."*
> *– Ursula Le Guin, American writer.*

But adaptation efforts are not the same as adaptive management. While shared visions and goals can enhance success, adaptive management helps ensure progress even in their absence, and even when the goals turn out to be faulty. Adaptive management is thus more focused on the journey of renewal, rather than the destination.

A good revitalization strategy will, of course, adapt to the challenges of a changing climate. That requires stronger, not weaker, environmental regulations. Likewise, a good climate resilience strategy will adapt to the challenges of a changing economy. A city can't thrive if its streets are under water. And it can't pay for climate adaptation projects if its economy is under water.

THE RISE OF FIXERS

> *"The most common way people give up their*
> *power is by thinking they don't have any."*
> *– Alice Walker.*

Our world has no shortage of people who want to renew communities and/or natural resources, or whose vocation or avocation it is to do so. I generally call them "fixers." Fixers are the ones who actually get it done, despite insufficient resources, political difficulties, bureaucratic obstacles, or social injustices.

It's similar to how there's no dearth of people who would like to be authors, but who find an plethora of excellent reasons why they can't write now. Writers write. Fixers fix. The ability to fix assets—or situations (such as depressed communities)—is often the only characteristic fixers share. They arise from all socioeconomic backgrounds, professions, and age groups.

So, the job of those who wish to revitalize places is simple: either become a fixer, or attract fixers. If one is successful at the latter, one joins the ranks of fixers. In our present-day world—which is more broken than at any previous time in history (even our climate is broken!)—no breed of individual or organization is more desperately needed than the fixer.

For most of the past century, community redevelopment has been a top-down activity. It was envisioned and run by political leaders and government agencies. When a public leadership vacuum existed, it was controlled by real estate developers, whose projects (both sprawl and redevelopment) were often at odds with the best interests of the community.

Over the past couple of decades, a strong movement towards bottom-up (resident-led) revitalization efforts emerged. Our modern times—characterized by ubiquitous and accelerating economic, environmental, and social crises—has collided with an onslaught of disintermediating technologies (such as crowdsourcing and crowdfunding) that bypass traditional command-and-control hierarchies. The result is that leadership of community revitalization has become diffuse, emergent, and opportunistic.

Is resident-led renewal a real thing? Here's an excerpt from an article titled "What Cities Looking to Shrink Can Learn From New Orleans" by Roberta Brandes Gratz in the April 5, 2012 issue of *The Atlantic*: "*American cities started losing population after World War II with the creation of suburbs. "Planned Shrinkage," no different from today's shrinkage strategies, was New York's solution to a South Bronx that looked like Dresden after the war and other failing neighborhoods. Fire houses, police stations, schools closed, garbage ignored, streets unrepaired. But residents citywide fought back fiercely, refused to leave, took over vacant buildings, fixed them up on their own, stuck it out with minimum city services and with mottos like "improve don't move" set about on a sweat equity path that was the catalyst for a slow, incremental citywide rebound. Developers followed the residents' lead. That is why New York grew again, instead of shrank. The same pattern of regeneration took hold in small doses slowly in Savannah, Pittsburgh, Cincinnati, San Antonio and more. Now, similar pockets of re-growth can be found in Buffalo, Detroit, Syracuse, Muncie, South Bend and elsewhere.*"

Anyone can have a great idea for renewing their neighborhood, city or region. This has always been the case. What's new is that people with such ideas can now take rapid, effective action, turning their ideas into projects with a facility never before seen. This is the root of the rise of fixers.

> *"What we think, or what we know, or what we believe is, in the end, of little consequence. The only consequence is what we do."*
> – John Ruskin, writer and philanthropist.

Fixers can be ordinary citizens, green/social entrepreneurs, mayors, community foundations, non-profits, or real estate redevelopers. Those communities that wish to tap 100% of their revitalization potential must learn to be both responsive to, and supportive of, fixers. The flip side is that they must also learn to resist initiatives that retard revitalization, whether they come from elected leaders or powerful developers.

This "fixer ecosystem" creates a redevelopment meritocracy that advances good projects, programs and policies, no matter from whom they originate. Healthy communities develop a "radar" for renewal—"redar" if you will—that quickly spots and responds to revitalizing ideas that don't arise through normal channels.

A fixer—as the purposely-prosaic name suggests—is a person (working individually or through an organization) who repairs the form and/or function of a dead, dying, or otherwise-distressed place or asset. These fixes could be in a city, such as renewing an empty building, decrepit park, or drug-ridden neighborhood. They could be in a rural area, such as restoring farmlands depleted by overgrazing or industrial agriculture. Or they could be in a natural place, such as reviving a damaged reef or estuary.

Prevailing wisdom is that people don't like change. This isn't true. Most people enjoy change; that's why the most popular category of non-fiction book in America is self-help. What they hate is being changed. So too, most people enjoy self-organizing into effective groups and teams. But they often don't like being organized by others. This explains why so many community engagement exercises yield so few lasting, measurable results.

Most fixers fix only the present (existing problems). Revitalization without resilience, in other words. These are often the private fixers. Public fixers also fix the present, but are also responsible for the longer term—fixing the future—so they must also identify and reduce vulnerabilities. People in many blighted or declining places are working hard to fix their present, but they're not doing it in a resilient manner. Many fail outright.

> *"If it can't be reduced, reused, repaired, rebuilt, refurbished, refinished, resold, recycled or composted, then it should be restricted, redesigned or removed from production."*
> — *singer/social activist Pete Seeger.*

Of those that succeed, many will achieve a burst of growth and renewal, only to see it fade. This can be even more painful and psychologically devastating to the citizens than outright failure.

Syncing your community or organization with the adaptive renewal megatrend involves two key areas of change:

- Leadership that effectively adapts to surprises in general, and to emergent resources/initiatives contributing to resilient prosperity in particular; and
- Implementation that renews, repurposes, and reconnects your existing natural, built, and socioeconomic assets, adapting them to both current needs and future threats/opportunities.

As we'll see a bit later, the RECONOMICS Process provides a context that facilitates both of these challenges.

The following passage appeared in an article titled "Slow Moving Miracle" by Sven Eberlein in the Winter 2015 issue of *YES! Magazine*: "'I think all the government projects [to revitalize Medellín, Colombia] are good in a sense,' says Juan Carlos Anadón, Project Coordinator for the nonprofit Fundación Pazamanos. 'But things are really complex when you work in the trenches of social development. You have to have flexibility to address problems you find along the way, which people who work in government often don't have.'"

Thomas Edison said "Our greatest weakness lies in giving up. The most certain way to succeed is always to try just one more time." Few disagree. But many places do give up, and citizens acquiesce. We seem to believe that—unlike individuals—some communities simply can't revitalize. That's usually been nonsense, though today, sea level rise is quickly destroying the future of many long-established communities...and even nations. But giving up on a location doesn't necessarily mean giving up on a community, as we'll see later.

Adaptive management has no endpoint. It keeps regeneration and resilience processes viable. Thus, it can't fail in the long run, though it might not succeed on your preferred timetable. But simply perpetuating efforts isn't enough: they must be the right efforts, organized in a way that identifies efficiencies and synergies.

For instance, infrastructure undergrounding beautifies an area—thus leading to revitalization—but it's also a major contributor to storm resilience. Identifying such overlaps early can greatly increase both funding and public support for expensive projects.

RESTORATIVE SPRAWL

I'll end this chapter by acknowledging that the world population is still growing—and urbanizing—quickly, and that some nations don't have enough cities to handle that growth, no matter how well they revitalize them. But these same places often have a wealth of damaged and depleted landscapes.

In that case, a model I call "restorative sprawl" is the way to go. It's an integrated approach to designing, funding, and building new suburbs and new cities that goes beyond the usual "green" and "sustainable" designs: it actually restores watersheds, biodiversity, and farmland. It would work almost anywhere—especially arid lands—as there are few places on the planet where the local water resources, wildlife, and topsoil have not already been significantly degraded.

CHAPTER 2 - THE CRISIS RESTORATION ECONOMY: RECOVERY, REVITALIZATION & RESILIENCE SHOULD BE ACHIEVED TOGETHER.

"The nation behaves well if it treats its natural resources as assets which it must turn over to the next generation INCREASED...in value."
– Colonel Theodore Roosevelt, President of U.S.

As President, Teddy Roosevelt was in an ideal strategist's position when he voiced the vision quoted above. At the time, many of the U.S. regions that are today well-forested (such as New England) were ugly, barren, muddy wastelands. Over a century of rampant, unregulated deforestation to build ships and cities had ensured that outcome.

Too bad Teddy never created a strategy to activate that vision. The U.S. could have started launched its restoration economy a century earlier.

The still-emerging field of regenerative economics was launched in 2002 with the publication of my first book, *The Restoration Economy*. Today, new approaches to restorative economic development are arising on a regular basis. The "circular economy" trend is one of the best modern iterations of the idea. The Ellen MacArthur Foundation defines a circular economy as *"a framework for an economy that is restorative and regenerative by design."*

The Restoration Economy was the first book to document the rapid rise of a broad spectrum of regenerative industries and disciplines.

Some of them were quite new at the time of its publication, such as restoration ecology and brownfields remediation.

In fact, the U.S. Environmental Protection Agency had just launched its revolutionary brownfields program (probably the single most efficient federal program in the nation's history, in terms of return on investment) in 1995, the year before I started writing The Restoration Economy.

Eight of the book's twelve chapters created a taxonomy of the restoration economy, categorizing eight sectors of restorative development. These eight sectors involve the regeneration of the natural and built environments.

Revitalization of the socioeconomic environment is a fairly automatic outcome of that work, if restorative development of the natural and built environments is done strategically, and with that goal in mind.

I addressed the global climate fifteen times in that first book, but it obviously wasn't enough, considering how much worse things are now. Since that book was published, we've had 9 of the 10 hottest years in recorded history. As I write this, Category 5 Hurricane Dorian just hours ago obliterated the Abaco Islands and Grand Bahama Island in the Bahamas...while the U.S. President was busy playing golf and denying that there's a climate crisis.

Here's that original eight-sector taxonomy of the restoration economy, updated to show its adaptive, carbon-negative relevance to restoring our global climate:

- Ecosystem and biodiversity restoration: restored ecosystems sequester carbon while stopping carbon from being released by dying ecosystems, and—done properly—they leave the land more resilient. So this sector is adaptive, mitigating and restorative vis-a-vis the climate.
- Aquifer recharging and waterway/watershed restoration: Nothing is more crucial to surviving climate disruption than the ability to generate fresh water when you need it, and absorb it efficiently when you're getting too much of it. And restoring a watershed is largely based on growing trees (which sequesters carbon), so this sector addresses climate restoration and adaptation.
- Estuary, reef, and pelagic fishery regeneration: the "blue carbon" sequestration approach focuses heavily on mangrove restoration, which also makes coastlines more resilient. So this sector also achieves both climate restoration and adaptation.
- Regenerative agriculture (ranching, farming and aquaculture): Regenerative farming and ranching sequesters about four times as much carbon as reforestation, so that restores the climate. And, since the industrial ag model it replaces is a huge greenhouse gas emitter, that makes it mitigating, as well. It tends to be far more resilient to drought, not to mention more profitable, so it's a form of climate adaptation. Regenerative mariculture with shellfish or seaweed leaves the water cleaner. Even better, the mollusks sequester carbon in their shells, and

seaweed sequesters five times more carbon than land-based plants, so this sector is both adaptive and restorative, climate-wise.
- Brownfields remediation and redevelopment: This is normally a form of infill development, so it mitigates climate change by reducing both commuting and deforestation (from sprawl). Extracting methane from landfills is also climate mitigation, as is the use of brownfields for producing renewable energy ("brightfields"). Removing contamination from riparian areas (many brownfields and Superfund sites are on rivers and lakes) reduces the spread of toxins during climate-related floods, so this sector is adaptive, as well.
- Infrastructure renewal: Nothing is more crucial to the climate crisis than renovating our global energy infrastructure from fossil fuels to renewables. Doing so in an underground and microgrid design is far more resilient that our current centralized, above-ground grids, so this is a form of adaptation. Renovating our transportation infrastructure to focus less on automobiles and more on public transit, walking and bicycling both mitigates climate changes and makes cities more resilient when disasters hit, so this sector is also adaptive.
- Heritage restoration/reuse: Renovating and/or repurposing the structures we already have mitigates climate change both by reusing the embodied energy and by eliminating the very significant emissions of new construction. So, this sector is more relavent to climate restoration than most people might assume.
- Catastrophe reconstruction: This sector is (tragically) a major growth industry, so we need to be sure we accomplish it in a resilient manner that takes all of the above sectors into consideration. The technologies and designs are already present, allowing us to rebuild in a way that adapts to, mitigates and restores our climate.

So, the restoration economy might now be called the climate restoration economy, since that's Job One, and the modality is virtually identical. The good news is that regeneration of our built, natural and socioeconomic environments exploded after *The Restoration Economy* first appeared. (I'm not claiming any kind of causal relationship, of course: it would have happened whether or not I put those words to paper. But I enjoy thinking that the book might have accelerated the trend just a teensy bit.)

What was exceptional back in 1996 is now pretty much the norm. Everyone wants to get on with restoring nature and regenerating our cities. We just need to add one rather major new agenda to that original mix: restoring our climate.

You say you don't believe that restoration is now ubiquitous? What's one of the least-likely industries you can think of as a sponsor of stream restoration? How about professional hockey? The NHL Foundation pledged to restore 1000 gallons of stream flow to the Deschutes River in Oregon for every goal scored during the 2011-2012 regular season. This was in support of the Bonneville Environmental Foundation's (BEF) Water Restoration Certificate Program...which is itself another indicator of restorative development's increasing maturity.

Regenerative economics was advanced six years later when McGraw-Hill Professional (a now-defunct division of McGraw-Hill) published my second book, *Rewealth*.

One way of differentiating the focus of *The Restoration Economy* from that of *Rewealth* is that the former was more about the "ingredients" of revitalization (the various types of asset renewal).

The latter, on the other hand, was more about the "recipe" for those ingredients: how one combines them to create economic growth and increased quality of life (revitalization).

The Restoration Economy was documenting a historic shift in the global economy, so it was more theoretical.

Rewealth contained case studies of places coming back to life in a dramatic and unexpected manner—as well as the professionals and businesses that help them do so—so it was more practical.

Regenerative economics was yet advanced again in 2012 by the great Marjorie Kelly with her book *Owning Our Future*, which was taglined "Journeys to a Generative Economy." It was published by Berrett-Koehler Publishers, the same wonderful folks who had published *The Restoration Economy* a decade earlier.

Although *Owning Our Future* is more about ownership models, and didn't focus directly on "re", it conveyed that message indirectly by categorizing economic activities as being either "generative" or "extractive."

That mirrored *The Restoration Economy*'s "destructive development" mode (based on sprawl and the extraction of non-renewable resources) vs. the "restorative development" mode (based on revitalizing the places we've already developed, and restoring the natural resources we damaged along the way).

Here's an excerpt from the Foreword to *Owning Our Future*, written by David Korten: "*Our well-being, indeed our future as a species, depends on restoring our relationships to one another and with the land, the water, the sky, and the other generative resources of nature that indigenous people traditionally considered it their obligation to hold and manage in sacred trust. The architecture of ownership is key.*"

Kelly and Korten were right that affecting the behavior of those who own capital and real assets is crucial to restoring both our planet and confidence in our economies. It's easy to understand people's distrust of big business when one looks at the blatant hypocrisy of large corporations. They preach the gospel of free enterprise while they're small and want unfettered access to markets. But as soon as they're large enough to pull it off, they use their money to get government to restrict the markets, so others can't compete with them.

The majority of economic activity worldwide now consists of gambling. It's called "investing" in polite company, but seldom are any real stocks or bonds involved: people and companies are merely gambling on derivatives, and derivatives of derivatives. There is no effective difference between these derivatives and making a bet at the horse track. They are merely a way for those with access to privileged information to siphon money out of the market.

If we want economic restoration, we need to first cleanse the economy of giant parasites. Otherwise, it would be like setting a boat on a new course, while ignoring the gaping holes in its hull.

> *"...we have devised a Ponzi scheme with the planet over the last couple of centuries, exploiting natural resources, other species, foreign cultures, and even future generations to keep those at the top of this pyramid scheme enriched. As we know from other, smaller Ponzi schemes, such frauds cannot last."*
> *– Thomas Fisher, Dean, University of Minnesota.*

The remedy for the Ponzi scheme described in Professor Fisher's above quote isn't to improve the scheme by making it more "green" and "sustainable".

Only altering the fundamental basis of wealth creation can subvert it. Economic activity that increases our resource base can flip that pyramid on its head, creating ever-greater health, wealth, and happiness for all.

What's especially encouraging is that the powers-that-be at the top of the current pyramid can maintain their wealth, if they too make this shift.

This minimizes disruption to our political structures, since money is the basis of political power. In other words, this is a revolution that can—in theory—be implemented without bloodshed.

RE: A PREFIX-BASED STRATEGY FOR GLOBAL REVITALIZATION VIA POLICYMAKING.

The regeneration of our planet could be reduced to a change in prefix. We need to replace "de" with "re". Transitioning to a global (or local) restoration economy happens when we move...

- ...from development to redevelopment
- ...from despoilment to remediation
- ...from depletion to replenishment
- ...from demolition to reuse
- ...from destruction to restoration
- ...from degeneration to regeneration.

In other words, we need to stop being degenerates, and start becoming regenerates.

The de-re shift could be greatly accelerated via a shift to true-cost (AKA: full-cost) accounting, but that would undermine far too many huge corporation with powerful political connections. The lack of true-cost accounting enables many archaic, inappropriate industries to live far past their sell-by date.

Fossil fuel firms continue to claim that renewables are too expensive. In fact, fossil fuels are many times more expensive, but their costs are hidden. Many other authors have written entire books on the subject, so let me just offer one example to the uninitiated.

Canadian tar sands extraction is a top contender for the most criminally-irresponsible industry on the planet. Their political influence enables them to enjoy freedom from normal business costs.

For instance, the good people of Toronto pay about $674 annually per household for their water. The tar sands companies pay $0, and they use the same amount of water annually (370 million cubic meters from a single river) as the entire city of Toronto.

A shift to true-cost accounting would automatically shift economies from degenerative to regenerative activities: the numbers would force it. But don't hold your breath waiting for it to happen: such a structural shift is too terrifying to entrenched power.

Instead, the current incremental approach is the only other option; more of a long-term economic gut renovation than sudden demolition and replacement.

REGARDING DEMOLITION

The repurposing, renewing, and reconnecting of existing natural, built, and socioeconomic assets has long been the foundation of my "restoration economy" approach.

That said, not everything is worth saving. Demolition can, in fact, make way for progress. But demolition without a follow-up revitalization strategy can lead to social and economic isolation.

Some buildings are simply too ugly or too badly-constructed to be worth saving, like the FBI headquarters here in Washington, DC. It could have been declared "blight" the day it was commissioned. The hideous architecture is bad enough, but it was also shoddily built, so it's a maintenance nightmare.

While I'm a passionate advocate of historic preservation, I don't believe trash is magically transformed to treasure on its 50th birthday (50 years is the age a building becomes "historic" in the U.S.; a standard seen as ridiculously low in older nations).

Other buildings are rendered un-reusable by water damage from poorly-maintained roofs, or by vandals (such as copper thieves).

But in general, planners and mayors often avoid the complexity of repurposing and renewing existing assets, and just go for the simplistic "wipe it all clean and start afresh" approach of mass demolition. This can sometimes make sense in places that desperately need to downsize their infrastructure maintenance budget to cope with a drastically lower population (like Youngstown, Ohio), but only if they have a strategic renewal process in place. Youngstown's "city shrinking" vision was both innovative and brilliant, but they apparently lacked a strategy for overcoming the obstacles to it, and/or a process to implement that strategy.

Speaking of Ohio, the Slavic Village neighborhood of Cleveland provides some insights into the relationship of demolition and rehabilitation. Slavic Village was the epicenter of the national foreclosure crisis: it had the highest number of foreclosures of any zip code in the country in 2008 and 2009.

The predominantly African-American neighborhood is now revitalizing nicely, thanks in large part to a not-for-profit organization called Slavic Village Development (SVD). Its Executive Director, Chris Alvarado, credits much of their progress to SVD's partnership with the Cuyahoga Land Bank, which was created in 2009 specifically to deal with the foreclosure crisis.

The land bank's economic impact over that decade is estimated $1.43 billion, based on restored property values accomplished via a combination of demolishing and rehabilitating distressed structures so the properties can be returned to Cuyahoga County's tax rolls, plus the jobs created in the process.

Until recently, federal and state funding assistance focused on demolition, so that's what they did. Now that these funds are drying up, the Cuyahoga Land Bank is shifting to what often makes far more sense: rehabilitation. They are also adding commercial properties to their historic focus on residential (a shift I've recommended to a number of land bank clients over the years).

WABI-SABI: SOME DECREPIT STRUCTURES NEED NEITHER RENEWAL NOR DEMOLITION TO REVITALIZE A PLACE...JUST PROMOTION.

In Japan, the aesthetic concept of wabi-sabi (first brought to most Americans' attention by TV's Bart Simpson, of all "people") is one of the characteristics that dramatically sets their culture apart from that of the United States.

In Japan, they tend to appreciate the uniqueness of a flaw or irregularity in a new product (it gives it personality: making it an object only one person owns), and the decrepitude of an old object. Wabi-sabi is a world view centered on the acceptance of transience and imperfection. The aesthetic is sometimes described as one of beauty that is "imperfect, impermanent, and incomplete."

Characteristics of the wabi-sabi aesthetic include asymmetry, roughness, simplicity, economy, austerity, modesty, intimacy, and appreciation of the ingenuous integrity of natural objects and processes.

Here in the USA, we worship visual perfection. And not just in inanimate objects, either: We warehouse our old people in commercial operations we like to call retirement "homes", so we don't have to see their physical deterioration on the street. Those with gross deformities, like goiters or facial cancers, don't dare go into public if they can't afford cosmetic surgery (which is common, what with our being in the only industrialized nation without universal health care).

In most other nations, by comparison, the ancient and the afflicted can walk in plain view down the street without drawing looks of disgust, horror or even outright anger at their polluting of our visual environment. In our drugged, commercial American cocoon—where pharmaceuticals and buying new stuff fixes everything—we don't like to be reminded that death and disease exist.

We Americans waste vast amounts of fresh produce because it isn't "perfect". An estimated 25-40 percent of all food grown, processed and transported in the United States is never eaten. We don't seem to care if it's loaded with toxic pesticides—or if it's rendered tasteless, nutrition-less, and potentially carcinogenic by genetic engineering—as long as it looks good.

"*Produce is art,*" says Jordan Figueiredo, solid waste specialist for the Castro Valley Sanitary District in California's Bay area. "*It's amazingly nourishing. It should be celebrated.*" He uses various social media accounts at @UglyFruitAndVeg to show lovable images of outcast fruit and vegetables. He says this helps people understand the issue better and makes them want to celebrate–rather than waste–produce.

As so often happens, North America trails behind Europe in embracing its love for ugly fruit and vegetables. France's third-largest supermarket chain, Intermarché, launched a campaign in March of 2014 to get consumers to see the beauty of ugly produce. Television and print ads hailed the attractiveness of "the grotesque apple," "the failed lemon," "the disfigured eggplant," "the ugly carrot" and the "unfortunate clementine." One aisle of a store just outside Paris is devoted to "inglorious" produce and sold at a 30% discount. It's hugely successful.

Of course, Americans aren't alone in demanding that even old things look new. Restoration of historic buildings and old artwork is a multi-billion-dollar per year business worldwide. In most cases, that's a good thing, since it enables them to enjoy a new life, often with a new, more relevant purpose.

But some ancient art is actually more beautiful in its aged state. And leaving a few well-built abandoned buildings unrestored adds a bit of age diversity to the visual environment.

In Gary, Indiana, they seem to get this concept. City Methodist Church, a grand, Gothic cathedral, has been abandoned for almost 50 years. Yet you can see it all over the internet, on Flickr and Instagram, and in movies like Transformers 3. It's billed as "one of the best known and most popular Midwest locations for urban explorers."

The church---which has been vacant since the 1970s as the steel industry bottomed out in Chicago and northern Indiana---has enjoyed an unlikely second life as a particularly beautiful, even sublime, decaying structure...what some call "ruin porn," the ugly American name for urban wabi-sabi.

The church was in the news recently after it became 1 of 33 winners of the Knight Foundation's Cities Challenge, which awards cities around the country with grant money for their best project ideas. Gary's Redevelopment Commission received $163,333 to transform City Methodist into a safer, more official tourist destination for the city.

The church is one of the most visited places in the city, despite the fact that it's not safe to explore. "*The fact that the building, in its current condition, is not structurally sound has not deterred visitors,*" says Sarah Kobetis, Gary's deputy director of planning.

"*So turning the space into a ruins garden felt like a mutually beneficial way to preserve what's left of one of the city's most notable structures, while also creating a new public amenity in downtown Gary for both tourists and community residents to enjoy,*" she continued.

Gary isn't the only Rust Belt city that has iconic "ruins" with considerable architectural value. And it's not the first city whose ruins have become popular tourist destinations in their decay. But Gary might be the first to use these ruins in a purposeful, strategic manner to boost their economy.

As mentioned in Chapter 1, the science of complex adaptive systems answers some important questions, such as how do living systems arise, how do they evolve, and how do they recover after massive disruption. Today, most of the algorithms that run massively complex tasks (financial trading, weather forecasting, Netflix recommendations, etc.) derive in whole or in part from the insights of complexity science.

Applying these insights at the human level is more of a challenge, but it can be done. For instance, politicians wishing to transform their city or nation should know that complex systems are best altered by changing the most basic decision-making rules of the system. These rules should guide individual "agents" in the desired new direction, while being flexible enough to allow decision makers in the field to adapt them to local needs and challenges.

Most urban planning instead tries to make arbitrary decisions for local agents. This is not a criticism of the concept of planning, only the practice, which is often based on centralized—rather than distributed—control, and on blind obedience to the plan (in those few cases where the plan is actually implemented).

> "*Let us green the earth, restore the earth, heal the earth.*" – Ian McHarg.

Sometimes, only one local rule needs to be changed. For instance, the struggling downtowns of many small U.S. communities are hampered in their efforts to compete with sprawl malls outside of town by archaic "blue laws" that ban sales of alcohol on Sunday, or that prohibit businesses from being open on Sunday. Eliminating those rules might be all that's needed to bring some downtowns back to life (though it's seldom that simple).

Two core problems that undermine sustainability and resilience worldwide are both related to accounting rules: 1) the aforementioned lack of full-cost accounting, and 2) lack of what I dubbed trimodal accounting and policymaking in *The Restoration Economy*.

Due to the lack of full cost accounting, both natural disasters and fossil fuel extraction go onto the books as economic growth, because we credit the jobs they create. But we don't debit the lost value in damage or depletion, which violates the basic principle of double-entry bookkeeping. The emerging field of attribution science is a step towards a solution to that problem.

The latter, trimodal accounting, recognizes three basic modes of development:
1) New Development (sprawl and virgin resource extraction);
2) Maintenance/Conservation (maintaining the built environment and conserving what's left of the natural environment); and
3) Restorative Development (redeveloping existing communities and replenishing natural resources.

Current government reporting only accounts for the first two modes: we're inundated with figures like "new housing starts", but redevelopment and restoration activities are largely invisible (or buried in maintenance as "capital improvements"). We can't manage what we don't measure. Restorative development is where almost all of the good economic news resides these days.

While we can certainly have too much sprawl and too much virgin resource extraction, we can't have too much restorative development or revitalization, provided they are done well. I've been doing this work all over the world for about two decades, and I have yet to hear someone say *"hey, we've got to slow down this community revitalization program: our incomes and quality of life are way too high!"* I've never heard anyone say *"hey, we've got to slow down this river restoration program: the water is way too clean, and has far too many native fish!"* I've never heard anyone say *"hey, we've got to slow down this brownfields redevelopment program: our community is running out of contaminated properties!"*

Too many people conflate population growth and economic growth. I'm always careful to specify that unlimited economic growth is possible if based on restorative development, but some people still take me to task, thinking that economic growth and population growth are intrinsically linked.

If there were 100 people on an island, and each person's income went up 10% annually—based on greater productivity and the enhancement of natural resources—and the population remained at 100, how would that be unsustainable? We could actually have economic growth and population decrease simultaneously, which would be the best of all worlds.

Many of those in power resist turning points (like the Paris Agreement), since it threatens their power base. But in the Anthropocene Epoch, restorative development will be—directly or indirectly—the source of most economic growth, so it's an irresistable shift. Embedding simple rules like repurposing, renewing, and reconnecting into policy can accelerate this transition to restorative development.

RECONOMICS

"Humanity has been destroying Earth's forests for millennia; the 2015 Paris Agreement (calling for massive forest restoration) means we've reached a fundamental turning point in that relationship." – Doug Boucher, IUCN.

Many folks rightfully bemoan the plague of obsolete, decrepit, vacant structures and toxic, degraded, depleted lands and water bodies. Here's a more positive and constructive way of perceiving the situation: we have a wealth of renewable assets. That massive inventory of renewable assets is fueling the $3 trillion/year global restoration economy.

Strategies and processes aren't just needed to revitalize cities and regions: entire nations require need them.

For instance, Wales has long been an economic basket case, exploited for centuries by England. They were heavily dependent on coal mining for almost three centuries, so the shift to cleaner forms of energy, and cheaper sources of coal, hit them hard.

But that's been the case for decades. During that period, the European Union repeatedly awarded Wales the highest level of economic aid (called Objective One) in 2000, 2007 and 2014. Since 2000, an additional £5.3 billion has been injected into Wales from the EU, on top of major grants from the British government. But the economic needle hasn't moved. Why?

I would posit that, while there's been an unending flow of ideas and tactics designed to revitalize their economy, there's never been a cohesive vision and strategy, or a process to deliver the fragmented visions they do have.

Some good approaches have been suggested, such as keeping the focus on energy, but shifting to renewal sources. But none of these visions were supported by a national strategy: they only had a long string of projects.

The turning point for long-suffering Wales will come when it has a process that links a regenerative program, regenerative vision, regenerative strategy, regenerative policies, regenerative partners and regenerative projects. And they will need an entity to house that program, because—believe it or not—Wales doesn't have an economic development agency of any sort.

We often hear economists "explaining" economic collapses, both local and national. Where we seldom see economists is in economic rebirth situations; either during or after the fact. Why is that? Most economists are similar to engineers, in both their love of control and their fear of surprises. This is why few degreed economists work in the messy fields of community revitalization or natural resources restoration.

> *"OK, sustainability advocates, first the good news: in a recent survey of business executives by BCG and MIT Sloan Mgt Review, more than 2/3 of respondents agreed that sustainability is essential to competitiveness. And nearly three-quarters said that their commitment will increase in the year ahead. The bad news? They may not actually be able to define sustainability."* – Paul Michelman, Harvard Business Review, 2/2012.

For three decades, well-meaning folks have been in the thrall of sustainable development. Many of the healthiest and most enlightened activities on the planet take place under the rubric of sustainability, but that's mostly for lack of a better term. Sustainable development was coined as a dialog tool, a compromise designed to bring together the forces of unbridled economic growth and the forces of environmental responsibility.

As a dialog, it has achieved some wonderful things. But that's all it is: a dialog: it lacks rigor. There's been no shortage of attempts to create sustainability metrics, but a shortage of such metrics persists.

At my university talks and workshops, I'm increasingly picking up a "sustainability sucks" vibe from students and recent graduates. They are increasingly seeing it as the failed paradigm of their parents and grandparents' generations.

Many online dialogs have been started in recent years by folks who recognize the problems with sustainable development, and who are looking for a better name. Smart growth, breakthrough economy, clean economy, conscious economy, cooperative economy, capitalism 2.0, sharing economy, experience economy, collaborative economy, information economy, knowledge economy, and so on.

Most of those descriptors exist only in the mind: you can't see them in action. On the other hand, we're surrounded by buildings and landscapes that are being—or have been—restored.

As is often the case, the terminological solution is hiding in plain sight: restorative (or regenerative, if you prefer) economic development. Reconomics, in other words.

RECONOMICS

"Should you find yourself in a chronically leaking boat, energy devoted to changing vessels is likely to be more productive than energy devoted to patching leaks." – Warren Buffett.

The redevelopment of existing communities and the restoration of damaged natural resources already accounts for at least $4 trillion annually, worldwide. But to tap its full potential, we need policies that establish it as the default mode of economic growth, and that establish some basic quality/ethical controls. The current default—which is encouraged by policy and subsidized in practice—is still mostly sprawl and virgin resource extraction.

Why do we put so much attention on the idea-of-the-month hyped by publishers, and so little on a multi-trillion-dollar reality that's staring us in the face? Part of the problem is that we assume restorative development is merely an aspect our normal economic paradigm, as opposed to an emerging alternative. As a result, the restoration economy's numbers are buried. Try to find government reports that break-out the "re" costs and benefits, separating them from the "de" costs and benefits.

You won't find them. Instead, you'll find redevelopment, regeneration, renovation, reuse, restoration, etc. buried under budgets categories like "maintenance" and "capital improvement", where they give the appearance of supporting the status quo, rather than subvert it.

Often times, "redevelopment" is simply used synonymously with "development", which is like not distinguishing between virgin materials and recycled materials when manufacturing a bag, bottle, or can.

We can see the wisdom of defining and measuring the difference between recycled and virgin paper, glass, or metal. So why can't we see the wisdom of being able to distinguish recycled land from virgin land...a recycled city from one built of virgin farmlands of forests?

Most large, publicly-traded real estate developers don't want that distinction to be made. They need to make their quarterly growth projections to keep Wall Street happy, and that's easier to do developing a few large tracts of greenfields than it is redeveloping many infill, adaptive reuse and brownfields projects.

They are quite happy being free to make money by sprawling a community in a way that kills its historic downtown and undermines its environmental health and quality of life. When they do take on the occasional redevelopment project, they are just as happy to be able to doff the black hat and don the white hat, playing the role of community hero. Thus, their conflation of the labels "developer" and "redeveloper". This confusion permeates all of economic theory and policy: academics perpetuate it and politicians implement it.

> *"If we don't know the difference between value creation and value extraction activities... we risk passing off anything included in GDP as value creation. In the process we reward those activities, so it becomes sort of a feedback loop: because they're valuable, we consider them valuable and they will be valued by society so policymakers will try to increase those activities, and that then also increases those activities' share of GDP."* – Mariana Mazzucato.

Complex systems evolve; sometimes incrementally, sometimes discontinuously, spasmodically, and asymmetrically. The incremental approach is the norm, with only occasional bursts of "punctuated equilibrium". Thus, we should expect the next mode of economic growth to emerge in parallel with the old mode. But politicians want us to believe we can fix everything by tinkering with the old model (thus, not threatening the old money that backs their campaigns).

If we're not willing to reinvent capitalism, we at least need to measure it accurately (full-cost accounting). If we do that, the insanity of fossil fuels, fission energy, sprawl, and unsustainable resource extraction becomes evident, and the sanity of restorative development and clean tech becomes equally evident. Then, we merely need to shift our policies and efforts from one existing reality to another: no "magic solutions", "global awakenings", or improvements to human nature needed.

The primary reason so many governments and major corporations have sustainability initiatives is because they know that it's just a dialog. It can't be measured, so government and corporate (and non-profit) sustainability programs can't fail. They love that.

> *"We talk of sustainable development and sustainable economies,*
> *but it is time to move on to restorative development and restorative economies."*
> – Richard Chartres, Bishop of London.

On the other hand, restoration, reuse, renovation, and most other "re" functions are eminently real. We can measure how much more a restored historic theater is worth. We can measure how many more fish are in a restored river. We can measure how much healthy topsoil has been rebuilt on a restored farm. We can measure how much more biodiversity inhabits a restored meadow. We can measure how much less toxicity is in the ground at a remediated old industrial site.

It's true that we can measure components of sustainability: waste reduction, energy efficiency, etc. But there's no metric for sustainability itself. We can't point to anything and say with surety "that's sustainable". Sustainable for how long: 100 years? 10,000 years? Sustainable with what population: 8 billion? 80 billion?

But we can easily point to what's unsustainable. For instance, as I write this on June 15, 2019, the Amazon rainforest has lost 739 square kilometers just during the past 31 days. That's equivalent to two football (soccer) fields every minute.

Due to our short life spans, each generation keeps ratcheting-down the notion of what a healthy world looks like: it's whatever existed when they were young. If we face up to how degraded, depleted, fragmented, and contaminated our planet is now, we would ask *"Who wants to sustain this mess?"*, as many young folks are now asking.

A major problem is institutional dynamics. The grants supporting many non-profits and academic programs are linked to the words "sustainability" or "sustainable development". Changing the organization's mission to "regeneration" or "restorative development" would quite literally threaten their economic survival.

So, they instinctively stop listening—or even go on the attack—when someone questions the efficacy of the sustainability dialog. As Upton Sinclair so famously said: *"It is difficult to get a man to understand something, when his salary depends upon his not understanding it!"*

The irony, of course, is that sustainability advocates frequently invoke Sinclair's insight when explaining the intransigence of fossil fuel executives, dam engineers, big box chains, etc. regarding climate change, river health, and sprawl, respectively.

About 24% of all usable (by humans) land on the planet is considered "degraded". The estimated economic loss of this degradation is about $40 billion annually, primarily from soil erosion by water and wind.

On September 24, 2013, a report was presented to to the UN Convention to Combat Desertification conference in Windhoek, Namibia. It stated that restoration and better management of degraded lands could deliver up to $1.4 trillion (USD) per year in increased crop production.

Sustainable development should have started at least two centuries ago. But it didn't, so the world is now far too damaged to speak of sustaining as a goal. The economic and social degradation—and opportunities—presented by this situation don't get as much attention as one might expect, given its vast size. This is mostly because it's primarily the rural poor who bear the brunt of the suffering: the 1.2 billion people worldwide who depend on small farms for both their diet and their income. Given the failure of both their national leaders and global NGOs to address it, people are taking arid land restoration into their own hands.

> *"Restoration, when combined with conservation and sustainable use, provides the critical missing link to enable human society to create a net positive impact on the environment."*
> *– Jim Hallett, Society For Ecological Restoration.*

"A more accurate economic evaluation is crucial to prevent and reverse land degradation by raising the profile of the issue with policymakers," says Richard Thomas, lead author of the study, and assistant director of the drylands ecosystems program at the UN University's Institute for Water, Environment and Health, based in Hamilton, Ontario, Canada.

Ecological restoration is a powerful economic revitalizer, but its full value is often underestimated because our metrics are too simplistic. For an example of folks who are trying to take a more intelligent, systemic approach to quantifying ecological restoration's economic impact, here's an excerpt from a March 2012 report titled "Economic Impacts of Ecological Restoration in Massachusetts" by the Massachusetts Department of Fish and Game's Division of Ecological Restoration:

"*Impacts can be observed in two phases:*
- *Short term effects: These are benefits associated with increased demand for employment, materials, and services in Massachusetts during the Construction / Installation Phase of a project. Examples include: construction labor, materials costs, engineering time, permitting activities.*
- *Long-term effects: These are benefits associated with the Operational Phase of a project. These may include, for example, expenditures associated with increased boating, hiking, birdwatching, or beach visitation that may result from the project implementation.*

Our study uses IMPLAN to examine the regional economic benefits associated with short-term construction/installation phases of restoration projects:

- *Direct effects are production changes or expenditures that result from an activity or policy. In this analysis, direct effects are equal to the costs of the MA DER project, which we assign to appropriate economics sectors.*
- *Indirect effects are the "ripple" impact of local industries buying goods and services from other local industries as a result of the project (e.g., restoration project requires purchasing plant seeds or cement) within Massachusetts. Additional impacts that occur outside of Massachusetts are not included in these effects.*
- *Induced effects are changes in household consumption arising from changes in employment and associated income (which in turn results from direct and indirect effects) in Massachusetts. For example, these may include additional spending by construction workers with their wages, as well as additional spending by seed growers or cement companies with income received from sales for use in the restoration project.A DER project, which we assign to appropriate economics sectors."*

Our societal learning disability vis a vis the shift from new development to restorative development is producing a societal earning disability, as our resource base crumbles.

Traditional economics is a never-ending search for the unicorns of stasis, equilibrium, and predictability. It arbitrarily assumes linear, mechanical effects in the system, and purely rational behavior in the individual agents. Both assumptions are plainly absurd, but without them, economists wouldn't be able to create the illusion that they know what they're talking about.

So, don't look to economists for insights into economic growth in general, or devitalization and revitalization in particular. As a January 14, 2019 article by Peter Coy in Bloomberg Businessweek stated, "*The open secret of the economics profession is that its practitioners don't have a theory for why expansions die. Or rather they have several theories, each of which contradicts the others, and none of which is fully supported by the data. Because economists don't know why recessions start, they can't predict when one will start.*"

Like reductionist disciplines, conventional economists are loath to recognize that the whole is more than the sum of its parts. Facing up to that obvious reality messes up the simplicity of their assumptions, and their ability to "explain". Economists' inability to make accurate predictions undermines its claim to be a science. That's why they normally stick to "explaining" what has already happened.

This, in turn, is why most economists either 1) teach economics, or 2) work for government agencies and large corporations. In the latter situations, their primary duties involve justifying whatever course of action has already been decided upon, and legitimizing previous actions.

Conventional economics is designed by economists for economists, and so has little relevance to the chaos and complexities of reality. But an economy—by definition—encompasses natural resources, infrastructure, agriculture, urban societies, information, technology, psychology and much more. This inherent holism makes an economics degree a wonderful background for anyone doing useful, high-level work (i.e. – not economics itself).

The more recent trend towards "complexity economics" is far more courageous. It attempts to understand a world where individuals react to patterns that their decisions have helped create, and how those patterns alter as a result of their reaction, which means individuals must react again.

In complexity science, it's generally recognized that negative feedback stabilizes systems (that's "negative" as in reducing, not as in bad). Thermostats offer a simple example of negative feedback. They monitor the temperature in a room, raising or lowering it when the temperature violates an established threshold. Negative feedback thus reduces fluctuations. The supply and demand dynamic in economies is another example. Equilibrium prices are established and maintained thanks to the negative feedback between the price of a product and demand for it (in the idealized world of accepted economic theory).

On the other hand, positive feedback tends to destabilize systems (that's "positive" as in enhancing, not as in desirable). The melting of polar icecaps from atmospheric warming is an example of positive feedback. The smaller surface area of ice reduces the albedo (energy-reflecting) effect of the ice, thus accelerating the melt by raising the average atmospheric temperature.

The recruiting process in honeybee hives is also an example of positive feedback. Scout bees dance to advertise a new hive site they find attractive, thus recruiting additional scouts to visit that site. The more bees that are thus recruited, the more will be advertising the new site, which recruits still more. Eventually, the number of scouts promoting a particular site passes a threshold ("tipping point"), and the entire hive swarms to the new site. That's maximum social disruption, at least in the short term. Long term, it's an effective resilience-enhancing mechanism.

In terms of community revitalization and resilience, it's negative feedback that stabilizes the society (such as via policing) or the economy (such as via budgets and policies) when perturbed. But it's positive feedback that drives the acceleration of either revitalization or devitalization. Positive feedback loops produce both increases and decreases that are far out of proportion to the inputs.

> *"In the field of sustainable cities, Herbert Girardet's name is legendary. ...But now he's left the concept of sustainability behind, moving on to define a new, more dramatic concept: the idea of regenerative cities."* – David Thorpe (2014).

Whereas traditional economic theories only acknowledge negative feedback loops (diminishing returns), complexity economics also accepts the reality of positive feedback loops (increasing returns). These are the primary source of economic surprises, like cities that suddenly spring back to life "for no reason." Of course, elected leaders usually attribute such scenaria to their own brilliance, and hire economists to prove it.

This emergent property known as an increasing returns situation is a synergistic "whole is greater than the sum of the parts"-type behavior: output increases by a larger proportion than the increase in inputs.

The increasing returns phenomenon has been known of since the time of Adam Smith, but conventional economists closed their minds to it, because it throws all of their most beloved theories for a loop (pun intended).

In 1939, Sir John Hicks, a founder of modern economics, said that acknowledging the reality of increasing returns would wreck established economic theory. It would rob standard economic models of the two qualities most prized by economists: determinism and simplicity. That's still the case today.

The courageous work of forcing economics to deal with reality was pioneered in the modern age by Stanford economist W. Brian Arthur.

This is similar to the way classical (e.g. Newtonian) physicists choose to believe that the quantum realm can't affect the physical realm (even though our physical reality is composed entirely of quantum reality). It's not due to any paucity of intellect to grasp the obvious (that they are just two views of the same universe, at different scales), but due to lack of courage to face the ramifications (which would admittedly shake our society, and many of its most revered institutions, to the core).

For those of you who are familiar with quantum dynamics, one might say that using the RECONOMICS Process (described in more detail later) helps a community select (on some unconscious level) the probability wave leading to a revitalized future.

Increasing returns doesn't just apply to economics, of course. Witness the small amount of "social currency" issued by individuals such as Martin Luther King, Nelson Mandela, or Gandhi, and the vast amount of that social currency that ended up in circulation.

Such movements could be considered "social revitalization", and they succeed due to the same three dynamics often found in successful economic revitalization: confidence, momentum, and alignment.

The opposite of such movements also arise—those promoting fear, ignorance, and separation—and these produce both social and economic devitalization.

Acknowledgement of the reality of increasing returns thus makes complexity economics the only form of economics that can deal with the dynamics of revitalization.

An obvious factor in devising any successful strategy is basing it on a reasonably accurate perception of the situation one wishes to change. Turning a blind eye to the messy, complex nature of economic revitalization—local, regional, or national—is not an option in the real world, as it is in academia.

In the summer of 1996, Harvard Business Review published one of the most influential articles in its long history: W. Brian Arthur's Increasing Returns and the New World of Business.

Two decades later, the December 7, 2016 issue of *Fast Company* magazine featured an article titled "A Short History Of The Most Important Economic Theory In Tech". In it, author Rick Tetzelli says *"the theory of increasing returns is as important as ever: It's at the heart of the success of companies such as Google, Facebook, Uber, Amazon, and Airbnb"*.

Business strategists rely on increasing returns, but the theory has yet to make any serious inroads in the practice of community economic revitalization.

A dreamed-of goal of all revitalization efforts is to trigger an increasing returns situation. That's what the RECONOMICS Process is designed to do. Combine an acceptance of increasing returns with the trimodal development perspective plus full-cost accounting, and one has a solid foundation for a new field of study: resilient economies, or reconomics for short. Its purpose would be to generate useful insights into the process of bringing places back to life, leading to better strategies and management.

FINANCE & TAX POLICIES FOR RESILIENT PROSPERITY

> *"As soon as the Adaptive Reuse Ordinance had been enacted, the problem of finding developers evaporated; they began looking for properties to convert. By 2018, 89 buildings with 10,278 apartments had been converted in downtown Los Angeles. Downtown LA is once again a mixed-use district, buzzing with life 24 hours a day."* – Alexander Garvin, The Heart of the City.

After strategy and program, policies are the most frequently overlooked aspect of revitalizing a place. When good policy gets translated into legislation, with teeth and/or sufficient funding, it can work wonders. A national policy of supporting the preservation of historic buildings created the federal Historic Tax Credit which—over its first 36 years—created 2.3 million jobs, leveraged $117 billion in investment, and rehabilitated over 41,250 buildings, which helped revitalize many downtowns throughout the U.S.

Any place that launches a revitalization or resilience initiative without creating supportive policies (and eliminating counter-productive policies) is inviting failure in the short term, and virtually guaranteeing failure in the long term. Such failures most commonly affect financing.

Financing for revitalization and resilience efforts is just as siloed and fragmented as are the many professions, organizational types, and government agencies. There's a great opportunity for innovative leadership in this area. We've so far documented many obstacles faced by those wishing to renew neighborhoods, cities, regions, and natural resources, but one challenge almost everyone shares is funding.

Most folks assume the primary problem is the quantity available, but that's an illusion: there's no shortage of money. As stated earlier, of the three sub-trends of the adaptive renewal megatrend—regeneration (revitalization), resilience, and adaptive management—revitalization is the most important focus, since that's where the majority of the current funding is targeted, usually labelled "redevelopment" or "capital improvements" in the U.S.—or "regeneration" in the UK—when the focus is cities.

The problem lies more in finding the appropriate funding when its needed. This is a great opportunity for a tech company. Linking it with mapping would be ideal, so maybe Google or Esri should be looking into this. A single source—localized and global—of information and links to regenerative foundation grants, government grants, community bonds, startup financing, bridge financing, equity investors, impact investors, individual investors, crowdfunding, institutional investors, tax credits, etc. would be magic.

Add in links to relevant tools and models such as land trusts, conservation easements, TIF, CDC, BID—all focused on "re" activities—and the fixers of the world could spend more time actually fixing things, instead of finding resources and reinventing wheels.

The map would allow filtering according to the type of renewable asset: brownfields, historic structures, damaged waterways/ wetlands, forests, degraded farms/ranches, depleted fisheries, obsolete infrastructure, rundown parks, vacant lots, etc. Such a tool would allow organizations like land banks to become far more holistic in their revitalization efforts.

And it would enable resilience efforts to more easily integrate with revitalization agendas.

> *"We need 2-3 good cases where money flows from businesses to river restoration to show the world that this can be done."*
> *– Joppe Cramwinckel.*

It often seems that there are too many sources of money—which complicates revitalization and resilience—but the real problem is the lack of a good tool for finding them. This is especially problematic in smaller communities lacking local agencies to attract state/provincial and federal funding. For instance, creating a park to revitalize downtown Greenport, NY (population 2200) was a $14.9 million effort that used the following financial tools (thanks to N. David Milder of DANTH and Andrew Dane of SEH for data from their Oct. 23, 2014 "Some More Thoughts on the Economic Revitalization of Small Town Downtowns"):

- $4 million of town money. This included $1.2 million from a general obligation bond offering to buy the foreclose property, $1.5 million from their Capital Improvement Fund, etc.;
- 25 grants from a local, state and federal agencies;
- Private funds from the estate of a local resident; and,

- Donation of a full-sized carousel by Northrop Grumman Corporation (to help fund park operation via $200,000 from the carrousel's projected 100,000 annual riders).

Many additional funding sources suddenly appear when project leaders climb out of their mental silos. For instance, a historic building is often viewed as just that: a heritage asset. But it's within a watershed, so installing a green roof—or bioswales in the landscaping—might qualify it for grants or tax credits related to restoring the watershed. It might be in a low-income neighborhood that would entitle it to New Market or other tax credits, depending on how it is going to be repurposed.

It might contain hazardous materials, entitling it to brownfield remediation resources. An unused portion of the property might be ideal for an urban farm or a farmers' market, entitling it to grants related to enhancing a locally-based food system, or fixing a "food desert" situation. It might be an ideal site for affordable housing, which opens up another realm of funding and tax credits.

> *"We refuse to believe there are insufficient funds in the great vaults of opportunity..."*
> *– Dr. Martin Luther King, Jr.*

The list of potentially-connected agendas that could lead to additional design, development, start-up, or operational funding is almost endless. Normally, the people proposing projects are unaware of these overlaps. Even when they are aware of them, they often lack the manpower and expertise to investigate or pursue them. But the kind of integrated funding locator described above would ideally suggest non-obvious agendas and related resources.

This could make all the difference in a project's financial viability. It would also improve the project's design and appeal: the more amenities a place offers, the greater the geographic area from which it will pull customers and visitors. A park with beautiful natural features will generally attract more users if it also has historic features.

Many federal and state funding sources focus on programs, not projects. An example in the U.S. is the HUD-DOT-EPA Partnership for Sustainable Communities. So, creating a local process that includes an ongoing program broadens your funding opportunities. This book's subtitle reads "The path to resilient prosperity" because resilient prosperity should be treated more as a path than a goal. The regenerative process you'll learn here doesn't suddenly achieve resilient prosperity at the end of your effort: it produces it in increasing amounts from the very beginning, as you apply the process. There is no "end of your effort," except maybe on the day you decide you no longer desire resilient prosperity.

Such national programs often focus on clean energy, resilience, poverty, etc. All relate to the creation of resilient prosperity, but most can't be accessed without creating a relevant local program. Governments and foundations are (finally) realizing that most of these societal and environmental challenges can only be addressed by ongoing programs, not by one-time projects. So the RECONOMICS Process gives you the necessary receptacle for such funding.

REVITALIZING TAXATION STRATEGIES

> *"Economists are an odd bunch. They believe that people respond to economic incentives...yet they tend to deflect criticism that they themselves could be negatively influenced by their gigs as consultants, board members, and advisors."*
> – Justin Fox, "Have Economists Been Captured by Business Interests?", HBR, September 8, 2014.

The second aspect of attracting new sources of funding is to tax only what you want to reduce in your community or region, so as to increase desirable behaviors. This approach isn't as simple as grant-writing, but has significantly greater potential for making the structural and policy changes your community needs to create resilient prosperity.

For at least a century, practical economists have recommended taxing those activities we want less of, and using some of the resulting revenue to encourage what we want more of. Using fossil fuel taxes to fund research and development of renewable energy (or the creation of public transit) is an obvious application of this approach. The use of tobacco taxes to fund preventive health care/education is another.

In the same manner, places can reduce sprawl and unsustainable resource extraction—while increasing urban revitalization and natural resource restoration—via sprawl and/or extraction taxes. In most cases, sprawl developers don't pay the full public cost of providing infrastructure and services to their projects. Even where they do, their projects usually decrease local quality of life by reducing greenspace, damaging watersheds, adding to traffic congestion, increasing air pollution, and devitalizing historic downtowns.

It's only fitting then, that—in addition to paying for infrastructure and services directly related to their projects—they also pay a "revitalization fee" to boost the local resilience and quality of life in ways that help offset the negative impacts of their sprawl development. Such a fund could boost public transit, brownfields cleanup, infill development, watershed restoration, historic structure renovation, etc.

Likewise, resource extraction companies (lumber, fossil fuel, mining, and ranching, etc.) often pay nothing (or a bare pittance) for the public resources they deplete and damage. They often aren't required to fund post-extraction restoration. Even when they are, they usually just declare bankruptcy and create a new corporate entity to avoid paying.

Requiring substantial restoration escrow accounts prior to mining, fracking, clear-cutting, etc.—in additional to fair compensation to the public for the value of lost natural capital—could go a long way towards funding resilient prosperity in the region. This has recently become the norm with mining in many U.S. states.

In a January 27, 2015 New York Times Op-Ed, David Brooks said, *"The big debate during the 20th century was about the relationship between the market and the state. Both those institutions are now tarnished. The market is prone to devastating crashes and seems to be producing widening inequality. Government is gridlocked, sclerotic or captured by special interests. ...many of the most talented people on Earth have tried to transform capitalism itself, to use the market to solve social problems. ...Impact investing is probably the most promising of these tools. Impact investing is not socially responsible investing. Socially responsible investing means avoiding certain companies, like tobacco... Impact investors seek out companies that are intentionally designed both to make a profit and provide a measurable and accountable social good."*

Private impact investors (as Brooks mentions above) can undo much of the existing damage, but local governments don't suffer as greatly from the problems he describes. They are far from helpless.

Property taxes offer an obvious area of reform. Currently, they are based on the entire property, both land and improvements (such as buildings). This has two problems: 1) It "punishes" property owners for adding value to the land; and 2) It rewards property owners for passively sitting on vacant or derelict properties, waiting for overall revitalization to boost their investment. Such "parasitic" real estate speculation thus retards the very revitalization they're hoping for.

A more intelligent way to tax land is called a "land tax", variously known as site-value tax, land value tax (LVT), split rate tax, and site-value rating. A few progressive governments around the world have adopted it, such as in New South Wales, Australia, Mexicali, Mexico, and Pittsburgh, Pennsylvania in the U.S.

This is one of the most revitalizing policy changes a place can make. The land value tax levies high rates on the land itself, but none on its structures. Speculators are thus punished for sitting on blight, and redevelopers are thus rewarded for improving their properties.

A fringe benefit is that most homeowners will see their tax bills drop, often by about a third. This helps prevent the negative feedback loop that kills so many places: devitalization reduces city revenues, so they raise property taxes, which drive out more residents, thus accelerating devitalization. The community doesn't experience a revenue drop when revenue from homeowners drops, because tax receipts from vacant properties go up significantly...often doubling. In other words, you're rewarding what you want more of, and punishing what you want less of. Put another way, such policy changes help retain the residents and employers you have, while attracting the investors and redevelopers you need.

The concept of a land value tax has been around since 1879, when Henry George suggested in it his book, Progress and Poverty. But it's not in wide practice. Why? The usual story: the influence of money on politics. Commercial and industrial property owners are normally among the wealthiest people in any community, and are thus major campaign contributors to mayors an city council members. Doing what's right takes more courage than one usually finds in elected officials.

"*Tax policy has always encouraged land speculators,*" said Ed Dodson, a former market analyst with Fannie Mae and professor at Temple University in a September 2019 GOVERNING article by J. Brian Charles. "*It makes it easy for speculators to acquire and hold land and wait for public-private partnerships to come along with funds to pay them their profit for speculating.*"

In the places where it has been tried and abandoned, the usual cause (other than lobbying by land speculators) is failure to reassess land values on a regular basis. Homeowners expect taxes to go up incrementally, and don't complain much when they do. But if a city or county only reassesses land once every 10 or 20 years, land-based taxes suddenly shoot up, causing voter backlash. Structures often lose value as they age, but land almost always rises in value.

In the places where it's still in use, the results have been spectacular. Pittsburgh has used land value tax in its Central Business District since 1997. Between 2009 and 2019, some $8.5 billion worth of downtown redevelopment has been completed or announced. But the major champion of land value taxation in Pennsylvania was Harrisburg mayor Stephen R. Reed.

Between 1960-1980, Harrisburg lost 800 businesses and a third of its population. In 1980, the U.S. Dept. of Housing and Urban Development (HUD) called it "One of America's most distressed cities." But by 2010, Forbes magazine was calling it "The second best place in the U.S. to raise a family." The single most important factor in that dramatic turnaround was the adoption of 2-tiered property taxation.

This was pioneered by Reed, who was Harrisburg's mayor from 1981-2010. He was frequently called "Pennsylvania's most popular and successful mayor." By reducing the "penalty" for improving property, Harrisburg catalyzed $3 billion of new investment. Rehabilitation of existing structures increased the city's taxable real estate from $212 million to over $1.6 billion.

It should be noted that Mayor Reed also borrowed hugely for many dubious projects like sports stadiums and an incinerator, which ended up bankrupting the city. But that was in no way the fault of the land value tax, whose success led to that "irrational exuberance" (as Alan Greenspan might have called it). More recently, Minneapolis has been considering it.

Why don't more cities use land value taxation? Once again, fear. Middle class and lower income property owners—in others words, most voters—are happy enough with the reduction in taxes the two-tiered system brings to them. But the wealthiest property owners/political campaign contributors see it (correctly) as a constraint on their speculative land investments. Value-capture funds and land taxes could go into the general tax revenues to fund education, police, fire services, etc. Or, they could go directly towards organizations doing revitalizing work.

For instance, Tybee Island, Georgia funds local non-profits from their 6% hotel/motel tax. The program has been so successful that—in January 2015—their mayor, Jason Buelterman, suggested raising the city's annual contributions from $57,902 to over $100,000. He says activities of groups like the Tybee Island Historical Society attract tourists, while enhancing the quality of life for year-round residents.

TAX INCREMENT FINANCING (TIF)

Tax increment financing (TIF) has financed far more redevelopment and revitalization work in the U.S. than any other tool or source. It's probably the only financial tool that is fundamentally rooted in revitalization. TIF allows communities to borrow from the value of future revitalization in order to fund the work needed to make that revitalization happen now. If that sounds circular and self-referential, that's because it is.

The basic process is this: the community draws a border around a blighted area and calls it a "TIF District". A baseline of current tax revenues (if any) from that area is documented. Then, an estimate is made of the tax revenues that the District would be generating in 20 or 30 years if it were successfully revitalized. The difference between that figure and the baseline is the "increment". The community then borrows against a portion of that increment, and uses the money to stimulate that revitalization.

Ideally, TIF funds don't fund actual redevelopment itself: that's mostly the role of the private sector. TIF funds are best used to pave the way for the private sector; performing infrastructure improvements and brownfields assessments (even remediation) that make a dead section of town more attractive to redevelopers.

One of the great benefits of tax increment financing: it enables "broke" communities to come to the public-private partnership negotiating table with cash. It also helps small places do large projects when necessary.

The first TIF was created in California in 1952. By 2004, all 50 American States had authorized the use of TIF. Due mostly to perceived risk, TIF has been slow to catch on in more-cautious nations.

As with any other good tool, people will find a way to twist it to their own selfish purposes over time. The practice of tax increment financing currently suffers from tremendous abuse, misuse and overuse. Political leaders abuse it by directing the funds to their friends, mostly in the form of unnecessary subsidies. Places misuse it to fund sprawl, rather than redevelopment. And some places overuse it to the point where their general tax revenues are depleted, making it harder to pay for essential services like schools and police. But none that malpractice detracts from TIF's intrinsic value.

All three of those problems tend to result from a combination of insufficient transparency and revitalization ignorance. TIF is what's known as a "value capture" mechanism. It's unique in that it captures enhanced future value, and makes it available to spend in the present, so as to make that future value enhancement happen. It's like economic time travel.

Many cities complain that overuse of TIF has damaged their school funding. But the Union Township of greater Cincinnati—recognizing the role of quality education in revitalization—announced in January of 2015 that a new high school would be constructed with TIF funding, using no taxpayer money. Sounds simple, but it's a revolutionary innovation. Here's a slogan that should guide all TIFs: "*No taxation without revitalization!*"

Each state has their own flavor of TIF. Some establish different qualifying conditions to allow for the creation of different types of TIF districts. Minnesota, for instance, allows for six district types: economic development, housing, redevelopment, renewal and renovation, soil condition, and hazardous waste substance subdivisions. Illinois allows TIF to be used for remediating blight, for conserving areas with many structures older than 35 years, and for promoting industrial parks in areas of high unemployment. With such definitional diversity, it's little wonder that the unscrupulous find so many ways to subvert it for personal gain.

Another reason TIF is so commonly misused is that the enabling state legislation often fails to define "blight" in a rigorous manner, as mentioned earlier. They are careful to use hard numbers in reference to blight, such as requiring that 60% of buildings in a prospective TIF District be substandard, or that 90% of the tax increment needs to be used to remediate blight. But they often forget to actually define blight well enough to avoid its being used for sprawl.

For an example of abuse, look at the billionaire Koch brothers. They've funded several foundations that extol the social benefits of free enterprise, while decrying government regulation, socialized medicine, public transit (they're in the oil business) and public assistance to the poor. But even with their vast wealth, they aren't above demanding unnecessary taxpayer subsidies to expand their businesses: they receive some $50 million in such handouts in an average year. Many see this as corporate socialism.

What does this have to do with TIF, you ask? In Enid, Oklahoma (population: 50,000), the Kochs planned to spend $1 billion expanding their Koch Nitrogen Plant (fertilizer). But they wanted the taxpayers of this small, working-class city to help them do it.

To accomplish that, the Kochs turned their private plant into a TIF District. This means that taxes which would have gone towards paying for schools, roads, police, etc. will go towards renovating their for-profit factory. This was blatant abuse of TIF, which should only be used to fund community redevelopment and revitalization. Large employers across America use similar forms of extortion. They threaten to leave communities that are desperate for jobs, demanding tax breaks, free land and subsidies...hardly the behavior of good corporate citizens.

In the old days, when most newspapers had investigative reporters, they would have blown the whistle on such a scheme. The only "exposé" of the Koch's TIF abuse I know of was a lonely tweet from me to my 26,000+ Twitter followers, which is a pretty pathetic excuse for investigative reporting.

The only newspaper coverage I could find was in the local Enid News and Eagle, which ran a puff piece extolling the virtues of the plan (without explaining the cost to citizens). The article sounded like it came straight from the Koch's PR team, sans editing. (It's estimated that between 80-90% of all articles in the U.S. news media come from corporate and government PR agencies.)

Most cities spend TIF funds on repurposing and renewing properties. When they spend it on reconnecting the TIF District, it's usually in the form of roads and telecommunications.

That's sometimes best, but Milwaukee, Wisconsin took an approach that's often smarter: public transit. While it's not unprecedented, using TIF for public transit certainly isn't common.

They used $59 million worth of TIF funding to build the first phase of their $124 million "Hop" streetcar system. In May of 2019, Milwaukee Mayor Tom Barrett presented his plan to add another 2.4 miles to the 2.1-mile system, using another $51.8 million of TIF funds.

To fund the first phase, Milwaukee simply extended the lifespan of existing TIF districts. For the second phase, which extends it to their lakefront, a new TIF district is being formed. $47 million of the $51.8 million would extend the streetcar. The remaining $5 million would create a new public plaza connected to their downtown convention.

Jeff Fleming, spokesman for Milwaukee's development department, explained that the city used federal grant dollars and TIF financing for the streetcar in order to keep local taxpayers from paying the costs. "*Doing so tapped into the increased property values immediately surrounding the streetcar,*" Fleming said in a September 13, 2019 Wisconsin Public Radio article. "*There's no question that property values are increasing within a quarter mile within the streetcar line.*"

GREENTIF

Green Bonds and other new tools for funding the restoration/creation of green infrastructure (often for climate change resilience) are obvious candidates for funding such projects on a large scale.

But the most overlooked source is that well-proven revitalization tool described above: tax increment financing (TIF).

We've talked about TIF's longstanding role in funding community redevelopment (its original purpose). But I believe it has tremendous potential for funding the restoration of natural resources and green urban infrastructure.

Now, with the rise of metrics for monetizing ecosystem services—combined with the growth of resilience programs that require greater integration of our built, natural, and socioeconomic environments—the time has come for a new breed of TIF to emerge, which I'll dub "GreenTIF™".

Instead of—or in addition to—the usual property and sales tax base of urban TIFs, the GreenTIF could be funded by a combination of specific natural resource industry taxes, water fees, climate disaster insurance, and/or a new disaster prevention tax. The latter will likely emerge soon, in these days of climate change-related superstorms, floods, droughts, etc.

> *"Our ability to redesign industrial systems to be restorative and regenerative, to transform waste into a nutrient for the next generation of industry...will be the measure against which our generation will be judged. The transition to a regenerative circular economy is now a declared objective of the European Union and of China..."*
> *– Tim Brown, president and CEO of IDEO*

In December of 2014, the U.S. EPA published an excellent guide, "Getting To Green: Paying for Green Infrastructure." Financing options and resources for local decision-makers." But it contained not a single reference to value-capture mechanisms in general, or to TIF in particular.

A GreenTIF would differ from a regular TIF in three basic ways:
- It would generate its incremental value increase in large part from renewing the natural environment;
- It would be applicable to far larger areas, possibly entire watersheds or estuaries (such as Chesapeake Bay); and
- It would derive revenue from sources other than property and sales taxes.

There's one more key differentiator: a GreenTIF would need to define "blight" in a different manner from the normal urban TIF. It might be based, for instance, on resource depletion, such as current oyster or crab harvest levels from a bay compared to historical levels.

Some major projects in the U.S. are already looking to apply TIF towards renewing the natural environment, though it's usually in an urban setting. The billion-dollar-plus Los Angeles River Restoration Project is one. The aforementioned 11th Street Bridge project here in Washington, DC is also looking at TIF-like value-capture mechanisms to fund the bridge repurposing, as well as nearby ecological restoration and park creation along the Anacostia River shoreline.

Just as urban TIF funding sets the stage for increased private redevelopment via infrastructure and brownfields renewal, so too would GreenTIF funding set the stage for increased commercial usage via environmental restoration. Of course, the performance specifications would need to call for the restoration of the diverse ecosystem in which those commercial species or ecosystem services are found, not just for the increased production of commercial species (like blue crabs or striped bass in the Chesapeake) themselves. In addition to simply being the right thing to do, this would help ensure the resilience of the harvest.

One current project that moves the TIF needle a bit in this GreenTIF direction is in Maine. As you probably know, salmon farms—whether based in rivers, estuaries or the open ocean—are usually environmental disasters. They pollute the water with excess food, concentrated fish excrement, antibiotics and growth hormones. They also contaminate wild salmon stocks with genetically-modified fish that inevitably escape. And, their food comprises vast quantities of smaller wild fish, thus depleting food stocks for wild salmon, mackerel and other species.

A new company called Whole Oceans wants to become America's premier, land-based producer of sustainable farm-raised Atlantic salmon. Their model is more sustainable than a normal salmon farm because it's a closed system: no pollution—or fish—can escape. In 2019, they started building a state-of-the-art Atlantic salmon recirculating aquaculture system (RAS) facility in Bucksport, Maine.

This project will be one of the largest land-based aquaculture projects in the world. On July 12, 2019 the Town Council of Bucksport voted unanimously to create a TIF for the site of the former Verso Paper Mill, where the Whole Ocean facility is being built.

Whole Oceans' development on a 90-acre portion of that site is expected to increase the property's value by $42.2 million. If taxed at the town's current tax rate of $16.30 for every $1,000 in property value, that increased value would translate into $13.7 million in new taxes paid by Whole Oceans in their first two decades of operation, amounting to $687,000 annually.

But with the TIF, the town will reimburse about 70% of the new taxes — $473,000 a year on average. That reimbursement would work out to $9.45 million over the 20 years. Whole Oceans will not have to pay property taxes for the first five years of the 20-year agreement on any new property value it creates from developing the salmon farm. It will pay 25 percent of its new property tax obligations over the subsequent five years and 50 percent for the remaining 10 years.

The first phase of the salmon farm's development, estimated at $180.6 million, could create as many as 75 jobs. So, this should be a win for the town, the company and the environment (although their website doesn't say what the salmon will be fed.) Granted, this isn't a GreenTIF as described above, but it might help people start thinking of using TIFs for natural resources, rather than just urban redevelopment.

The ideal host for a GreenTIF would be an organization that has already embraced a holistic approach to environmental restoration, regenerative agriculture and rural economic revitalization. There aren't any, you say? Take a look in Amsterdam, where a non-profit called Commonland was founded in 2013 by the IUCN Commission on Ecosystem Management, the Rotterdam School of Management of the Erasmus University, and a private foundation.

Commonland facilitates long term support to local people to restore degraded landscapes and ecosystems, generating inspirational, social, natural, and sustainable financial returns: what they call the "4 returns framework". Commonland is closely aligned to the UN Decade on Ecosystem Restoration. Its focus is on developing Landscape Restoration Partnerships, and on developing businesses that are regenerative and nature-restorative, while capturing carbon and beautifying landscapes.

Over the past five years or so, they have focused in the field on building a "proof of concept" track record in four landscapes in South Africa, Spain, Australia and Netherlands. In 2018, the first "4 returns" company was listed on the Australian Stock Exchange.

In an email to this author, the CEO of Commonland, Willem Ferwerda said "*Our strategy is to build bridges among farmers and local landowners, investors, companies and governments. That is our way to restore living and productive landscapes. It is not an easy way, but after six years of testing we believe that this 4 Returns approach is the best way to achieve long-term landscape restoration successes.*" Of course, Europe isn't yet TIF-friendly, so if the GreenTIF ever takes off as a concept, it will more likely do so here in the U.S, the home of TIF. But Commonland shows that restoration economy organizations are emerging that aren't restricted to the usual silos.

It's too early to go into any more detail about this nascent GreenTIF™ effort, but I intend to assemble a team to develop a basic, replicable, customizable model for just such a funding mechanism. Interested individuals and institutions are invited to inquire about involvement.

ADAPTIVE FUNDING

There's one advantage to the fuzziness surrounding the definitions of revitalization and resilience: it makes it easier to "adapt" money from well-funded sectors to important under-funded sectors.

Just as repurposing, renewing and reconnecting physical assets revitalizes communities, so too can repurposing narrowly-targeted, short-term financial assets and reconnecting them to serve broader, long-term agendas. In the process, we can also renew and expand project funding to serve programmatic goals.

The majority of such opportunities arise with infrastructure funding. This is partly because infrastructure projects are typically large, so earmarking 1% for resilience, for example, could yield millions of dollars. It's also because infrastructure is the connective tissue of the urban and regional bodies, so it's often a direct path to a strategy for renewing, repurposing, and reconnecting distressed or vulnerable properties and neighborhoods.

In 2012, U.S. Conference of Mayors estimated that American cities will invest some $4.8 trillion on water and wastewater infrastructure renewal in the coming 20 years. If just 1% of that got "repurposed" to more effectively connect to local resilience and revitalization agendas, the ROI of this money could easily be doubled.

As noted earlier, with the right strategy, many types of revitalization activities can also build resilience: infrastructure renewal, brownfields remediation / redevelopment, heritage renewal / reuse; watershed restoration; restorative agriculture; etc.

Whenever natural, built, and socioeconomic assets are renewed, repurposed, or reconnected to create a greener, more inclusive economy, both revitalization and resilience are advanced.

In the February 2015 issue of *Municipal World*, an article titled "Heritage Builds Resilience" by Natalie Bull said, "*...if infrastructure includes 'the range of structures that enable, sustain, or enhance societal living conditions' then governments need to think—and invest—more broadly. In fact, funds earmarked for infrastructure can and should include funding envelopes for investments in a community's heritage assets. Certainly, Canada's towns and cities are full of examples where investment in 'heritage infrastructure' has successfully generated economic vibrancy, as well as cultural and social benefits—all part of the recipe for resilient communities.*"

An "adaptive funding" approach could help create a local resilient prosperity process with serious funding. If resilient prosperity is (as described earlier) "a feedback loop of rising levels of optimism, equitable wealth, quality of life, and environmental health, usually deriving from an ongoing, adaptive process of regeneration," then it's obvious that budgets focused on renewing virtually anything could fall within its purview.

This wouldn't necessarily mean defunding any existing agency. But the adaptive renewal megatrend will make it easier rectify some of the inefficiencies and dysfunctions arising from the current fragmentation of urban and regional governance and management.

> *"We're building a restoration economy here in Massachusetts and advancing Governor Patrick's goal of promoting smart public investment that spur economic activity." (2012)*
> *– Environmental Affairs Sec. Richard Sullivan Jr.*

A resilient prosperity agency, department, and/or director could be given some level of oversight over all such funding, helping to ensure that they comply with the strategic vision and goals.

Adaptive funding isn't yet a formal practice: it's currently just a practical expedient...something intelligent, creative people do when the project they love is starving. This lack of formal recognition doesn't mean it's small potatoes, though. Hundreds of billions of "re"-oriented dollars per year are "up for grabs" for managers of adaptive renewal.

A CLIMATE RESTORATION ECONOMY BASED ON NUMBERS, ASSETS AND PEOPLE

Since *The Restoration Economy* came out in 2002, I've had some clients—like Montana governor Brian Schweitzer—who grasped the need to quantify the economic and employment benefits of restoring watersheds and brownfields. He published the landmark *Montana Restoration Economy* report in 2009.

But that was primarily focused on watershed, fishery and brownfield regeneration: no one has properly documented the holistic revitalization of whole communities or regions, which would also include the regeneration of heritage, infrastructure, agriculture, ecosystems and disaster zones.

In 2012, The Nature Conservancy and Oxfam America held a Restoration Economy summit in Thibodeau, Louisiana for over 100 local leaders. Its purpose was to explore the job creation and economic revitalization potential of the post-BP oil spill restoration activities. In 2013, researchers at Yale and the University of North Carolina published a narrowly-focused Restoration Economy report. So did US Fish & Wildlife in 2014. But it wasn't until resilience joined the agenda that places worldwide finally started getting the message.

On a finite planet with a growing population, basing economic growth primarily on renewing the capacity of our existing natural and urban assets is obvious. Restoring our climate is an equally-obvious agenda (and growth industry), since not doing so will undermine virtually every investment we make. Since it might already be too late to reverse the cycle (no one knows for sure) then adapting to climate change and making places more resilient is a logical adjunct.

But the shift to healing and rebuilding is primarily happening locally, not at state or national levels. Restorative economics is gaining momentum, hopefully leading eventually to a rigorous "Revitalization On Investment" (ReOI?) metric. But we can't capture those values until we climb out of our silos and get a better handle on that mysterious—but oh-so-desirable— outcome called "revitalization".

Some cities run out of room for sprawl before others. Some countries (especially small island nations) run out of natural resources before others. In both cases, they are forced to switch to regenerative economic growth. If they go into adaptive renewal mode—using a reliable process for resilient prosperity— such places will become our "windows on the future."

This doesn't always mean renewing natural and built assets, however. Tiny, natural resource-poor Singapore became a global model of sustainable economic growth by regenerating their governance—making it more transparent and competent (accomplished in part by paying public servants very well, which reduces corruption)—and by regenerating the capacity of their citizens (via universal, high-quality education).

So let's review what a non-resilient economy looks like. If your economic growth...

- ...isn't inclusive and equitable, it's not resilient: lack of economic justice foments social unrest and crime;
- ...isn't based on regenerating natural resources and agricultural lands, it's neither resilient nor growth: the productivity of watersheds, fisheries, biodiversity (such as pollinators), and topsoil must be restored to drive economic growth, not merely sustained. ("Fortunately," most are already so damaged and deleted that significant improvements are readily attainable by even modest restoration efforts);
- ...isn't supported by good infrastructure and connectivity, it's not resilient: the global economy is changing too fast to forgive inefficiency; and
- ...is based on tax incentives, subsidies, and marketing, it's not resilient: artificially-induced economic growth is usually ephemeral.

All of the above factors, when missing, lead to instability, insecurity, and inertia. This reduces confidence in the future, thus undermining economic growth.

Merely tweaking the current economic and political system—rather than overhauling it into a regenerative model—is like having someone pointing a gun at your head, and trying to remedy the situation by making sure the gun is in good working order.

REGENERATIVE CAPITALISM

> *"If we measure the wrong thing, we will do the wrong thing. If we focus only on material wellbeing—on, say, the production of goods, rather than on health, education, and the environment—we become distorted in the same way that these measures are distorted."*
> *– economist Joseph Stiglitz.*

Adam Smith's widely misunderstood concept of the "invisible hand" of the market—a Godlike force he tossed into his book to mollify the Church, which ran the government and the economy at the time—has led most cities to believe, consciously or not, in a "magic hand of revitalization".

They hope it will miraculously transform their haphazard renewal activities into revitalization, without their having to put any overt focus on achieving that outcome. In other words, they work for redevelopment, but pray for revitalization. As it says in the Bhagavad Gita, *"We are kept from our goal not by obstacles, but by a clear path to a lesser goal."*

For decades, business leaders (especially Americans) have hewn to the gospel of the high priest of dollar-worship: the Nobel prize-winning economist, Milton Friedman. In response to activists who were calling on corporations to do less social and environmental harm, he said in 1970, "There is only one one and only one social responsibility of business: to engage in activities designed to increase its profits."

Over the past decade or so, as business leaders have been forced to adopt at least the appearance of real social and environmental responsibility, myriad modifiers for the word "capitalism" have been suggested: "compassionate capitalism", "conscious capitalism", "shared value capitalism", "green capitalism", etc. My contribution to that ingredient-rich stew is "regenerative capitalism".

Why? Because, as pointed out in *The Restoration Economy*, basing profit-making on activities that restore natural resources and revitalize communities doesn't require any change of consciousness or human nature in order to do good. If they are done well, it's an automatic outcome.

CHAPTER 3 - THE PROBLEM: MUCH ACTIVITY AND PLANNING; NOT MUCH STRATEGY, PROCESS OR PROGRESS.

"Amateur in the art of running government: Lots of horse trading, but little or no strategy."
– Institute for Government describing British Treasury (The Guardian, Nov. 25, 2015)

I often ask city leaders what strategy their comprehensive plan is based on. You'd be shocked how many times their answer is some thing like, *"Well, I'm not sure what the strategy is, but we've got a great plan."* This is like having a great airplane, and lots of passengers who want to go to the same place, flown by a pilot with no knowledge of the process by which to get there. Simply knowing where you want to go isn't enough...although you might be equally shocked at how many communities don't even know that.

There are many factors that can contribute to community revitalization:
- Tourism
- Food culture
- Brewing / distilling / winemaking
- Heritage renewal
- Artists and other bohemians
- Streetscaping / façade improvements
- Mobility enhancements
- Trees and urban forestry
- Daylighting streams and enhancing water features;

- and dozens—if not hundreds—of others.

But these are just factors: trying to base a city's revitalization on just one or two of them is a fool's errand. It would be like basing your strategy to live longer solely on switching from white bread to whole wheat. Revamping your personal health necessitates lifestyle changes...a holistic learning process that improves diet, exercise and attitudes.

Likewise, revamping the future of a place necessitates a holistic learning process that improves attitudes, guides decision-making and facilitates implementation. But, too often, city leaders allow their momentary enthusiasm for one of the above factors to override common sense. They launch a revitalization effort that's far too simplistic, and failure usually ensues. At best, that failure might leave a few improvements in its wake, but not revitalization. Often, the only lasting evidence of the effort is a plan, and the cobwebs attached to it.

A vision is a destination. A renewable asset map reveals opportunities to advance that vision. A plan is a collection of suggested activities. A strategy is what enables those activities to succeed. A strategy thus helps dreams become reality.

When presidents, mayors, CEOs and consultants promise success to their constituents and clients, they tend to focus on one or two key elements. It might be vision: having an aspirational, well-defined goal is the key, they say. Or it might be strategy: knowing how one is going to overcome obstacles to achieve that goal is the secret, they say.

Others advise that it's all about creating supportive policies to motivate the desired behavior. Or that the magic is in the plan: detailing the needed activities. Others focus on resources and support, claiming that the ultimate source of success is in forging good partnerships.

Still others will scoff at all of the above, saying it's all useless, and that one must focus on action: diving straight into actual projects. Or, the advice could be that success comes from sustained activity, so it's essential to form an ongoing program; a series of coordinated efforts that lead to long-term success.

So, who's right? Is the secret to success found in program, vision, strategy, policies, partnerships or projects? The answer is all of them. The key is a strategic renewal process: a complete, integrated system of elements needed to produce the desired result. Each of the six elements named above is crucial to the process of producing resilient prosperity.

For instance, the policies you need are determined by your vision and strategy. The partners you need are determined by the combination of your vision, strategy, policies, and local renewable assets (as in: who owns them). And the projects you'll do are determined by the combination of your program, your vision, your strategy, your policies, your partners and your assets.

Many worthwhile initiatives struggle in vain to make a difference, due to lack of strategic skills. Among them are urban / rural regeneration; natural resource restoration; renewable energy; catastrophe recovery, sustainability, smart growth, climate resilience; corporate social responsibility; brownfields/infrastructure renewal; and social / economic / environmental justice.

For instance, in 2010, FaceBook founder Mark Zuckerberg donated $100 million to fix Newark, New Jersey's public school system. It was matched by another $100 million, mostly raised by then-Mayor Cory Booker and then-Governor Chris Christie. The simple, sensible tactic? Pay the best teachers better.

But there was no strategy for dealing with established teacher contracts or state laws. For want of a strategy, $200 million was lost.

Similarly, Zappos CEO Tony Hsieh threw $350 million into revitalizing downtown Las Vegas, which desperately needed it. But he did so with no knowledge of the community revitalization process, no apparent desire to learn about it, and no perceptible strategy.

A decade later, a few urban improvements are evident, but no revitalization momentum has been generated. For want of a strategy, $350 million was lost.

Simply having a strategy won't suffice, of course: it needs to be the right strategy.

On June 12, 2017, Jeff Immelt was fired from his job as CEO of General Electric. GE stock shot up 4% on the news. Why? Because his 16-year tenure was marked by good vision, bad strategy, and poor timing.

For instance: in 2015, he rightly saw that the world needed more power generation, so he decided to expand the GE Power division. That was a good vision. But his strategy was to do it by buying Alstom—a company that made fossil fuel-powered turbines—for $10.6 billion. That might have been a good strategy a few decades ago.

Today? Not so much. And he did it just as renewable energy became cost-competitive, compounding a bad strategy with poor timing.

GE Power's profit dropped by 45%, and GE itself is now in such bad shape—after a long series of good vision / bad strategy fiascoes—that the current CEO is breaking it up and selling the pieces. On June 20, 2018, GE was dropped from the Dow Jones Industrial Average. For want of the right strategy, one of the world's great companies was lost.

Everyone uses the word "strategy", but few understand it.

Everyone says they have a strategy, but few can state it.

Everyone knows what a tactic is, and assume a strategy is a collection of tactics.

Nope: that's a plan.

Some dictionaries even define strategy as a "plan" for achieving a goal. Little wonder, then, that folks are confused as to the difference between a strategy and a plan.

One of the differences is that people with a strategy tend to take action. With planning, as mentioned above, the norm in most cities is "plan and forget." Too many places substitute planning for action. Delivering the plan often becomes the measure of success. Too many "leaders" forget the learning value of action (which is the raw material of adaptive management). A good strategy can be created in minutes, by the right person with the right awareness. Action can follow immediately. With adaptive management, you can start now. With planning, you can only start when the plan is done.

Action leads to action....and to insight. Many times, it's action itself that reveals what needs to be done, far better than a bunch of folks brainstorming in a room. As the 13th century Persian poet Jalāl ad-Dīn Muhammad Rūmī said, "*As you start to walk on the way, the way appears.*" Thinking often leads only to more thinking, and meetings to more meetings.

Even among those who know they need a strategy, few know how to create a good one. And even fewer know how to implement one.

THE DEVITALIZING POWER OF SILOS

Maybe the biggest obstacle to creating revitalization strategies is siloing: everyone works on the pieces, no one on the whole.

Silos are dysfunctional vestiges of the Industrial Revolution, alien to today's hyper-connected, partnering-oriented, stakeholder engagement world. Strategists usually facilitate the emergence of a strategy, rather than craft one in isolation. With today's communications technologies, such "emergent strategies" can often be devised, tested, and revised at a lightning pace.

For instance, you'd think that increased employment would be a key component of revitalization, right?

Here's the reply I got from the CEO of a county economic development council, when asked if he had been involved in any revitalization successes: "*Hi, Storm: I am not in an urban revitalization role. We are a non-profit. Our focus is recruitment, retention, expansion, entrepreneurship, workforce development, international trade/FDI, and competitiveness. Revitalization and redevelopment is handled by county staff.*" The staff in that same county told me that redevelopment and revitalization are handled by developers and non-profit partnerships.

In case you think this was an isolated case, or one from the distant past, here's a reply I received from a Director of Economic Development in Colorado on February 27, 2018: *"We are not currently involved in any economic revitalization, brownfields reuse or community redevelopment that you should feature in REVITALIZATION."*

Here's part of my reply to her: *"Most economic development agencies bring new employers to town, which is a form of economic revitalization. Some of those new employers reuse old buildings or brownfield sites, which makes them even more interesting to us."*

But it gets worse: many economic development agencies are decades behind in their thinking, and still consider sprawl and tax holidays to be the only way to grow an economy. Here's a reply I got on January 17, 2018 from an economic development agency official in South Carolina, when I asked if they had been involved in any local redevelopment: *"Unfortunately I'm not much help. Our services are focused primarily on greenfield opportunities – incentivizing companies to build brand new facilities, normally on property that has not been developed before."*

Economic revitalization agendas often fall into the interstitial spaces among the silos. Translation: it's nobody's job. Folks have talked about the silo problem for decades. Does it still exist? You be the judge: On May 3, 2016, I asked a "Chief Economist" if he had any urban revitalization-related material to contribute to REVITALIZATION. His answer was "no" because *"my work on urbanization is mostly related to economic development and inclusive growth."* Being an academic, the distinction might be useful, so he knows what journal to submit to. In the real world, it's the opposite of useful.

Reductionism, the belief that we can understand (or worse, control) the behavior of living systems by isolating and analyzing their parts, is a form of insanity. One thing it leads to is isolated specialization of knowledge: understanding the trees, but being clueless about forest dynamics. This means we don't really understand the trees, since context pretty much defines everything.

Physical silos are handy when we wish to keep our barley separate from our hops. Beer makers can access those silos and combine their contents to brew ale. But communities aren't so good at accessing their institutionally-siloed resources and expertise when they wish to brew community revitalization.

Housing authorities are another type of siloed local agency that has huge potential as a community revitalizer, but most heads of housing authorities look at me blankly when I ask what neighborhood revitalization initiatives they've initiated or contributed to.

Managing and funding our parks separately from our water infrastructure might make sense, but those two agencies need to be able to coordinate when a watershed restoration effort is underway. The right revitalization process taps these stakeholder and resource silos, without requiring established institutions to change their structure or behavior.

It's insane for a revitalization initiative to focus on just one or two realms, whether economy, jobs, society, health, justice, environment, infrastructure, heritage, brownfields, and buildings. But most do.

Silos can also be defined geographically. It might not be insane to revitalize a downtown or a Main Street without including suburbs and surrounding rural areas in the process, but it certainly wastes a lot of potential, reduces resilience and hamstrings success. That's like trying to improve the health of your heart while ignoring the health of your body.

Why do so many disciplines confine themselves to ever-narrower silos? Part of it is the modern human tendency towards shutting out more and more of the world, in order to come up with simpler and simpler—often non-fact-based—explanations for how it works. Another part of it is turf-protection, which is similar to warfare: as other disciplines make inroads, the borders are withdrawn to a smaller, more-defensible perimeter.

Most professional societies and associations inhibit integrative approaches, usually while proclaiming their support of them. One of the goals of association managers, for instance, is to create a microcosm in which their members can be important, influential, and honored. This is done by tightly focusing on the one area of knowledge or expertise in which they excel over others, and by giving them the opportunity to earn impressive titles within that organization. This is nice for the members, but often not so nice for the world they effect, as they become more inwardly-focused.

A focus on integrative approaches widens their field, diluting their uniqueness. For instance: the members of an association focused on ecological restoration might know that their discipline and projects benefit greatly when integrated with community or regional economic revitalization programs. But they will still resist making such integrative approaches a core focus, as that would mean people with expertise in the other components of revitalization might upstage the core members' expertise.

All that being said, organizational silos do tend to contain many resources and a lot of expertise. So, rather than busting silos, maybe the more productive approach would be to effectively (re)connect them. Here's a quick example of how a good strategy can connect the problems and resources trapped inside two professional silos, solving the problems of both.

All over the world, drinking water and agricultural water professionals professionals have long bemoaned the vast quantities of valuable water that evaporate from canals and irrigation ditches.

Meanwhile, renewable energy professionals have long bemoaned the fact that very large solar arrays usually cover arable land or wildlife habitat (such as deserts), and that getting access to large amounts of fallow land is expensive and/or time-consuming.

In the state of Gujarat, India (where REVITALIZATION's web team is based), someone decided that there must be a strategy that would solve all of these problems. That forced them to link the silos, and—sure enough—a simple strategy emerged.

They decided to put solar arrays over the canals. This greatly reduces evaporation by shielding them from the sun. It also provides almost unlimited surface area—with built-in right-of-ways to speed approvals—without infringing on farmland or ecosystems.

This is just one example of a larger trend: repurposing idle or contaminated land for renewable energy production (called "brightfields" in the U.S.).

This is a great option for places that don't have the money to redevelop or remediate such properties. They can earn revenue from selling or leasing such properties to energy companies.

Or, better yet, they can follow the example of Kimberley, British Columbia, and build a community-owned solar farm on the brownfield (in this case, mined land). This converts a liability to an asset, simply by bringing the brownfields silo into contact with the renewable energy silo.

While this trend towards integrating renewable energy production with the repurposing and renewing of fallow land has a lot of momentum, don't think for a moment that most public or private leaders are clued-into this most common sense of approaches.

For instance, Washington, DC's Georgetown University currently (2019) plans to clear-cut 240 acres of Southern Maryland's largest forest to build an industrial-scale solar facility. They are encountering a lot of flack over the proposal from better-educated leaders—such as at Preservation Maryland and at Smart Growth Maryland—so we can hope their plan will be thwarted. Maryland has a wealth of brownfields and previously-mined land on which to put solar panels.

Before we move on, let me address that other brilliant aspect of that Kimberley, BC brightfield: the fact that it's community-owned. This is an element of resilience and revitalization that's too often ignored. Nothing is more crucial to the functioning of a city and the welfare of its people than infrastructure: power, transportation, telecommunications, wastewater, drinking water, solid waste, etc.

Most places understand this, so they keep it publicly-owned, but usually farm out the maintenance (and sometimes the operation) of it to private companies.

The one area in which this is not the case is internet access: most cities have one or two corporate providers who take advantage of their near-monopoly to provide the least service for the most money. But internet access is now as crucial to the economic health of a place as any of those other forms of infrastructure. To compete, cities need the fastest-possible access at a price that makes it affordable for all residents. The obvious solution is public ownership, which enables the community to select the best ISP, and cancel their contract if they fail to deliver first-rate service.

Don't think it can be done? What U.S. city do you think has the fastest, most sophisticated and most affordable fiber-optic network? Boston? Austin? Portland? Nope: it's Ammon, Idaho, which has a grand total of some 16,500 residents. Why? Because it's community-owned, so they have the power to demand the best service for the best price from competing ISPs.

Before going with public ownership, residents paid an average of $99/month with a 3-year contract. Now they pay $9.99/month with no contract for a 1 Gbps connection. And all residents have the option of a free 15 Mbps connection if they are hard up. They also have far more options. For instance, both residents and businesses can actually own their own fiber, paying either $3200 up front or $20/month for 20 years. They also have the choice of eight local ISPs, and can easily switch among them.

Such is the power of a truly free market with intelligent, responsible government management. For any entrepreneur or existing business looking to relocate to that part of the country, Ammon would stand out for that reason alone, making community-owned fiber infrastructure a significant contributor to economic revitalization. And, since redundancy is a core component of resilience, having eight ISPs makes the community more resilient to boot.

BOOSTING YOUR STRATEGIC AWARENESS

To strengthen your strategy-making muscles, a good exercise is to make a game out of perceiving strategies at work around you. If you watch police dramas on TV or read detective fiction, watch for the moment one of the characters comes up with the strategy. Even though serial killers are fairly rare in the real world, they are prolific in crime fiction. Why? Part of the reason is that the cops have to strategize in order to catch them. A common scenario is this: the police have no idea who the serial killer is, or where he is. Someone will inevitably say "So, if we can't go to him, let's get him to come to us." That's a strategy.

The tactic might be to put a pretty policewoman on the street as bait in the killer's favorite hunting ground. If that doesn't work, another common tactic in fiction is to insult the criminal in the news media, and get them to attack the detective in charge of the case. The tactics can keep changing, but the strategy stays the same until it succeeds, or until someone comes up with a better one.

If a lot of manpower or logistical support—over a long period of time—is needed to execute the tactics, then a plan might be needed. In the "bait" scenario above, a checklist might suffice as the plan: 1) recruit female cop; 2) arm her and put her in costume; 3) drive her to the hunting ground; 4) observe surreptitiously. A true professional uses checklists constantly, but in the above example, the team leader is unlikely to write anything down. Plans are optional. Strategies are essential.

The role of plans is often to deal with conflicting constraints. Sticking with bait tactic in the above police scenario, the team leader's primary goal is to catch the killer. But his/her secondary goal is to keep the bait unhurt. These goals could conflict: if the safety goal were primary, the female cop would never be asked to be bait for a serial killer. Conflicting constraints are normal and common: dealing with them well is a mark of a good leader. The "joke" sign one often sees in service businesses gets to the heart of conflicting constraints: "You can have it fast, cheap, or good. Pick two."

What I constantly find amazing is how seldom local governments "get" the role of strategy. In truth, few really understand the whole goal/strategy/plan/tactics taxonomy in any formal manner. As with most things, the various parts usually get siloed. One group set goals. Another writes the plan. Another prepares to execute the tactics. But seldom does strategy get addressed, because that's the magical moment of clarity.

Since it only takes a moment for it to emerge, strategy gets no respect. No formal team is created, due to its ephemeral nature. Since anyone in the room could channel the strategy, no Director of Strategy is usually assigned. All of that is understandable. With the right people in the room, one meeting should be all it takes to come up with a viable strategy.

But why, then, do so few communities even have a strategy meeting when planning their revitalization? Some do, of course, and I've attended a few of them. What usually happens is that everyone uses the word "strategy" a lot, but no real strategy is formulated.

These days, communities are considered enlightened if they have a visioning session, as if it's somehow optional to know what it is you're trying to achieve. But even those "enlightened" towns that create a vision usually forget to map their renewable assets and create a strategy. They go straight into designing and/or planning, without ever having the key insight upon which their success will rely.

Strategy is such an intrinsic part of planning in corporate and military organizations that suggesting the creation of a strategy would get a "well, duh" response from them: it's a no-brainer.

But the planning profession somehow got so focused on the business of delivering products (plans) that they lost track of the process, and strategy largely fell by the wayside. I've reviewed countless city, county, and state development plans over the past decade or so, and can count on my fingers the number that actually had a clearly-defined strategy...and I'd have enough fingers left over to pick my nose while eating corn on the cob.

Most corporations at least understand the role of strategy, even if they aren't particularly skilled at strategizing. They know that a strategic analysis is a logical first step in the process. But when was the last time you heard of a city, county, or state/province commissioning a strategic analysis? Beyond my own clients, I rarely hear of it.

Once we get attuned to the dynamic, we can find strategic lessons everywhere, whether raising children, raising crops, or being entertained.

In the 2015 movie, *Sicario*, for instance, Emily Blunt's character is bewildered when she must abandon the FBI's tactical approach of intercepting drug smugglers and adopt the CIA's more-strategic approach of assassinating cartel bosses. At one point, Benicio Del Toro's CIA character tells Blunt's FBI character, *"You're asking me how the watch works. For now, let's just keep an eye on the time."*

Note: I say "more strategic"—rather than "strategic"—because a truly strategic approach would destroy the drug cartels' raison d'être, either by 1) getting 20% of Americans to stop using illegal drugs, or 2) legalizing drugs (the only strategy that's been proven to work). But the latter approach also threatens the multi-billion-dollar drug enforcement and incarceration industries, so it's not politically feasible in the U.S.

Another example: environmentalists have long despised coal mining companies, and the feeling is reciprocated. Renewable energy champions want to build a fossil fuel-free economy, while coal miners want to feed their families. Neither is likely to shift their position, and both have tactics for fighting the other. It's not just economies that go through transition, but the finances of individuals. That's where the real pain is, and thus the resistance to change.

But a strategy is free to ignore all of that baggage, and solve everyone's problems. An ideal strategy would, for instance, make the transition to clean energy while restoring damaged mine lands AND keeping coal miners employed.

Is a strategy to close coal mines while keeping coal miners working even possible? Yep: The $26 million Ehrenfeld Abandoned Mine Reclamation Project in Pennsylvania employs out-of-work coal miners to do the environmental restoration. What's more, Ehrenfeld is a federally-funded pilot project that—if successful—could unleash $1 billion of federal funds to replicate the model nationwide.

We're already making the renewable energy transition. At the turn of the millennium, the most optimistic projections for wind power were that by 2010, the world would have 30 gigawatts of capacity. Instead, we had 435 gigawatts. Similarly, the optimists predicted that we would be installing one gigawatt of solar capacity annually by 2010. In 2010, we actually installed 17 gigawatts. In 2015: 58 gigawatts.

The numbers are even better when we look at what's coming soon, and not just at what has already been installed. As of this writing (October 2019) the pipeline for contracted utility-scale solar energy projects in the U.S. has mushroomed to 37.9 gigawatts. This is the largest solar pipeline in U.S. history, according to the U.S. Solar Market Insight Report from Wood Mackenzie and the Solar Energy Industries Association. This growth is mostly the result of solar's cost-competitiveness: Prices are lower than ever, averaging just $18-35 per megawatt.

But fighting the climate crisis isn't just about cleaner energy sources or more-efficient cars and buildings. Simply lowering carbon emissions—or even achieving carbon-neutrality—aren't going to fix the problem: they'll just slow it down.

Climate restoration can only come from carbon-negative strategies. The best of these are based on restoring natural resources, since they have multiple fringe benefits and few or no negative unintended consequences. These include reforestation, of course, but there are many kinds of reforestation, some more efficient at carbon sequestration than others.

One of the most efficient is mangrove forest restoration (AKA "blue carbon"), which sequesters 10 time more carbon than terrestrial forests. And then there's regenerative agriculture, which—as mentioned earlier—sequesters three or four times more carbon than terrestrial reforestation.

The worst of the carbon-negative approaches fall under the category of "dumb engineers' tricks." These are the single-purpose technologies that remove carbon from the atmosphere either through "active air capture" or "passive air capture"), but have no fringe benefits. Worse, they usually take huge amounts of carbon to build, and take huge amounts of energy to operate.

The best of these air capture technologies turn the carbon into something useful, like gasoline or diesel fuels (usually by combining it with hydrogen from renewable energy-powered electrolysis). Or building materials: In September of

2019, the UK-based company, Cambridge Carbon Capture, developed a process called CO2LOC. It's a 2-stage mineralization process that reacts magnesium hydroxide (MgOH2) with CO2 to produce rock-like magnesium carbonate (MgCO3).

The dumbest of the carbon-capture technologies don't even repurpose the carbon: they just inject it into the ground, hoping it doesn't escape or have any negative effects, like aquifer acidification or earthquakes. The primary purpose of such technologies is to enrich engineering and manufacturing firms. They will get built though, because such firms have vast resources with which to buy or rent politicians.

Urban redevelopment strategies are just as central to climate restoration as technologies...maybe more so, since urban areas are responsible for an estimated 75% of CO2 emissions worldwide. As David Owen said in his 2009 book, *Green Metropolis*: "*A sprawling suburb is a fuel-burning, carbon-belching, waste-producing, water-guzzling, pollution-spewing, toxin-leaking machine, and, unlike a Hummer, it can't be easily abandoned for something smaller and less destructive.*"

As a result, a city can have a large number of green buildings, and still not be green. Its growth strategy creates inefficient horizontal structure that no amount of efficient vertical structure can overcome. One might call it "green flesh on brown bones".

It's not just about efficiency; it's also about vitality. Fissionable materials release vast energy when sufficiently compressed. So too do cities release more creative, productive energy as they densify.

Most ordinary folks can figure out that a strategic nuclear weapon is designed to win the war, while a tactical nuclear weapon is designed to win a battle. Thus, they can surmise that strategies achieve overarching goals, while tactics achieve sub-goals.

So, if strategies are so simple, why do most cities and regions not have a revitalization strategy? The primary reason seems to be because few public (or private) leaders know how revitalization works.

Generals know that battlefield success comes from killing the enemy or disrupting their logistical flows.

CEOs know that business success comes from growing revenue while shrinking expenses. They grow revenue via strategies that either increase market share, or that pioneer new markets.

But ask 100 mayors how to revitalize a city, and you'll get 100 answers. How can they devise a successful strategy if they don't know what leads to success?

PLANNING WITHOUT A STRATEGY IS PLANNING TO FAIL

In May of 2016, the city of Rio de Janeiro, Brazil released its excellent resilience "strategy". I call it excellent because it contains many essential actions. But I put "strategy" in quotes because it's not a strategy: it's a treatise...maybe even a plan. It doesn't even contain a strategy. Just the overview of this "strategy" is over 1200 words...more than 10 times the length of a good strategy.

A strategy is the core technique that guides decisions to help ensure success, so it must be brief and memorable. The Rio folks come closest to stating one when they say "Connection, collaboration, and the identification of co-benefits are the foundation of our strategy." But they call the entire 50-page document a strategy.

Most cities' expensive "comprehensive plans" are similarly devoid of strategy. It's like buying a Rolls Royce, and finding the transmission missing. But it's not just comprehensive plans: most of the "strategic plans" I've seen in the past two decades also lacked an identifiable strategy.

THE PROBLEMS WITH PLANS: MOST ARE JUST A FORMALITY, AND OVER 95% HAVE NEITHER A STRATEGY NOR AN IMPLEMENTATION PROCESS.

> "I have always found plans to be useless,
> but planning is indispensable."
> – Gen. Dwight D. Eisenhower, President of U.S.

Let me start this section—which is likely to be controversial—by pointing out that it's not so much a criticism of planners, as it is a criticism how they (and their plans) are used by their clients—if they are in private practice—or by their bosses (usually mayors) if they are on the public payroll.

In the Introduction, I described the minimum viable process for reliably producing revitalization and/or resilience: a regenerative program, a regenerative vision, a regenerative strategy, regenerative policies, regenerative partnerships and regenerative projects.

"*Where's the plan?*", planners are no doubt asking. The act of planning is good. But plans are often counterproductive to success. In the two decades I've been working in the field of regenerative economics, I've encountered literally hundreds of successes and failures in communities worldwide. What I noticed was that many of the successes had no plan, and many of the failures did have a plan.

Most urban, rural and regional plans are never implemented. Most plans that are implemented fail...despite having skilled personnel, and despite spending millions, even billions, on projects. As Kevin Bacon said in the movie, Tremors: "We plan ahead. That way, we don't have to do anything right now."

This sad track record is seldom the fault of the planners: neither strategy nor implementation are in their job description. Worse, mayors often commission plans as ends unto themselves, rather than as a means to an end. Creating a plan is a quick, failure-proof political "win", requiring only the writing of a check. Implementation introduces the risk of failure, so it's safer to shelve the plan. Another guaranteed glorious achievement can be had 5, 10, or 15 years later, with the commissioning of a new plan.

Thus, most plans go onto a shelf, and the ritual is repeated 5 or 10 years later. Planners earn a living and politicians avoid risk. Everyone is happy...except the community. [Please Note: This discussion of plans ONLY relates to their role in the revitalization process. Plans and planners have essential roles in many other crucial aspects of managing a community.]

Planning firms understand that their products are mostly for show, which is one reason they seldom bother with strategy, and focus instead on pretty pictures. This view might be just a bit overly-cynical, but it's closer to the truth than most planners would like to admit.

In a remarkable moment of frankness during a conversation on the subject of whether plans improve revitalization outcomes, an American Planning Association (APA) executive (who, prior to going to work at the APA was a professional planner, and had won national awards) told me, "*most plans are just a list of crap that no one ever looks at.*"

When we talked about the need for process, he totally agreed that communities had no real process for revitalizing themselves. He also said that he knew of no efforts within APA intended to study or facilitate such processes. Apparently, the only process in which planners have any interest is the process of creating a plan.

Most folks assume that a plan is essential to achieving revitalization or resilience, but they are actually optional. As mentioned above, plans are often present in success stories. But they're just as often missing. At best, they seem to be somewhat irrelevant; at worst, they substitute for action, and can even undermine success.

I should declare up front that the research I've done regarding the process of reviving places is mostly anecdotal, deriving from almost two decades of constant, intimate exposure to it. Academics reading this will, no doubt, be dismayed. But this is actually the norm as regards this subject.

That research reveals that there seems to be little or no correlation between a city's having a comprehensive plan, and the success of their revitalization or resilience efforts. I had long assumed that to be the case, but to confirm it, I consulted several other high-ranking executives at the American Planning Association, of which I used to be a member.

Professional planning firms benefit from the lack of implementation too, since they don't want anyone saying that their plan failed. Truth be told, there's little chance of that: post mortems on revitalization efforts are extremely rare.

Since one of APA's missions is to promote and advance the practice of planning, I asked one of them if the organization had ever done any research showing that places fare better when they have a plan. The answer was "no." She said such a research project had been discussed from time to time, but it would be hugely complex, since the relevant data is either hard to access or nonexistent.

That's because no one does forensic research on plans. Why? One reason is that there's no one in city government—the most common client or employer of planners—who has any motivation to document whether their plan worked. Such research would likely show that it had never been implemented, or that it had failed. It's one thing not having information that confirms the value of your work. It's far worse to have data proving that your work isn't as valuable as you want people to believe it is.

I encountered a similar situation back in the late 90s, when I spent five years as the Director of Strategic Initiatives at the Construction Specifications Institute (CSI). The Building Owners and Managers Association (BOMA) had an informal initiative that was trying to figure out why the functional (as opposed to aesthetic) design of buildings never seemed to improve much. Materials often improved, but the underlying design flaws were repeated decade after decade, resulting in massive additional maintenance and energy costs.

They determined that these repeated architectural failures were due to the lack of forensic analysis. There was no data because there was no feedback process: building managers had no way to communicate problems back to the designers. As a result, the architects never become aware of deficiencies in their work. In other words: the architectural profession lacks an effective learning mechanism.

One property owner decided it was time to fix that problem. Their RFPs started including a clause whereby X% (I think it was about 10%) of the architects' fees would be withheld for a year or so. After that period, a survey of the building manager and the occupants would be taken, regarding their happiness with the building from a comfort and maintenance perspective. If the score didn't exceed a certain threshold, the balance of the fee would be forfeited.

Architects were, of course, horrified that "ordinary people" would be judging their work, and fought back vigorously. As a result, this feedback loop of evaluation-learning-improvement was never established. The same situation exists with planners: no one judges or measures the outcome of their work, which is why my research is anecdotal. Children stop touching hot stoves when they feel pain. Both the planning and the architectural professions lack pain receptors.

For many years, I've habitually asked planners how much of their work they feel was successful. I was initially impressed when most of them replied "almost all of it". Then I discovered that their idea of "success" was the creation of a plan, not the impact of that plan.

But I don't want to be unfair: turning a plan into actual revitalization or resilience is not in their job description. Here's one official definition of what IS in their job description: *"Urban and regional planners design, promote, or administer government plans or policies affecting land use, zoning, public utilities, community facilities, housing, or transportation. They supervise or coordinate the work of urban planning technicians or technologists. They recommend approval, denial, or conditional approval of proposals. They might also create, prepare, or requisition graphic or narrative reports on land use data, including land area maps overlaid with geographic variables such as population density. They advise planning officials on project feasibility, cost-effectiveness, regulatory conformance, or possible alternatives, and discuss with planning officials the purpose of land use projects, such as transportation, conservation, residential, commercial, industrial, or community use. In addition, they keep informed about economic or legal issues involved in zoning codes, building codes, or environmental regulations."*

Notice that there's no mention of being responsible for outcomes in that exhaustive list. So, let's not blame planners when plans fail, or fail to even to be read.

Most folks with long experience in community revitalization know there are only two things worse than not having a plan:
- not implementing your plan, and
- implementing your plan.

That's because the traditional approach to planning a major redevelopment project is to throw money (usually in the 6 figures) at a professional planning firm. I specify "major redevelopment project" to distinguish this outsourced work from staff planners' normal day-to-day work of approving or denying permits. The result is often a plan that's 70% boilerplate, with some token "community engagement" exercises (like design charrettes) thrown in along the way.

> *"Unfortunately, we are excellent at developing award-winning plans and ignoring them. And that really needs to change."*
> *– Druh Farrell, Calgary City Councillor (2019).*

Sometimes, plans are done in-house by local government. This has the advantage of being done by people who are more in tune with the community's needs. But it has the disadvantage that the local planners might lack an objective perspective, and are often out of tune with the latest revitalization trends, tools and success stories from around the world.

The reason observation #2 (above) often holds true is because so many plans are bad and/or out of date. Virtually every disastrous urban mistake you've ever heard of was professionally planned. Many of the urban plans of the past half century have done far more damage than would have been done in their absence.

Not planning usually results in ugly, damaging, traffic-inducing sprawl. The downtown will often be devitalized in the process, but is seldom obliterated. Bad planning often obliterates, removing the restorable assets the city would have used to revitalize itself when it finally came to its senses. Not having a good inventory of assets (such as historic buildings) that can be repurposed, renewed and reconnected reduces investors' confidence in the revitalized future of a city. Such places are deficient in renewal capacity, but that capacity can be boosted via the adoption of a strategic process.

The planning profession has improved in recent years, but nowhere near as much as they think they have. They look back on the planning atrocities of the "urban renewal" disasters of the 50's, 60's, and 70's with disdain, proud that they now understand the value of old buildings, and proud of not being as overtly racist as those earlier planners, who assumed the best place for demolition or new highways was wherever poor people—especially people of color—lived.

But that's a mighty low bar. A higher bar would be to define an ideal strategic revitalization or resilience process, and to measure themselves by how close they are to being able to facilitate it.

Here's an excerpt from a December 7, 2012 article by Sarah Fecht in *Scientific American*: "*In 1961 urbanist Jane Jacobs didn't pull any punches when she called city planning a pseudoscience. 'Years of learning and a plethora of subtle and complicated dogma have arisen on a foundation of nonsense,' she wrote in The Death and Life of Great American Cities. Fifty years later the field is still plagued by unscientific thought, according to urban theorist Stephen Marshall of University College London. In a recent paper in Urban Design International, Marshall restated Jacobs's observation that urban design theory is pseudoscientific and called for a more scientific framework for the field.*"

In that same article, Michael Mehaffy, an urban designer at Portland, Oregon was quoted as saying: *"In urban planning, we're like physicists without a particle theory or doctors without a germ theory. We don't have a unifying idea about the nature of what we're looking on. We say we're artists but it's as if we're medieval doctors with potions.... We need to recognize that we have a responsibility to use models that are more likely to produce better outcomes."*

> *"(UK) Communities Min. Andrew Stunell has said that planning 'isn't brain surgery' and should become a community-owned occupation." – Jamie Carpenter (2011).*

To be fair, it wasn't planners who came up with the disastrous idea of revitalizing cities by demolishing historic buildings and poor-but-healthy ethnic neighborhoods. But they did implement it. Whose idea was it?

Here's the Abstract from a paper by Alexander von Hoffman in Issue 3 of Volume One (2008) of the *Journal of Urbanism*, titled "The Lost History of Urban Renewal": *"Contrary to common understanding, the US government's policy of 'urban renewal' was conceived as an alternative policy to slum clearance. Bitterly opposed to public housing, conservative housing industry trade associations sought a way to reform the urban redevelopment formula of clearance and public housing established in the Housing Act of 1949. In the early 1950s, the industry groups seized on citizens' neighborhood fix-up efforts, particularly the Baltimore Plan, to conduct a national campaign to popularize code enforcement, rehabilitation, and private low-cost housing development as methods to restore and stabilize city neighborhoods."*

He went on to say: *"At conferences organized by House and Home magazine and in the President's Advisory Committee on Government Housing Policies and Programs, the housing industry associations fashioned policies, now named 'urban renewal,' which were codified in the Housing Act of 1954. But private industry's venture in urban policymaking failed in implementation. Home builders proved reluctant to participate in the new programs, public housing hung on, and hundreds of thousands of homes fell to the wrecking ball. As urban renewal became synonymous with slum clearance, neighborhoods continued to decline. In the end, ironically, housing rehabilitation reemerged as a populist tool for reviving the inner city."*

One California city is finally getting around to restoring the downtown that urban planners obliterated half a century ago. This story has some personal interest: I graduated from Pioneer High School in nearby Campbell, California (a suburb of San Jose) in 1969. During my many trips to San Francisco via El Camino Real, I often wondered whether any of the identical-looking commercial areas labelled "Sunnyvale", "Palo Alto", "Santa Clara", etc. actually had a real downtown.

The following excerpt from an Opinion piece by Dan Ondrasek in the Mercury News on June 9, 2018 answers my question regarding Santa Clara: "*In the 1960s, a wrecking ball crushed the last of downtown Santa Clara. Citizens looked on in bewilderment and sadness. Within 10 years, any hope of promised benefits of urban renewal were dashed with the result — a two-block concrete strip mall. Only 13 of the 120 original merchants returned. The Mercury News called the demolition of downtown Santa Clara one of the "Worst Decisions in Silicon Valley in the last 50 Years."*

What followed was even worse. The city engaged in parcel-by-parcel development. This approach replaced the charming downtown with a jumble of unrelated office buildings, strip malls, a 1980s apartment complex and a traffic court...all surrounded by a sea of surface parking lots. It left many Bay Area residents wondering if Santa Clara had a downtown, and if so, where was it?

Santa Clara is now on the verge of fully restoring its downtown, but it will only happen if the city council stops parcel-by-parcel development and fully funds an integrated plan. This effort to restore downtown began two years ago. Rod Dunham got things started by posting a Facebook page called "Reclaiming Our Downtown." What began with a meeting attended by five Santa Clara natives has now grown into a force of more than 3000. All want Santa Clara's heart back. Past bickering has been replaced by unity among a diverse group of residents and groups working to plan and build a nationally significant and economically viable downtown.

Most planners spend so much time working on zoning that many think planning and zoning are pretty much synonymous. Zoning controls how land is developed, and redeveloped, so it's the key tool for implementing plans. But zoning isn't planning.

In its ideal form—which is seldom, if ever, seen in the real world—the planning discipline would conform to this description by Peter Park, former planning director of Denver and Milwaukee (as quoted in an October 17, 2019 interview by James Brasuell in Planetizen): "*Planning is the process of broadly, meaningfully, and effectively engaging communities to define their collective vision and aspirations for their future. This process culminates in the adoption of plans and policies for future development as the basis for regulatory changes and capital infrastructure investments. Planning and establishing a future vision should precede zoning changes.*"

FROM PERPETUAL PLANNING TO RESILIENT PROSPERITY

As with economic development departments, your community's planning department is likely to be an obstacle to establishing a strategic renewal process. Not that they don't understand its value, but because they fear it will reduce their influence and/or infringe on their turf. But—again as with economic developers—there are many enlightened planners who are quite ready to abandon their antiquated, unproductive current practices as regards revitalization and resilience.

While writing a plan is sometimes appropriate, it often brings things to a standstill while it's happening, and is ignored after its done. A plan is too voluminous to guide decisions. For that, you need a strategy, and that should fit on the back of an envelope.

> *"I don't have business plans...I have a back-of-the-envelope idea of what I want to do."*
> *– Richard Branson, CEO of the Virgin Group.*

Even worse, many people think planning IS the revitalization process. The planning process produces a plan. If it's done well, it also produces community engagement. And that's it. A plan is not a community revitalization process any more than a map of the world is a globetrotting adventure.

The key to turning a plan from an expensive ritual to a component of revitalization is to embed it in an effective renewal process. And the key to doing that in a way that doesn't screw-up the process is to make the plan an adaptively-managed living document. If your municipality has money that must be spent on a document, a study is often more useful than a plan. A good study will inform your strategic renewal process, rather than restrict it (as does a plan.)

Plans are usually the centerpiece of any renewal initiative, but they are the element that takes the most time (and—aside from projects—the most money) to produce and approve. Plans are also likely to be the element that's rendered obsolete the soonest.

Complex systems (e.g. cities, economies, ecosystems) resist rigid, imposed order, which is what most plans attempt to do. The other downside is that plan-based regeneration puts too much control in the hands of the planning department, which cities do at their peril.

"There have been hundreds of plans, and none... have really gotten to the change that we need."
– Dawveed Scully on revitalizing Chicago's Woodlawn neighborhood.

Planning falls into the category of "official activity": most places are required to write one (or buy one) because they assume it's essential to success. It isn't.

Freed of following a formal plan, the focus tends to shift from activity to performance; one might say from official activity to effective activity.

To recap: the act of planning is a positive, but the possession of an official plan is often a negative that stifles both innovative solutions and agility (responsiveness to changing challenges and resources).

But again: don't confuse my criticism of plans with a criticism of planners. Used properly, they can do wonders. But they do have to at least show up.

In Chicago, newly-appointed (as of September 2019) planning commissioner Maurice Cox has repurposed 20 of the city's urban planners to focus on neighborhood revitalization, specifically to support the new Invest South/West initiative. But at the announcement meeting, 11th Ward Alderman Patrick Daley Thompson emphasized that his ward was revitalizing just fine without the city's planners. He pointed out that the planners never attended the neighborhood's redevelopment meetings.

At the other end of the showing-up spectrum, you have planners like Tyler Hinkle in Virginia. Kim Woodwell, Executive Director of the Alliance for the Shenandoah Valley, noticed a face that kept showing up at all of the Alliance's meetings. Introducing herself, she found that he (Hinkle) was the county's planner. I'll bet he's a good one. On the other hand, when she asked him what the most exciting thing was that he would be working on in the coming year, he said it was updating the comprehensive plan. Sigh.

So, create a plan if you want to, or if you're required to, but know that it probably won't improve your chances of success, and might well hurt them. You could add it as an element in the minimum viable process we're describing in this book, or you could just treat it as one of the projects. If you do add it to the process itself, I recommend putting it at the end, just before the "Projects" element.

I realize that this advice will rub many planners the wrong way, but you'll soon be learning about a practical alternative to the traditional plan-forget-plan-forget cycle that has devitalized so many places. When planning is properly integrated into the RECONOMICS Process, it will likely revitalize the profession, along with the communities.

Why learn the roles of visions, strategies, tactics, plans, programs, and projects?

Many projects are actually revitalization efforts, and fail because they don't realize it. They often fly under banners like "renewable energy", "sustainability", "ecodistrict", "innovation district", "economic development", "infrastructure renewal", "beautification", "affordable housing", "workforce development" or "brownfields remediation." All can be forms of revitalization, but approached from different angles.

The fact that "community revitalization" or "regional resilience", etc. isn't in the vision statement of those more-focused efforts means that it isn't in their strategy. As a result, untapped resources, reduced stakeholder buy-in, and limited success ensue.

For instance, many cities these days are spending millions—even billions—on making their downtown more pedestrian/bicyclist-friendly, more transit-oriented, and less car-centric.

Few activities are more revitalizing for an urban center, yet many of these vast investments of time and money go by utilitarian names like "transit-oriented", "trail-oriented", "mobility", "walkability", "complete streets", etc.

But those names are all tactical: the vision and strategy should be focused on contributing to resilient prosperity. It's increased quality of life and economic growth that people really want, not just another mode of transport. The right vision leads to the right strategy, which boosts the project's funding and stakeholder support.

In the U.S., conservatives often oppose public transit, since they associate it with serving primarily lower-income families, people of color and immigrants. But progressives and conservatives alike desire revitalization.

In the 50s and 60s, Washington policymakers and professional urban planners did more damage to American cities than all foreign enemies combined, via the aforementioned urban renewal tragedy. Why? Because they didn't know the difference between a tactic and a strategy.

They blindly assumed that, if they demolished all the empty buildings, new development would automatically sprout in its place. The "destroy it and they will come" assumption of "urban renewal" didn't work.

Most of those cities (such as Hartford, CT) are still plagued with vast, lifeless downtown surface parking lots as a result. Their "restorable assets" were removed.

Cities that didn't partake in the madness—like Charleston, South Carolina—revitalized via strategies that repurposed old buildings, while also renewing green spaces and reconnecting to their waterfronts.

But now, some American "Rustbelt" cities are again enthusiastically demolishing blighted neighborhoods, again with federal money. Let's hope they have a regenerative strategy this time, because demolition is only a tactic.

This urge to wipe the slate clean is irresistible to many urban planners and architects. I pointed out in my 2008 book, Rewealth, how the New Urbanism movement had quickly abandoned the regenerative principles laid out in its birth, and had become sort of a new version of urban renewal. Many historic downtowns have been demolished to make way for often-sterile, hyper-commercial (but walkable!) New Urbanist developments, where everything is new and nothing is charming or quirky.

An article titled "Paper Utopias" by Monte Reel in the November 5, 2018 issue of *Bloomberg Businessweek* explained the origins of urban planners' destructive tendencies thus: "*Embedded in the cerebral folds of every city planner who's ever lived, there's a cluster of neurons that lights up like Las Vegas when confronted with the possibility of a blank slate. It started with Hippodamus, the man Aristotle claimed was the father of urban planning. When the Persians destroyed his hometown of Miletus, Hippodamus discovered a bright side to catastrophe: The attackers had erased all the regrettable improvisations that, over the centuries, had made a mess of the place. Tasked with rebuilding, he seized his chance to impose order upon chaos. And so the concept of the urban grid was born. Ever since, the dream of carte blanche has proved an all-but-irresistible seduction.*"

The parts of a community that people often love most are the unplanned parts; the sections that have been filled-in by local entrepreneurs and neighborhood activists, rather than by design-from-above. Brazil famously (or infamously, depending on one's perspective) built an entirely new capital city—Brasília—in 1960, using the oppressive, Brutalist architectural style popular at the time.

Monte Reed said in that same article, "*Cities are organisms that undergo constant evolutions, inevitably responding to stresses in ways planners can't predict. The most vibrant part of Brasília today isn't the faux-futuristic corridor of government buildings that dominated the city plans; it's all the neighborhoods and restaurants and clubs that occupy the spaces left blank.*"

Unless a historic property is dangerous or disgusting, local residents usually prefer renovation and reuse over demolition. The city of Waterloo, Ontario, Canada created a very good process for engaging local stakeholders in the writing of their 2015-2018 Strategic Plan. It was documented in an excellent 2019 Case Study by the Tamarack Institute.

Waterloo started off correctly by forming a vision statement for their Neighbourhood Strategy: "Waterloo is a city of caring, vibrant, engaged neighbourhoods where everyone belongs." They then documented six principles/values to guide the creation of their Neighbourhood Strategy (also a good practice):

- Residents and neighbourhood volunteers are at the root of a great neighbourhood;

- Every resident is a neighbour and can help build strong neighbourhoods;
- Neighbourhood community building should be resident-led;
- Neighbourhood community building should aim to be inclusive;
- City departments must work together to help support resident-led and delivered neighbourhood initiatives; and,
- Collaboration with community partners is key to achieving the strategy's vision.

Here then, is the "strategy" (their term) that Waterloo created:
- Goal 1: Encourage neighbourhood interactions;
- Goal 2: Empower Neighbours to lead; and,
- Goal 3: Commit to a corporate City culture that supports neighbourhood led and delivered initiatives.

Each of the above goals was accompanied by a to-do list of actions that would help accomplish the goal. For instance, here's the list for Goal #1:
- Encourage Neighbourliness;
- Support neighbourhoods seeking to build stronger relationships through a program that sparks neighbourhood community building;
- Nurture place-based neighbourhood pride, belonging, identity and placemaking;
- Inspire those living in multi-unit buildings to connect with their neighbours;
- Continue to build neighbourhood cohesion in areas with a high concentration of post-secondary students; and,
- Clarify the City supports available to homes associations and residents in these areas.

So, after three years, they created three goals with recommended actions. But no actual strategy to help ensure success. On the one hand, its heartening to see a community put so much excellent, sincere, grassroots effort into improving their situation. Their resulting document is far more thoughtful than what most communities have. On the other hand, it's tragic to see so much work get started without someone ever asking *"do we know what a strategy is?"*

My suspicion is that—as in most such situations—the primary value of that 3-year exercise in Waterloo will derive from the exercise itself (no small thing), not from the resulting Neighbourhood Strategy document.

Moving south, New Orleans' former Chief Resilience Officer Jeff Hebert was largely correct some years back when he said *"resilience is, for us, synonymous with being strategic."* But resilience itself is actually a goal/objective, not a strategy. For resilience efforts to be strategic, one needs an actual strategy for achieving resilience. Unfortunately, Resilient New Orleans—the city's 88-page "strategic plan" (published in 2015 as part of the Rockefeller Foundation's now-defunct 100 Resilient Cities program) lacks a clearly-defined strategy.

There are 50 occurrences of the word "strategy" in that document, but no actual statement of the strategy itself. It's not New Orleans' fault: the problem seems to be endemic to all of the "strategic plans" from the 100 Resilient Cities program. Little surprise, then, when the New York Times reported on March 29, 2019 that the program was being disbanded. It was a brilliant idea, but poorly managed and implemented.

The New Orleans plan almost makes a concise statement of strategy when it says they will "*Promote sustainability as a growth strategy.*" But, like resilience, sustainability is a goal, not a strategy.

If flood-prone places were really thinking strategically, one of the "re" words that would come up frequently would be "retreat". Just as it makes sense for an individual to walk out of a spot that's flooding, so too does it often make more sense for a community to move out of a floodplain (where they never should have been in the first place). You could call it a "strategic retreat" to make it more palatable, because most folks—certainly Americans—don't like that word. During the Korean War, when asked if his troops were retreating, Major General Oliver Prince Smith replied "*Retreat, hell! We're not retreating; we're just advancing in a different direction.*"

The New Orleans Strategic Plan often refers to "this strategy", such as when they say "We are moving beyond our recovery to focus on our future, and this strategy outlines many deliberate steps forward." What they are referring to as "this strategy" is the 88-page document itself, which is actually a plan. The closest that plan comes to making a concise statement of an actual strategy is in what they call their "three visions":

"We will:
- Redesign our regional transit system to connect people, employment, and essential services;
- Promote sustainability as a growth strategy. Improve the redundancy and reliability of our energy infrastructure. Integrate resilience-driven decision making across public agencies. Invest in pre-disaster planning for post-disaster recovery;
- Develop the preparedness of our businesses and neighborhoods."

Of course, a vision is supposed to describe what the strategy is meant to accomplish: it's not a statement of what you will do to accomplish it. But, with a little re-wording, the above could be a good vision statement.

I recently heard the leader of a multi-billion-dollar regional environmental restoration program tell local stakeholders, "If our Master Plan is the vision, our

Annual Plan is where that vision becomes reality." This confusion of "vision", "strategy", and "plan" is what happens when smart, knowledgeable, well-meaning folks are asked to draft a strategic plan, without first ensuring that they understand the key terminology. Each element (program, vision, strategy, policies, partners, projects) should be defined, and the role of each in the overall process described.

Without that, one gets the New Orleans situation: when asked what their strategy is, they hand over a hefty document.

In March of 2017, Pittsburgh, Pennsylvania—another of the 100 Resilient Cities—released their beautifully-produced Strategic Plan. Despite a couple hundred uses of the word "strategy", no strategy is ever stated. Again, the assumption is that the entire 61-page document is a strategy.

Likewise their 91-page "strategic plan" for Los Angeles, which was released in March of 2018. It has 29 uses of the word "strategy", but never once says what that strategy is.

I alerted the 100 Resilient Cities folks to the problem right after the first "Strategic Plans" were released—and offered my assistance pro bono to rectify it—but both the warning and the offer fell on deaf ears.

About two years later, on April 29, 2019, the District of Columbia—across the Potomac River from where I live—released its own "resilience strategy." At about 150 occurrences, they managed to triple the number of times New Orleans used the word "strategy." Unfortunately, it's just as strategy-free as the other 100 Resilient Cities strategic plans. An indication of their confusion of "strategy" with "plan" is in their statement "The 68 initiatives in this strategy…"

If Rockefeller had named the program "100 Resilience Plans," it could have claimed success, since plan-writing seemed to be their primary skill. The demise of 100 Resilient Cities was a tragedy, because many good people put much hard work into these plans.

History is littered with losers whose strategy wasn't as good as their opponents'. But at least they had one. For leaders not to even know what a strategy is…that's just plain scary. The 100 Resilient Cities program had lots of company, unfortunately.

Here's a fairly-recent example: the Philadelphia Land Bank's 2017 Strategic Plan has some excellent ideas for dealing with the city's 43,000 vacant lots, and their dearth of affordable housing. But, like most strategic plans, it was strategy-free.

As in New Orleans, the Philadelphia Land Bank confuses their strategic plan with a strategy. Thus, they have a 77-page "strategy", which means they have no strategy at all.

The plan makes several references to a strategy, such as an "acquisition strategy". They sometimes refer to specific tactics as a strategy (such as acquiring community gardens). But no strategy ever appears.

Here are two representative sentences from the plan: "*The Land Bank provides a strategy to address the blight and bring the land back to productive use, reducing public cost and increasing tax revenue.*" and "*The proposed Land Bank acquisition policy and strategy outlines a process by which low-income and affordable housing developers can seek assistance in assembling land for development.*"

The good news is that these strategy-less "strategic plans" aren't a waste of time. They can be fixed. A strategy can be devised to fit the plan after the fact. I know that sounds silly...like figuring out where you want to go on vacation and how you're going to get there after you've bought the airline tickets. While it's certainly not the ideal order, it's doable.

After all, the plan represents a lot of thought about what you want to do and what you're capable of doing. A pre-existing plan does impose constraints, but that could actually be seen as making strategizing easier. I've occasionally been asked to do "plan repair" in this manner, and it's not as hard as it might sound. Remember: the strategy's sole purpose to simply, speed, and secure success via good decisions. We can thus derive a plan from a strategy, or derive a strategy from a plan. There's no chicken-or-egg-first conundrum.

An understanding of strategy is the basis of being effective in any endeavor: personal, organizational or municipal. For those involved in improving their community or restoring nature, it's the primary determinant in success or failure. Does having a good strategy guarantee success? Not if your opponent (which many communities falsely assume they lack) has a better one. But not having a strategy virtually guarantees failure.

WHAT TRIGGERS DEVITALIZATION?

The list of devitalizing factors is as long as the list of factors that contribute to revitalizing a place. Whether it's pollution, crime, corruption or decrepit infrastructure, in the end, the devitalizing influences all boil down to insufficient health, beauty, safety, opportunity and/or efficiency. One factor that has brought down societies repeatedly over the millennia has now reached critical level again: gross economic inequity.

Smart mayors of declining places acknowledge that population flight is a symptom, rather than the underlying problem (what's making them flee?). And, as explained elsewhere, a city can revitalize while shrinking: quality beats quantity.

But those same people tend to fall back on "loss of jobs" as the real problem, rather than the poor quality of life or lack of confidence in the local future that's causing those jobs to disappear.

That's often because the only tool they have is an economic development agency, so every problem looks like lack of employer incentives. The basic tactic of the economic developer is to make his or her city cheaper, but every marketer know that lowering one's price is the weakest form of marketing. Quality of life and confidence in the future are ignored because leaders in general—and economic developers in particular—have no inkling of how to fix them. Such maladies can only be cured with a strategic renewal process.

THE ZERO-SUM APPROACH TO REVITALIZATION

Many folks renew and reuse historic buildings. Others clean and redevelop brownfields. Some restore watersheds, ecosystems, farmlands, or greenspace. Others improve public transit, or make communities more pedestrian-and-bicycle-friendly. Some renew infrastructure. Some specialize in catastrophe recovery and resilience. Others activate vacant lots with community gardens, farmers' markets, pop-up functions, and pocket parks. Wonderful activities all...but none focus on the whole. And few—if any—of those folks have any training in revitalization.

Economic development directors would say "Hey: I'm in charge of revitalization, and I have training!" However, "economic development" is traditionally just sales. The pitch to employers is "move here: we're cheaper", but price competition is usually an act of desperation.

But most relocating firms have already chosen a new location before demanding public sector handouts ($80 billion/year in the U.S.). Wooing employers from another city might revitalize winners, but it devitalizes losers. It's a zero-sum strategy.

In New Jersey, Governor Chris Christie gave $40 million in tax incentives to Cooper Health System to relocate 353 jobs from a Camden suburb to downtown Camden. Now, I'm all in favor of downtown revitalization, but does it really make sense to move jobs from one place in your own state to another, while eliminating the tax benefits of having that employer?

> *"In politics, we presume that everyone who knows how to get votes knows how to administer a city or a state. When we are ill... we do not ask for the handsomest physician, or the most eloquent one."* — Plato

Governor Christie also gave Lockheed Martin $118 million in tax incentives to move 250 jobs from another Camden suburb to the downtown. How much tax revenue is New Jersey expected to earn from Lockheed Martin over the next 35 years? A grand total of $248,000. Sounds more like economic suicide than economic development. [Critics say Lockheed Martin got a $118 million return on the $50,000 they donated to Christie's Republican Governors Association.]

There's certainly no net gain for the nation: it's a zero-sum game (actually, a negative-sum game) that merely shuffles jobs around while sucking revenue from vital public services. The good news is that GASB, the Governmental Accounting Standards Board is proposing new rules that would require local governments to annually report on the revenue they've lost to economic development subsidies.

Growth of good jobs is a joy to the unemployed, and a key component of revitalization, but it's not revitalization. I specify "good" because an excess of demeaning, low-paying jobs demoralizes communities, and many economic developers focus only on quantity, not quality. The system is perpetuated by lack of rigorous metrics: economic development agencies tend to take credit for any jobs that arrive, regardless of provenance. As an economic developer in North Carolina once said about his state's strategy: *"We shoot anything that flies and claim anything that falls."*

Some economic development organizations (EDOs) rise above this old job-recruitment mode. Examples include InvestAtlanta, and the Philadelphia Industrial Development Corporation (which led redevelopment of Philly's old Navy Yard). Some of them, like the Urban Redevelopment Authority of Pittsburgh, even use "redevelopment" rather than "economic development" in their names.

The International Economic Development Council (IEDC) is encouraging evolution of the profession, but "re"-focused EDOs are still the exception: far from the norm. In fact, the Executive Summary of the IEDC's 2014 report "Looking Around the Corner: The Future of Economic Development" unfortunately didn't contain a single "re" word (redevelopment, revitalization, regeneration, remediation, reuse, renewal, restoration, etc.). To its credit, it does say *"It is likely* that *[economic developers] will play a key role in reinventing their communities, and even their own organizations, several times over."* But it doesn't say how.

EDOs say new employers give cities the money to do redevelopment, but experience doesn't support that hypothesis. How can cities pay for renewal if they've forfeited all corporate and property taxes for decades? One problem is that the name—economic development—tends to inhibit focusing on social, infrastructure, or environmental agendas.

> *"Politicians respond to noise and money."*
> *– Rina Cutler, Philadelphia Deputy Mayor,*
> *who has served 7 mayors and governors.*

Another problem is their bosses: mayors and city councils often want the "quick fix" of new employers, so that's how they measure the EDO's success. Yet another problem is that anyone can call themselves an economic development professional. So the majority—those who "steal" jobs from other communities, or who base economic growth on destructive sprawl—can bask in the halo of the minority who base economic growth on restorative development.

REVITALIZATION IS MESSY

> *"Throw an ashtray in any direction, and you'll hit a messy, complex challenge. It's difficult to escape the persistent feeling that while our problems are already big and bad, they're in fact getting bigger and badder. It's harder and harder to believe people who tell us things are actually getting better. The future is changing in our lifetimes from a magical place to a place best avoided..." - Zaid Hassan.*

Before we leave this chapter on common problems encountered in communities that are trying to revitalize, let me point out that revitalizing a place is always going to be messy, and likely to generate controversy. A good strategy and a good process will maximize the efficiency and minimize the discord, but some messiness and controversy will be unavoidable. Here's a brief story to illustrate.

After decades of largely-unsuccessful design and developer-based attempts to revitalize their downtown area—including streetscaping, sidewalk-widening, and a huge failed infill project—Clearwater, Florida is now trying a small business-based strategy. I lived in Clearwater and St. Petersburg for 15 years, so I'm quite intimate with the redevelopment history of Pinellas County in particular, and the Tampa Bay area in general.

After long-pursuing development along US 19 (the central north-south artery of Pinellas County), and along SR 60 (the major east-west artery of Clearwater), they finally want to make downtown the easiest and most profitable place to open a business in the city. They'd especially like to see more art galleries, microbreweries, and restaurants.

On June 12, 2017, the Clearwater Community Redevelopment Agency (CCRA) approved the Anchor Tenant Incentive Program to provide incentives of up to $250,000 each for both property owners and commercial tenants via a loan-to-grant program. The loans can be applied to business startup costs, such as rent, furniture, fixtures, and equipment, as well as for interior refurbishment.

The loans have 5-year terms. Here's how the loan-to-grant aspect works: for each year that the business stays open, 20% of the loan is forgiven. Thus, at the end of 5 years, the businesses will owe nothing if they're still operating.

This is a strategy that has worked in some places. But it has also failed in many places when there weren't enough downtown residents. All the up-front incentives in the world won't keep a business alive in the long run if it doesn't have enough customers. Incentives and subsidies can be considered the "artificial stimulant" approach to retail revitalization: progress tends to disappear when the "drugs" wear off. Resident-based retail revitalization, on the other hand, could be considered the "organic" approach to downtown economic growth.

The wisest retail growth strategies thus focus first on downtown housing (especially affordable), and only then do they incentivize the businesses that will serve these residents. A family can survive a lot longer without a nearby grocery store than a grocery store can survive without nearby customers. Residents have far more "revitalization patience".

Fortunately, Seth Taylor, Director of Clearwater's Community Redevelopment Agency, is aware of this danger. They are wisely focusing their strategy on attracting established local brand names that have a strong following in the Tampa Bay area, and will thus be less dependent on downtown residents.

In a June 16, 2017 phone conversation, Seth told me they aren't overlooking the need to boost the downtown's residential capacity. They already have over 400 units of new market-rate rental units under construction. This is especially good because rental units tend to be far more revitalizing than condos which—in resort areas like Clearwater—tend to be occupied only seasonally.

But wait, there's more: Clearwater (not to be confused with Clearwater Beach, which is on the other side of the beautiful Intercoastal Waterway) has long put its public administration offices on the waterfront. This was a rather self-serving decision on the part of city officials in decades past, since it boosted their quality of life at the expense of the downtown's economic health. Public infrastructure—whether government offices, parking lots or sewer plants—is seldom the highest and best use of a good view.

Thus, the city's new $55 million Imagine Clearwater master plan will move these offices off the waterfront, freeing that valuable space for huge amounts of multi-story residential redevelopment. They'll make even more room for residents by demolishing their failed waterfront convention center.

Our phone conversation took place only 5 days after the Anchor Tenant Incentive Program was announced, and Seth said they had already received 25 inquiries from Tampa Bay area entrepreneurs.

Many local folks say that one of Clearwater's most intransigent challenges is that the largest and most important downtown heritage building—the Fort Harrison Hotel, which opened in 1926—has for over 40 years been occupied by the highly-controversial Church of Scientology. Their strong association with downtown Clearwater has, in some folks eyes, diminished its attraction as a business location.

Others point out that the Church of Scientology saved and restored a derelict-but-beautiful building that might have otherwise have been demolished, and that Scientology staff and visitors have helped support downtown businesses. In addition, unlike most tax-exempt churches, they currently pay over $205,000 annually in property taxes on the hotel.

In a June 26, 2017 letter to me, Church of Scientology Director of External Affairs Ben Shaw said: "*over 12,000 Scientologists now live in the greater Clearwater area, fully 10% of the Clearwater population. ...a 2013 report by economists at Florida State University (said that) the Church and its related activities had a $917 million annual positive impact on the local community. The Church has seen even further expansion in Clearwater since that study was published in 2013, and the figure is now well over $1 billion. ...In total, the Church's contribution to the beautification and redevelopment of downtown would have exceeded $65 million by the end of 2017.*"

Either way, the church/city relationship has been messy from the very beginning. The Church of Scientology secretly acquired the dilapidated Fort

Harrison Hotel property in 1975, purchasing it under the false names "Southern Land Development and Leasing Corp" and "United Churches of Florida Inc." In 1976, the Church of Scientology's connection with the names on the purchase was reported by the St. Petersburg Times, as was their plan for a $2.8 million restoration and upgrade of the hotel. Reactions ranged across the spectrum, from anger over their surreptitiousness to joy over the salvation of the much-loved building.

I wish Clearwater all the best, as I love the city, and the Tampa Bay area in general. This downtown revitalization has been a long time coming.

FRAGMENTED RENEWAL

> *"The U.S Congress, mired in partisan discord, has ceased to perform even basic functions of governance, let alone address major national challenges around immigration, climate change, competitiveness and growing inequality."* –
> Bruce Katz & Jennifer Bradley, Brookings (2014)

Just in the past few years, efforts to actually measure and map revitalization have stepped up considerably. One of the striking initial insights to come out of this research is the high level of what might be called "fragmented renewal".

We live in a fractal universe of macrocosms and microcosms. Cities are microcosms of states/provinces, which are microcosms of nations, which are microcosms of the world. Just as the world comprises nations on their way up and others on their way, so too do nations comprise states that are revitalizing, and others that are devitalizing. States, in turn, comprise cities whose futures are bright, and others with trouble on the horizon.

Likewise, cities comprise neighborhoods that are getting better, while others are simultaneously getting worse. Many cities that have received a lot of good publicity about their successful revitalization are being revealed as having only isolated pockets of renewal, such as the downtown or a few neighborhoods. It's not just that other parts of the city haven't yet been revitalized, but that they have been devitalizing while the others are revitalizing.

Researchers mostly seem content to have documented the phenomenon: they usually make little—if any—attempt to explain why it happens. None of this was new to me. Not because I'm any smarter than any of those researchers (I'm sure the opposite is usually the case), but because I've been exposed to literally thousands of revitalization success and failure stories—and real-world experiences—over the past two decades, as described earlier.

Given the focus of my work on identifying the missing elements in the failures, and the component elements of the successes during this time, you won't be surprised when I say that the cause of both of those situations is the same: lack of a community-wide strategic renewal process.

If a forensic analysis were done on those cities, going back 20 years or so, I suspect that you'd find grand pronouncements about how the city was going to be reborn, starting with X area. And in all of those situations, I suspect that revitalizing "X" was the only part of the city that had a vision, or policy change (like TIF), or funding (like CDBG or TIGER) or a significant P3. No city-wide strategy or process was in place, so—even when the effort was successful—the revitalization stopped at the borders of the project.

In other words, that fragmented revitalization was planned. Maybe it wasn't intended. Maybe they really hoped it would magically spread beyond the target area. But professionally planned it was.

CHAPTER 4 - EQUITY & INCLUSION: REVITALIZING OUR INSTITUTIONS TO CREATE RESILIENT PROSPERITY FOR ALL.

"Let the Anthropocene not end as it started, as a time of immense misery for nature and society. Rather let it be a time when we as a species morally mature, and embrace an ethical vision of restorative justice for people, animals and nature." – William S. Lynn, Rewilding Week.

Economic revitalization that reduces the inventory of affordable housing doesn't result in resilient prosperity. It produces a nice blip of improvement in the economy and quality of life, to be sure. But it undermines those results by driving away the blue-collar and service workers—and young workers just entering the workforce, white-collar and blue-collar alike—on which that economy depends.

So, efforts to preserve and increase affordable housing have a solid economic justification: they don't need to rely on moral appeals for equity and inclusion. That's a good thing, given that national governance is increasingly by billionaires, for billionaires.

One mayor who seems to understand that dynamic better than any other in the U.S. is Jenny A. Durkan of Seattle, Washington. As of this writing, REVITALIZATION: *The Journal of Economic & Environmental Resilience* has already documented a number of her affordable housing initiatives, despite her only having been in office since 2017. On December 9, 2019, she accelerated those efforts when she announced that the city will invest $110 million to create 1944 new affordable homes in neighborhoods across Seattle, the largest investment—and the largest number of affordable homes ever created—in Seattle in one year in the city's history.

Since she entered office, the City has directly invested $250 million and—together with its partners—nearly $1.5 billion in public and private resources to create and preserve affordable homes. That includes repurposing, renewing and reconnecting an old military base as an affordable new community and public park (with waterfront views!). Unfortunately, Durkan is a rarity.

As noted in the Preface, I've been a professional speaker on community revitalization and natural resource restoration full-time since 2002. The usually-enthusiastic ovations after my talks and workshops fooled me into thinking I was changing the world. The critical distinction I failed to make was that it was individuals who were applauding, not institutions. The people who applauded my message usually found themselves stymied to apply it in their institutions, no matter how high in the hierarchy they were.

Some of the problem was terminology, as we've already discussed. Individuals are normally happy to adopt new terms when they encounter better ones. Institutions often can't. For instance, a non-profit or NGO that has spent 30 years branding itself as a "conservation" or "sustainability" organization has a huge vested interest in those words. Abandoning "sustainable development" for "equitable, inclusive redevelopment" or "restorative development" is a non-starter in the executive suite. Likewise, abandoning "nature conservation" for "nature restoration" is unthinkable: it would be throwing away decades of effort defining the group and communicating its mission. Worse—again as mentioned earlier—it often shuts off the funding spigot, since government and foundation grants are often based on those same labels.

Strangely, this dynamic holds true even after an organization has reached the point where they are actually doing more regenerating than sustaining...more restoration than conservation. As a result, relatively few purely regenerative organizations (such as the Society for Ecological Restoration) have managed to emerge. The "big boys" try constantly to subsume restoration by expanding their catalog of disciplines. What usually happens is that their mission statement gets amended from "protecting nature" to "protecting and enhancing nature", or some such edit. That works fine, provided they have an adaptive renewal process for their organization, to ensure the change goes deeper than their slogan.

It's not just terminology, though. Most institutions are either locked into a very narrow silos of focus, or their existence is based on their controlling a certain part of a process. Calls to integrate the management of our natural and built environments—or to address equity and inclusive in our socioeconomic environments—are thus highly threatening to the status quo if one's organization is defined as being focused only on nature, or only on structures.

Disruptive events—such as catastrophes—often provide excellent opportunities to dissolve such silos, as urgency of action takes precedence over form. Managers are allowed to bypass normal procedures, making disasters an excellent time to set new precedents. A good disaster is a terrible thing to waste.

Revitalization efforts don't always come from gradual economic deterioration: they often derive from post-disaster reconstruction, restoring peace after war, or simply a desire to make a place safer, cleaner, and more beautiful.

As a result, regeneration and resilience efforts often arise together. Resilient prosperity efforts thus encompass a broad spectrum of coordinated activities, falling into three general categories:
- Attracting new and better opportunities;
- Preventing or reducing new damage or loss; and
- Repairing existing damage and renewing existing assets.

Whether a city or nation is moving ahead can be determined by what—and who—it is leaving behind. If it leaves contaminated land and vacant properties in its wake, it's on the way down. If it leaves immigrants or lower-income families sick, homeless or hopeless in its wake, it's on the way down. If it leaves repurposed, renewed and reconnected assets—along with increased confidence in a better future for all—in its wake, it's on the way up.

While individuals can instigate the necessary changes, it's institutions that have to deliver them. So, how do we expand from regenerative, inclusive, equitable individuals to regenerative, inclusive, equitable public and private institutions? The private side is usually easier, because they follow the opportunities. If the public side makes such activities easier and more profitable, private investment will follow. If the public side specifies that those regenerative activities must be designed and delivered in an inclusive, equitable manner, the private side becomes a true believer in such agendas.

We shouldn't underestimate the degree to which our dominant institutions and professional practices are based in processes designed specifically to create social injustice. Take the planning profession—as you've seen, one of my favorite punching bags (along with economic developers and civil engineers)—for example.

Granted, there are many wonderful, ethical, conscientious folks working as planners today, but here's an insight into the modern birth of the discipline from Stuart Meck, professor of urban planning at Rutgers University, from "A Brief History of the Birth of Urban Planning" by Amanda Erickson in the August 24, 2012 issue of The Atlantic Cities: "*City planning, along with zoning, was a vehicle to control where African-Americans, the poor, and immigrants lived, and to keep them out of the areas where middle and upper class people resided. It is no coincidence that the initial efforts to adopt land use controls in the U.S. were aimed at enacting racial zoning—zoning that segregated cities by race. The first city to adopt racial zoning was Baltimore in 1910, and racial zoning spread to other eastern and southern cities (e.g., Atlanta, Louisville), even though the U.S. Supreme Court declared it unconstitutional in 1917, in a case titled Buchanan v. Warley."*

Communities will be better-equipped to tackle redevelopment and economic growth issues when they tackle social issues. And they will be better able to tackle social issues when they have an inclusive, efficient, equitable process for renewing their built and natural environments. In other words, if the process for renewing a place is itself inclusive and equitable, the end product tends to be so.

Currently, the focus of social and economic justice efforts tends to be on policies and projects, for the simple reason that most places don't have an actual program or process to improve. This presents a wonderful opportunity, since communities now have the opportunity to create their resilient prosperity process from scratch—without resistance from an existing such institution—so it can be equitable and inclusive from Day One.

If other public and private institutions want to be players in that process—which they would have to be in order to remain relevant and viable participants in the community's revitalized future—they usually need political and/or financial motivation. So, those individuals wishing to instigate change should focus on getting the place to adopt a process for creating resilient prosperity, which is a non-partisan, economic growth-oriented goal. All else flows from that vision, and from its associated map of renewable assets.

It's important for that process to be focused on resilience—and not just the more easily-sold revitalization—in order to address the needs of future generations while we're addressing current problems. Equity and inclusion is not just about adults: we need to include—and be fair to—our children and the not-yet-born.

For instance, are we building in a way that will allow our children to have their own restoration economy? Is your community or nation producing restored (or at least restorable) assets? Here in the U.S., my generation inherited a wealth of gorgeous buildings from the 19th Century and first half of the 20th Century. Given the disposable trash that passes for much of today's construction, our children will be taking most of our legacy to the landfills. But we're doing a great job of providing opportunities to restore our devastated natural resources. We shouldn't be proud of that.

The good news? We're discovering that almost everything can be adaptively repurposed, often with the help of new technologies. We're increasingly deconstructing—rather than demolishing—buildings, and Apply now has a robot that disassembles old iPhones to reuse the materials for new phones.

For instance, big-box stores, fast-food joints, and even banks have been covering the world with disposable buildings of no substance or architectural value for decades. Now, we're seeing many innovative communities and architects ignoring the ugliness and flimsiness of the structure and are focusing on the value of the sites. For obvious reasons, these throwaway buildings are usually in high-traffic locations. Former burger and pizza joints are becoming "doc-in-a-box" clinics, schools and city service. Even huge, abandoned big-box stores—which folks previously thought were only good for retail—are now being transformed into indoor skate board parks, BMX tracks, drone racecourses, and other such public venues.

They won't be here in 100 years, but at least adaptive reuse is wringing all the value out of them while they're standing. Just 20 years ago, such structures were automatically demolished, even if no new use of the property had been identified. Repurposing and renewing is finally getting institutionalized. Of course, there's nothing revolutionary about a new business moving into a space left vacant by a failed or relocated business: the revolution is in the scale and level of innovation. And in the level of green retrofitting, which is aided greatly here in the U.S. by the PACE program.

Even the "Brutalist" eyesores excreted during the architectural nightmare of the 60's and 70's are being repurposed, often being made significantly less ugly in the process. In North Atlanta, Georgia, a sterile former IBM office building—built in 1977 and abandoned in 2010—was repurposed into a high school. The addition of copious new glass improved its aesthetics, making it look less like a Soviet prison. And the community got a new school in a great location, while simultaneously ridding the area of a blighted property which had been driving down real estate values.

That project is representative of a national trend that's helping to revitalize neighborhoods in a way that benefits all: the conversion of empty office buildings into schools.

Commercial buildings are often built "on spec" (as speculative investments), and real estate investors are like most other investors: sheep-like. They all dive into the same opportunity at the same time, and a glut of office space emerges.

Intelligent places, like Fairfax County, Virginia, are turning that problem into an opportunity by repurposing these financially-distressed structures to meet the growing demand for safer, more-easily-secured elementary schools.

The other trend is the increased focus of big-box retail chains on smaller stores in urban centers, which often involves repurposing existing structures. When done intelligently, this strategy has been paying off nicely.

Target, for instance, now has over 100 such locations. They typically bring in almost $900 per square foot, about triple what the company generates from their suburban and rural locations. Like most good strategies, this approach has additional long-term benefits for Target: 1) it provides them with well-located distribution hubs for the fast-growing online portion of their business; and 2) these locations seldom suffer competition from their nemesis, Walmart.

THE STRATEGIC IMPORTANCE OF EQUITY AND INCLUSION

> *"Social advance depends as much upon the process through which it is secured as upon the result itself."* – Jane Addams

The words "equitable" and "inclusive" have appeared numerous times in this book. That's not just because pursuing them is the right thing to do: it's also because improving those factors improves our ability to achieve resilient prosperity for the entire community or region.

Why? Let's look at some U.S. statistics. 1% of Americans (the aristocracy) have 42% of the wealth. The lower 80% of Americans (the serfs) have 4.8% of the wealth. If a personal emergency arose tomorrow, and $500 in cash were needed to address it, half of all Americans couldn't come up with it

Since 1978, college tuition has increased by 1,120%. CEO pay has increased 937%. Healthcare costs have increased 601%. Housing costs have increased 380%. Food costs have increased 244%. Worker pay has increased 10%. The federal minimum wage has decreased 5.5%. Those numbers speak volumes about the root cause of our widening social and racial divides, and the rise of mental and emotional problems at all levels of our society.

Why aren't our elected leaders ensuring equity? As wealth is ever-more concentrated into the hands of billionaires, democracy becomes more of a sham. It costs $50 million to become a U.S. senator. As a result, virtually 100% of their time and attention is on raising money for the next election, and on rewarding those who funded the last election. Any time focused on the public good (documented to be less than 1%) is mostly for the sake of appearances.

In our money-driven political system, we need to stop thinking of lobbying as something politicians do after they leave office. Members of Congress are lobbyists from the first day they enter office. Government has long been the most common target of militants, because all governments eventually devolve to protect the wealthy from change...if they weren't set up to do that from the beginning (which most were). So, any meaningful solution to economic equity is far more likely to emerge at the local level than from "on high".

Unfortunately, local conversations focused on "equitable" and "inclusive" are noble and essential, but even they are often unproductive. The best such initiatives usually just fix the problem on a tiny scale: usually a neighborhood or even just a particular redevelopment project. They seldom result in the policy changes necessary to prevent non-inclusive, inequitable redevelopment from happening again, elsewhere in their community.

Safety and security don't just come from good infrastructure and resilient design. For a very large portion of Americans—immigrants, those "of color", those with non-standard, non-binary sexual identities, etc.—the primary threats derive from their fellow local residents, and even from their police.

Safety is a key factor in revitalizing any place, and city leaders need to face up to the fact that some people are far less safe than others. Here in the U.S., we are experiencing a long-overdue recognition of the disparity between how law enforcement agencies deal with blacks versus whites.

The next step will be to do the same with Latinos/Latinx, who also experience police abuse, but who have the added worry of being deported if they call the cops, which happens even to those in the country legally. Being a less-confrontational culture, they also largely lack the kinds of louder, in-your-face civil rights organizations enjoyed by African Americans, such as Black Lives Matter.

A major step forward for Latinx justice would be for Americans to better understand their relationship with their North American neighbor to the south: Mexico. Most of what Americans think they know about Mexico is wrong, based on our fairy-tale history books, racist Hollywood stereotypes, and disinformation from the (formerly low-profile) white supremacists who permeate our government.

The fact-free description of the 1960 John Wayne movie, *The Alamo*, on IMDB.com is *"In 1836, a small band of soldiers sacrifice their lives in hopeless combat against a massive army in order to prevent a tyrant from smashing the new Republic of Texas."*

Few Americans know, for instance, the real reason the white farmers and ranchers in the area now called Texas called for independence from Mexico: they were operating farms and ranches using slaves, and Mexico outlawed slavery (half a century before we did). So, those brave defenders of the Alamo were actually land thieves defending slavery.

This led to the "Mexican-American War," which slaughtered thousands of Mexican men, women, and children, and which led to our theft of the lands now called Texas, New Mexico, Arizona, and California. It's hard for most Americans to form a healthy relationship with Mexican immigrants when their heads are full of propaganda and fairy tales, rather than facts. We've proven we have the courage to pull triggers; do we have the courage to apologize?

Our neighbors to the north were luckier. England and France came to the rescue of Canada during the frequent attempts by the U.S. to steal their land. This is why the national capital was relocated from Toronto to Ottawa: Toronto was too close to the U.S. border. The largest of our invasions—the War of 1812—was effectively lost by the U.S., but you won't find that defeat in our public school history books.

Drive into Canada over the Niagara River on the Queenston-Lewiston Bridge, and you're greeted by a 185-foot-tall statue of Major General Sir Isaac Brock. He was the Canadian commander who defeated the Americans when we tried to steal Niagara Falls, and much of southern Ontario. Brock died in the battle, and his bones lie at the base of the monument. That was just one of our many invasions during that war, every one of which ended in defeat for the U.S. forces. To help restore a cordial relationship, the Canadians eventually gave us Maine so we could save face.

Americans also have very selective memories regarding African American history, with most thinking that racial segregation only happened in the South. As long as northern Americans in "blue states" think racism only infects southerners and "red states," little progress will be made.

In an article titled "What it's like to being a cop now" in the August 24, 2015 *TIME* magazine, Philadelphia Police commissioner Charles Ramsey said, *"If you were in the South, you might have been tracking down slaves. Who enforced Jim Crow laws? Police. So just as our democracy has evolved, so have we. But what about those people who were on the other side of that? That baggage is still there. It ain't gone away. So why is there more tension in one community vs. another community? A lot of it has to do with the history of policing. Now I'm not saying you spend your life looking in the rearview mirror, but I am saying you can't move forward until you understand where you've been."*

REVITALIZING OUR INSTITUTIONS TO REVITALIZE OUR WORLD

> *"The goal is not always meant to be reached, but to serve as a mark for our aim."*
> – Joseph Joubert.

We've talked a lot about renewing communities and regions, but what about renewing institutions? More specifically, how does one go about revitalizing an organization whose purpose is to revitalize your community? In my experience, the majority of regenerative agencies and non-profits could themselves use some regeneration.

The 3Re Strategy (repurpose, renew, reconnect)—which you'll learn more about later—is ideal for revitalizing a community or region. But it's also ideal for regenerating an institution, or even a whole class of similar organizations. The example we'll use here is land banks.

While land banks were invented in the USA and are primarily found here, the lessons should be applicable to organizational leaders anywhere on the planet. They are a powerful, fairly recently-created tool to help revitalize cities suffering from depopulation, often combined with deindustrialization. In other words, shrinking communities with large inventories of vacant, tax-foreclosed properties.

That's the theory, anyway. In actuality, far too many of them have devolved from a strategic revitalization entity to a tactical blight removal entity, with little ability to facilitate the revitalization that's supposed to follow demolition.

I said "devolved" because the enabling legislation that created the very firsts land banks originally envisioned that they would house local revitalization programs, not just blight removal mechanisms. In 2002, U.S. Congressman (D) from Michigan Dan Kildee sponsored the LAND BANK FAST TRACK ACT 258 of 2003.

The key text reads, *"The legislature finds that there exists in this state a continuing need to strengthen and revitalize the economy of this state and local units of government in this state and that it is in the best interests of this state and local units of government in this state to assemble or dispose of public property, including tax reverted property, in a coordinated manner to foster the development of that property and to promote economic growth in this state and local units of government in this state. It is declared to be a valid public purpose for a land bank fast track authority created under this act to acquire, assemble, dispose of, and quiet title to property under this act."*

That makes it pretty clear that the Michigan legislators were focused on the ends, not just the means. But few organizational leaders are visionary or strategic: most are actually just managers.

Applying the 3Re Strategy, land banks could be revitalized by:
- repurposing them from blight removal to revitalization;
- renewing them via the additional funding this higher-and/better mission should attract; and
- reconnecting them to the assets they are meant to renew via partnerships with other organizations whose mission contributes to revitalization, but who don't have sufficient access to properties.

As you know by now, the foundation of any revitalization program is the vision, and the strategy to achieve that vision. This is just as applicable to organizations as it is to communities. The vast majority of land banks I've encountered have neither vision nor strategy. They just do real estate transactions; taking in vacant properties on one end and disposing of them (via sale, donation or demolition) on the other end. (What they do often have is a map of renewable assets, though it's usually limited to their inventory of vacant houses.)

In other words, rather than working consciously to achieve neighborhood revitalization, they merely remove what they perceive to be the problem, and hope that revitalization magically appears as a result. But hope is a beggar, not a creator.

About 70 percent of the approximately 160 land banks that currently exist in the United States were created pursuant to comprehensive state-enabling statutes that authorize local governments throughout a state to create land banks.

According to the Center for Community Progress (CCP), the following eleven states have passed comprehensive state-enabling land bank legislation as of August 2015: Michigan (2004), Ohio (2009), New York (2011), Georgia (2012), Tennessee (2012), Missouri (2012), Pennsylvania (2012), Nebraska (2013), Alabama (2013), West Virginia (2014), Delaware (2015).

Founded in 2010, the Center for Community Progress is the only national nonprofit specifically dedicated to building a future in which vacant, abandoned, and deteriorated properties no longer exist. They serve as a sort of national association for land banks.

You're probably wondering *"If they've only been around since 2004, why do they need to be reinvented already?"* Excellent question! I'm glad you asked.

As you saw in the enabling legislation, land banks were meant to be community revitalization entities. But people and organizations tend to gravitate away from risk, and towards money. As mentioned earlier, regarding the Cuyahoga County Land Bank, most of the federal and state funding made available to land banks has been strictly for blight removal, which usually involves widespread demolition. People usually do what they're paid to do.

Demolition is relatively quick, simple, and risk-free. The opposite is true of community revitalization. It tends to be slow and complex, with uncertain outcomes (risk). Little wonder then, that so many of these community revitalization entities have devolved into little more than demolition agencies. Or, as Dave Allen, Executive Director of the Kent County Land Bank Authority in Grand Rapids, Michigan told me, they've become *"a repository for everyone's crap."*

Kalamazoo County Land Bank's visionary Executive Director, Kelly Clarke at Prairie Gardens. This site of a former mental asylum got the 3Re Strategy treatment: repurposed as affordable housing, renewed with restored native prairie habitat, and reconnected to the community with new infrastructure.

Back on October 2 and 3, 2017, I delivered a keynote and a workshop at the annual conference of the Michigan Association of Land Banks in Battle Creek, Michigan. That was followed a day later by a workshop for the Kalamazoo County Land Bank.

The Battle Creek keynote focused on the latest trends in community revitalization strategies. The workshop on the following day focused on what I dubbed "Land Bank 2.0: defining the next generation of land banks.

One of the attendees at that conference was the above-quoted David Allen. He understands that the simplest—not necessarily the easiest—way to harness a land bank's physical assets to a vision and strategy is to partner with (or at least collaborate with) other organizations that have a vision and strategy, but lack physical assets.

Here's how he described the benefits of such an approach, in an email to me prior to the conference: *"The Grand Rapids Community Foundation (GRCF) has a major initiative called Challenge Scholars It is a multi-million dollar investment on behalf of the GRCF. However, once launched a very negative unexpected consequence occurred. Property values and rents in the Challenge Scholar neighborhood immediately soared! Soon the very families they made a multi-million investment to help were being priced out of the neighborhood. The GRCF and the KCLBA partnered together to assemble multiple parcels literally adjacent to the Challenge Scholar middle school, Harrison Park. The KCLBA brought in a well established non-profit housing developer and a rather significant LIHTC project is about to break ground on this site. The GRCF PRI was used to purchase the key piece of property in this development. This only happened because the KCLBA was in regular communication with the GRCF."*

Allen takes a similarly-collaborative approach to working with the for-profit sector, as well. Here's how he described his land bank's mission and approach to me: *"KCLBA provides tools to local units of government—as well as nonprofit and for-profit developers—to revitalize and stabilize communities throughout Kent County. By*

purchasing and facilitating acquisition and rehabilitation of bank-owned and tax-foreclosed properties, the KCLBA helps:
Kent County's local units of government:
- *stabilize neighborhoods;*
- *eliminate blight;*
- *increase property values;*
- *create economic development opportunities; and*
- *preserve neighborhood character.*

Nonprofit developers:
- *revitalize properties by giving them...*
- *access to tax- and bank-foreclosed properties in their development areas.*

For-profit developers:
- *quickly clear title on properties;*
- *obtain brownfield designation on contaminated properties;*
- *fully inspect and make an educated decision on purchasing tax-foreclosed properties; and*
- *provide access to purchase bank foreclosed properties".*

That all sounds good, but it all went bad. The Kent County Land Bank is no more: one of the few land banks to be publicly executed. In the previous chapter, I cautioned that revitalization can be messy. This is a good example.

The Kent County Land Bank had a deal with the city of Grand Rapids that enabled it to purchase tax-foreclosed properties before they went to public auction. The trouble arose because the land bank reportedly avoided buying blighted properties, and bought marketable properties instead. It was accused of behaving like a private real estate investment firm and failing to address blight in Grand Rapids, so it was decommissioned.

In the land bank's defense, the county claimed that the land bank was acting strategically: they bought non-blighted properties in key locations to help ensure that they didn't fall into the hands of speculators who would sit on them, or of flippers who would sell them without making improvements or even bringing them up to code. They wanted the properties to go to people and companies who would reuse them in a way that actually revitalized the neighborhood.

So, who was right: the city or the county? Both arguments make sense. I tell this story to emphasize that revitalization is messy, and that the only thing that can substantially protect you from that messiness is a transparent, strategic process.

As you can see, not all land banks see themselves only as blight removal agencies. One of my clients, the Kalamazoo (Michigan) County Land Bank, for instance, is on the leading edge of community revitalization. They've adopted the 3Re Strategy not just as a tool, but as their official slogan.

As the Kalamazoo County Land Bank's projects reveal, the process of becoming more beneficial to their community isn't just about repurposing, renewing and reconnecting. They also looked at scale, and realized that focusing on individual residential properties was far too limiting: as the Prairie Gardens example (above) shows, they are creating entire new neighborhoods out of blight.

And it's not just about increasing the physical scope: extending the chronological scope is key, too. They aren't just taking in houses and disposing of them as quickly as possible: Prairie Gardens also shows that they are into their properties for the long haul.

Kalamazoo County Land Bank's office is on a revitalized old commercial property. Its landscape is primarily a bioswale full of native plants. Using the 3Re Strategy, the property was repurposed and renewed, and was reconnected to the community via a river trail.

For a land bank that truly understands how to revitalize a place, holding on to properties while they revitalize the entire neighborhood offers a major new revenue stream. Everyone wants to invest in a neighborhood that's coming back to life, which means the land bank would enjoy actual appreciation of assets that most people see as liabilities.

Changes are also afoot at some of the nation's largest land banks. Here are two paragraphs from a recent *Next City* article about the Philadelphia Land Bank:

"*The land bank has a five-year goal of reactivating roughly 2,000 properties. So far, according to the city, the number of properties sold through the program is 196, and most were vacant lots. Any streamlining Rodriguez does will have to cover mastering the agency's elaborate acquisition policies. As outlined in the strategic plan, released in February, the criteria for whether or not the land bank can transfer certain parcels depends on the intended re-use. The re-use category also determines the approval process and which city offices and organizations have to weigh in.*"

"'*The ability to be strategic is key*', *says Frank Alexander, co-founder of Center for Community Progress, a national nonprofit that focuses on vacant properties. While Philly's five-year targets forecast that the land bank will add 7,727 publicly owned parcels to its holdings, it will also acquire another 1,650 tax-delinquent properties. The agency also has outlined a mix of types of properties for its disposition process. Sixty-five percent of land returned for active use will be for housing, and in an effort to ensure affordability, only 25 percent of that won't be restricted by income brackets.*"

The next generation of land banks should be more efficient at dealing with brownfields. This would likely require their becoming more involved in TIF (tax increment financing). Some day, I hope to see an app invented that allows entities like land banks to more-quickly and easily create a "mini-TIF", which would provide the financial resources to do renewal on a grander scale, including brownfields cleanup, affordable housing and infrastructure renewal.

LAND BANKS + COMMUNITY LAND TRUSTS: AN INCLUSIVE, EQUITABLE, REVITALIZING MARRIAGE?

Maybe the best strategic partnership for a huge land bank like Philadelphia's would be with Community Land Trusts (CLT), which have the mission of providing permanently affordable housing, usually in neighborhoods and communities that are revitalizing. There are 225 CLTs in the U.S., and they've experienced significant growth in the past few years, due both to the expansion of community revitalization efforts, and to the resulting crisis in affordable housing.

They are natural complements to each other: land trusts have a property disposition problem, while CLTs have a property acquisition problem. Land banks are strong on tactics (cleaning encumbrances from vacant properties), while CLTs are strong on strategy (usually focused on affordable housing / displacement solutions).

Maybe states should rewrite their land banking legislation to enable the creation of either a hybrid organization—land bank + CLT—or to at least allow more effective partnerships between them. This would combine proven tactics with proven strategies, and would help address the full lifecycle of vacant property reuse.

Land banks and community land trusts (CLTs) are often perceived as "off mission" or antithetical...not suited for the same environments. Conversely, they also sometimes conflated as effectively one and the same. Neither perception reflects reality.

Land banks are public entities, usually public nonprofit or governmental entities, which specialize in the conversion of vacant, abandoned and foreclosed properties into productive use. On the other hand, CLTs are traditionally private nonprofits that hold land in trust to provide affordable housing and other community assets in perpetuity.

The Center for Community Progress and the Grounded Solutions Network (the national group that promotes and supports CLTs) have done some pioneering work in setting the record straight, and in exploring how land banks and community land trusts might coordinate to optimize equitable development outcomes. Theoretically, a land bank-CLT "property pipeline" can achieve both lasting stabilization and affordability, despite fluctuations in the market. John E. Davis argues that CLTs and land banks are each the potential solution to the other's problem. Together, they could complete the "pipeline".

Most land banks consider their work to be done once properties have cycled through the land bank "laundromat". What happens after their return to private ownership is typically outside the land bank's purview. Affordability is left to the whim of the marketplace; upkeep is left to the whim of the new owners; occupancy is dependent upon the owners' ability to meet monthly mortgage payments.

Community land trusts, on the other hand, do a good job of sheltering lands, homes, gardens, stores, and facilities brought beneath their protective umbrella, but they do a poor job of building that portfolio in the first place. Without access to monies and powers made available to land banks, most CLTs have remained small. Few have managed to acquire enough lands and buildings to transform the neighborhoods they serve. They have not gone to scale.

While there are currently few land bank and CLT collaborations across the U.S., the good news is that we see a lot potential for effective partnerships.

So, what's the best way to revitalize an organization that supposed to be revitalizing your community? Again, the same way it should be revitalizing your community: via the 3Re Strategy: 1) find a viable new (or enhanced) purpose for the organization; 2) this will attract the funding and other resources needed to renew it; 3) then reconnect it to the community via effective partnerships.

MOTIVATING, RECOGNIZING & TRACKING REVITALIZATION

The climate crisis threatens Miami's future on 3 fronts: 1) more frequent/more powerful storms; 2) flooding from sea level rise; and 3) saltwater intrusion in the aquifer (also from rising seas).

If, as author Ben Arment says, *"We are motivated by two conflicting fears in life— the fear of failure and the fear of insignificance"*, then getting better at making our world better should solve that conflict.

People in prosperous places don't feel a need to revitalize, which puts them at risk. All around the world, many towns, regions, and nations that used to be healthy, wealthy, and happy are now either basket cases, or are becoming one.

Comfort makes them complacent: they ignore regenerative opportunities, which undermines their future. They are on their way down, and don't feel it or see it. Their broken future is shrouded in a haze of contentment.

The 2015 Global Risk report from the World Economic Forum revealed that environmental risks outnumber economic risks among the list of major threats identified by senior business leaders, with water issues leading the pack.

In the near-two-decades I've spent speaking, advising, and listening at revitalization, restoration, reuse, regeneration, redevelopment, and remediation conferences and meetings all around the world, I've observed that every one of those nations and cities had different challenges, legal frameworks, cultures, dreams, and resources.

Simultaneously, I observed that similar—often identical—factors were contributing to all of their renewal successes...and to their failures. The signs of downtown revitalization, for example, are fairly universal: prolific pedestrians, bicyclists, waterfront access, trails and retail activity are obvious indicators. Water and air quality are a bit harder to perceive, but no less important. All of those factors are measurable.

They are all just snapshots of the present, however: for it to be revitalization requires a baseline to measure against. If a stream that was buried a decade ago is now daylighted, that was a revitalizing project. Likewise with brownfields that are now clean, vacant lots that are now activated, empty buildings that are now full of life.

Other common revitalizing factors include heritage renewal; restored connectivity (e.g. dam or urban highway removal), the arrival of immigrants, and fiber-optic telecommunications. Broadband internet access has quickly gone from nice-to-have to must-have for community revitalization.

Here's what Darrell M. West said in *Brookings Focus* "way back" in 2011 (it's far more true now): "*Broadband is viewed in many places as the key driver of economic development, social connections, and civic engagement. ...Fifty-four percent of the area's (Dundas County, ON) businesses that had access to the fiber-optic network reported job growth, compared with 27 percent of businesses that had dial-up Internet access and 5 percent of those with no Internet access. ...diverse, multilateral stakeholders use broadband technology to work for solutions to a range of health, environmental, and social problems. These enterprises form the backbone of the new knowledge economy and use information and communication technologies to stimulate higher-level economic growth.*"

Activation of dead spaces is crucial, so "growth of users" on vacant properties or unused parks (such as via pushcart food vendors) is an easy metric. Property values and tax revenues are the two most common metrics, of course. But revitalization begets revitalization, creating a positive feedback loop, so that dynamic should itself be measured.

How? The pivot point is often when the free market takes over, and public leaders no longer have to push so hard for revitalization. This can be tracked by comparing public to private investment, which would produce valuable trending data related to the renewal process, not just the "economic snapshots" everyone relies on today.

Maybe the best way to measure revitalization is to kill two birds with one stone: create a regenerative tool that would both trigger renewal and provide hard data to track progress. For instance, in July of 2013, a bill was introduced that would allow the Dublin (Ireland) City Council to introduce a levy on vacant and derelict land in the Inner City of Dublin.

The bill's goal is to *"incentivise and accelerate its [re]development...prevention of dereliction, encouragement of economic development and job creation, tourism, and with the sustainable benefit of encouraging new inner city housing and reduced long distance commuting"*, to quote directly from the bill. It further says *"there is no disincentive to a landowner leaving a site vacant for many years [which is] is not in the best interest of the city, the city economy, and the national economy."* This would provide a wonderful starting point for a regeneration tracking system.

The list of tangible and intangible measures of revitalization is almost endless. They also vary with the place. If your city has many vacant, abandoned, or foreclosed properties, then measuring the rate at which they return to productive use is a vital measure. A place with poor air quality, or too many contaminated properties, could measure the cleanup process as a revitalization/resilience indicator. Any measure of "better" will probably be valid, if only in a narrow sense. But those narrow indicators are often what concern people most, as anyone hacking their lungs out in Beijing can attest.

The measurement challenge is compounded by the fact that revitalization comprises both qualitative and quantitative components. Many standard metrics can be applied: home sales/rentals, business startups/recruitment, business/resident retention, etc. But can we measure what inspires an 8-year-old to speak at a public hearing on saving a historic building? (true story) Do we need to? So many factors CAN be quantified that we can leave unsullied the magical aspects that touch our hearts and souls.

Many cities spend vast sums on "magic bullet" redevelopment projects intended to revitalize a downtown, waterfront, etc. These projects sometimes succeed in temporarily raising real estate values in the redeveloped area, but usually fail to revitalize the community.

Such situations help explain why few places measure their revitalization progress: politicians would rather hide their failures...and failures abound. Revitalization in particular—and planning in general—needs more forensic investigation.

This resistance to transparency also explains the popularity of sustainability initiatives in government and corporations. The lack of rigorous metrics makes sustainability efforts "failure-proof". Virtually any reduction in waste, toxicity, or energy use—or increase in talking about it—qualifies as "sustainable".

Such reductions are good, of course, but slowing down the rate at which we destroy our planet isn't sustainability: it's just less unsustainable. It's an importance difference, because settling for the latter is a recipe for disaster. The planet and climate are too far gone to rely on token progress.

> *"The more we do, the more we can do. Prosperity is a great teacher; adversity a greater." – William Hazlitt.*

Even if we do eventually define and gather rigorous data that tells us when we've hit our revitalization and resilience goals, these successes should be seen only as waypoints—and reasons to rejoice—not as places to stop. In mountain climbing, "false summits" are a frequent cause of despair. In revitalization and resilience, there is no ultimate summit, so we should celebrate each achievement along the way.

Since the state of being revitalized is relative to where one started, don't forget to fully-document (anecdotally, photographically, and statistically) your local "before" condition. Otherwise, your new data will lack the context needed to be fully appreciated (and celebrated).

I once met someone who had just visited a city following its dramatic rebirth. When I asked him what it was like, he said "Seemed kind of dead to me." It wasn't the first time I'd heard such a report about a place that was making great progress. Why the mismatch between perception and reality? No frame of reference. The visitor had no way of knowing how much worse things had been recently.

If you want to attract fixers, employers, and new residents to your place, you need to make your momentum visible. It's not just to impress visitors, though: Many places are revitalizing nicely, and their own residents don't know it. Their government has no system for tracking and reporting revitalizing activities and outcomes.

The leaders might know things are improving, but to the citizens, that progress is often invisible. The qualitative value governments most often fail to measure is confidence in the future (both baseline and periodic surveys). This sounds fluffy and imprecise, but it might be the most crucial of all resilient prosperity metrics.

Being based here in Washington, DC, I'm in frequent contact with the folks who run federal grant programs for community or regional revitalization and resilience. I've asked a number of them if there are any factors that tend to determine the winning grant recipients.

They usually explain that their internal goal is to be able to cite success stories, so recipients are chosen not so much on the basis of need. They are selected based on the likelihood that their use of the funds will produce a feather in the federal agency's cap (which, in turn, strengthens that agency's ability to justify their budget, and ask for increases).

What factors convince these federal agencies that one community is more likely to put the funding to good use than another? In conversations at HUD, EPA, FHA and FTA, three were cited repeatedly:

- A clear strategy for applying the funds, preferably based on resident-derived goals (vision);
- Pre-existing public-public partnerships (neighborhood-city, city-county, suburb-metro, rural-urban, county-state, etc.); and
- A trusted non-profit or public agency capable of creating a program that will persist when the grant is exhausted.

It's no accident that the above list includes four of the six elements of the RECONOMICS Process that you'll learn more about soon. Even the feds know what's important; it's just that all the pieces have never before coalesced into a complete process.

Of those three factors, the first is by far the most important. Why? Because creating a shared vision and effective strategy is the most effective way to achieve the other two factors: creating partnerships and finding the right organization to run the program. Partners and supporters (both residents and political leaders) can be divided into two groups: early and late adopters. The former are involved in the visioning and strategizing work. The latter come to the table as a result of the confidence inspired by your vision and strategy.

RECIVILIZING

"It can be argued that investing in girls education is the ultimate investment in positive change." – Erna Solberg, PM of Norway.

For the society as a whole to be regenerative, its parts (individuals and institutions) must be regenerative. And not just regenerative, but properly connected and empowered to boot. For many human societies, that means ceasing to marginalize the half of their society that can contribute most to that recivilizing process: women.

As you've no doubt heard by now, many "poor" societies have a higher level of happiness than wealthier societies. Global research firm Ipsos' 2012 results from its annual world happiness poll—based on interviews with 18,687 adults in 24 countries—showed Indonesia, Mexico, and Brazil with the world's happiest citizens. At the other end of the happiness spectrum (misery territory) were Russia, South Korea, and Hungary. In general, Latin American countries are happiest, as are people with high levels of both income and education (but not one or the other).

So, what makes happiness? Health. Beauty. Trust. Quality of life. Diversity. A feeling of belonging. Being of service and value to others. Accomplishment. Knowing ourselves. Expressing ourselves. Something to look forward to.

In Victorian England, art critic John Ruskin believed that the key to a satisfying life was the mental challenge of designing something combined with the physical challenge of making it.

So, the modern makers movement that is revitalizing many old industrial neighborhoods might also be a significant contributor to enhancing community happiness.

If civilizing is the process of creating circumstances that tend to make us happy—such as those eleven factors just listed—then recivilizing is the process of restoring those factors when a civilization is no longer producing them.

I believe that societies with a healthier respect for feminine energy in its leadership is better positioned to advance all of those factors.

> *"The single biggest problem in communication is the illusion that it has taken place."*
> *– George Bernard Shaw.*

Lip-service stakeholder engagement generally produces stakeholder enragement. The "inclusive" aspect is especially confusing to many local leaders, maybe men more than women. They often confuse "inclusive" with "engaged."

Stakeholder engagement is a Good Thing, but it doesn't necessarily lead to inclusive economic growth. Nor does the lack of stakeholder engagement necessarily lead to economic injustice. "Inclusive" is a goal. "Engagement" is a practice.

What's not on that list are those things we can have too much of: Money, security, and people (including children). Sure: we need a certain amount of money, security, and fellow humans to be happy.

We might begin this journey by replacing our normal Santa Claus-style prayers for health, wealth, and happiness with the Buddhist prayer "*Bless me into usefulness.*"

Will human civilization devise an effective strategy for restoring our global climate? If not, will we at least devise an effective strategy for thriving on a massively disrupted planet?

In Chapter 6, you'll see how how Chattanooga, Tennessee's dramatic, long-lasting revival started when the people worked together to restore their air quality back in the late 70s. Prior to that, they had the nation's worst air, and were paralyzed by racial and political divisions. Maybe restoring our planet's climate together offers a similar opportunity for human civilization. Maybe it's an opportunity for us to recivilize.

As noted earlier, constant regeneration is at the heart of keeping a complex system whole and healthy. When resistance to renewal arises within a system, it's a disease process, making the system brittle, slow, and vulnerable. So, recivilizing would derive from the constant regeneration of society. Which would, of course, require a replicable process.

> *"Owing to past neglect, in the face of the plainest warnings, we have now entered upon a period of danger... The era of procrastination of half-measures, of soothing and baffling expedients, of delays, is coming to its close. In its place we are entering a period of consequences...*
> *We cannot avoid this period; we are in it now."*
> *– Winston Churchill, warning of the rise of Nazi Germany in November, 1936.*

The above quote could be perfectly applied to today's climate crisis. Just as British Prime Minister Neville Chamberlain did during the build-up of the Nazi war machine prior to World War II, so are American politicians (and the public, thanks to massive disinformation campaigns by fossil fuel companies) wallowing in willful ignorance, fear and denial regarding anthropogenic climate change. Unlike a war, though, the climate crisis won't go away by declaring peace.

FIXING OUR BROKEN FUTURE

> *"Those who have never experienced anything but decline may have difficulty even conceptualizing a different reality."*
> *– Alan Mallach*

I've referred to "fixing" the future rather than "reinventing" or "reimagining" or other soft concepts because "fix" implies "broken". When I say "broken", I don't necessarily mean that the entire city or organization is broken: it might just be a significant aspect or function. This is a normal use of the word.

After all, when we say our car broke down or our computer is broken, we know that it's usually a single component that's the problem, like the car's alternator or the computer's power supply.

Too many of us don't realize just how broken our future is. Many who are comfortable assume they will remain comfortable, but most will be wrong. Many who are presently uncomfortable optimistically assume their future can only get better, but most of them are wrong, too.

Many ocean economies are pulling the last of the high-value, easily-caught fish out of the ocean, but have no strategy for what comes next;

Many farming economies are down to their last inch of near-lifeless topsoil, thanks to chemical and till-intensive farming techniques. Their climate is changing at an unprecedented rate, making traditional crops obsolete, and most have no strategy for what comes next; and

Many extraction industries are in their last decade of plundering public minerals and fossil fuels at virtually no cost (beyond what it takes to buy politicians), and no responsibility for restoring the damage (such as fracking's polluted aquifers). Few have a strategy for what comes next.

For the past century, the model has been for politicians to give private resource extraction firms free access to public resources, and then use public funds to clean up the mess left behind. As smart phones, web-connected sensors, and drones become ubiquitous worldwide, mining and energy firms are finding themselves in an uncomfortably transparent, far more costly world.

As fishing, farming, and industrial economies all cruise blindly into catastrophe, they take our illusions of a safe, comfortable future with them. And that's just at the macro level.

> *"The ancestor of every action is a thought."*
> *– Ralph Waldo Emerson.*

What happens when most people worldwide lose their faith in the future? What happens when real estate investors and entrepreneurs around the globe withdraw from the market? What happens when everyone everywhere stops putting time and money into making the world a better place, because they've lost confidence in the ability of government, the economy, and even nature to sustain us? We lose our resilience. But disease is resilient. Poverty is resilient. So, it isn't resilience itself that we want, but resilient prosperity.

Bringing it back down to the level of institutional revitalization—especially for national and international organizations—the easiest path for most would simply be to add strategic renewal process expertise to the repertoire of their local representatives or organizations.

It wouldn't matter if their focus were historic preservation, nature restoration, water quality, disaster preparation, infrastructure, brownfields, policy work, community management, or whatever: sending a single person around to train all of the organization's members, branch offices or affiliated groups would build on their existing skills. This would enable them to fit that expertise into the process of revitalizing their local area, and/or making it more resilient, thus supercharging their organization...making it more relevant to the pressing needs of each city, region or nation.

PART B - STRATEGY: MASTERING THE MISSING KEY TO SUCCESS, TO FIX YOUR PRESENT AND FUTURE TOGETHER.

Would you stand on a 3-legged stool that had a missing leg? Most communities and non-profit organizations do. They usually have a vision/mission and a plan, but no strategy. In other words, they know what they want to achieve—and they know what activities they want to perform—but they don't know how to succeed. Even worse, most labor under the illusion that they do have a strategy, making the problem harder to fix.

Even otherwise-excellent organizations suffer from this. For instance, go to the website of Colorado's Big Thompson Watershed Coalition (BTWC), and you'll find well-crafted vision and mission statements. BTWC's vision is "*A healthy and resilient Big Thompson Watershed that benefits the fish, wildlife, and people it serves.*" Their mission is "*To protect and restore the ecological health of the Big Thompson Watershed for the use and enjoyment of our community today and for future generations.*" They even include their four values. But no strategy. It's possible that they wish to keep their strategy secret—there are often good reasons to do so—but if they are like most of their peers, they probably don't have one.

When revitalization and resilience efforts encounter budgetary shortfalls, they tend to put most of their attention on raising money. That's usually because they're focused on their projects, which are the most capital-intensive aspect of fulfilling their mission. When they fail to find funding, they often fail as an organization. Instead, they should devise a strategy for success using what they've got, which often has the fringe benefit of being the best way to raise more funding.

Strategy and program are the least capital-intensive portions of any process. They are the elements that magnify the impact of all the other components. And they are the two that are most commonly missing, usually because they are outside the knowledge and comfort zone of the leaders. This makes them insecure, to the point where they dismiss strategy as being less important than whatever they are good at (such as project management). Strategy is a mystery to them.

Strategy is an executive mindset. But most executives rose up from managerial positions, and never received any actual training in strategic thinking. They are so familiar with the word "strategy" that they assume they know what it is. Nine times out of ten, that assumption is wrong. It's the Peter Principle in action, and might be the single most common cause of failure.

If you're a business executive, you've likely heard someone (usually a corporate culture consultant) say "*Culture eats strategy for breakfast*". But the decision to make an organization successful by creating a great culture is a strategy. Other popular versions include "*Execution trumps strategy*", "*Structure trumps strategy*", or whatever organizational characteristic that particular consultant is selling.

They pick on strategy because 1) they don't understand it, so it's a safe whipping boy; and 2) strategy evokes long-term thinking and military training, so using the word makes them feel intelligent and macho. All of those other organizational characteristics are worth focusing on, but success usually depends on strategy. It's not either/or, of course: that would be like saying "air trumps water"...the lack of either will kill us.

> *"If you see the world in black and white, you're missing important grey matter."* – Jack Fyock.

A far more insightful perspective comes from successful tech entrepreneur, Whitney Wolfe Herd. She's the founder and CEO of Bumble, and a co-founder of the dating app Tinder. Herd says "*Mission eats culture for breakfast. You have to have a purpose.*"

Mission and purpose are embodied in a good vision, which should drive any strategic process. Herd likely knows that culture is one those things that paternalistic CEOs focus on when they don't know what else to do. I say "paternalistic" because molding their corporate family's personality is like a parent trying to control their children's character development. The rate of success is similarly dismal.

Again: it's a false dichotomy. The CEO who focuses on strategy and ignores culture—maybe allowing a toxic workplace to evolve—is an idiot. It's like asking a parent "are you going to focus on developing your child's intelligence or their personality?" What sane parent would think they have to sacrifice one for the other?

The October 2017 issue of WIRED magazine contained an article by John Malta titled "Venture Ball: Silicon Valley shoots and scores." Based on a book titled Betaball by Erik Malinowski, it illustrates this strategy vs. culture point perfectly. The article describes how Joe Lacob was ridiculed for paying $450 million for the Golden State Warriors basketball team in 2010. At that point, most considered the Warriors to be the worst team in the NBA, worth no more than $315 million.

Seven years on, the Warriors had won two national championships, and were valued at $2.6 billion. Here's an excerpt from the article describing the team's regeneration: *"...the slingshot turnaround (was not due) to Steph Curry's swishing three-pointers, but to Lacob's application of Silicon Valley strategies to revitalize a sluggish team. First off, Lacob used his newcomer status to build a thriving corporate culture."* Lacob also had a crystal-clear vision driving his strategy: to win a championship within five years. They won their first championship in four years and seven months.

Strategizing is an intensely-creative process that allows—even demands—that one think outside one's industry, professional silo, geographic area, political prejudices, etc. Unlike tactics, strategies aren't limited to dealing with the practicalities of the immediate situation. Strategies are only constrained by the requirement that they make success more likely.

A plan without a strategy is like a car without an engine. Yet fewer than 10% of community and regional plans have an actual strategy, much less a process to bring it all to life. But, before we dive into process, let's fix that strategy problem.

CHAPTER 5 - REVELATION: SEEING STRATEGIES THAT ARE INVISIBLE TO OTHERS.

"The revitalization of Harlem in the 1990s and early 2000s demonstrated that well-designed revitalization efforts, which included programs for small business and job creation, along with low-income housing targeted at local residents, can improve neighborhoods both physically and economically, while keeping the vast majority of residents in place." – Glenn Robert Erikson

So, are there any good examples of strategies actually at work in communities? For over three decades, possibly the world's most successful downtown revitalization program has been run by the National Main Street Center (NMSC), created by the National Trust for Historic Preservation.

From the beginning, they recognized that hundreds of hard-working non-profit groups across America were reinventing the same wheel in efforts to revitalize the centers of their towns and cities via the repurposing and renewal of historic buildings.

What they all needed was a strategy, so NMSC devised a simple, generic strategy that all could apply.

They call it the Four Point Approach: Organizing (e.g. – creating an ongoing program); Promoting (e.g. -recasting the image and perception of downtown from rundown and dangerous to vibrant and safe); Designing (e.g. – making downtowns more beautiful and interesting); and Economic Restructuring (e.g. – linking the renovation and reuse of old buildings to expanding business activity downtown).

The result? The states that have well-organized Main Street Programs have seen significant economic revitalization.

STRATEGIC THINKING ON MAIN STREET

Kentucky has the oldest state-wide program, and Iowa might have the best. The 44 communities in the Kentucky Main Street Program reported $76,126,662 of cumulative investment in their commercial downtown districts in 2015. In 2016, it was estimated that the Texas Main Street Program had generated some $3 billion and 30,000 jobs during the course of its existence.

Nationwide, the Main Street Program has triggered some $65.6 billion of public and private investment in physical improvements to downtowns since 1980. About 556,960 jobs were created and over 260,000 buildings were repurposed and/or renewed in the process. The return on investment averages about 26:1.

The Main Street program also has eight Guiding Principles: 1) Comprehensive; 2) Incremental; 3) Self-help; 4) Partnerships; 5) Identifying/capitalizing on existing assets; 6) Quality; 7) Change; and 8) Implementation. These, too, are excellent.

"Incremental" means a confidence-building process that constantly gains momentum; "Self-help" means equitable, resilient bottom-up efforts, rather than fragile, big-budget top-down efforts driven by the wealthy. "Partnerships" make efforts more politically-and economically resilient. "Existing assets" means working with what you have, rather than waiting for some savior or silver-bullet project. These eight principles comprise the basis of their tactics.

And they're not resting on their laurels, having recently updated their Four Point Approach. There's still room for improvement, of course. I find the relationship of the four points and the eight principles to be a bit of a jumble: any future re-do should focus on process, in order to add some flow and logic to its structure.

You might have noticed a crucial missing element: reconnecting. They are repurposing and renewing existing assets, but there's not one mention of the word "connect" on NMSC's pages explaining the Four Point Approach or the Guiding Principles. Reconnecting downtowns to suburbs (such as via corridor revitalization), and to surrounding agricultural regions (thus creating local food systems) can supercharge a downtown. For instance, in Britain, it's well-documented that real estate prices near farmers' markets are 26% higher on average. A similar dynamic can probably be found in most cities worldwide.

Is the Main Street program an ideal revitalization strategy? Not by a long shot. Why? Because, by design, its primary goal is preserving our built heritage. Wedding that goal to the broader goal of downtown revitalization is the brilliant strategy. But communities are much more than just old buildings: they are natural resources, infrastructure, business, cultures, suburbs, farms, disaster zones, industries, and so forth.

The "Comprehensive" guiding principle should address this, but seldom does, due to the vision and goals being primarily focused on downtown and historic preservation.

Should the Main Street program thus be expanded to include all those things? Probably not. It would likely lose its key supporters, and would likely lack the expertise, resources, and political ability to successful address that far-more-complex goal. Nonetheless, it does serve as a great example of how much more successful a community can be when a strategic and programmatic approach supplants a stop-start, project-by-project, tactical approach.

The real magic—and the lesson to be learned here—is that Main Street has been wildly successful not because they have a perfect strategy, but because they HAVE a strategy, AND an ongoing program to support its execution. That's incredibly rare.

So, what would an ideal strategic approach to revitalizing an entire community or region look like? First off, it would embrace all of the aforementioned basic modes of action: top-down (driven by government and/or large developers); bottom-up (driven by residents); and middle-out (efforts that start life as partnerships, drawing support from all directions).

As will be explained later, partnerships can and are used by both top-down and bottom-up initiatives. What makes middle-out initiatives unique is that they are partnerships from the beginning: partnering isn't just a means to an end that's employed at some point to boost buy-in or funding.

Some generic principles can inform the process of renewing any place, anywhere, at any time. Visions and goals vary from place to place, but most are related to improving quality of life, health, wealth, happiness, heritage, safety and/or justice (economic, social, and/or environmental). The strategies also vary, but the best ones will be based on repurposing, renewing, and reconnection existing natural, built, and socioeconomic assets.

STRATEGIC THINKING IN SOUTH AFRICA

Many metropolises around the world are belatedly realizing that excessive automobile traffic can kill their downtown. As a result, they are closing key streets to automobile traffic while boosting public transit. But many older people love their cars, and can't imagine living without them.

So, a good strategy would address that lack of imagination. To boost public support for pedestrianization and public transit, communities are declaring car-free days or weekends. The hope is that, when residents see how much quieter, cleaner, and safer their neighborhoods are without car traffic, they support more enlightened policies.

You might have read about the EcoMobility Festivals sponsored by ICLEI. One took place in October of 2015 in Sandton, a traffic-congested district of Johannesburg, South Africa. The festival lasted an entire month, which cost millions of dollars. Why so long? Strategic thinking. The vision ICLEI wanted to achieve was lasting change for the better.

If a street is closed for a day, people might visit it out of curiosity, but they'll probably drive there. If an area is closed to traffic for a week, people needing to get there—such as for a dental appointment—might reschedule the visit to avoid being inconvenienced in their car.

But if an entire district is closed to cars for an entire month, people will have to find another way in. They might take a bus for the first time. Or they might become aware of the paucity of local options, and demand more buses, trolleys, or subways. That can lead to lasting change.

> *"If you plan cities for cars and traffic, you get cars and traffic. If you plan for people and places, you get people and places."*
> *– Fred Kent, Founder, Project For Public Spaces.*

The key was to devise a strategy ("close an entire district to cars for a month") that would help ensure that the tactic ("reducing car traffic") actually accomplishes the vision (revitalizing the city center). Most places just set a goal, and rush right into writing a plan. That plan might be expertly detailed as to the best tactics for closing a place to cars for a day or weekend. But it will fail, because nobody took the time to create a strategy to ensure that the tactics achieved the vision.

STRATEGIC THINKING IN SPECIAL FORCES

The time factor mentioned above is often another differentiator between a tactic and a strategy. Too few communities and organization remember that time is a resource. If one is not in a hurry, time can substitute for resources that are in short supply, such as money.

When I was with the U.S. Army's 7th Special Forces Group (AKA "Green Berets"), we were taught how to deal with vastly superior forces. Since Green Berets operate in 12-person teams behind enemy lines, the best tactic was usually to run away: "shock and awe" was seldom an option. Going undetected is a key element of an A-team's strategy, both for survival, and because it enables the element of surprise.

But if a mission requires engaging a large force—say a 500-person battalion— a good strategy might employ multiple tactics over time. Sniping a few of them daily, so they are afraid to be in the open. Killing a few in their tents every night, so they are afraid to sleep. Contaminating their food or water, so they are afraid to eat or drink. Setting booby traps, so they are afraid to move. Living in constant fear is exhausting, and exhausted soldiers make mistakes, or give up entirely.

Let's take a moment to use the above example to ensure that you're really clear about vision, strategy and tactics. For an A-Team taking on a battalion, the vision (goal) might be to render them ineffective as a fighting force. Various strategies could achieve this, two of them being: 1) kill all their officers and senior NCOs; or 2) demoralize and exhaust them. If strategy #2 is chosen, the tactics ("projects" in the civilian world) would be the above-mentioned sniping, sleep kills, poisoning and booby traps.

In warfare—or any competitive situation—strategies are often more effective if kept ulterior, for obvious reasons. Strategies and tactics sometimes look very similar, and are differentiated both by timescale and intention. For instance, an arsenal of Intercontinental Ballistic Missiles (ICBM) is designed to prevent wars, or if that fails, win wars. Thus, each of those missiles is a "strategic nuke". A nuclear warhead fired from an artillery piece over a distance of 50 miles—or one carried in a backpack—is designed to win a battle, so those are called "tactical nukes".

But it can get more complicated than that. It might be believed that the threat of using a tactical nuke on the enemy might scare them into ending the war. In that case, the tactical nuke was used strategically: the goal was primarily to end the war, not just to wipe out a particular battalion. Wiping out a one or two cities would normally be considered tactics within a larger war. But the bombing of Hiroshima and Nagasaki were (officially) about scaring the Japanese into surrendering and (unofficially) about dissuading the Russians from expanding their control of the region. Neither city was a military target. Thus, those two bombs were strategic.

Tactics and strategies are often nested. The Pentagon might have a strategy for winning a war that includes occupying a particular city (tactic). But the general charged with taking that city needs a strategy, and that will involve many individual tactics for taking key buildings and infrastructure. So the general creates a strategy to achieve the Pentagon's tactic. A squad leader assigned by the general to take a particular building will need to devise a strategy for doing so, which will involve tactics executed by members of the squad. The general's tactic thus requires a strategy to execute.

Sometimes, a mode of action can be either tactical or strategic, depending on scope, and depending on complexity. Transit-oriented development is often just a tactic for boosting the value of a project. But applied at the scope of an entire city, metro area, or region, it becomes strategic.

You've probably heard of "tactical urbanism," such as pop-up parks in streets that show local residents how much nicer life would be with fewer cars. One of the people who helped coin that term, Mike Lydon, defines it as "an approach to neighborhood building and activation using short-term, low-cost and scalable interventions and policies."

My favorite example of long-term revitalization deriving from tactical urbanism is the Incredible Edible Todmorden project in Todmorden, Yorkshire, England, whereby residents planted vegetables and flowers in every barren city-owned piece of land they could find without official permission.

The resulting improvement in quality of life was so dramatic that the local government eventually endorsed and supported it (though not without a fight). Pam Warhurst, one of the Incredible Edible organizers, did a wonderful and very popular TED talk on it in 2012.

From the standpoint of complexity (not to be confused with complicatedness, which is a negative), transit-oriented development can be quite simple, and thus more of a tactic. Transit-oriented revitalization is always strategic, no matter what the scale, since it incorporates many of the elements that go into bringing a place back to life—social, economic, natural, heritage, infrastructure, etc.—and is thus far more complex than transit-oriented development.

A California governor's strategy for revitalizing his/her state might thus include revitalizing the state capital, Sacramento, as a model to be replicated statewide. So Sacramento's revitalization would be a tactic of the governor's strategy. But whoever is put in charge of revitalizing Sacramento is going to need a strategy. So, distinguishing strategy from tactic is often based on context, perspective and hierarchy.

This nesting of tactic and strategy is natural and normal, and is not as confusing in real life as it probably sounds here. I explained it here to prevent folks from getting too wrapped around the axle trying to figure out what's a strategy and what's a tactic during their work. Academics studying it might be frustrated by the fuzziness, but soldiers in the field don't worry about labels. In fact, the nested nature of strategy and tactics is the key to scalable solutions, such as are needed to address the global climate crisis.

In 2016 an article titled "Special operations forces: A global immune system?", Joseph Norman and Yaneer Bar-Yam said this: "*...we apply this multi-scale framework to provide a control theoretic understanding of the historical and increasing need for Special Operations Forces (SOF), as well as conventional military forces. We propose that the essential role distinction is in the separation between high complexity fine scale challenges as opposed to large scale challenges. This leads to a correspondence between the role SOF can best serve and that of the immune system in complex organisms—namely, the ability to respond to fine-grained, high-complexity disruptors and preserve tissue health.*

Much like a multi-cellular organism, human civilization is composed of a set of distinct and heterogeneous social tissues. Responding to disruption and restoring health in a system with highly diverse local social conditions is an essentially complex task. SOF have the potential to mitigate against harm without disrupting normal social tissue behavior. ...SOF might be leveraged to support global stability and mitigate against cascading crises."

And the much-quoted Field Marshall Helmuth Karl Bernhard Graf von Moltke (1800 – 1891) had this to say about strategy: "*Strategy is a system of expedients. It is more than science, it is the translation of science into practical life, the development of an original leading thought in accordance with the ever-changing circumstances.*"

He went on to say this about the relationship of tactics to strategies: "*The tactical result of an engagement forms the base for new strategic decisions, because victory or defeat in a battle changes the situation to such a degree that no human acumen is able to see beyond the first battle.*" Lastly, he had this to say about plans: "*No battle plan ever survives contact with the enemy.*" In fact, plans are despised by most combat-experienced military leaders. This is an attitude that would probably benefit many mayors and city managers.

Not surprising, then, that Napoleon said: "*I have never had a plan of operations.*" While most think of Napoleon in terms of his losses in Russia and at Waterloo, it was his many successes on the battlefield that made his few losses so memorable. This is similar to how we mostly remember dinosaurs for their extinction—and thus speak of them as emblematic of failure—rather than for their having ruled the Earth for 100 million years. Just because their biology and ecology lacked the resilience to deal with a massive asteroid strike doesn't mean they failed. They had zero control over cosmic bombardment. We, on the other hand, have total control over our greenhouse gas emissions.

STRATEGIC THINKING ON GENTRIFICATION

OK: back to civilian applications. One compelling reason to learn strategy is to resolve conflicting constraints (described earlier). Gentrification is such a controversial aspect of revitalization these days that the American public often uses the two terms as if they were synonymous. That's just plain wrong.

Just because mildew often appears when a room is too moist doesn't mean that mildew and water are the same thing. Mildew is a sign of badly-managed moisture, just as gentrification is a sign of badly-managed revitalization.

In the November/December 2019 issue of the Washington Monthly, Will Stancil wrote an article called "The Gentrification Panic". It was subtitled "The media's obsession with a handful of trendy neighborhoods obscures the real story of urban America." The article was primarily a review of the new book, "Newcomers: Gentrification and Its Discontents" by Matthew L. Schuerman, published by the University of Chicago Press.

Here's an excerpt from Stancil's article: *"Gentrification itself is a notoriously fuzzy term. Almost everyone agrees that it encompasses some mix of a place becoming wealthier, whiter, better educated, and more expensive, but these don't always happen together. There is little consensus about which factors are required and which are simply side effects. There's also a dispute over the connection between gentrification and the displacement of poor people. In many economically growing neighborhoods, the low-income population does not fall by much. This can happen because new investment leads to new, higher-density housing, or because the area was a deserted industrial quarter to begin with, such as New York's DUMBO. Schuerman settles on what he admits is a simple definition of gentrification: the process by which a neighborhood goes from having below-average to above-average incomes for its region."*

Note that last sentence. If it's accurate (I haven't read the book), we've got the author of an entire book on gentrification who confuses it with revitalization: no mention at all of displacement in that definition. Little wonder then, that ordinary citizens are so confused.

One of the rare commentators who doesn't conflate the two terms is Amy Greil, a Community, Natural Resource and Economic Development Educator for the University of Wisconsin-Madison. In an article titled "Weighing revitalization with gentrification" in the July 20, 2019 edition of The Kenosha News, she says:

"*Revitalization is an inclusive change process most often viewed positively within a neighborhood. This is community activism sponsored by the people, for the people, usually accompanied by new public or private investment that adds value to a neighborhood. Gentrification, on the other hand, tends to be an exclusive change process of areas historically inhabited by marginalized groups such as diverse racial/ethnic or low-income populations. Into these areas come destabilizing investments from a resources group into areas that have seen long-term, structural disinvestment.*"

British sociologist Ruth Glass coined the term "gentrification" in her book *London: Aspects of Change.* (1964). She was referring very specifically to the displacement of lower-income residents with higher-income residents. Although the term derives from the "landed gentry", the "displacers" in these regenerating London neighborhoods were usually only middle class. So, when the middle class is displaced by the upper class, should that also be called gentrification?

I've been to countless community meetings on the subject of gentrification, and almost all of them have devolved in a confused mess. Participants one moment were confused when someone said "gentrification" meaning revitalization, which most people wanted. The next moment, they were confused when someone said "gentrification" meaning displacement, which few people wanted.

So, the first step in solving the gentrification problem is fixing the dialog around it. I propose that we immediately stop using the word. The problem is displacement, so let's just call it that. "Gentrification" won't appear again in this book, unless it's part of someone's quote.

Much of the heartbreaking social displacement of revitalization is easily avoidable when mayors, planners and developers simply care enough to create a strategy to avoid or minimize it. For instance, a city council might say that they are concerned about displacement, but then they sell-off all their excess city-owned properties in an area that's about to revitalize. Some city-owned properties might well be crucial to successful revitalization, and should thus be sold to redevelopers, but certainly not all of them.

If they were really concerned about displacement, they would hang onto some of those properties for future affordable housing development, after the revitalization is underway. That would make the area's rebirth more resilient, and would provide those who are displaced with a newer—probably nicer—place to move to in the same neighborhood, close to friends, family and favorite amenities.

A December 2014 study, "Lost In Place", by the urban think-tank City Observatory, examined population and income changes between 1970 and 2010 in large cities. They found that poverty concentration, not displacement, is the central problem for the urban poor. But revitalization ignorance leaves many leaders fighting the very regenerative results they seek.

Many displacement debates are actually based on two false assumptions:
- That economic growth and affordable housing are conflicting goals; and
- That higher-income people moving into lower-income neighborhoods is always a Bad Thing.

In fact, boosting affordable housing—especially in downtown areas—is a fairly reliable strategy for lasting revitalization. And mixed-income neighborhoods are generally more resilient and socially-healthier than concentrated poverty. I say "generally" because it can be unhealthy when wealth is injected into a poor area in a way that rubs the lower-income folks' noses in what they don't have.

Recent research by Michael J. Hicks, PhD, and Dagney Faulk, PhD, of Ball State University proved that in today's economy, jobs tend to move to people, whereas people often moved to jobs in the past. Many communities' strategies are based on that old assumption, so they launch revitalization with commercial redevelopment, rather than residential. Or, they forget to include sufficient affordable housing, so there are too few nearby customers (or employees) to attract retail businesses.

Affordable housing isn't just a feel-good social responsibility tactic: it's often at the heart of successful revitalization strategies. Zappos CEO Tony Hsieh's previously-mentioned $350 million downtown Las Vegas revitalization fiasco failed not only because it lacked a strategic process, but also because he didn't provide sufficient affordable housing (which a strategic process would have identified as essential).

As a result, the area remains somewhat lifeless. It didn't help that some of his key partners didn't get the "re" concept: that points out the need for up-front education of your team. Too many people rush into community revitalization without a clue as to what they don't know. Apparently, the fact that they live in a city fosters the illusion that they know how it works.

Back to displacement: Poor ghettos and wealthy ghettos are both undesirable. Just as injecting affordable housing into wealthy neighborhoods is socially revitalizing, so too is injecting wealthier residents into poor neighborhoods. Mixed-income, mixed-ethnicity, mixed-age, mixed-use, mixed-transit (foot, bike, car, bus, train, etc.) neighborhoods will define healthy 21st-century cities.

While locally-appropriate strategies are crucial, it's important to remember that some challenges are almost universal. Racial and economic equity are two of these...especially here in the United States, where both problems are worsening as the middle class shrinks and anti-immigrant rhetoric infects the public soul.

As a result of the universality of many challenges, it's very likely that another city has already hit on a strategy that will work in yours. Joining organizations like the Government Alliance on Race and Equity (GARE) helps avoid reinventing that wheel. GARE is a national network of governments working to achieve racial equity and advance opportunities for all.

That said, the process at arriving at a solution is sometimes as important than the solution itself, so be wary of shortcuts.

In the 50s and 60s, the standard line uttered by white suburbanites when a "family of color" moved next door was "there goes the neighborhood!" Today, the same sentiment is often uttered by people of color in traditional "ethnic" neighborhoods when a middle-class white family moves in next door.

Given that mixed-income and mixed-race neighborhoods are seen by many as a "cure" for concentrated pockets of urban poverty, it helps neither of those agendas if locals start screaming "displacement" the first time a wealthier white family arrives.

Just as species migrate to different environments as ecosystems evolve over time, so too do residents move as cities evolve. Healthy neighborhoods usually have healthy amounts of resident turnover. So displacement is generally only bad in excess, except when new arrivals flaunt their wealth, or isolate themselves in gated communities.

Displacement via revitalization is a high-profile problem that rightly deserves attention. But a much larger problem is being ignored: displacement via devitalization (neighborhood abandonment due to decline). It's true that elected leaders need to learn how to revitalize without excessive displacement. But the bigger need is for local leaders to simply learn how to revitalize, period.

At least 95% of the displacement in the U.S. derives from devitalization, not revitalization. Devitalization displaces far more people (via crime, drugs, poor schools, bad infrastructure, lack of opportunities, etc.), but people only talk about revitalization's displacement, for two reasons:

- It happens more suddenly, so it's more perceivable; and
- There are identifiable "bad guys": real estate developers and newly-arrived people with more wealth.

Mayors who talk constantly of the displacement problem are often like teenagers discussing how to put a car into a power slide, when they haven't yet learned how to drive. Too many mayors and city councils think that achieving revitalization is simply a matter of getting out of the free market's way, so developers can do what they want. This is mostly due to ignorance: they simply don't know any other path. No one ever taught them a process for revitalization.

As with so many seemingly-intractable community problems, displacement suffers from a paucity of metrics, and we can't manage what we can't measure. For instance, when places do visioning exercises, they are often forced to relegate the anti-displacement goal to some fuzzy and useless line in their vision statement like "we will revitalize with no displacement" (which is probably impossible in most cases.)

All of the other measures of revitalization—economy, security, education, health, etc.—are relatively easy to define and measure. Displacement is the big bugaboo. It drives people crazy, because they think they have no control over it. But that's because they don't quantify how much is acceptable up front, which means they can't measure and have some degree of control over the results.

Here's a simple way to add a bit of rigor to the anti-displacement portion of your revitalization vision: divide neighborhood revitalization into three categories, as relates to displacement. (I'm specifying "neighborhood" because it's primarily at that level of revitalization—not community-wide or regional—that displacement takes place.)

All three of these categories result in an improved local economy and better quality of life. It's only the level of turnover in local residents that distinguishes them:

1. Low Displacement: retains 80% or more of the original residents;
2. Medium Displacement: somewhere in between the two extremes; and
3. High Displacement: inflow and outflow results in 20% or fewer original residents.

In most communities, fewer than 20% of the people create over 80% of the problems, so some replacement of existing residents is usually acceptable, and even desirable (such as thieves, pimps, gang leaders, drug dealers and slumlords).

Categories #1 and #2 are easily measured and defined, but the third has significant wiggle-room. The value of the arbitrary numbers (change them as you see fit) in this taxonomy of neighborhood revitalization is that it gives local stakeholders a metric they can add to their vision statement. Choosing the "Medium" level, for instance, says that reducing displacement isn't the top priority, but is a concern.

Embed one of the above three displacement categories of revitalization into your vision, and you now have the ability to know when you are achieving or violating it. It's not a solution for displacement, of course: just a tool to help you better manage it.

In recent years, Denver, Colorado has done a wonderful job of revitalizing its downtown, and—as you'll see in a later chapter—they've used light rail to spread that revitalization across their metro region. As a result, residential rents have skyrocketed from below the national average to 12.6% above average. "Before we've realized it almost, we're a high cost housing city," says Ismael Guerrero, director of the Denver Housing Authority. "We're new to that club, but we're clearly there, because the wages haven't kept up."

Stimulating property value enhancement—without anticipating and making some attempt to ameliorate the predictable negative impacts on lower-income families—indicates a lack of concern by public leaders. These dynamics are universal: they should take no one by surprise. But Ismael isn't to blame: revitalization is a systemic process that should be addressed at higher levels of public management than a housing authority.

> *"A dream you dream alone is only a dream.*
> *A dream you dream together is reality."*
> *– Yoko Ono*

Displacement, as I'm using it here, is the traumatic disruption of long-time residents' lives due to a suddenly-higher cost of living deriving from revitalization. It's caused by rapidly-rising property values, which raises property taxes and rents, meaning that both low-income homeowners and low-income renters are forced from their homes.

But wait: isn't increasing the value of property—and boosting public revenues—the whole goal of revitalization? No, it isn't. That's the whole goal for most private redevelopers (as opposed to developers, who do sprawl projects), and that's fine: that's a market force that can be harnessed for revitalization.

But if market forces are the only forces at work, then there's a failure of government. In the emotion-packed, fact-free, money-driven chaos that passes for political dialog in the United States these days, Americans seem to have forgotten the vital role of government.

It's the job of the government (together with the justice system) to watch over the welfare of their citizens. That means:

- raising the quality of life for all;
- increasing job and business opportunities for all;
- boosting health, safety, and social justice for all;
- restoring natural resources, reactivating abandoned properties, rehabilitating heritage, and regenerating the economy for all; and
- constantly renewing, repurposing, and reconnecting the community's assets to keep it vibrant and relevant in a changing economy.

All of those factors together comprise the definition of true revitalization, and that's far beyond the remit of real estate investors and developers.

The simple fact of the matter is that traumatic, unjust displacement is preventable. What's more, it's easily preventable. Yes: it's a complex problem. But the solution is dead simple: the government simply has to WANT to prevent it.

Once that desire is established, the tactics and strategies that can produce revitalization with a minimum of trauma and dislocation are numerous. Desire is the key. Add social justice to your local revitalization vision, and it will flow through into your program, strategy, policies, partnerships and projects.

In my 2008 book, *Rewealth*, I documented two simple, preventive displacement tactics that were used by conscientious private redevelopers (who stepped in to fill the gap left by unconcerned local government officials). One of them used tax increment financing (TIF) to ensure that any increased taxes came back to those communities in the form of neighborhood improvements. The other set up a non-profit fund using a surcharge on the sale of new residences, which refunded any increase in property tax paid by the long-established residents.

So the solution is more in changing HOW we do revitalization, not in changing its basic dynamics. In a personal communication, Aksel Kargård Olsen, Senior Planning Analyst at the San Francisco Bay area's Metropolitan Transportation Commission told me "*I think this is generally true: all manner of things are policy failures at their core. Income inequality? Sure, folks like to blame greed as if it were an anomaly in markets, the just once in a blue moon occurrence requiring swift and public denunciation. Markets do what markets do, which is why we have policies shaping them in the first place. Gentrification and its expressions is a great example of that.*"

Does this mean that private redevelopers are blameless? Of course not. Some are brazenly insensitive to the needs of lower-income residents, especially ethnic minorities. Some buy influence on the city council, sometimes to the point of not just getting their own project approved, but also to enact unhealthy changes to zoning, building codes, and development incentives that undermine the community for decades. That's just who they are. But when they get their way, it's a failure of government.

Charlotte, North Carolina is currently building a massive greenway system that is revitalizing neighborhoods throughout the area. They are basically trying to produce the High Line Effect on a metropolitan area scope, which includes many low-income communities. This is a wonderful opportunity to apply strategic thinking to the creation a more-humane form of revitalization that doesn't let displacement run riot. If they want to.

GOOD STRATEGIES ARE SO SUCCINCT, THEY LOOK LIKE NO-BRAINERS

Baltimore, Maryland's famous Inner Harbor revitalization had a brief, simple strategy: create a critical mass of retail, restaurants, waterfront paths, and tourist attractions in one fell swoop, rather than piece by piece. That strategy worked beautifully.

These days, many folks are championing incremental revitalization strategies over such "Big Bang" approaches. In many cases, this is sound advice: too many redevelopment initiatives are driven by a politician's need for publicity—or a developer's ambition—and the resulting projects are often too large and too fast (read: poor public engagement and lack strategic process). The point isn't that one is better than the other, but to avoid becoming too dogmatic about either strategy.

"Critical mass" is thus a two-word strategy. "Incremental" is only one word. The brevity of a good strategy often makes it seem as if not much thought went into it. In Baltimore's case, that might actually be true: the public-private partnership behind this spectacular success in Baltimore failed to create a strategy for ensuring that the revitalization spread from the Inner Harbor to the rest of the city. Oliver, for example.

The Oliver neighborhood of Baltimore was in rough shape even before the 2015 protests and unfortunate riot following the brutal death of resident Freddie Gray at the hands of the police. Reportedly, some 250 businesses (most of them minority-owned), were looted or destroyed. Over 150 innocent residents' cars were vandalized, and over 100 fires were set that damaged local residents' homes. Innocent victims are what distinguish a riot from a protest.

Now, Oliver's starting to come back to life, thanks to a visionary local developer, and to a program funded by the Annie E. Casey Foundation.

Their strategy comprised just three words: Build On Strength. "Build On Strength" might seem hopelessly simplistic and generic, but remember that a strategy guides project and partnership decisions in a way that fulfills the vision. This includes both formal decisions made in meetings, and on-the-fly decisions made in the field.

Let's say you must choose one of two neighborhood revitalization proposals. #1 is a big-budget project. #2 is less capital-intensive, but requires significant grassroots organizing to succeed. If your community has financial resources, but citizens are fractious or apathetic, the "Build On Strength" strategy points to proposal #1. If your community is weak at finance or fundraising, but harmonious and effective at working together, the "Build On Strength" strategy selects #2.

Without a strategy in mind, you might spend months debating the features and benefits of each proposal, with two likely results: the wrong proposal is chosen, or neither proposal is acted upon. Strategy puts your focus on the elements that are vital to success, such as overcoming or bypassing obstacles.

On January 5, 2016, first-term Republican Governor Larry Hogan announced that Maryland would provide $75 million to help Baltimore demolish thousands of vacant buildings. That would be worrisome if there were no strategy for filling those vacant spaces into new residences and employers. But he also announced $600 million in state subsidies to encourage redevelopment of those spaces. Sounds good, right? Wrong.

Two powerful tactics—getting rid of old stuff + subsidizing new stuff—were announced, but community revitalization isn't just about stuff. It's also about factors like trust, justice, health, education, connectivity, etc. There was no apparent strategy in Baltimore to address such issues. Worse, some of the demolition funding came from the Community Legacy program, which supports rehabilitation. Thus, this approach actually reduced their ability to revitalize these neighborhoods.

> *"Strategy requires thought, tactics require observation." – Max Euwe, Chess Champion*

Connectivity might be West Baltimore's greatest strategic need: lower-income residents must be able to get to jobs, schools, and shops without owning a car. But one of Governor Hogan's first acts was to kill the Red Line, a long-planned transit project that would have finally connected West Baltimore to the rest of the city. Thus, his $675 million investment in demolition and redevelopment will likely fail to produce lasting revitalization, due to a lack of strategic thinking.

Recently, a coalition of neighborhood groups called the Baltimore Housing Roundtable offered a strategy for reducing displacement of citizens during these mass demolitions. I hope it works.

In a May 28, 2019 email to me, Rick Rybeck, Director of Just Economics, told me the following New York City story during our discussion of Baltimore's revitalization challenges: *"In the 1980s, the Nehemiah Housing Project redeveloped several square blocks of vacant and boarded-up properties in Brooklyn for workforce housing. The project began with land assembly. Much of the land was owned by the city through tax defaults. Most of the rest was owned by banks through mortgage default and there were a few private owners still holding on here and there."*

He continued: *"They all readily agreed to relinquish their sites for $1 in exchange for Nehemiah's redevelopment commitment. For most owners, the sale was a release from* potential liabilities. The project was completed with donated materials and labor. Homes were quickly occupied and there was an outcry for more. Nehemiah approached New York City for land in adjacent blocks and the City was happy to sell additional parcels for $1."

Rick concluded: "However, the banks and private owners resisted, saying "This is a thriving neighborhood. Our land is worth much more than $1." Thus, Nehemiah was forced to pay premium prices to obtain access to the land that Nehemiah had made valuable in the first place! Baltimore should legislate tax reform so that the community (and NOT speculators) profit from the redevelopment of these vacant properties."

Obviously the organizers were so focused on succeeding that they forgot to create a strategy for dealing with success.

Try this test: the next time you are getting onto an elevator with your mayor, or whoever is leading your regeneration initiative, ask him/her what their strategy is. If they haven't finished reciting it by the time you reach your destination floor, they don't have one.

For instance, the strategy for my revitalization consulting practice is both simple and generic: it's the universal two-step consultant's strategy. Step One: Fool people into thinking you know what you're talking about. Step Two: Convince them they'll be better-off after sending you money than they were when they still had the money. That's a simple strategy. It works for massive Fortune 500 consulting firms and independent practitioners alike.

Seriously, though: a strategy that can't be remembered without consulting a document is too complicated—or too undefined—to succeed.

STRATEGY FAILURES AT THE NATIONAL LEVEL

The need for an effective strategy isn't limited to neighborhoods and communities, of course.

Angela Merkel has been Germany's chancellor for over 13 years, but it's clear (as of this writing: January 29, 2019) that she's on her way out. The beginning of her political demise can be traced to a private meeting with her own party's lawmakers on June 12, 2018.

As she was attacked relentlessly for her increasingly-unpopular support of allowing refugees into the country, her response was totally ineffective.

A *Bloomberg BusinessWeek* article titled "How Merkel Lost Her Grip" cited one of her aides asking another. "*What's the strategy?*" "*I don't think we have one*," was the reply. And thus did her end begin.

Look at America's Vietnam War for a prime example of failure on both the shared vision and the strategic front. We won most of the battles, and lost the war. What was our strategy? God only knows.

If you had asked that question of any 100 military and political leaders at the time, you would likely have received 100 different answers.

If any of the answers had been the same, such as *"to prevent the spread of Communism in southeast Asia"*, the similarity would have derived from the fact that it's a vision/goal, not a strategy.

Towards the end of the Vietnam conflict, we actually had three very different visions/goals in place nationwide:
1) American military leaders were still focused on the original goal of winning;
2) Many of America's business leaders (the "military industrial complex" that President / General Eisenhower warned us about) on the other hand, had become addicted to the military spending (about $950 billion 2011 dollars between 1965 and 1973), so their goal was to keep the war going as long as possible; and,
3) American citizens (and a few political leaders who listened to them) had the primary goal of getting out of the conflict as soon as possible.

Little wonder, then, that we had no cohesive strategy: we had no share vision of the goal.

FIXING THE PRESENT AND FUTURE TOGETHER

"We are stealing the future, selling it to the present, and calling it GDP." – Paul Hawken

Are the rapidly-growing current efforts to increase resilience "real", or they just another policy fad promoted by journalists and foundations?

On the one hand, the need for physical resilience to the storms, droughts, floods, and blizzards ensuing from our destabilized climate is very real, and is intensifying. Just ask the flood insurance companies that are beginning to wonder how long they'll be able to hike their premiums before their business model gives up the ghost and entire regions are designated "uninsurable".

On the other hand, politicians seldom push expensive initiatives with delayed benefits to voters: the optics aren't good. So, to help the resilience movement grow and thrive, we thus need to give it both short-term and long-term benefits.

This would make resilience economically appealing to elected leaders and voters alike.

This is exactly what a resilient prosperity program would do, by fixing the present and the future together. A resilient community renews its natural, built, and socioeconomic environments together. A resilient community creates a vision of their desired future together, so the resulting strategy benefits all.

Resilient prosperity programs often include the repurposing of social, economic, and human assets via training in new skills and technologies. These are often best derived on-the-job from regenerative projects. Good strategies enable places to achieve their goals with what they have. A strategy for resilient prosperity is usually one that reconnects, renews, and repurposes the assets of today to meet the needs and threats of tomorrow.

The resulting projects fix the present by reusing old buildings, undoing previous planning mistakes, cleaning and reusing contaminated sites, restoring natural resources, and the like.

They fix the future by ensuring that these projects are designed and located in a way that adapts the place to known future threats and opportunities, while also making it more adaptive in the face of unknown threats and opportunities.

When Hurricane Irene unleashed devastating floods in Vermont in 2011, it was found that some of the culverts under the roads were too small to handle the flows, causing the roads to fail. The village of Townshend did what any sane place would do, and rebuilt them larger.

But, in 2012, FEMA refused to reimburse them for that upgrade. FEMA knew how to rebuild the past, but didn't quite get the concept of fixing the future. It took a lot of arguing, but Vermont Governor Peter Shumlin and Vermont's congressional delegation announced in 2013 that FEMA had reversed their policy and would pay for such upgrades. In such small steps do institutions start incorporating strategies for the future into rebuilding the present.

Virtually all places worldwide are in a "fix the present" mode. This manifests as a broad assortment of mostly-uncoordinated public and private redevelopment projects. The simplest way to perceive the difference between revitalizing your present and revitalizing your future is to see the former as tactical and the latter as strategic.

Most communities with tight budgets understandably tend to focus entirely on tactics: projects that provide immediate functional or economic benefits. But in today's increasingly broken, rapidly shifting world, not paying attention to the future can leave a community high and dry, despite a plethora of excellent projects.

> *"You have a goal you've been putting off. ...You've been meaning to take real action on it, but could use more motivation. Let it go. It's a bad goal. If it was(sic) a great goal, you would have jumped into action already. ...Goals are not to improve the future. The future doesn't really exist. ...Judge a goal by how well it changes your actions in the present moment."* – Derek Sivers.

Though usually unstated as such, the universal desired end result is resilient prosperity. Places that don't have prosperity want it. Those that do have prosperity want it to last. If they're wise, they'll want it to be enjoyed by all, because the more widespread prosperity is, the more resilient it is. Resilient prosperity is best achieved through a constant process of regenerating communities and nature. But that work has two parts, tactics and strategies. As we've seen, most places are long on the former, and short—or completely lacking—in the latter.

Stereotypes are dangerous, but not necessarily wrong. Canadians love peace, order, and good government. The English just need a good "cuppa" when the sky is falling. The French are philosophers and lovers, not fighters. Americans are fighters and doers, not thinkers: we prefer immediate fixative action to long-term, preventive planning. But maybe we shouldn't be too worried about that. Peter Drucker, the late, great management consultant, once said: *"Planning is actually incompatible with an entrepreneurial society and economy. Planning is the kiss of death of entrepreneurship."*

Most people seem to have a pretty good grasp of the difference between the present and the future, so let's just refer to tactics as "fixing the present", and strategy as "fixing the future". A good strategy is an adaptive, high-level technique for using available resources to achieve one or more goals under uncertain conditions. A good tactic is an action that advances a strategy.

Strategies tend to attract and organize resources, whereas tactics expend resources. Tactics make sense at their point of action: a strategy ensures that they make sense for the whole. Strategies can adapt and evolve, but not frequently. Tactics can and should adapt to the challenges and opportunities of the moment. Strategies guide. Tactics deliver.

For the sake of clarity, here are working definitions of fixing the present versus fixing the future:
- Fixing the Present ("tactical renewal"): Relatively short-term projects that renew, replace, reconnect, and/or repurpose natural, built,

socioeconomic, or human assets. The goal is to produce immediate new value.
- Fixing the Future ("strategic renewal"): Long-term initiatives or ongoing programs that renew, replace, reconnect, and/or repurpose natural, built, socioeconomic, and/or human assets. The goal is usually to redesign or restructure an entire place to better cope with upcoming challenges, and/or reposition it to better respond to upcoming opportunities.

Most projects that fix the present also fix the future to some degree, but not all. How can we determine if a project is solely tactical or if it also serves a strategy? Here's a hypothetical example.

Let's say your community has an old industrial waterfront with ugly but still-functioning public infrastructure, such as a power plant or sewage treatment facility. If you decide to renovate and "green" that infrastructure—making it less polluting or more aesthetically pleasing—that would be a tactic that contributes to your community's "green" or "sustainability" initiative. That would help fix the present.

> *"Established population centers, rich in cultural heritage, have been, and continue to be, going through radical transformation, as their economic bases evolve, their populations shift, and their entire reason for being is in question. ....It is without dispute that America's older legacy cities and their revitalization are critical to the country's economy and its international economic competitiveness."*
> *-Advisory Council on Historic Preservation.*

The future? Not so much. But revitalizing that waterfront—creating a public park, entertainment facilities, and mixed-use redevelopment with good transit connections—might revitalize of the entire city for decades to come. But who wants to live, work, or play next to a power or sewage plant...or a noisy, pollution-rich urban highway?

In that case, the strategic approach would relocate the infrastructure, not just improve it. You could still make the new facility green and beautiful, but relocating it would fix your present and future together. The balance of "fixing the present" vs. "fixing the future" depends on current conditions:

A place that's in wonderful condition, whose citizens and leadership are "fat and happy", is at risk if they're not fixing their future. Their resilient prosperity program would likely be skewed—at least in the early years—towards strategy. Any activities that fix the present would likely focus on specific problem areas, rather than on the entire city or nation;

A blighted, highly-distressed place will probably skew strongly towards the present. Their renewal activities will be more focused on the entire community or nation, and will be more tactical in nature, due to the urgency of their situation; or

An "OK" place might hypothetically have an equal distribution of present and future priorities, but is more likely to be doing nothing at all. Places that are "just getting by" are often stagnant and fear spending money, doing little to fix either present problems or future vulnerabilities.

Whatever the balance, fixing the present and future together is the path to resilient prosperity. Or, to paraphrase poet Khalil Gibran, "*Progress lies in enhancing what is, while advancing toward what will be.*"

Strategy makes the timing, sequence, and integration of projects important. That's the realm where efficiencies and synergies are to be found. In a strategic vacuum, leaders say things like "Who cares about strategy or timing? Cleaning up a brownfield or restoring a historic building is always good, right?"

That's true enough, but strategy is what can turn those good projects into what's really desired: resilient prosperity. A strategy for fixing the future makes it easier to finance huge projects, such as "green infrastructure", or transportation initiatives that remake and reconnect entire cities or regions. This can open avenues to new social and economic improvement opportunities, while making those places more physically resilient.

In the 20th century, we adapted our cities to prioritize automobiles. As discussed earlier, we now realize that excessive cars kill cities (not to mention pedestrians). There are three proven strategy/tactic combinations that help undo the auto-centric urban planning mistakes of the 20th century:

1. Provide increasing amounts of affordable / free public transit;
2. Make cars more expensive and less-convenient, such as by increasing pedestrian-only streets, by increasing parking fees and by charging for inner-city usage; and,
3. Reduce the need for cars by planning cities better, such as getting rid of single-purpose zoning and increasing affordable housing near centers of employment.

Portland, Oregon is adapting to this new reality: their newest Willamette River bridge, Tilikum Crossing, accommodates pedestrians, bicyclists, and public transit, but not cars. Helsinki is going a step further, with plans to make their downtown effectively car-free by 2025.

Paris has repurposed and renewed the ugly highway along the River Seine into a people zone—no cars allowed—thus reconnecting the neighborhoods to the water. The revitalizing effect on both quality of life and property values has been dramatic.

All three cities are thus renewing their present and future together, which characterizes most great community strategies.

There have been few points in the history of our world when people weren't saying *"we are beset by crises of unprecedented scale and frequency."* We're certainly saying that today. Young people especially are worried—and angry—that their future has been so undermined by the climate crisis. Fixing the present and the future together is essential, as far as they're concerned.

In this world of ubiquitous, accelerating local and global crises, strategies must be more adaptive than ever. The November 2, 2017 issue of *Strategy + Business* (published by PwC) contained an article by Marissa Michel. Its title was "Why Your Company's Disaster Recovery Plan Needs a Strategy".

Here's a brief excerpt: *"Strategy development, even in crisis mode, provides critical opportunities. It gives you a chance to hit pause, even for an hour, on the chaos around you. You can take stock of the facts and decide what your values and priorities are. Your strategy keeps you on a path but also enables you to adjust course, and to appropriately and meaningfully shape, expand, or limit your response as the situation unfolds. No crisis starts and ends in the same place; crises are by definition unpredictable and overwhelm your coping mechanisms."*

Money can fix some problems, which leads those looking for simplistic solutions to assume it can fix all problems. The reality is far more complex, and can only be addressed with an adaptive, strategic, process-oriented approach.

COMMUNITY LEADERS AWAKEN TO THEIR STRATEGIC VACUUM

> *"The way I define the job is, firstly, in setting the strategy for the company, and then leading the allocation of capital to that strategy—because until you put money where you say your strategy is, it's not your strategy."*
> *– Emma Walmsley, CEO, GlaxoSmithKline.*

The good news is that local governments are starting to realize how planning without a strategy wastes both resources and opportunities. Where I live, in Arlington County, Virginia, County Board Chair Libby Garvey said (on November 14, 2015) that one of her top priorities is to craft a strategic plan for the county. "*We really don't have one,*", she admitted.

In truth, Arlington County doesn't need a strategic plan as much as most places. Why? Because of a simple strategy devised in 1968, which can be reduced to a single sentence: "*Focus most new development around our subway stations.*"

The Washington Metropolitan Area Transit Authority originally wanted to route the Orange Line of the DC area's new Metro system down the median of Interstate 66. This clueless bit of planning would have largely isolated pedestrians from subway access. The County Board rejected that plan, forcing the underground line right through the heart of the county.

The key element of this strategy was to focus almost all new residential and commercial development around 4 of the county's 6 Orange Line stations. About 25% of Arlington residents now use transit to get to work (the national average is under 5%), and 10% don't even bother owning a car. The county has grown dramatically, both economically and population-wise, yet its charming old neighborhoods and copious parks remain largely intact, thanks to a one-sentence strategy.

This has begun to change, with influential developers destroying some healthy lower-income neighborhoods for high-end projects (as was proposed for the historic, mixed-income Westover neighborhood). And 898 old, supposedly-protected trees have been removed by just eight public projects in the past 4 years alone. But this isn't a failure of strategy: only of political will.

RECONOMICS

> *"The truth about a city's aspirations isn't found in its vision. It's found in its budget."*
> *— Brent Toderian, TODERIAN UrbanWORKS.*

A December 3, 2015 news release from New York State said this: "*Governor Cuomo (designated) 11 new Brownfield Opportunity Areas in communities across New York. The program helps participants develop revitalization strategies focused on returning dormant and blighted areas into productive communities of economic growth and development.*" That's unusual: the norm is to throw money at projects or plans, not strategies.

So again, what is revitalization? Speaking literally, it would be a return to a state of vitality after a period of devitalization. But in normal usage, it generally means any significant improvement in quality of life, economic vibrance, environmental health, social justice/harmony, and optimism.

Can a project—no matter how large—deliver all of those benefits? Not bloody likely, mate.

If your community isn't planning to revitalize, it's planning to devitalize. Regeneration should be budgeted for as automatically as is maintenance: not just as a reaction to crises. In fact, the constant repurposing, renewing, and reconnecting of assets is the best form of crisis prevention.

The second law of thermodynamics states that the total entropy of an isolated system can only increase over time. Thus the need to continually reconnect to heal divisions, and constantly regenerate to restore functions.

Author Jim Rohn says *"Your life does not get better by chance, it gets better by change."* The same could be said of communities *"A city's quality of life and economy don't get better by chance, but by change."*

In a poll taken by the Myrtle Beach (South Carolina) Area Chamber of Commerce of local residents at a revitalization forum in February of 2018, 80% of residents said they wanted to close a major downtown boulevard to cars, and 83% said they were excited about the future of their downtown.

Taken together, I'd say downtown Myrtle Beach probably has a bright future. They are both open to change and optimistic about it.

Better futures are created by better actions in the present. But these days, people worldwide have been demoralized by the relentless globalization of social, economic, and environmental problems that used to appear only locally.

You now know three essential factors in creating resilient prosperity:
- Have a regenerative strategy to help ensure success. Ideally, it will repurpose, renew and reconnect a previously-used or underused site;
- Have a regenerative process to implement the strategy; and

- Have as one of your goals the creation of confidence in the future of the place.

Even a little bit of awareness of those three factors should help you avoid embarrassing, expensive failures like Kenya's "smart city", Konza Technopolis. Kenya violated all three of these rules in their creation of their "Silicon Savannah":

- First, they knew that their government agencies were excessively slow and bureaucratic, but they had no strategy to address that key obstacle.
- Second, there was no renewal process because there was nothing regenerative about this project: it was just old-fashioned sprawl.
- Third, they didn't understand that investors are only attracted to places that inspire confidence in a better local future. They allowed delays to erode all confidence that this project will ever succeed. More than a few government and business leaders bit the dust on this massive strategic failure.

CHAPTER 6 - THE PARTIAL SOLUTION: HOW TO CREATE A VISION AND A STRATEGY...AND WHO SHOULD DO IT.

"Without a vision there is no strategy."
– David Rixter, U.S. Treasury (personal communication with this author).

We humans like to control things, even those things we don't understand and that can't—by their very nature—be controlled. We assign roles, budgets, and missions that pack ambitious, dynamic agendas into tight little packages, and then wonder why good stuff seldom comes out of those boxes.

As already stated, resilient prosperity is the goal of a most intelligent places, whether or not they use the term. It could be considered a "universal" target for community and regional futures. Most places already have everything they need to create resilient prosperity, but it can't manifest because they try to pack that grand mission into a narrowly-focused existing agency that can't handle it. Such places assume that revitalization must emerge from their economic development or redevelopment agency, or real estate investors, or their planning department, or their mayor's or governor's office, etc. In other words, they're prioritizing structure over function.

As a result, when the right vision, strategy or resources emerge from an effective-but-unofficial local leader—such as a neighborhood group, a community foundation or a student group—opportunities often die on the vine. But even when renewal efforts sprout within an "approved" entity, they usually get constricted by the limitations of that agency.

At some level, public leaders are aware of their ignorance regarding complexity. This is why you seldom see an agency charged with revitalizing the entire community. No one wants to be in charge of an activity they can't define; whose principles, models, and cycles they can't explain. Better to break it down into controllable specialties, and hope that the overall goal magically takes care of itself.

Economic revitalization strategies are sometimes simple to describe, but seldom easy to implement. One accepted strategy, for instance, is called "plugging the leaks." It comprises the filling-out of local supply chains and/or the strengthening of local industries. When companies purchase good or services from outside the region, revenue is "leaking" out of the region's economy. A good example of plugging such a leak is the way many U.S. regions that have a strong craft brewing industry are now growing their hops locally, rather than buying them from England or Germany, or from the other side of the U.S. The current rebuilding of local food systems is that same dynamic on a more holistic scale.

"No one else but an architect could solve the problems of the contemporary city." This pronouncement by the 1994 Pritzker Prize winner, architect Christian de Portzamparc appeared in a 2017 *ArchDaily* interview by Vladimir Belogolovsky. No one but an architect would say such a thing.

Few architects are able to get their heads out of the building envelope, except to see how their design might fit with the architectural vernacular of the city. An architect who even cares about—much less understands—the economic, ecological and cultural complexity of an urban area and its rural surroundings is a rare bird indeed.

On the other hand, putting an architect is charge would probably be vastly preferable to putting a civil engineer in charge: the architect would likely do less damage. Now, if Portzamparc had said "landscape architect," he would have been a bit closer to the mark. But only a bit: their scope is more holistic, but they are generally no more knowledgeable of process or strategy.

Strategies live in the mind: they die on paper. Many folks confuse strategies with plans. But plans are just thoughts frozen in time. Other folks confuse strategies with actions. But actions are just tactics: strategies determine tactics. Others confuse strategies with goals, such as when they say "our strategy is to make this a more sustainable / equitable / prosperous community".

The first step in creating an effective strategy is to make sure you're addressing the problem, not the symptom. For instance, a city suffering from "blight" makes it sound as if vacant and derelict buildings are the problem.

In reality, poverty might be the problem and the buildings are only the symptom (or, to be medically correct, the "sign"). Of course, poverty is not the only cause of blight: bad planning (especially bad transportation planning, like urban highways) is also a common cause.

Determining the underlying problem that needs to be addressed by your strategy can only be done if you have a very clear vision of what you're trying to achieve, and a well-researched map of the renewable natural, built and socioeconomic assets you have available. (Note: "renewable assets" are also referred to as "problems" or "blight".) Working from the right starting point is essential.

A strategy is a technique that simplifies, speeds, and/or helps secure the achievement of a goal. A strategy can be devised for ANY situation. If it fails, it's because it didn't fit the situation (or didn't have an implementation process: more on that later). For instance, your project didn't fail because it lacked sufficient funding, but because its strategy didn't take your available funding into account. Your program didn't fail because your citizens lacked sufficient motivation, but because your strategy didn't take their level of motivation into account.

The need for a strategy depends on the goal, not the activity. For instance, let's say you're in charge of renovating an urban park. Refurbishing a park is fairly straightforward, so you might not need to devise a new strategy.

But if you don't have the necessary funding, you need a strategy to rectify that. Your strategy might thus be to tie the park renovation to a larger goal that has broader support, such as revitalization of the adjacent neighborhood.

But, if you make advancing neighborhood revitalization a goal of your park project, you'll need a strategy to make sure it happens. Of course, there's a chance that the renovated park will be all that's needed to trigger adjacent revitalization, but what kind of professional relies on chance?

THE RIGHT VISION AND MAP DIRECTS US TO THE RIGHT GOALS. THE RIGHT STRATEGY DRIVES US TO SUCCESS.

Many factors contribute to success, of course, like design, efficiency and quality of work. But, as mentioned earlier, strategy is the only element of an endeavor whose sole function is success. If it's a bad strategy—or if the competition has a better strategy—failure is still possible. But without a strategy, failure is likely.

In the world of marketing, maybe the best-known strategy is "price skimming." Every consumer is familiar with it too, even if they don't know its name. Price skimming is the strategy of setting a high price during the launch of a new, innovative product and then lowering the price over time to access different points on the demand curve. Some call it the "early adopter" strategy, since there's usually a subset of buyers who will pay extra to be the first on their block to have your new widget.

This strategy works like a charm. Most consumers largely ignore advertising copy and judge the value of a product (or service) primarily by its price. So, starting with a high price is the most effective way to elevate the market position of the product, and thus boost what people are willing to pay. Marketers know that they can always lower a price, but can seldom get away with raising it. Like all good strategies, price skimming is simple, effective, and broadly applicable.

The same strategy can often be applied to multiple communities, despite differing strengths, weaknesses, and cultures. How is that possible? That's where the vision comes in: if it addresses the unique needs and dreams of the place, the strategy can be relatively generic. Dreams + research + deadlines = goals. Cohesive set of goals = vision.

Why do so many cities write plans and start projects without a strategy or vision? Because few public leaders understand how programs, visions, strategies, policies, partnerships and projects (tactics) all fit together.

But not all visions are created equal. Some are deeply flawed. Why? Because they are based on daydreams, rather than data. Visioning should be a research process. Daydreams will reveal what you want, but data will help reveal what you need. That's why the map of renewable assets is combined with the vision portion of the process. If data drives your vision, it will *ipso facto* drive your design, strategy, plan, etc.

Mapping tools have evolved tremendously in recent years, and are becoming more affordable. Likewise, having a GIS (geographic information systems) expert on staff is now normal for all but the tiniest of communities: it wasn't long ago that only large cities had such capabilities.

Detroit launched its Motor City Mapping Project in 2014, in order to get a handle on its vacant properties. It's a city-wide initiative, and the Detroit Land Bank now uses it to determine which vacant structures should be demolished, and which should be rehabilitated. Two years later, the Western Reserve Land Conservancy implemented that same technology to create "property dashboards" in Columbus, Cincinnati and Cleveland, Ohio.

Imagine the regenerative power of having dashboards that include all of the eight sectors of renewable assets documented in *The Restoration Economy*:

infrastructure, brownfields, heritage, disaster, ecological, watershed, fishery and agricultural.

GIS isn't just crucial for urban areas: the restoration of natural assets is increasingly managed by such systems. For instance, the Western Association of Fish and Wildlife Agencies (WAFWA) is a not-for-profit organization that coordinates the strategic, science-based conservation and restoration efforts of public agencies in 19 U.S. states and 5 Canadian provinces, which together manage some 3.7 million square miles of North America's wild and scenic territories. They have created an online mapping tool called Crucial Habitat Assessment Tool (CHAT) to dynamically reveal strengths, weaknesses, opportunities and threats related to their missions.

Mapping technologies are also becoming more affordable: even ESRI, the leading (and traditionally most expensive) vendor is now offering less-expensive cloud-based tools such as ArcGIS Online to replace dedicated local servers. Their new ArcGIS Hub is especially exciting: it makes sharing open GIS data with public and private partners far easier. This, in turn, is the key to creating a complete resilient prosperity program—ideally based on the RECONOMICS Process—online. That will be the game-changer.

So, both your vision and your strategy must be based on research, not assumptions. Your vision is your dream and your map is your present reality, but the dreamers must be knowledgeable and aware. One might say that the vision maps the "soft stuff" while the renewable asset map maps the "hard stuff" (tangible assets).

But, even if informed by research and mapping, a vision without a strategy is still nothing but a dream. And a strategy without a vision is meaningless. A vision/map and strategy together can change your world (if you have a proven process for implementing them).

> *"The dream of a better city is always*
> *in the heads of its residents."*
> *— Jaime Lerner, former Mayor of Curitiba, Brazil.*

There's nothing grand about visions and strategies: we all create, use, and change them constantly. Here's a totally superficial example to show how mundane and ubiquitous strategizing is. Let's say you're the male host of a talk show, and an upcoming guest is an actress with a reputation for being narcissistic and obnoxious. You decide to take her down a notch on your show, so you research embarrassing facts from her life. Thus, your vision is to publicly humiliate her, and your strategy is to ambush her with facts she'd rather keep secret.

But she is expecting this, and has a strategy of her own: to make you like and desire her. She deploys tactics that charm you. It works. Suddenly, your goal changes. Your vision is now to marry her. Your quickly-adopted new strategy is to charm her. Your tactics are to compliment her and avoid embarrassing her. Her strategy trumped your strategy. She wins.

Again, the strategy's purpose is to achieve the goal: if the goal changes, so might the strategy. But one should be cautious of changing a strategy if the goal remains unchanged. The primary mechanism of a strategy is to guide decision-making. Decisions often have to be made in stressful or chaotic circumstances, so we're tempted to "wing it". Those who are able to keep their strategy in mind under pressure are often the victors.

A November 29, 2016 article by Lyneir Richardson in the National Real Estate Investor was titled "How the Strategic Opening of Retail Stores Can Revitalize City Neighborhoods". It described six examples of struggling Chicago neighborhoods that had been revitalized by the opening of new retail in the right place, at the right time.

The inclusion of "strategic" in the title was telling, given the long history of failed attempts to revitalize places via new retail. So, was it the retail or the strategy that revitalized these places? Both, of course: a strategy without tactics (action) is useless, and action without a strategy is often counter-productive.

Since downtowns are the most common focus of revitalization efforts, let's use them to illustrate a common lack of strategic thinking. It should obvious to anyone that 1) businesses need customers, 2) customers who return frequently are best, and 3) customers are more likely to visit frequently if they live nearby. But as glaringly-obvious as those statements are, many downtown revitalization initiatives ignore them.

Local leaders look at their downtown's paucity of stores and restaurants and think "we need more stores and restaurants." So they launch incentives—from tax breaks to cash handouts—to artificially stimulate the opening of more businesses. A year or two later, those businesses are usually dead. Why? Because they didn't have enough customers. The downtown needed customers, not vendors.

As mentioned in the Clearwater story, residents have far more "revitalization patience" than retailers. Someone renting a downtown loft in an repurposed warehouse can go for years without a downtown hardware store: they just drive or take the bus to one elsewhere. But a downtown hardware store can't survive long without customers. An exception is downtown "central markets": they can attract shoppers from a large geographic area by adding entertainment, cultural elements, and critical mass to retail, and can thus be excellent revitalizers.

That's the simplest form of strategic thinking, yet time after time, downtown revitalization efforts focus on commercial redevelopment, rather than residential. Thus the rise of mixed-use redevelopment. But even mixed-use can be overdone: sometimes, all that's needed is residential redevelopment.

Create the customers, and businesses naturally follow. Retail is an outcome of downtown revitalization, not a cause (as with all rules, there are exceptions to this one, as we'll see in a moment). Hundreds of millions of dollars are wasted annually, simply because cities rush into action without a trace of strategic thinking.

But places that recognize the value of this simple "customers drive retail" strategy tend to produce dramatic results. Kansas City, Missouri enjoyed 39% growth in downtown residents from 2010 to 2018, versus 7% growth in its metro areas. Chattanooga, Tennessee added 14% more downtown residents in the same period, versus 7% growth in its metro areas. Both cities previously had downtowns on the verge of death.

HOW ARE THE RIGHT STRATEGIES CREATED?

Countless streetscaping and façade renovation projects go by the grand name of "revitalization." If they are, in fact, a tactic/project in a larger revitalization strategy/program, that's fine. But if they are just isolated, one-time projects, then citizens will likely be disappointed when the project is over, and revitalization hasn't manifested. Regeneration is an ongoing process, not the result of a quick fix. Moreover, it's a journey, not a destination: the process of regenerating is itself revitalizing.

Sometimes, an experienced person possessing deep familiarity with a place will be able to intuit the right strategy on the spot (making it look deceptively easy). Other times, a long series of public engagement, visioning, and partnership meetings is needed for the right strategy to emerge.

An option between those two extremes is to conduct (or commissioning) a process analysis. A process analysis provides the locally-appropriate perspective and understanding needed to design an entire comeback process: regenerative program + regenerative vision & map + regenerative strategy + regenerative policies + regenerative partners + regenerative projects.

Visions can be good, bad or mediocre. Visioning is a very different activity from strategizing, and we're focusing here on the element of strategy. But let me toss in one tip about creating a vision. A vision that's inspiring, appropriate, and achievable often derives from asking two questions: 1) Under what circumstances would our problems become assets? and 2) What opportunities emerge when we combine (integrate) our problems?

Take Detroit, for example. It's a huge city (140 square miles), and—after half a century of population loss—two intrinsically-linked problems emerged: too much vacant land and too few people.

Applying Question #1, vacant land becomes an asset if repurposed to produce food or energy, and low population becomes an asset if reducing food or energy consumption is a goal.

Applying Question #2, the juxtaposition of low population with copious amounts of food-and-energy-generating space means Detroit is uniquely positioned to become the world's first food-and/or-energy-independent major city. Not just planting a few urban gardens (like everyone else), but 100% self-sufficient via industrial-scale production. With all of the spin-off jobs and economic benefits that come with any industrial hub.

That might be an inspiring, appropriate vision. It wouldn't be an answer to all the city's problems, of course, but it would dramatically reposition the city in the eyes of the world.

Rather than being an iconic victim of the decline of the manufacturing economy, Detroit would be an icon of the global restoration economy: repurposing old assets, renewing quality of life, and reconnecting citizens to their food sources.

NOTE: That's only an example of the visioning process; not an actual recommendation. Detroit is doing a lot of things right these days, and might well become an icon of the restoration economy without any significant focus on urban farming. Repurposing their industrial buildings for new forms of manufacturing—such as small-scale, artisan or robotics—is one option that already has some local traction, for instance.

WHO SHOULD CREATE YOUR STRATEGY?

Planners plan, just like writers write. But some writers are also publishers, and so too are some planners strategists. But we must avoid the very common tendency to conflate strategizing with planning. They are two very different processes, and two very different skill sets.

It's relatively easy to write a plan if given a clear vision and strategy. So, planning can—and usually should—be a separate process run by different people. Planners have skills and perspectives (especially if they are engineers by training) that are often not appropriate for strategizing. If your goal in writing a plan is to go through a visioning, strategizing, and planning process, good on you. But if the goal is simply to produce a plan, boo on you. In a stable world, a plan could be a good thing, if well-researched and written by someone with deep insight. But who has a stable world?

Strategy is where the process of changing a complex adaptive system is simplified. It's where uncertainty and surprise are both expected and welcomed.

A healthy, living river pulses with periodic floods (surprises) that erode banks in some places, and deposit that sediment in others, so it's always changing its shape (more surprises). To an old-school civil engineer, a good river is one that never floods and never changes its shape. In other words, a dead river.

As mentioned earlier, a basic function of all engineering is to remove surprises from a system. This changes healthy complex living systems into unhealthy complicated mechanical systems. Complex systems have distributed controls; engineers tend to want centralized control. Strategizing requires a risk-taking mindset. Engineers are risk-eliminators, not risk-takers.

Los Angeles has been trying to restore the ugly, lifeless concrete ditch they call the Los Angeles River for well over a decade. They also want to revitalize the properties and neighborhoods bordering it, which have been devitalized and fragmented by this monstrosity.

While the U.S. Army Corps of Engineers did respond with a restoration plan about a decade ago, many city leaders feel that the Corps is the major obstacle to their dream.

In February of 2019, they demanded that the federal government give them back their river. They felt that the only agenda of the Corps of Engineers was flood control.

LA officials claim that the Corps' mission *"does not include myriad issues his agency's County Flood Control District regards as essential: water conservation, movement of sediment, graffiti removal, ecosystem friendly vegetation, homeless encampments and recreational opportunities."*

The good news? A new generation of civil engineers—arising from the modern dam-removal and climate resilience trends—is far more collaborative. They bring in biologists and community revitalization experts who are well-versed in the complexity of living systems. This combination of skills can yield wonderful surprises.

So, strategies should be created by people who aren't intimidated by complexity or terrified of surprises. They should also be intimately involved in the visioning process, and they should have a vested interest in the outcome (provided it's based on shared community goals).

The bottom line is that there's no "right" profession that should create the strategy. What's important is that it's the right strategy. What's also crucial is ensuring that all stakeholders are invited to help create the vision that the strategy delivers.

The person or organization responsible for the strategy must be identified. If everyone is responsible, no one is responsible.

But we shouldn't just toss the job to the first person (such as the planner) who comes to mind.

If your community or organization hires a strategy director, know that their job isn't to sit around dreaming up strategies: it's primarily a research position. Awareness precedes insight. They must be supremely aware of the environment in which you operate: trends, technologies, players, etc.

> *"The role of the CSO (Chief Strategy Officer)...is growing increasingly popular. Companies large and small...recognize the value of having a member of the C-suite who is primarily oriented to the long-term future of the company, and to sustainability and profitability. Unlike the CEO, whose day job often focuses on short-term performance, the CSO can concentrate on the future." – Paul Leinwand, Nils Naujok, and Joachim Rotering in PwC's Strategy + Business.*

I spent 6 years as the Director of Strategic Initiatives for a professional society in the construction industry. The organization had some 16,000 members (architects, engineers, and product manufacturers), but it hadn't done anything new in 25 years, and was on the brink of bankruptcy.

The new Executive Director wisely knew that he would have his hands full restructuring the organization, and wouldn't have time to focus on strategic research, so he hired me to do that. Part of my job was attending industry conferences to get a better feel for where our organization fit in the scheme of things, both present and future. A superior strategy derives from superior awareness.

This applies to communities, as well. It's vitally important to provide both strategic leadership training and a learning environment for local residents. Like so many important and mysterious elements of life, leadership is an emergent quality of living systems: we never know when or where in the community a leader will pop up, so we should invest in as many people as possible.

Success isn't just about who creates the strategy: it's also about who implements it. Personality counts, so don't become so dependent on your strategy (or process) that you forget to put the right people in charge. As with football teams, political, business, and non-profit leaders tend to be strong on defense or offense: seldom both. Economic revitalization often requires an offensive strategy. Climate resilience often requires a defensive strategy. Achieving both simultaneously requires a strategy that produces more of what you want while protecting what you have.

Putting a defensive strategist in charge of an offensive operation can be disastrous, as we discovered in the Battle of Anzio during World War II. The amphibious landing took place on January 22, 1944, and the operation ended June 5, 1944 with the capture of Rome.

On the surface, that would seem to be a success, but the goal wasn't just to take Rome: it was to weaken German forces and prevent them from rejoining their main force. In that, it was an abject failure. It also should have taken far less time and cost far fewer American lives to accomplish what it did.

The problem was U.S. Army Major General John P. Lucas. After taking the beach with almost no resistance, he went into defensive mode, digging in on the coast to protect against counter-attack.

He should have taken advantage of the element of surprise and moved swiftly towards Rome, flanking the Germans and cutting them off from support. Instead, the Germans moved their forces to the beach and bombarded the U.S. soldiers mercilessly for weeks. The Army finally sent Lucas home, and brought in Major General Lucian K. Truscott. Truscott had an offensive mindset, and swiftly got the troops moving towards Rome. Truscott wasn't necessarily smarter than Lucas: he simply had a personality that was appropriate to the job at hand.

HOW QUALIFIED ARE YOU TO CREATE A STRATEGY FOR YOUR CITY? MAYBE MORE THAN YOU THINK.

While simply having a strategy sets a community or region apart from most of its peers, it's not enough to guarantee success. To state the obvious, your strategy must be 1) appropriate for your place and time, 2) better than your competitors' strategies, and 3) well-executed.

Let's take another quick look at an strategic example from the business world. Three new airlines—all funded with oil money and all with ambitions of global dominance—have arisen in the United Arab Emirates: Emirates (founded 1985), Qatar Airways (founded 1993), and Etihad Airways (founded 2003). As the latecomer to the party, Etihad has been playing a game of catch-up.

In 2011, Etihad's CEO, James Hogan, decided that the fastest way to catch up would be via a strategy of acquisition, rather than "organic" growth. It made sense, on the surface.

But his timing was bad, due to a drop in oil prices (probably unavoidable). And his execution was bad, in terms of choosing their purchases (definitely avoidable). The company spent billions on major stakes in struggling airlines, only to see them become worthless as badly-managed airlines (like Alitalia) filed for bankruptcy, and badly-positioned airlines (like Air Berlin) posted huge losses. In May of 2017, Hogan was fired and replaced.

Some public leaders might find that story depressing. After all, if a sophisticated chief executive at a multi-billion-dollar company can screw up a strategy, what chance does a small-town mayor have of getting it right?

A very good chance, in fact. A unique characteristic of strategy is that one's ability to do it right is highly dependent on one's intimacy with the players, dynamics, and trends of a specific situation. It's far less dependent on one's education or overall experience. In other words, strategy is extremely context-sensitive. Hogan had a background in regional carriers, but the players, dynamics, and trends of the global carriers were new to him. Likewise, just because a mayor successfully revitalizes a village doesn't mean s/he is qualified to revitalize a nation.

TACTICS VERSUS STRATEGIES

"Do what you can, with what you have, where you are." – Teddy Roosevelt, U.S. President.

While we're on the subject of the airline industry, let's look at a more-recent disaster created when a CEO abandoned a good long-term strategic decision for a short-term tactical decision. As mentioned earlier, the duration of the action and intended impact is often the only differentiator between a tactic and a strategy.

In early 2011, Boeing chair and CEO James McNerney intended to design a totally new aircraft to replace the ancient 737. That was the right strategic decision. But by August of that year, it was clear that customers didn't want to wait for a new design, and five airlines placed orders for 496 re-engined 737s.

So McNenerny abandoned his strategic decision, and made a short-sighted tactical decision to stick new engines on slightly-modified version of a plane that first flew in 1967. The problem is that short, wide high-bypass modern engines don't fit well on low-slung aircraft designed for long, narrow, low-bypass engines. The multiple hardware and software "fixes" added to the plane to manage that bad design didn't work very well, and hundreds of people died in the subsequent crashes. McNenerny lost his job in 2015.

The result of abandoning that good long-term strategy for an expedient tactic is the greatest crisis in Boeing's history. The company went through the entire month of April 2019, without selling a single airplane. And that loss of income comes as massive lawsuits are being filed by airlines hurt by their inability to fly the 737 Max aircraft they have, or to take delivery of new equipment that were counting on. In December of 2019, they suspended production of the MAX, and a week later, the current CEO, Dennis Muilenburg, was fired.

Othertimes, a truly strategic decision is made, but it's the wrong one. Scana Corporation used to be South Carolina's largest public energy utility, tracing its history back to 1846. A single bad strategy devised a decade ago resulted in the company's disappearance in 2019.

Around 2008, they had to decide between upgrading a dangerous nuclear power plant or expending into safe, renewable energy. Nuclear was what they knew, so they stuck with it.

But the cost of that renovation ballooned to over $20 billion, and they abandoned the project. That left them in dire financial straits, and they were acquired by Virginia's Dominion Energy in January of 2019.

Around the same time Scana was making that fatal decision, NextEra Energy—the largest U.S. producer of renewable power—was doubling-down on their strategy. Given that photovoltaic energy is now about 1/100th the cost of nuclear (when full-cost accounting is applied), that would seem to be a no-brainer, strategy-wise. In stark contrast to Scana's crash-and-burn, NextEra's shares have doubled in value since 2014.

Public leaders are always admonishing unemployed or underemployed citizens to enroll in education or training course that will match their skills to the changing economy.

But sometimes, entire communities need to be retrained for a new economy, especially when they've been overly-dependent on a single industry. Worker retraining for in-demand skills is just one of several revitalizing tactics for a community, but that same training is strategic for the individual. It's also an example of fixing the present (tactics) and the future (strategy) together.

Again: tactics are for achieving short-term goals, such as a platoon of soldiers taking a hill. Strategies are for achieving long-term goals, such as winning the war, which involves deciding which hills need to be taken.

To recap: the first step to creating a strategy is to know what you want (vision). If you're now saying "well, duh", you'd be shocked at how many places are spending millions on projects without knowing what they're trying to achieve, other than "more".

TIMING, SCOPE, AND STARTING POINT

> *"Action is a great restorer and builder of confidence. Inaction is not only the result, but the cause, of fear."* – Norman Vincent Peale.

The right strategy can arrive at the wrong time.

While there are always ways to boost the economy and quality of life of a place, some times are better than others to launch all-out revitalization programs. Revitalization is like farming: there's a time for preparing the soil, a time for planting, a time for harvesting, and a time for resting.

There's also a time for restoring farmland back to the original wetland to achieve flood resilience, and a time for repurposing exhausted farmland, such as for renewable energy production. Of course, not all old assets need to be repurposed, but we should explore any such opportunities before embarking on renewing their current form.

Repurposing can also involve expanding a project's scope by adding new purposes to a viable current function. For instance, a switch from toxic, soil-depleting industrial agriculture to regenerative agriculture keeps food production as the central purpose. But it adds carbon sequestration, soil rebuilding, watershed restoration and enhanced biodiversity to the mix of goals.

The right strategy at the right time can still fail, if you get the scope wrong. Too often, scope is taken for granted. An organization focused on downtown will automatically devise a downtown revitalization program. A city or county agency will automatically create a citywide or countywide program. A good strategy will take scope into consideration. In fact, adjusting the scope of an effort (up or down) is sometimes all that's necessary to revive a faltering initiative.

For instance, if your goal is to boost quality of life—including air quality, water quality/quantity, human health, safety, recreational opportunities, etc.—that usually can't be done at a downtown, or even a community level. You'll need to regenerate your surrounding neighborhoods, watershed, family farms (local food system), green spaces, and so on. That would require at least a countywide scope, if not a regional or even statewide scope.

But even finding the right time and scope isn't enough if your starting point is wrong. A good strategy will identify the right focal point to begin the revitalization process.

You want to score some quick and early "wins" to boost confidence and gather momentum. Few communities have the funds to repurpose, renew, and reconnect all their assets at once.

Much reconnecting is now needed in cities worldwide, after decades of unplanned or badly-planned sprawl. Thus, public transit is often most efficient starting point: it can unify physically-isolated neighborhoods and other assets into a vibrant community.

In some places, heritage will be the starting point, such as restoring a historic downtown theater. In other places, remediating brownfield sites should be first, in order to create "shovel-ready" opportunities for redevelopers.

Elsewhere, restoring natural resources—fisheries, farmland soils, watersheds, ecosystems, etc.—will be the obvious first step towards revitalization. All too frequently these days, disasters are the genesis of revitalization and resilience initiatives.

Identifying your ideal timing, scope, and starting point are all functions of a strategic analysis. But they will accomplish nothing if they don't lead to action.

For both individuals and communities, action is often the best therapy for inertia and depression. This advice might seem at odds with the earlier advice to create a vision and strategy before acting, but if your first goal is activate the populace, completing a successful physical project might be the best strategy for achieving it.

But creating a vision is also action, so choose carefully. In some cases, creating your renewable asset map will be the best first step: it's an easily-understandable goal, and the process of creating it—especially if you primarily use local volunteers—will boost the residents' awareness of their opportunities, thus inspiring new hope.

REFRAMING ASSUMPTIONS

> *"If you want to make small changes, change the way you do things. If you want to make big changes, change the way you see things."*
> – regenerative rancher Gabe Brown.

Good strategizing, especially when dealing with social issues, often involves reframing our perceptions and assumptions.

For instance, many cities are being redesigned for the convenience of humans, getting away from previous plans that prioritized the convenience of deadly 3000-pound steel projectiles (cars). Creating an effective strategy for making a place safer and more efficient for pedestrians might thus mean reframing the problem from "pedestrians crossing streets" to "cars crossing sidewalks".

Planner Brent Toderian takes it a step further, and refers to cafes and street seating as "pedestrian parking". That perspective makes it clear who has priority, which helps keep decision-making properly focused.

Since strategies are driven by vision + challenge (what one wants plus what one must overcome to get it), identifying the actual challenge is crucial: too often, we confuse cause and effect, as mentioned earlier.

For instance, is your affordable housing crisis driven primarily by a paucity of inexpensive residential units? Or is the real problem too many people with low incomes? If the latter, then equitable economic revitalization becomes the primary challenge, not cheap housing.

Or maybe the real problem is that too much of your citizens' income goes to car payments, car insurance, car repairs, and gasoline. If so, the challenge might be creating more public transit and transit-oriented redevelopment. Don't start strategizing until you've examined your assumptions.

A vision can actually be written so as to embody (or at least imply) a strategy. For instance, Mark Gerzon's new book from Berrett-Koehler is titled *The Reunited States of America: How We Can Bridge the Partisan Divide*. In it, he describes a vision/strategy for restoring good governance and social cohesion, which would greatly boost socioeconomic revitalization in the United States.

He calls citizens and leaders who put the nation's interests above political interests "transpartisans". Here's his combined vision/strategy: "*Transpartisans are open to learning from each other, instead of insisting they already have all the answers. They work respectfully with people they disagree with, instead of vilifying and avoiding them. They're willing to try new solutions, instead of clinging to the old* approaches. And after the campaign is over, they insist their elected representatives come together to govern, not to just continue campaigning."

The social fragmentation problem he's addressing in that book in no small thing. In 1960, a poll asked Americans if they would be displeased if their children married someone of the opposite political party. 4% of Democrats and 5% of Republicans said "yes". When the same poll was conducted in 2010, it was 30% of Democrats and 50% of Republicans. Just a few years ago, a study showed that Americans of all stripes would pay money to avoid having to listen to the opinions of someone from the opposite party. If members of a society consider each other the enemy, and won't even speak to each other, that's a society on its way down.

Nature conservation is one traditional area of disagreement between conservative and progressives. But consider that there are no truly pristine ecosystems left on the planet: all conservation now requires some degree of restoration, even if it's only reconnecting to other ecosystems. Consider also that restoration is a far less partisan issue than conservation—almost everyone loves to make ugly, dying places more beautiful and productive—and that partisanship is blocking much progress these days.

Therefore, my recommendation is to focus on the "re" stuff that people already agree on, rather than trying to convince people to embrace conservation. The more we restore, the more we understand the true cost of not conserving, so one leads to the other.

There are three types of organizations that desperately need their own unique strategies for advancing—or becoming a part of—the process of enhancing revitalization and/or resilience: governments, foundations and institutions of higher education.

THE ROLE OF GOVERNMENTS IN ADVANCING RESILIENT PROSPERITY

"Coming together is the beginning.
Keeping together is progress.
Working together is success." – Henry Ford.

As originally suggested in *The Restoration Economy*, there are three basic personality types at work in the world (from the development perspective). They

correspond to three basic modes of wealth creation, and three corresponding types of government policy:
- Sprawlers expand cities and extract virgin resources;
- Sustainers maintain cities and conserve nature;
- Revitalizers renew cities and restore nature.

Where do real estate developers fit in that scenario? Developers are usually Sprawlers. Redevelopers are usually Revitalizers. The fact that densification ("intensification" in Canada) is replacing sprawl in most nations means that Revitalizers are displacing Sprawlers.

I say "usually" because not all redevelopers revitalize. Even a lot of "new urbanist" redevelopments are highly destructive, replacing interesting urban environments with hyper-commercial sterility. Many of them are the urban equivalent of replacing a forest with a tree farm. The right thing (walkability, in this case) can always be done badly.

Poor implementation aside, a taxonomy such as the one above can greatly simplify the process of crafting policies and choosing policymakers. If you're building a new nation and need new cities, Sprawlers are the folks you need. But who on Earth is in that situation these days?

What we've got is a planet burdened by badly-planned, unplanned, or simply obsolete cities. For them, we need the Sustainers and the Revitalizers. Sprawlers are counterproductive when one is heavy on damaged or underused built assets, heavy on overused natural assets, and light on healthy greenspace and agricultural land.

So, an initial step on the path to a brighter future is for governments to realize that derelict natural and built assets are doorways—not obstacles—to urban and rural economic growth.

> *"A leader takes people where they want to go. A great leader takes people where they don't necessarily want to go, but ought to be."*
> *– Rosalynn Carter, former U.S. First Lady.*

Some U.S. states are blessed with governors who understand the key role urban revitalization plays in state economies. For example, on January 15, 2015, New York Governor Andrew Cuomo announced a $1.5 billion Upstate New York Economic Revitalization Competition. Three years earlier, he had offered $1 billion over 10 years to restore the greater Buffalo economy, a program that's working wonders. Cuomo also has an annual $100 million Downtown Revitalization

Initiative, which awards $10 million to the one community in each of ten regions that comes up with the best revitalization proposal.

But, for the most part, citizens everywhere are rightly disgusted with their state and national "leaders". The good news is that the quality of mayors seems to be improving. Nonetheless, serious problems remain, and a very large percentage of them are directly or indirectly related to revitalization and/or resilience. So, what almost all places need it someone to create a more coherent focus on these areas, so weaknesses / threats can be identified, and strengths / opportunities can be leveraged. For now, let's call these imaginary professionals "RE Facilitators".

Government-appointed RE Facilitators could help redevelopers by providing real-time mapping of local property renewal, repurposing, and reconnection opportunities. They could land-bank them to speed property assembly for large projects. Granted, communities can do all this without creating any new positions or departments. But why should something as crucial as renewal be homeless, lacking a dedicated champion?

> *"A community is like a ship;*
> *everyone ought to be prepared to take the helm."*
> *– Henrik Ibsen, Norwegian playwright.*

In this disorganized, vision-less environment, many developers become professional devitalizers. Instead of aiding local regeneration, they foster degeneration (professional degenerates?). But we shouldn't blame them. We kept electing people who let developers create places without hearts, populated by over-medicated, underpaid, socially-isolated, traffic-numbed commuters seeking joy as consumers. Together, they often built places not worthy of the work it would take to revitalize them.

Fixers are ready and willing to invest in your place, IF you inspire confidence in your local future (they want your rising tide to raise their boat), and get out of their way. Many distressed places can't afford capital-intensive projects to fix their present. But they can afford a strategy to fix their future, which inspires the necessary confidence.

In her article, "It Takes a Village: The Rise of Community-Driven Infrastructure" in *The Atlantic* (January 30, 2015) , writer Greta Byrum says, "*A decade ago, Philadelphia's outdated sewer system...was crumbling, causing a nasty brew of storm-water, raw sewage, and pollutants to flow directly into local waterways. But the cash-strapped metropolis... couldn't afford to build a new system. So the city decided to think small—and local, and cooperative—to construct something big and different. The city rolled out its "Green City Clean Waters" plan in 2011: a 25-year effort to let residents take the lead in creating a web of small interconnected "green" infrastructure projects like roadside plantings, green roofs, porous pavements, street trees, and rain gardens...The key to the "Green City Clean Waters" plan was building layers of community engagement and partnerships over technical and governance systems. ...schools and libraries will teach kids about water with hands-on active learning projects like rain gardens, while the city enforces requirements for the replacement of non-porous surfaces, offers funding and support for neighborhood initiatives, and streamlines bureaucratic procedures to facilitate their approval and success."*

Despite the focus on dysfunctional leadership in this chapter, it should be acknowledged that the right leader at the right time can do wonders. My 2008 book, *Rewealth*, showed how Bob Corker was the perfect mayor for Chattanooga at the perfect time, arriving with his big-money friends just as a resident-led revitalization program had perfectly set the scene for investment in redeveloping the downtown waterfront. Ten years earlier, he would likely have been a disastrous mayor for Chattanooga.

Another example was California Governor Jerry Brown's terms as mayor of Oakland from 1999 to 2007. Brown's "10K Plan" successfully attracted 10,000 new residents to Oakland's ghost town city center. This was a high point for a city long-plagued with bad governance, the highest per-capita crime rate in the country, and possibly the nation's worst police department.

Despite a boost during the Brown years, Oakland is a classic example of how an inept government can undermine even the most opportune of circumstances. After all, Oakland has sunnier weather than its wealthier, fog-plagued neighbor across the bay: San Francisco. Accessible waterfronts are powerful revitalizers, yet this desperate city has more waterfront than 99% of U.S. cities. Oakland enjoys an excellent harbor, the fifth-busiest container port in the U.S. (with excellent freight rail connections), and it's surrounded by lovely hills that boast glorious views of San Francisco and the San Francisco Bay.

It also enjoys another proven revitalization factor: tremendous racial diversity: African-American, Latino, Asian, and Caucasian. Top this off with the fact that it's within one of America's most prosperous regions, and it's a city that has everything going for it.

Yet it doesn't. Today, the only thing Oakland seems to have going for it is cheap real estate. The city is attracting many wealthier residents from San Francisco, one of the most unaffordable cities in the nation. This should be a positive, yet poor governance has managed to turn it into a negative. Instead of guiding the redevelopment so that all citizens benefit from it, the city has allowed developers to build isolated islands of prosperity. This has inflamed resentment in a city that already suffered from a high degree of economic inequity.

One thing I've noticed in virtually every city in which I've worked is that newcomers are often the most valuable participants in a revitalization process. This is especially true in cities with a long history of struggle: newcomers aren't plagued with the "we tried that and it didn't work" syndrome. In Oakland, tons of newcomers bring desperately-needed money, and what do the natives call them? Invaders. With poor governance, blessings can turn into curses.

Progressives are tired of corporate control of government. Conservatives are tired of government inefficiency. But both want to see their communities revitalized, and their children growing up healthy, happy and secure. That makes the pursuit of resilient prosperity a path to more functional governance.

Unfortunately, too few government leaders have a clear idea of what factors contribute to revitalization and resilience, and which ones retard them. This makes it difficult for them to create initiatives that stimulate, manage, monitor, and report efforts to create resilient prosperity.

THE ROLE OF FOUNDATIONS IN ADVANCING RESILIENT PROSPERITY

In his 2014 book, *Rebalancing Society: Radical Renewal Beyond Left, Right, & Center*, Henry Mintzberg says that healthy societies are built on three balanced pillars: 1) respected governments; 2) responsible enterprises; and 3) robust voluntary associations (nonprofits, NGOs, foundations, etc.).

When local, state, and federal funding for community improvement decreases to a crisis point, foundations often step in. There are several varieties of foundations, though they generally fall under two general labels: private or public.

Private foundations get their funding from an individual, a family, or a company. The best-known are those set up by the industrialists and robber barons of the 19th and early 20th centuries: Rockefeller Foundation, Ford Foundation, Carnegie Foundation, and so on.

Private foundations created by commercial banks often focus on community revitalization. This benefits the community and the bank, since revitalization increases both the value of real estate and the success of businesses. This reduces mortgage and business loan defaults. The Bank of America Charitable Foundation was created in 1958. Its mission statement says "*the Foundation funds (local) institutions to help enrich the community and advance overall community revitalization.*"

A more-recent such creation is the TD Charitable Foundation, created in 2002 by Canada's TD Bank. Their stated mission includes "*community revitalization and the preservation and development of affordable housing.*"

There are two kinds of public foundations: grant-making charities (often fighting diseases or social problems on a national or global basis), and community foundations. What they have in common is funding derived from diverse sources; individuals, corporations, public agencies, and other foundations. An example of a grant-making charitable group is the Foundation for Rural and Regional Renewal (Australia), which has a "Repair-Restore-Renew" disaster recovery program.

Community foundations (often referred to as "place-based foundations") are also grant-making public charities, but they differ in two ways: 1) their focus is defined by geography, rather than by issues, and 2) they tend to focus more on providing logistical support to local non-profits, rather than just handing out money. In a few cases—such as one of my clients, the Calgary Foundation—a community foundation is so successful that they start handing out grants far afield from their initial geographic scope.

This section will focus primarily on the revitalizing roles of private foundations. We'll return to community foundations later, since they are especially well-positioned to lead communities into the next generation of effective, efficient and equitable resilient prosperity programs.

For the past two or three decades, most philanthropy related to helping communities and the natural environment has been focused on "greening" or "sustainability" efforts. This is all well and good, but let's face it: it's a bit late. As noted earlier, sustainable development should have been our mode for many generations already. Our world is now so degraded that only restorative development can give us a healthier, wealthier, more beautiful future, especially in the face of rising populations.

In many cases, restorative philanthropy is hidden behind the labels of "sustainability" or "resilience". As mentioned earlier, reducing new damage and new waste is vital, of course. Anyone who's satisfied with sustaining the world as it is just isn't paying attention. Their heart's in the right place, but we need to revitalize the communities we've already created, and replenish the natural resources we've damaged and depleted.

Now, restorative philanthropy is taking hold, joining the government and business spending that has long-dominated revitalization efforts. Philanthropic organizations increasingly realize that revitalizing communities and restoring natural resources is by far the most effective use of their precious funds.

The trend can only grow, since recycling and retrofitting our cities—plus repairing our natural resources—is the ONLY sure way to increase health and wealth in our broken world. Today, it's hard to find a major private foundation

that isn't focusing on renewing the natural, built, and/or socioeconomic environments to some degree. A few quick examples:
- The New York Restoration Project is developing a shareable model for community revitalization with $250,000 from the Knight Foundation;
- The C.S. Mott Foundation funds the Flint Area Economic Revitalization for that stricken city;
- The Kellogg Foundation has given $2.4 million to LINC Community Revitalization Inc. in Grand Rapids, Michigan, and is supporting many revitalization efforts in Detroit;
- The distressed Anacostia area of Washington, DC wants to repurpose the remains of an ugly abandoned river bridge as a public park. The 11th St. Bridge Park combines four powerful revitalizing elements: connectivity, water, greenspace, and pedestrianism. Early foundation backers included the Educational Foundation of America, Horning Family Fund, Prince Charitable Trusts, and Fetzer Memorial Trust.

While generally a negative, socially-destabilizing force, today's wealth concentration trend has one positive effect: a growth in philanthropic funding. Zachary Mider, in the May 12-18, 2014 Bloomberg Businessweek, says "Over the past few decades, the rise in fortunes of the country's richest people has created a golden age of philanthropy, comparable to the one that spawned the Carnegie and Rockefeller foundations a century ago. ...Because Congress offers tax deductions for philanthropy, this growing breed of donor is deciding the fate of billions of dollars that would otherwise flow to the government."

In the U.S. in 2013, university business schools received 67 single-donor gifts of over $1 million, the most ever in a single year. A 2014 study from the Boston College Center on Wealth and Philanthropy projects that a record $27 trillion is expected to be donated by Americans to charities between 2007 and 2061.

It's not just "rising money meets rising need": there's a supreme level of satisfaction that comes with bringing dead or dying places back to life, and this motivates donors.

> *"Brain scans reveal that the mere thought of helping others by planning to make a donation makes people happier."*
> *– Bruce DeBoskey, Denver Post, May 11, 2014.*

Restorative philanthropy is now regenerating, renovating, renewing, remediating, replenishing and revitalizing more of our world with each passing year. Add to this grant-making the rapid growth of restorative impact investments—often by the same philanthropic entities—and the numbers start to get serious.

As regards revitalizing—or at least supporting—poverty-stricken neighborhoods, government programs tend to focus on what's urgent, often at the expense of what's important. Addressing needs that are both urgent and important—such as food assistance, healthcare, etc.—tends to be capital-intensive, but they help make poverty survivable. Making poverty escapable is a bit less urgent than eating, but no less important. It's also less capital-intensive, which is why that tends to be the focus of many foundation and other privately-funded efforts.

Some private foundations—such as the Walton Family Foundation, Orton Family Foundation, and Kresge Foundation—have practiced restorative philanthropy for decades, often focused on the U.S. "Rust Belt". The Surdna Foundation is unique in that they focus on both community revitalization and nature restoration.

The best way to describe how private foundations can put a distressed city on the path to rapid, resilient renewal is via a dramatic success story. Let's revisit Chattanooga, Tennessee for a moment.

In 1969, Walter Cronkite announced on national TV that Chattanooga had been labeled "the dirtiest city in America" by the U.S. government. Air pollution was sometimes so bad that people had to drive with their headlights on in the middle of the day. Motivating by a potent combination of humiliation and regulation, the city spent the next decade remedying the situation.

Chattanooga eventually won the EPA's first Clean Air Award. In the process or restoring their air quality, the people realized that they could actually work together productively. That led to what the city did after they cleaned their air, which earned them global renown.

By the early 80's—despite their cleaner air—the city was still losing 5000 manufacturing jobs annually. Crime was high, racial problems were rife, and the city was dysfunctionally divided...except those stakeholders who had worked together on the air pollution problem.

In 1986, that group helped form a revitalization process that took they city from basket case to a revitalization "poster child". Two private foundations—both built on the fortunes of independent Coca-Cola bottlers—were directly responsible: The Lyndhurst Foundation and the Benwood Foundation. Their funding kicked off two years of public engagement and visioning, via the non-profit Chattanooga Venture. Virtually every good thing that has happened to the city in the past 30 years has its roots—directly or indirectly—in Chattanooga Venture's network of "fixers", and in their ongoing revitalization program.

The Lyndhurst Foundation, led by Jack Murrah (now retired), provided catalytic funding for virtually every major initiative that ignited Chattanooga's rebirth. The Benwood Foundation provided follow-on support for most of these renewal initiatives, with a heavier focus on arts and culture. Chattanooga Venture created stakeholder cohesion.

Venture's mission was to engage the public in the creation of a shared vision of the community's future. That vision integrated the renewal of their natural, built, and socioeconomic assets with their dreams. It provided a home for that vision, and the resulting continuity allowed renewal momentum to build. Besides visioning, Chattanooga Venture provided learning: lectures by revitalization leaders from other cities, and field trips for local leaders to revitalized cities.

Crucially, Chattanooga Venture also provided a forum for effective, transparent public-private partnering, using a simple-but-effective process. They created a task force whenever new challenges and/or opportunities were identified. They chose people for these task forces—each possessing unique resources of potential value to the solution—who were in a position to do something about it. As a result, they had ready-made public-private partnerships when the task forces made their recommendations.

Chattanooga's best-known feature, the Tennessee Aquarium, was added to their revitalized waterfront in 1992. The 21st Century Waterfront initiative was created when the aforementioned Bob Corker (now U.S. Senator) became mayor in 2001. It expanded and renovated the aquarium, Discovery Museum, and Hunter Museum of American Art, and created pathways from the Hunter to the waterfront. By 2005, when the 21st Century Waterfront plan was finished, the Tennessee Riverwalk had been expanded to 11 miles of trail down to the Chickamauga Dam, and over 1100 trees had been planted on this old industrial land.

Every $1 of public money invested in recreational space and art tends to attract about $13 of private investment. Chattanooga spent $9 million remediating the waterfront site of an old enameling plant. Via ecological restoration, they created the 22-acre Renaissance Park. Developers have now surrounded the park with $110 million worth of condos, stores, restaurants and a LEED-certified shopping center.

In 2011, Volkswagen opened the world's only LEED Platinum-certified auto manufacturing plant on what was previously a highly-contaminated waterfront brownfield. The 1400-acre parcel was once an ammunition plant, manufacturing up to 30,000,000 pounds of TNT per month for World War II, the Korean War, and the Vietnam War.

The transformation is dramatic: the new plant has 33,000 solar panels generating 9.5 million watts. VW went beyond green, to regenerative: they restored two creeks on the property to enhance habitat for native species, providing a wildlife corridor around the plant.

How did Chattanooga clinch this $1 billion, 3200-employee prize, over the dozens of cities vying for it? They offered $577 million of incentives to VW, but other cities made similar offers. The clincher: VW wanted the waterfront trail extended to their site, so employees could enjoy walking to the downtown. Quality of life and connectivity were the differentiators.

> *"People move for reasons besides employment. Pittsburgh's net gain may point more to quality-of-life advantages than economic opportunity because the city's job growth has not been that much better than the state's...."*
> *– Kurt Rankin, PNC Financial Services Group.*

Mayors and public leaders from around the globe make pilgrimages to witness the "miraculous" rebirth of Chattanooga. All of this came about because a private foundation funded the creation of what became a very effective revitalization program that included all of the elements of the RECONOMICS Process. But they accidentally killed the ongoing program element of their process, as described in the case study in *Rewealth*.

In Jane Jacobs' 1984 book, *Cities and the Wealth of Nations*, she advocated for both ongoing efforts and for adaptive management: "In its very nature, successful economic development has to be open-ended rather than goal-oriented, and has to make itself up expediently and empirically as it goes along." That's what Chattanooga did for almost two decades, and it worked beautifully.

PARTNERING WITH A COMMUNITY FOUNDATION FOR RESILIENT PROSPERITY

Many foundations that attempt to revitalize a community—or make it more resilient—have a problem: When the only tool you have is money, every problem looks financial. Money is what most foundations bring to the table.

At the worst foundations, it's the only thing they bring to the table. At the best foundations, money is primarily used to help birth and perpetuate good ideas until they can feed themselves. And those good ideas are often promulgated by the community training provided by those same foundations. Community foundations are often very good at this, so they can make ideal partners for revitalization efforts.

The first community foundation (The Cleveland Foundation) was created by Frederick Goff in Ohio in 1914. There are now over 1700 community foundations around the world, with 700+ in the U.S. Community foundations tend to have a high level of public trust and a broad focus (often related to quality of life). They engage all levels of public and private leadership, and seldom operate in silos.

My first encounter came in 2007, when I keynoted a conference sponsored by the Buffalo Community Foundation (NY). But I didn't realize their true potential until I keynoted the Vital City event held in 2014 by The Calgary Foundation (Alberta, Canada) and met their CEO, Eva Friesen. The range of projects they sponsor that contribute to resilient prosperity is truly inspiring.

The Calgary Foundation is playing a key role in shifting a city best known as an "oil town" towards more-diversified economic growth based on renewing their existing assets. They've funded a wide array of projects that renew their heritage, neighborhoods, green infrastructure, arts, education, and more. In other words, they're perfectly positioned to be the heart of an resilient prosperity program.

For example, after the catastrophic flood of June, 2013, the Calgary Foundation's Flood Rebuilding Fund granted nearly $8.5 million via 125 grants to groups across Alberta. Environmental stewards Friends of Kananaskis Country was one of those recipients. I was kindly taken on a hiking tour of the flood-damaged Heart Creek Trail, which was magnificently rebuilt with both Calgary Foundation and provincial funding.

Most community foundations already have an extensive and functional network of both funders and fixers in place. They only need to add an appropriate process to turn these valuable resources into a renewal engine.

On October 2, 2014, the Council on Foundations (Washington, DC) published an article by Scott Westcott titled The Community Foundation of Greater Des Moines played a key leadership role in developing and executing a long-range community improvement plan.

Here's an excerpt from that article that illustrates how well-positioned community foundations are as the nexus of a resilient prosperity program:

"A few years back, leaders in Des Moines, Iowa, faced a common dilemma. While there was no shortage of people and organizations working to better the community, there was little alignment or master planning to coordinate the efforts. 'The city had a plan, Polk County had a plan, the United Way had a plan – there were lots of plans,' says Kristi Knous, President of the Community Foundation of Greater Des Moines. 'What was lacking was a process that involved community input and tied everything together to create an

integrated approach to moving the Greater Des Moines area forward.' Recognizing the potential of a more integrated approach, the Community Foundation saw the unique opportunity to play a key leadership role in creating a sustainable future vision for Greater Des Moines."

Community foundations would need training to better-understand revitalization, resilience, and adaptive management. But for most, this added responsibility would involve few new activities: just a strategic process for better-integrating, focusing and delivering what they're already doing. The downside is community foundations' lack of official authority.

But cities and counties could endow them with power via a public-private partnership. The legal mechanism to do so would vary with local laws. For instance, Iowa has statute 28E.4, which says "Any public agency of this state may enter into an agreement with one or more public or private agencies for joint or cooperative action."

The result? A public-private resilient prosperity partnership. In fact, a formal partnership between a city or county government and the local community foundation might well be ideal. Such partnerships would enable elected leaders to instantly create a resilient prosperity program using a trusted, existing infrastructure. In one fell swoop, the funding mechanisms and project evaluation / implementation processes of the community foundation would enable the city to launch a system with no added bureaucracy, and little new public expense. It would also open significant new public and private funding sources to the community foundation.

States, provinces, and nations don't have such a shortcut available to them. But most have the resources to create their resilient prosperity program from scratch, which would give them the control they usually demand. Such higher-level partnerships could actually be fairly simple, with very small budgets. If they did nothing more than encourage and facilitate the creation of local resilient prosperity partnerships—and then supported them—they'd be performing a valuable service, likely with an impressive ROI.

One of the most important factors in creating a prosperity partnership would be making it resilient in the face of changing political administrations. For instance, Philadelphia's Delaware River Waterfront Corporation (DRWC) was formed in 2009 to revitalize the city's waterfront. Then-mayor Michael Nutter appointed all board members. But at its October 2014 meeting, the DRWC board changed its bylaws so that ten Board members would be chosen by the board itself, with the mayor choosing just three.

In a November 17, 2014 article by Jared Brey in PlanPhilly, Matt Ruben, chair of the Central Delaware Advocacy Group said *"Our biggest concern moving forward was, 'How do we ensure continuity at the DRWC when a new mayor comes in?' Now DRWC has effectively made itself mayor-proof, and we can stay focused on the waterfront."* The best leaders know when it's time to share or transfer power.

This partnering approach suggested here could be considered a repurposing of existing social infrastructure. With those 1700 community foundations worldwide, a global network of local resilient prosperity partnerships might be the quickest and most politically-resilient path to revitalizing our planet.

THE ROLE OF HIGHER EDUCATION IN ADVANCING RESILIENT PROSPERITY

When did you last meet someone with a Ph.D. or a Master's in revitalization? Or resilience? Or adaptive management? Despite trillions of dollars spent annually worldwide on bringing places back to life—and despite the high rate of failure of such expenditures—academia largely turns a blind eye to regeneration.

They don't mind teaching and researching the technical disciplines that renew specific assets: there are many courses in historic preservation, brownfields remediation, infrastructure renewal, and the like. But when it comes to the process of reversing the stagnation or decline of a place, our institutions of higher learning seem content to allow their students to remain in a state of ignorance.

If you wanted to appoint someone locally to head-up your revitalization and/or resilience efforts, wouldn't you prefer to hire a person with relevant training, certification, or degree? That's how all other hiring works.

Universities must take seriously this challenge of creating professionals who revitalize in a world that's simultaneously experiencing rapid urbanization, agricultural depletion, natural resource collapse, not to mention the global climate crisis. They must realize that urban planning degrees don't address revitalization. Nor do degrees in public policy, public administration, public works, architecture, landscape architecture, civil engineering, and so on.

The best launching point for such a degree would be one grounded in the real world, not in academic theory. This could start with a partnership between a university and the city in which it's based. The school would get access to local data, lessons learned, and government internships. Local officials could do classroom lectures, while getting access to new research and curricula.

How could a discipline and profession focused on revitalization and/or resilient prosperity come about? There are three standard routes:

- Academic: This would require a benefactor to endow a chair to fund and advance research, curriculum development, and degrees;
- Governmental: A national agency (such as HUD or EPA in the U.S.) might perceive the need for such a discipline at the local, state, and national levels, and provide funding to schools or organizations to create the appropriate research, curricula, and certifications;
- Private: A professional association could be formed for this purpose. Its members would come from the myriad fragmented current disciplines that address revitalization. This could be a new organization, or a new focus of an existing organization. One such is revealed in Chapter 12.

It's not that universities don't study strategy, adaptive management, revitalization or resilience: the problem is that they don't teach it in a way that produces people prepared to manage the renewal of a place. This is a waste, because there are myriad academics doing work of crucial importance to advancing strategies and processes for both revitalization and resilience.

For instance, in his Harvard Business Review article "The Execution Trap", Roger Martin, former dean of the University of Toronto's Rotman School of Management, says separation of strategy and execution is a major flaw in executive thinking. We are all arguing the relative importance of good strategy versus good execution as if they were unrelated, so thinkers and doers work in dysfunctional isolation from each other. Communities suffer a worse problem. Not only do they separate implementation from strategy, but what they refer to as "strategy" is often just hope.

Martin says separation of strategy and execution is promulgated by management consulting firms. Why? Because it allows them to blame failures on clients' flawed implementation of their genius strategy. Urban planning firms also tend to avoid implementation. When a plan fails, they blame the mayor, the city council, unruly developers, or the citizens (NIMBYism, etc.) for screwing up their plan.

The psychological and health benefits of living in a revitalizing place are legion. Some are surprising. Did you know it cuts your electricity bill? Research led by Ping Dong of the University of Toronto found that people who feel more hopeless about their economy and employment opportunities prefer brighter lighting. 20.6% more power is used per 1 point less hopeful (9-point scale) folks feel about the future.

Another insight into the revitalization dynamic that we wouldn't know without academic research is why post-disaster cities are often more-resilient cities. In 2012, Eiji Yamamura of Japan's Seinan Gakuin University published a paper called "Atomic bombs and the long-run effect on trust: Experiences in Hiroshima and Nagasaki", based on researching survivors of those 1945 atomic bombings.

He found they were 16%-17% more likely than normal to trust other people. Trust is a crucial element of revitalization. It's the transactional lubricant of all economies: the more there is, the more efficiently they operate. Those leading post-disaster rebuilding projects should tap this silver lining.

Due to the lack of academic and practitioner rigor, a large "superficial revitalization" industry has emerged, as described earlier: mayors desperate to be seen as "doing something" commission comprehensive plans with no intention of implementing them. Or they buy instant "revitalization" in the form of street banners, planters and façade renovations.

> *"Council reviewed proposals to revitalize major thoroughfares...Revitalization proposals include a slogan contest, hanging banners and planters, brochures and street landscaping. Borough Manager Don Curley requested ... $1,000 for brochures and $6,000 for banners and planters."*
> *– Times Herald, July 21, 2015 (Bridgeport, CT).*

Some folks criticize downtown or Main Street façade improvement programs as superficial revitalization strategies that don't address underlying problems. They say they just provide visual revitalization. But as long as they call them façade improvement —and not revitalization—such efforts are worthwhile and honest. The fact is, most "revitalization" initiatives are themselves a façade.

Some say that commissioning a new comprehensive plan will revitalize the community. Some say a community-led visioning session will do the job. Others say that tax breaks for employers will do it. The list goes on, and they are all façades...all are superficial efforts that—lacking a strategic process—don't change the fundamentals, and so won't change the socioeconomic trajectory.

The social impacts of revitalizing a place are probably far deeper and broader than we know. I'd love to see graduate students comparing the health and psychological factors in revitalizing versus devitalizing places. Even better: randomized controlled trials for various revitalization tools and factors. A great step towards this hard-data direction is the new ISO 37120 standard, comprising indicators for city services and quality of life. This combines government-collected "Big Data" with citizen-acquired data. As wearable technology becomes more ubiquitous, these quality of life indicators will come closer to real-time.

Many cities are being hit with rapid population growth at the same time they're experiencing rapid aging, deterioration, and design obsolescence of their infrastructure. So, we encounter places that brag about their growth while they are actually in decline. The traditional assumption is that loss of population leads to economic decline, but it's not that simple. In 2019, Maxwell Hartt of Cardiff University published "The Prevalence of Prosperous Shrinking Cities", which explored the results of his research into this dynamic in U.S. cities.

Here's an excerpt from that paper's Abstract:

"The majority of the shrinking cities literature focuses solely on instances of population loss and economic decline. This article argues that shrinking cities exist on a spectrum between prosperity and decline. Taking a wider view of population loss, I explore the possibility of prosperous shrinking cities: if they exist, where they exist, and under what conditions shrinking cities can thrive. Examining census place data from the 1980 to 2010 U.S. Census and American Community Surveys, 27 percent of 886 shrinking cities were found to have income levels greater than their surrounding regions."

So, places can shrink and grow simultaneously. That's not news to those of us who have studied revitalization for decades, but it's news to most public leaders. They not only don't understand how to revitalize: they don't even understand the dynamics that drive devitalization. Most young people want to leave the world a better place, and choose studies in various forms of public management and policymaking, but few universities teach anything directly related to revitalization. Seems like a mismatch. So again: why isn't community revitalization taught in universities? Money and (again) fear.

Money because most universities only have one mode for entering a new realm of research and curriculum development: If someone walks through the door with a big check and asks them to focus on a subject, they will endow a research chair and create coursework. Otherwise, forget it. Academic institutions (with very few exceptions) have almost no internal capacity for institutional innovation.

Fear because revitalization is an emergent quality that seems magical...thus non-intellectual and non-academic. Why do all medical schools teach brain structure and function, but few teach consciousness? Fear of ridicule. Consciousness is also an emergent phenomenon, reeking of mysticism.

Appearances are everything in today's image-conscious, corporate sponsor-driven world of academic research. The best place to develop a revitalization discipline might be at one of the 40+ universities that study and teach complexity science. They are already comfortable with the concept of emergence.

Many academics are happy to work on a piece of the urban, rural, or environmental revitalization puzzle. But they shy away from taking responsibility for understanding the whole. It's the same with public leaders: If a place revitalizes, they get the glory. If it doesn't, it's not their fault: they did their part of the puzzle.

Fear of failure is also why we can't earn a degree in revitalization: academics perceive its complexity and worry that it's not understandable. So why risk studying or teaching it? (Then again, they teach economics and psychiatry, both of which suffer far worse from lack of logic, rigor and predictive ability.)

An article by Kate Kilpatrick titled "A promise yet to be delivered in West Philadelphia" (Al Jazeera America, Jan. 21, 2015) said: *"I don't have any faith at all," said Jimmy Allen, 66, a former gang member who works with neighborhood youth. He says many of the people involved with the Promise Zone don't come from or represent the community. "I think the companies will do well. I think the universities will do well, (and) some of the organizations that do their reports. But the neighborhood is going to still be stagnant." He wants to see funding go to grass-roots groups "so we can make sure our children, residents and businesses come up."*

Places are like people: About 1% are born into great wealth, and thrive no matter how poorly they perform. But for most places and people, life comprises a pattern of initial growth, followed by alternating devitalization and revitalization. The causes, frequency, and amplitude of these economic, social, and ecological tides vary from one place to another. But the underlying dynamics are universal, and deserve to be studied rigorously.

Since resilient prosperity programs work by regenerating the natural, built, and socioeconomic assets of a place, they touches on many scientific and engineering disciplines. Such work needs to be supported by an appropriate economic, legal, and policy environment, so it also touches many academic areas that might be less obvious.

Adaptive management can be seen as bringing the scientific process to management: hypothesize, experiment, document, adjust hypothesis if necessary, experiment again, and so on. In other words, adaptive our assumptions and our methods quickly and reflexively as experience reveals their inadequacies.

Today, many universities offer certificates, undergraduate areas of focus, and graduate degrees in the disciplines that are growing in size and importance as a result of the adaptive renewal megatrend: restoration ecology, infrastructure renewal, urban regeneration, urban planning, brownfields remediation, and the like. But the schools of management and schools of public policy have been largely left out.

Researching, developing, and teaching the process of creating resilient prosperity in virtually all coursework related to the natural, built and/or socioeconomic environments would be a great way to adaptively renew current curricula for the challenges of the Anthropocene. It's an appropriate skill set for academic, business and government leaders alike.

PARTNERING WITH A BUSINESS FOR RESILIENT PROSPERITY

> *"Monsanto should not have to vouch for the safety of biotech food. Our interest is in selling as much of it as possible. Assuring its safety is the FDA's job." – Philip Angell, Director, Monsanto.*

Those readers whose primary motivation for learning about the revitalization process is to improve environmental health might shudder at the title of this section. The thought of becoming financially dependent on corporate support for such work is perceived as rife with danger.

As the Monsanto (now Bayer) quote above indicates, their suspicions are well-founded. Too many corporate social or environmental responsibility efforts start and end in the marketing and public relations departments. That said, there tends to be a fairly direct correlation between public ownership and ethics: publicly traded firms are far less likely to factor the public good into their decisions. But that means the reverse is also true.

A local, small-to-medium-sized (SME) employer might well be a good home—or at least sponsor—for your resilient prosperity efforts. This could be in addition to partnering with a community foundation or public agency, but possibly stand-alone. Larger private firms could offer this service to multiple communities, wherever they have offices.

Given the outcry against excessive corporate influence in state and federal governments, this might sound unlikely. But local political dynamics are usually healthier than national, since public and private leaders have more face-to-face interaction. Plato knew this: he warned that democracy doesn't work with more than 10,000 citizens, since they wouldn't personally know—or know someone who personally knows—the candidates.

Mayors are very different animals from senators and presidents (watch Benjamin Barber's TED talk on "Why mayors should rule the world"). So too do local employers behave differently from those lobbying national politicians, even within the same firm. Some corporations that push national policies that are against the public interest are wonderful employers, and responsible local community members.

Change arises from individuals. Stasis arises from institutions. This is despite the fact that so many institutions say they exist to change things for the better. An institution's survival is based on the current system, not on change. When polio was eradicated, the entire reason for the existence of the March of Dimes disappeared. They cleverly reinvented themselves to fight something that would never disappear, something that had myriad causes: birth defects.

Other such institutions take a different approach to institutional survival. They actively suppress promising new innovations that might prevent the problems they solve, thus maintaining the status quo on which their existence is based.

Here's an excerpt from an article by Gus Speth in the July 2011 *SOLUTIONS* Journal, titled "American Prospect: Decline and Rebirth": "*...there is a deepening sense that this nation's challenges have grown so large that they exceed current capabilities. ... in a 20-country group of America's peer countries in the OECD, the U.S. is now worst, or almost worst, on nearly 30 leading indicators of social, environmental, and economic well-being. Even a well-intentioned and highly capable government in Washington, DC, would have severe difficulty successfully addressing the current backlog of major challenges. And, of course, the good government the American public needs is not the one that it has or is likely to have anytime soon. ...(however) Americans are already busy with numerous, mostly local initiatives that point the way to the future.*"

But a more practical approach for many places is to simply adapt to this new reality. Facilitating a local resilient prosperity program goes far beyond mere philanthropy, which is the hands-off way most companies try to help their local communities. This would be a much more intimate and far-reaching relationship, designed to tap the many assets a firm can bring to a community. At the same time, it avoids the abusive "company town" dynamic common in lumber, mining, oil, and steel-making communities of the 18th and 19th Centuries.

This approach might work best in small communities that don't have the capacity to do what needs to be done, and in larger areas lacking effective regional governance. It would, of course, necessitate the presence of a trusted, civic-minded firm with both the necessary will and resources.

With the growth of Corporate Social Responsibility (CSR), many companies offer employee volunteer programs, giving them a number of paid hours per month to work on local civic, environmental, or humanitarian projects. In most cases, the employees choose the project. It might be helping house-bound old folks, cleaning up a stream, renovating a derelict house for the homeless, assisting in a shelter for battered spouses, and so on.

Think of how much more effective these hundreds or thousands of annual volunteer hours might be with a little more focus and strategy. Hands-on labor, such as converting a vacant lot into a community garden, will always be valuable. But knowledge workers from the white-collar ranks could apply their management and computer skills to provide the usually-absent programmatic side of the equation.

They would become the "connective tissue" bridging the disparate Top-down, Bottom-up, and Middle-Out efforts to improve the community. They could also help bridge disconnects among the various projects that improve the local natural, built, and socioeconomic environments. Such integration is where efficiencies and synergies will be found. This multiplies community benefits with no budget increase, simply by effectively connecting isolated initiatives.

The private partner could even provide an executive as a part-time RE Facilitator, at least until a full-time position can be created in government. All of this free labor is a form of funding on the part of the company, but direct funding—such as impact investments—would also be a possibility.

Since the company's own employees are directly involved in the projects, they will be motivated to bring investment opportunities to the attention of the firm's management, whether it's start-up money, bridge financing, or for expansion. The company could create a revolving loan fund for such needs, giving employees discretion over how it is used, which would both improve and speed decision making.

One way the company could help ensure that projects are truly desired by the community would be to offer matching funds, and let the community crowdfund the qualifying amount. The Michigan Economic Development Corporation is using exactly that model for community redevelopment projects, via a partnership with crowdfunding platform Patronicity.

With proper training, the community would then have a RE Facilitator, plus a program, a team, and funding that can't be interrupted by elections. This could be a permanent arrangement, or an interim fix as the city or region builds its own capacity.

These days, cities privatize many previously-public services, such as water, fire, jails, and even police. If they are open to that, they should be open to the idea of outsourcing a needed service that isn't being provided—growing resilient prosperity—especially if it's being done as a voluntary public service, rather than to generate profit.

The story of Cummins in Columbus, Indiana provides evidence that some companies can be trusted to this degree.

When I was doing some work in the very rural Ohio town of Grand Lake St. Marys a few years back, several folks encouraged me to visit the city of Columbus, Indiana, about a 3-hour drive from there. They said it might be the most beautiful small city in the Midwest. Unfortunately, my schedule didn't allow it. But I've since learned why Columbus is so charming, and why it's a beacon of economic stability in a generally-distressed region.

Columbus is a small city (population: 46,000), but local employer Cummins is no small company. Its 2014 revenues were about $19.2 billion. It was founded in the proverbial garage in 1919 by Clessie Lyle Cummins, a Columbus native who worked as a chauffeur and auto mechanic. He had heard about the new diesel technology invented by Rudolf Diesel in Germany, and was convinced it was the future of truck engines.

Today, Cummins employs 17% of the local workforce. Indiana's unemployment rate is 5.8%. In Columbus, it's just 4.4%. An article titled An Engine Maker's High-Tech Makeover in the June 15, 2015 issue of FORTUNE magazine quoted Jason Hester, executive director of the Columbus Economic Development Board as saying "When I was growing up, my hometown of Anderson, an hour north of here, had 20,000 GM employees, and 30 years later, it has none. Right now, in this community, if you want a job, you're hired."

Many one-company towns can tell horror stories related to the abuse of power in such situations. Not Columbus. From 1929 to 1977, the CEO of Cummins was J. Irwin Miller, another Columbus native. During his reign, the firm grew from $26 million in revenues to $1.26 billion.

He wasn't just focused on his company: he loved Columbus, and knew that a thriving community would help his company thrive. Unlike so many modern executives, his attitude wasn't "Hey: I'm providing job. What more do you want?" To ensure a constant supply of talented engineers and managers, he created the Cummins Foundation, which put millions of dollars into improving local schools.

He wasn't just focused on things, either: Miller was a major champion of the Civil Rights Act of 1964. And, unlike today's slave-wage employers that make families rely on government handouts to make ends meet, he was strongly pro-union. Miller died in 2004, but some 40% of Cummins' global workforce is still unionized.

Miller paid architects' fees so that the town could afford beautiful buildings from the best designers. Columbus is now considered a national architectural showcase, which gives it a far better tourism economy than any other city in the region. Their library was designed by I. M. Pei. A local church was designed by Eero Saarinen. A school was designed by Richard Meier. Hester says "Cummins can attract employees who, but for these amenities, would not come here."

But this isn't just a story of good corporate citizenship: it's a story of adaptation, resilience and ery good strategic thinking. For Cummins to remain a stable employer, they needed to maintain healthy profit margins. The firm's greatest crisis came in 1997. Diesel engines are inherently "dirty", and the U.S. Environmental Protection Agency found that Cummins engines were being built in a way that enabled truck owners to easily disable the emissions controls. The EPA fined the company $83.4 million, the largest civil penalty in environmental enforcement history.

An even greater challenge was that EPA accelerated the deadline for lower-emission engines from 2004 to 2002. This threw all U.S. truck engine manufacturers into crisis, not just Cummins. But, under the leadership of then-CEO Theodore M. Solso, Cummins reacted differently from the others. He knew his competition's strategies would all take the normal route of fighting the environmental regulations, so he took a different path.

While other firms fought and sued the EPA, Cummins created a strategy that turned the situation to its advantage. It became the first company to meet the new standards—which most industry players were saying was impossible—thus giving them a competitive advantage. He boosted R&D spending 60%, which produced their breakthrough "deep spray" fuel injection process, which met EPA standards without hurting fuel economy.

By 2010, their two largest competitors in the big-rig engine market—Detroit Diesel and Caterpillar—had given up, leaving Cummins dominant, with today's enviable 39% market share. In fact, one of their most profitable divisions makes components that help other engine manufacturers reduce emissions.

This combination of civic investment, worker respect, environmental responsibility, and institutional adaptability makes Cummins a candidate for "ideal employer". Not all communities can attract such companies, but all communities can seek—even demand—similar values and behavior, especially when offering economic development incentives such as tax holidays.

If they are fortunate enough to land a Cummins-style business, they will likely have an idea partner or host for their resilient prosperity program.

CHAPTER 7 - THE 3RE STRATEGY: REPURPOSE. RENEW. RECONNECT.

> *"The idea of 'liveability' (has) given rise to numerous indices. In fact, there are now more indices covering...liveability than any other area."* – World Economic Forum

Horace said "*Whatever your advice, make it brief.*" Shakespeare said "*Brevity is the soul of wit.*" It's also the soul of wisdom. Strategies should be short enough to write on a napkin; preferably three sentences or less. But just three words can suffice, if they are the right ones, at the right time, in the right place.

Why so brief? Excuse the repetition, but this is crucially important: the primary function of a strategy is to guide decisions. Executing a strategy over time means making a constant stream of decisions that move you in the right direction, even under trying circumstances (such as being shot at, or watching your company lose money).

You've now heard it repeated *ad nauseum* that your vision should drive your strategy. While that's true, it doesn't mean that every vision must have a different strategy; only that the strategy should achieve the vision. In reality, there's a single, "universal" 3-word strategy that works well in almost any place whose vision is to create resilient prosperity.

Improving our quality of life (the "livability" of a place) usually boils down to three actions regarding your outdated and/or distressed assets (or institutions): 1) repurposing; 2) renewing; and 3) reconnecting. Together, they comprise what I refer to as the "3Re Strategy".

Repurposing is a key process in adaptively renewing a place. As described at the beginning of this book, for the past 12,000 years of the Holocene Epoch, we've been repurposing the planet to our own needs. That involved building a lot of stuff. When that stuff needs renewal, it's often because outlived its original purpose.

In the face of relentlessly-growing human populations, repurposing properties is often the best way to boost the capacity and resilience of our urban environments. At the institutional level, repurposing is often the path to survival in a rapidly-changing world that is rendering the organization irrelevant.

But not just buildings and infrastructure: sometimes we must repurpose farmland to earn money in a way that restores the biodiversity and productivity of damaged ecosystems, or that helps restore our climate. These repurposed lands might still produce food, so repurposing sometimes means adding an additional purpose, rather than replacing the original purpose. Switching from toxic, depleting industrial farming to regenerative agriculture is a perfect example.

Repurposing most often happens to "real" assets—either built or natural—but is increasingly happening to "soft" assets, such as socioeconomic or human (e.g., repurposing a workforce that was trained for a now-obsolete industry).

It can also be applied to smaller items—such as upcycling, rather than recycling, consumer goods—and to industrial equipment. For instance, the whole magic of building places out of old shipping containers derives from repurposing and renewing: you're giving new life to something that would have become trash. One of the few bright spots in downtown Las Vegas is the Downtown Container Park. Just one problem: they purchased brand new containers for the project. The reuse concept seems to have eluded them.

Maybe they just had too much money, so they had no motivation to buy used containers. Excessive funding is a real problem in some cities (such as several in China), where their wealth prevents them from valuing the efficiency of reusing existing buildings. This leads to the wanton destruction of heritage, as happened in Shanghai.

With natural assets, repurposing sometimes means restoring the original function, such as recovering ecosystem benefits:
- A buried urban stream that became an ugly urban highway can thus be repurposed as a natural asset that provides revitalizing green public space for a city;
- A dammed rural river that was repurposed a century ago as a power-generating or agricultural water source can be repurposed to its original function of providing fish, recreation and ecological health;

- In a world of sea level rise, waterfront residential properties can be repurposed as green barriers to storms for coastal cities.

With built assets, repurposing is often called "adaptive reuse", and often means creating an entirely new function:
- A historic bank building becomes a restaurant. An empty office building a school. An abandoned church a coffee shop;
- A derelict rural railway becomes a biking/hiking trail. A disused urban railway becomes a linear park that revitalizes adjacent properties;
- A contaminated former industrial property is cleansed and repurposed as a vibrant, mixed-use urban neighborhood and/or affordable housing. And so on.

In a private communication with me on September 23, 2019, Bruce Rasher, Redevelopment Manager at the RACER Trust—which revitalizes disused GM automotive manufacturing properties in the U.S.—said *"Adaptive reuse can generate numerous benefits, including revitalization of neighborhoods and cities, restoration of employment and tax base, utilization of existing infrastructure and the avoidance of investments in sprawl in an environment of limited resources."*

He continued, *"Implementation of Federal and state policies and incentives encouraging adaptive reuse and measures to reduce financial risks enacted since the mid-1990s is growing and becoming more so the conventional mainstream for both the public and private sectors. There is no reason this practice should not continue to expand and become permanently embedded in planning and investment principles throughout the U.S."* That kind of increasing policy support is making the 3Re Strategy more appropriate than ever.

When applying the 3Re Strategy, repurposing usually comes first: finding a viable new use for a derelict asset leads to funding, which enables renewal. That's pretty common these days. What too many places forget is the third step—reconnecting—which is where the projects' value can be multiplied many times over. So, reconnecting is usually the third step, after repurposing and renewing.

Most of the science, planning, and engineering of the 19th and 20th centuries was focused on separating or splitting things. Many of the most important sciences and disciplines of the 21st century will be focused on putting things back together. Maybe the most metaphorical example of this is nuclear energy.

The most toxic and expensive (when full-cost accounting is applied) form energy production of the 20th century was based on fission, which splits (disconnects) large atoms of rare elements such as uranium. This is the method that today's antique nuclear power plants are based on, and which are still being built, thanks to the political pull of the companies that build them. The non-toxic, almost perfectly efficient nuclear power of the future will be fusion, which fuses (connects) small atoms of common elements, such as hydrogen.

We already have one working fusion reactor: the sun. So, until we figure out how to make our own, it makes sense to use the one we have to its fullest extent, via photovoltaic, concentrator, wind, wave, etc. We might as well throw in lunar energy (tidal) while we're at it, since orbits are sun-powered. The renovation of our energy grids to solar power meets the repurposing trend in the form of "brightfields", where brownfields that no one wants to grow food on, or build on, become solar farms.

CAN A 3-WORD STRATEGY REALLY BE EFFECTIVE?

Before we dive more deeply into the 3Re Strategy, let's acknowledge that we humans seem to have a compulsion to reduce our solutions to three words. For instance, ICLEI recently introduced the Nature Pathway, a new tool to help integrate nature into cities. It's based on three phases: Analyze, Act and Accelerate. Despite its use of verbs (like a strategy) that's a methodology, not a strategy. Why? Because those three actions are too generic to produce any specific kind of result: they can be applied to anything.

I used to do a bit of flying, and one of the first things you're taught as a student pilot is a 3-word strategy for success (and survival): aviate, navigate, communicate. In that order. In other words: stay in the air, stay on course and stay in contact.

There are 3-word tactics, too. If your clothes are on fire, the recommended tactic is Stop. Drop. Roll. Again: if people can't remember a strategy after you've told it to them once, it's virtually useless. And if they can't remember it in an emergency, where a crucial decision must be made, it's totally useless. Thus, the magic of 3-word strategies and tactics. They work for flaming wardrobes and flying vehicles alike.

Moving up in scale from a strategy for individuals to a strategy for states and nations, the most successful growth strategy in the history of civilization comprises just three words: divide and conquer. Global empires have been built on that 3-word strategy. Just ask the British.

The United States has a severe backlog of infrastructure renewal and replacement projects, as the American Society of Civil Engineers has been measuring and reporting for some two decades. I documented this in my 2002 book, *The Restoration Economy*, which had an entire chapter on infrastructure renewal.

Given the threat to public safety, many states aren't waiting for the U.S. Congress to start functioning again, especially concerning what should be a nonpartisan issue. These states are behaving responsibly, and are moving forward with infrastructure renewal on their own. They're using federal funding where they can get it, and using public-private partnerships (P3) where they can't.

The state of Kentucky, for instance, has recently launched their Bridging Kentucky Program, a statewide initiative designed to improve the safety and soundness of bridges throughout the state. It will restore over 1,000 bridges in six years. Their three-word strategy? "Restore. Renew. Replace."

Moving down to the community scale, Columbia, South Carolina's mayor, Steve Benjamin—current president of the U.S. Conference of Mayors—is coping with challenges like opioid addiction, homelessness, immigration and trade. He has his own 3-word strategy for success: Infrastructure. Innovation. Inclusion.

Granted, that's more of a checklist than a strategy, given that it comprises nouns rather than verbs. But hey: if it works for Mayor Benjamin, that's what counts. Remember that the sole function of a strategy is to increase the likelihood of success. All other definers are either less important or totally irrelevant.

For those of you who are used to writing 100-page "strategies," the idea of a 3-word strategy must seem ludicrous. But you've probably encountered others without realizing it. For instance, FEMA has a 3-word strategy for effective natural disaster planning: Prepare. Respond. Recover.

Urban designers love 3-word strategies, as well. Two of the most successful downtown redesign strategies of the past two decades have been "Live. Work. Play." and "Transit-Oriented Development." In fact, the latter is often reduced to just three letters: TOD. Simple. Memorable. Effective.

So you might be wondering, why can't you just use one of those strategies to revitalize your community? Who needs the 3Re Strategy? The difference is that "Live. Work. Play." and TOD are both primarily urban, project-oriented strategies.

3Re, on the other hand, is a strategy that can be used by one-time projects or ongoing programs. It can be applied by almost any kind of entity: public or private, for-profit or non-profit. And it can be applied at any scale, from a single building, to a watershed, to a nation, to the entire planet.

For instance, many national economies will need to be repurposed in the coming years. This will most likely take place in countries that are heavily-dependent on unsustainable resource extraction, such as fisheries, old-growth timber, oil, or mining. At the very least, they need to be repurposed to value-added production, which simultaneously boosts profits and reduces imports.

All that being said about the power of 3-word strategies, the important thing is that your strategy works in your situation, not how many words it has. For instance, you might want to capture the ongoing, programmatic dynamic in your strategy. Adding one more "re"—repeat—would do that, so you would have the 4Re Strategy: repurpose, renew, reconnect, repeat.

3RE: REVITALIZATION STRATEGIES FOR NATURE, NEIGHBORHOODS, AND NATIONS

Just as our energy sources are moving from being based on splitting to a basis in fusing, so too must our thinking shift to fusing (reconnecting) our pathologically-fragmented economies, societies, and ecosystems.

For instance, water is a powerful revitalizer in both the urban and natural environments. Any community that has a significant waterfront, and that isn't revitalizing, probably isn't trying very hard. Or they don't have the right strategy (if they have one at all). Or they have an incomplete implementation process.

The key to tapping water's revitalizing power is often the 3Re Strategy. Sometimes we must repurpose a body of water (such as from serving manufacturing to serving recreation). Sometimes we must renew it (such as cleaning, undamming and restoring a near-lifeless river). Sometimes we must reconnect people to it (such as removing or burying a waterfront highway).

All three together can yield regenerative magic, as we'll see in a moment.
- Manhattan's High Line Park
- Atlanta's Beltline
- Chicago's Bloomingdale Trail
- Philadelphia's Rail Park
- Seoul's Cheonggyecheon
- Detroit's Dequindre Cut Greenway
- Paris' Promenade Plantée
- Toronto's The Bentway
- Jersey City's The Embankment
- Rotterdam's Hofplein
- Singapore's Green Corridor

What do the revitalizing, leading-edge projects listed above have in common? All are based on:
- Repurposing (adapting) old infrastructure and unused spaces;

- Renewing and greening those spaces for pedestrian and/or bicycle usage; and,
- Reconnecting isolated and/or distressed neighborhoods.

The same 3Re approach is also being used to revitalize our natural environment, such as repurposing abandoned farms or golf courses as public parks; renewing their biodiversity and ecological structure; and reconnecting isolated, dying ecosystems (such as via dam removal) to allow seasonal migrations and nutrient flows.

For instance, the term "regenerative agriculture" was coined in the 1980s by the Rodale Institute, a Pennsylvania-based research and education nonprofit. By the time I described it in my 2002 book, The Restoration Economy, it was just starting to pick up some steam, on its way to becoming the major trend it is today. Back in 2002, it had three core purposes: 1) to restore the quantity and quality of topsoil; 2) to restore native pollinator populations; and 3) to restore watersheds.

But recent research has revealed that regenerative farming and ranching techniques also sequester vast amounts of carbon from the atmosphere: even more so than reforestation. This adds a fourth purpose—climate restoration—which opens up a vast new realm of funding and partnership opportunities.

Why can those three words—repurpose-renew-reconnect.—serve as a "universal" core of resilient prosperity strategies? Because worldwide, our most basic urban, rural and environmental challenges similarly universal: obsolete, damaged / depleted, and fragmented assets. If it's obsolete, it needs to be repurposed (or removed, and the underlying site repurposed). If it's damaged or depleted, it needs to be renewed. If it's fragmented or isolated, it needs to be reconnected.

As mentioned before, repurposing is usually the first step: finding an appropriate new use for an old asset or property attracts funding and public support. That funding and support then enables renewal (restoration, redevelopment, etc.). Finally, reconnecting that asset provides access, which unleashes social and economic vibrance. Repurposing and renewing are mostly done at the local level, but the most important reconnecting can often only be done at the county, regional, or even national levels.

What happens when repurposing, renewing, and reconnecting meet? Sheer magic. Just look at the High Line Park.

New York City planned to spend millions of dollars demolishing this defunct elevated railway. Keeping the ugly relic made no sense, until two local citizens—Robert Hammond and Josh David—envisioned repurposing it as a linear park. The mayor at the time, Rudy Giuliani, thought it was a silly idea, and kept moving towards demolition. Then, Michael Bloomberg came into office, and saw the idea's potential.

That repurposing-based vision unleashed funding for renewing the structure as a beautiful green pedestrian space, which more than doubled nearby real estate values. Everyone now wanted to live or work near the High Line, so many adjacent, long-vacant buildings were suddenly reborn. In its first decade, the High Line generated $2.2 billion in new economic activity. The city expects over $1 billion in increased tax revenues over its first 20 years. It's enjoyed by over 5 million people annually, making it the city's 2nd most visited cultural attraction.

But that's not all. By reconnecting neighborhoods along the lower west side of Manhattan with the Hudson Rail Yards, the High Line (together with an extension of the No. 7 subway line from Times Square) enabled the city to do something they had envisioned for decades: cap and develop the space above the rail yards.

This has now happened: the $25 billion Hudson Yards revitalization is the largest real estate transaction in New York City history, and the largest mixed-use redevelopment project on the planet. That's the power of the 3Re Strategy at work.

Here's the key lesson from the High Line: Repurposing, renewing, and reconnecting are each powerful and effective on their own. Many communities have been revitalized using just one of these tactics. But the real magic occurs when all three are combined to reinforce each other, thus forming a truly regenerative strategy.

While repurposing often precedes renewing, it's not always needed. For instance, restoring vital flows to a place that's been isolated can trigger renewal of its original function, with no need to repurpose it. This isn't new knowledge: the Latin root of the word "affluence" means "to flow toward"...which is why well-designed reconnection adds so much to achieving your resilient prosperity goals.

Such flows might be water, nutrients, pedestrians, shoppers, traffic, migrating wildlife, etc. Many of today's most revitalizing global trends are based on this dynamic, such as reconnecting neighborhoods by removing or capping badly-planned urban highways, as is happening in dozens of cities as you read this.

Sometimes, only minimal renewal is needed to make a dramatic difference. For instance, the Pennsylvania Horticultural Society launched the LandCare non-profit in 2003. It works with community groups to ameliorate the effects of "hypervacancy" in depopulated neighborhoods via the simple expedient of cleaning-up, mowing and fencing-off vacant lots.

Today, they are using contractors to maintain about 12,000 of Philadelphia's 40,000 vacant lots. Most of these lots are chosen strategically, based on their proximity to schools, parks, residential areas and business corridors. As a result, some 20% of those long-vacant properties have now been redeveloped, and a 2012 study determined that the $15.3 million invested in LandCare at that point had yielded a $3.5 billion increase in residential values for the city. Not a bad ROI (revitalization on investment).

RECONNECTING STRATEGICALLY

It's also not unusual for reconnecting to be the first step, rather than the last, as Tampa's downtown waterfront revitalization illustrated. That said, there's often tremendous overlap. For instance, reconnecting a city to its waterfront usually means repurposing and renewing waterfront properties. So, we shouldn't get too pedantic about the order of things.

Even the most successful of current revitalization approaches are usually good at only one or two of the 3Re elements. I already mentioned how the Main Street Program, and many other historic preservation groups, have nailed the "repurposing" and "renewing" elements, but tend to be weak at "reconnecting".

This wastes much of their revitalizing potential. Pedestrian and bicycling trail groups, such as Rails To Trails, are great at "repurposing" and "reconnecting", but tend to be weak both at "renewing" and at devising strategies that maximize the economic revitalization potential of their trails.

Talk to people who are knowledgeable about urban revitalization or ecosystem restoration, and you'll hear one word repeatedly: connectivity.

Adaptability (AKA: "resilience") arises in part from a healthy level of connectivity. This is why network or team models will sometimes be more appropriate for resilient prosperity program. This is as opposed to creating formal departments or agencies, which often add bureaucracy without increasing connectivity. Effectively connecting assets—and those who can repurpose, renew and reconnect them—is often the most cost-effective revitalization strategy. Compared to actually renewing those properties, reconnecting your existing assets is usually cheap.

For example, connecting a housing project to a waterfront makes living there far more attractive, without having to change either the housing project or the waterfront. The housing, the waterfront, and the connective corridor are all revitalized in the process.

Likewise, a dying mountaintop ecosystem can be connected to a dying river ecosystem by restoring a wildlife corridor through the farmland that separates them. This restores the biodiversity of both ecosystems (by allowing species to make essential seasonal migrations), without the expense of actually restoring the mountaintop or the riverbanks themselves.

One more example: Many downtown revitalization initiatives focus exclusively on the center of the community. But, as mentioned earlier, downtowns are the heart of a community, and healthy hearts need healthy blood vessels.

Wise communities also focus on revitalizing the corridors leading to the downtown. This reconnects downtown and suburbs to restore healthful flows of residents, shoppers, employers, and employees.

One of the most common reasons that cities and regions fail to turn a flourishing redevelopment project into community-wide or regional revitalization is that they have no way to scale-up the success. The project sits in its own little bubble, with no program or process to flow that revitalization outward to catalyze similar work elsewhere.

Innovation has been a buzzword in urban planning circles for some time now, and many cities have incubators to support new businesses and social entrepreneurs. Some excellent results have been achieved, but almost always at a very small scale.

At Stanford University's Graduate School of Business, professor Charles O'Reilly notes that a similar dynamic occurs in the corporate world. He says that legacy companies that are trying to revitalize after being adversely affected by technological change must succeed at three disciplines: ideation, incubation and scale. "*Everyone ideates,*" he said in the June 1, 2018 issue of *FORTUNE* magazine. "*Every CEO spends money on innovation, and that's great. Some companies are OK at incubation. But scaling is the hard part.*"

COMPETITIVE VS. COOPERATIVE: THE 3RE STRATEGY CAN BE EITHER.

> "*(creating) mega-regions...might benefit the development of intercity and high-speed rail corridors linked to America's global facilities and other multi-state transportation networks, as well as the protection, restoration and management of large environmental systems and resources, and the development of economic revitalization strategies for underperforming regions.*" – IDB & UN-HABITAT.

The appropriate strategy to achieve your vision is determined by your capabilities, resources and constraints. In many cases, the 3Re Strategy will suffice, powered by your renewable asset map, which reveals what needs to be repurposed, renewed and reconnected. In other cases, a modified version of the 3Re Strategy will be ideal. In still other cases, a completely different strategy is needed.

Strategies come in two basic flavors: competitive and cooperative. The former gets most of the attention, and seems to be supported as the more effective of the two in our normal societal and scientific narratives. But this is mostly an artifact of predominantly-male leadership in both government and science. In truth, nature relies just as much—if not more—on cooperation as it does on competition.

Cooperative strategies are actually common in business, finance and government. But they are seldom discussed because they rely in large part on secrecy. They are far more effective if the people you're competing with don't know what you and those you're cooperating are up to.

Another name for a cooperative strategy is "conspiracy." When a husband and wife want to stop their daughter from seeing a boyfriend they dislike, they often decide it will be more effective to influence her individually, rather than as a united front. That's a conspiracy. Any secret decision to cooperate is a conspiracy. It's normal behavior for all individuals and organizations.

Imagine the ramifications if communities, regions and nations started cooperating in their mutual revitalization using the 3Re Strategy. What if we all started repurposing, renewing and reconnecting our natural, built and socioeconomic assets simultaneously? What if we were all focused on actually succeeding, rather than on going through the motions?

We would likely see a massive increase in economic growth, quality of life and biodiversity. We would also likely see a corresponding massive decrease in poverty, resource-based conflict and climate refugees.

LESSONS FROM TAMPA, FLORIDA

I lived in the Tampa Bay area for 15 years, and still love it, so my wife and I visit frequently. In the 50s, 60s, and 70s, downtown Tampa was devitalized by horrendously destructive, insensitive urban planning and redevelopment projects. As a result, a typical, sterile "roll up the sidewalks at 5 o'clock" sort of office-rich, resident-poor city center that nobody visited who didn't have to (unless it was to go to the wonderfully-restored Tampa Theater).

Over the past 30 years, city leaders and redevelopers made many bold attempts to undo the mistakes of earlier planners and politicians. The successful ones include a downtown residential towers; the Tampa Bay Aquarium; the Performing Arts Center (on a redeveloped waterfront site); and a trolley (which almost got decommissioned because it was so badly planned) that connects the downtown to the fascinating Ybor City area, and the star of the show, the gorgeous Tampa RiverWalk.

But along the way were some massive failures. The retail component of the huge Harbour Island redevelopment failed. The nicely-located new convention center endured many years on the brink of failure. The Channelside redevelopment failed (and is now being reborn yet again).

All of them failed for the same two reasons: bad timing and lack of connectivity. The bad timing came from the lack of an ongoing revitalization program, which would have ensured that each project created synergies with the others.

For instance, the new convention had to endure years before nearby hotels were added. Harbour Island, despite a nice monorail, was too poorly connected to a downtown that had too few people. Likewise with Channelside, despite the trolley.

Tampa is an example of a place that should have focused on reconnecting first. Had the Tampa RiverWalk been the first—rather than the last—project to be completed, it's likely those other projects wouldn't have failed. The RiverWalk now provides both many downtown visitors and many connections from formerly-isolated properties to those visitors.

The essence of strategy is often timing. Tampa did all the right things, but in the wrong order, with poor timing, and little or no integration. They never had a strategy that I ever heard of. As a result, all those ambitious projects never produced the desired revitalization.

Each one was usually at death's door by the time the next one started. There was no logical sequence to produce efficiencies and synergies, so vast sums of public and private money were lost. All that has now changed with the completion of the RiverWalk, and billions of dollars are pouring into downtown redevelopment.

Many developers and entrepreneurs (downtown stores and restaurants) lost their shirts along the way, all for lack of a vision-based strategic process. The irony is that those missing vision, strategy and program elements are the least cost-intensive: it's the projects that consume 99% of the funds. No one can say *"we lack a strategic process because we can't afford one."*

Tampa never even tried to create a process during that frustrating period. They had no program to capture the momentum of each project, or to create efficiencies and synergies that added value to each renewed property. They just lurched from one isolated project to another.

> *"These challenges form the impetus for the country's current urban reform efforts, a policy overhaul looking to turn Mexico from "3D" – distant, dispersed, and disconnected—to "3C"— connected, compact, and coordinated."*
> – The City Fix, December 31, 2014

Using the 3Re Strategy would have made it obvious that they needed to revitalize by repurposing and renewing the waterfront properties in a way that reconnected the downtown to its most attractive feature—the river—creating a new destination that drew from far and wide in the process.

More good news: Tampa's resilience efforts are getting off to a better start than did their earlier revitalization efforts. Their approach is holistic (defining eight community dimensions) and it has both pre-disaster and post-disaster components. If they were to launch a strategic renewal process, their resilience team would likely be an excellent nexus for it.

This is especially true in coastal cities like Tampa, whose very survival is now in question, thanks to the climate crisis. Resilience initiatives also have the advantage of being recently born, thus tending to embody new thinking with less bureaucracy. With the addition of their resilience goal, Tampa is finally fixing their present and future together to create resilient prosperity.

LESSONS FROM RYERSON UNIVERSITY

I lectured at Ryerson University back in 2010, and fell in love with the campus, which is in downtown Toronto, Ontario, Canada. The attraction wasn't due to grand architecture—as one would find at almost any old European university— and it wasn't the result of beautiful green spaces and grand old trees, as one finds at Davidson College in North Carolina. It was because they epitomize the 3Re Strategy that urban planning and public policy students worldwide need to be learning.

Ryerson University's campus has expanded incrementally, primarily by repurposing and renewing existing buildings like the abandoned, historic hockey venue, Maple Leaf Gardens. In this manner, they have: 1) preserved heritage; 2) boosted downtown revitalization; 3) saved money on new construction, and 4) avoided wasting the embodied energy and materials of these solid older buildings.

As a result of this opportunistic expansion strategy, it's a bit hard to distinguish the campus from the adjacent neighborhoods. If you don't see the banners, you probably won't know you're on the campus. Since Ryerson's buildings weren't originally designed as part of the school, there's little shared architectural vernacular. The school inexpensively addressed that visibility problem via banners that let people know when they are on the campus.

My earlier criticism regarding street banners is only directed at places that confuse such purchases with actual revitalization. Banners are certainly useful in providing visual cues to behind-the-scenes revitalization activities. They can also provide visual cohesiveness for revitalized urban districts, especially those that reuse existing buildings.

Banners were a good stop-gap measure for Ryerson, but now—after many years of repurposing and renewing a large collection of miscellaneous buildings—Ryerson is finally reconnecting them. This being done both to form a more cohesive campus, and to better integrate it with the adjacent neighborhoods they've helped revitalize. So, their 3Re Strategy is now complete.

Construction on Gould and Victoria Streets is underway as I write this, as part of their Campus Core Revitalization project. It's designed to enhance the quality of safe, accessible spaces and implement infrastructure upgrades, resulting in a campus that's greener, more accessible, more pedestrian-friendly and better connected to the community.

The central design theme is the permanent pedestrianization of Gould Street: raising the roadway to make it level with the walkway, prohibiting vehicular access except for emergency services, and establishing cycling dismount zones. Other improvements include additional outdoor lighting, increasing opportunities for public art installations, adding biodiverse plantings, replacing end-of-life trees and other site furnishings to improve the safety and accessibility of our shared public spaces.

Ryerson defines the "public realm" as the publicly accessible, exterior campus spaces, including streets, pathways, right-of-ways and parks; the spaces where students, staff, faculty and local residents move, meet and celebrate together. Most of Ryerson's public realm is owned by the City of Toronto, so partnering with local government is required for any improvements on public right-of-ways.

Other universities took a very different approach, and are now paying the price. Many actively encouraged the devitalization of the neighborhoods surrounding their campuses so they could buy the properties cheaply when they needed to expand. Johns Hopkins University in Baltimore discovered the downside of that strategy when they found themselves surrounded by pervasive drugs and crime, to the point where they started having trouble attracting students and faculty.

Over the past decade or so, Johns Hopkins has been pushing a grand—and expensive—campus and neighborhood revitalization project. Some of the elements are very good, but it's been rather poorly organized—with little sign of an actual process—so the ROI (revitalization on investment) has been low.

Many schools teach sustainability, enlightened urban planning, and heritage preservation, while simultaneously expanding via sprawl and demolition. Ryerson is thus a rare example of a university that teaches by example.

They aren't alone: other schools that have grown their campus by repurposing and renewing existing (often historic) buildings include Point Park University in Pittsburgh, Pennsylvania, Wilfrid Laurier University's campus in Brantford, Ontario, and SCAD (Savannah College of Art and Design) in Savannah, Georgia. The latter is housed in 70 renovated buildings, having single-handedly revitalized the city's Victorian District.

LESSONS FROM DENVER, COLORADO

In Chapter 11, you'll see how, in Denver, a single private redeveloper (Dana Crawford) brought about the revitalization of an entire urban district. Here, let's instead focus on how enlightened public leaders have repurposed, renewed and reconnected their way to the spectacular rebirth of that city.

Depending on one's focus, a starting point for Denver's revitalization could be assigned to a variety of dates over the past forty years. I'll choose 1974, which is when their Greenway Foundation was created.

At that time, the city's waterways were badly polluted, and—thanks to the proliferation of impervious surfaces—has become flood risks. In fact, the major motivation behind the creation of the Greenway Foundation was to become more resilient to prevent a repeat of the disastrous flooding of 1965.

They set about creating that resilience by restoring and redeveloping the urban corridors of the South Platte River and Cherry Creek. Where those two waterways met used to be the industrial heart of the city, back in the 1800s. At that point, it was a dead zone ringed by vacant and underutilized factory buildings and warehouses.

The Greenway Foundation repurposed and renewed that dead zone into what is now Confluence Park. It features performance venues, kayaking, trails and scenic points that attracted folks from throughout the region. In 2016, a $9 million renovation to the park was finished, but the foundation has never stopped ecologically restoring the two waterways, making them healthier and more attractive with each passing year.

Cherry Creek has a 12-mile footprint in downtown Denver, and the South Platte River has a 10.5-mile footprint. So restoring them has had a huge impact on the local quality of life. It soon became abundantly clear that these water features were the true heart of the city, so two new riverside parks in the late 90s, one 35 acres and the other 20 acres. Both connect to Confluence Park, with each park thus magnifying the value of the others.

There was a monetary payoff, too...a big one. Those vacant factories and warehouses around Confluence Park have all now been either repurposed as housing or demolished and replaced with housing. The other two parks have similarly been surrounded with new market-rate housing, since virtually everyone prefers living near greenspaces and flowing water. Those many thousands of new downtown residents are, in turn, economically revitalizing downtown businesses.

If one were forced to identify the date of another inflection point in Denver's revitalization, it would have to be 1982, which was when the 16th Street Mall opened. The city made 18 blocks of 16th Street pedestrian-only (except for the free bus service), and ran that free bus along the entire 1.4-mile length of the street.

It's a marvel of repurposing a street from serving primarily cars to serving primarily people. It's also a marvel of reconnection: virtually every major attraction—not to mention the vast majority of downtown workers—are within four blocks of the 16th Street Mall.

But that was just the beginning. When that 16th Street Transitway (the free bus) was connected to the new RTD Light Rail System (FasTracks), the entire metro area started to coalesce as a functioning whole.

Then they beautifully restored and redeveloped the historic downtown Union Station, repurposing it as a regional transit hub. As anyone who ever rode a taxi from the airport to the downtown in the "old days" (as did I) can attest, the icing on the cake came with the long-needed addition of rail service to the far-flung Denver International Airport.

With that, Denver was really cooking—and they still are—thanks to a constant focus on repurposing, renewing and reconnecting their natural, built and socioeconomic assets.

WANT TO SEE A LIST OF GOOD STRATEGIES?

You won't find that list here. That would be like a doctor listing good treatment regimens, without knowing who the patient is, and without knowing anything about their medical history, age, gender, or current condition. "Good" is defined by context.

Since your strategy is their to help you succeed, it's dependent on the local situation and impediments: politics, history, economy, ethnicity(s), geography, resources, attitudes, mores, superstitions, traditions, expectations, etc.

So, the strategy for a resilience initiative might have nothing to do with resilience *per se*: the resilience elements are in the vision, design, projects, etc. Likewise, a strategy for revitalization might have little to do with revitalization. A strategy for social justice would have little to do with social justice. The strategy is only about the path to success, not the nature of the goal.

A common element found in most resilience plans is the expansion and improvement of green infrastructure. If one Googles the definition of "green infrastructure", a vast array of variations on a basic definition is displayed. But one word that's common to almost all of them is "strategic."

Here's a composite definition that pretty much represents them all: "*Green infrastructure is a strategically planned and managed network of natural areas and other open spaces that conserves and restores natural ecosystem values and functions, provides clean air and water, and delivers a wide array of benefits to people and wildlife.*"

Strategy is what turns a bunch of rocks, dirt and plants into green infrastructure that successfully serves the resilience goals.

Sea level rise, ocean acidification, and increased frequency/severity of storms are rapidly rendering the future of many coastal economies non-viable. The climate crisis is undermining many once-productive farming regions, which might need to repurpose by switching to crops that do better in hotter, drier climates, rather than abandoning agriculture altogether. This repurposing challenge applies to forestry economies, fishing economies, tourism economies, and almost all others.

But they can't stop at finding a viable new purpose. That new purpose should inspire confidence in the local future which—in turn—inspires investment in the place. That investment pays for the renewing and reconnecting that's needed to complete the transition to resilient prosperity. Repurposing, renewing, and reconnecting is the only way many of these places will adapt and survive in the Anthropocene.

Let's finish this chapter by pointing out that the 3Re Strategy can be applied to any kind of system, not just communities. For example, repurposing, renewing, and reconnecting our centralized, fossil fuel-based energy infrastructure into a distributed one based on diverse, renewable sources is an obvious starting point for anyone concerned with the climate crisis, sustainability, or resilience.

CHAPTER 8 - REGENERATIVE STRATEGIES: EXAMPLES, THOUGHTS & INSIGHTS

The purpose of this chapter is to further attune your mind to strategic thinking, before we move from strategy to process. We'll do this primarily via 1) brief descriptions of places that are revitalizing by repurposing, renewing and reconnecting their assets, and 2) brief insights that reflect the kinds of revitalization and resilience challenges that strategic thinking can overcome.

Let's start with a few recent examples of the 3Re Strategy in action:
- On June 25, 2019, the new Willingdon Linear Park in Burnaby, British Columbia, Canada won the Envision Silver award for sustainable infrastructure from the Institute for Sustainable Infrastructure (ISI). To create the linear park, the city repurposed and renewed overgrown dead space alongside the roads to reconnect and revitalize the neighborhoods.
- On July 1, 2019 in London, England, the Museum of London unveiled the design for its revitalizing new home in West Smithfield. They will repurpose, renew and reconnect a group of derelict-but-attractive historic market buildings into a new, world-class, 24-hour cultural destination in the historic heart of the capital.
- On May 6, 2019 in New York City, the Waterfront Alliance released its latest plan for repurposing, renewing and reconnecting Governors Island—a former military property in New York Harbor—in order to further revitalize it. The essence of the plan focuses on activating the island's periphery via ferry and freight service while renovating the historic ship berths, kayak and small boat docks, recreational facilities, and educational facilities/activities.
- In May of 2019, the housing association L&Q Group (London & Quadrant) and the private redeveloper Countryside received planning consent for the 3,000-home Beam Park regeneration site in East London, England.

This £1 billion project is revitalizing the 29 hectares (71.7 acres), site of an old Ford factory by repurposing, renewing, reconnecting it (via multiple public transit points) into a vast new residential neighborhood, with 50% of the housing units being affordable.
- Most efforts to revitalize urban centers focus, not surprisingly, on the urban centers themselves. This means that only a relatively small area receives the majority of designers' attention. In Moscow, Russia, the peripheral areas aren't being ignored or forgotten. A new strategy called "Dvorulitsa" (Yardstreet) was proposed in May of 2019 by Russian architecture firm Meganom, aiming to shift that focus. If accepted, it would repurpose, renew and reconnect the properties of the urban periphery to revitalize the city center, without ever actually working on the city center itself.
- One of the most common ways in which cities have revitalized themselves in the past three decades has been by repurposing and renewing old waterfront industrial properties (or infrastructure, like water treatment plants) in order to reconnect the community to its water. A wonderful recent (2019) example of that is Brooklyn's new Domino Park, which reconnects the Williamsburg neighborhood to New York City's East River for the first time in 160 years. As part of the overall revitalization of the 11-acre former Domino Sugar Factory, this new five-acre park celebrates the history of one of New York's most iconic industrial waterfront sites by integrating over 30 large-scale salvaged relics, including 21 original columns from the Raw Sugar Warehouse, gantry cranes, screw conveyors, bucket conveyors and syrup tanks into an interpretive and educational "Artifact Walk." They are further regenerating the neighborhood by adaptively reusing some of the industrial buildings to provide 700 units of affordable housing.
- On March 15, 2019, the township of Bloomfield, New Jersey held a groundbreaking ceremony for the upcoming Lion Gate Municipal Complex project. The $13.3 million project will repurpose, renew and reconnect the 18.2 acre brownfield site of the former Scientific Glass Factory. What will emerge will be a soccer field, a children's park and walking paths along Third River. The project, which Mayor Michael Venezia's administration has been working to adopt for over three years, also includes restoring historic and ecologically important wetlands that will reduce the impact of floods in the area, and the soccer field will feature an underground water drainage system.
- In the long-struggling city of New Haven, Connecticut, city officials are now showcasing the latest developments of their Long Wharf

revitalization project. As in many cities along the Northeast Corridor of the U.S., for the past half century, the city's vital connection to water at Long Wharf has been largely cut off by poorly-planned highway infrastructure and industrial-scale land uses. As a result, a process of repurposing, renewing and reconnecting is needed to revitalize the area. That's what's happening now, as projects—such as the Food Truck Paradise, the Info Center and the Canal Dock Boathouse—have just been completed in 2019. All of these properties are being reconnected to the city via new walking trails. Spurred by climate threats of storm surge and flooding, the revitalizing design also boosts disaster resilience via green infrastructure and a "living shoreline", plus an ecologically restored park and wildlife refuge.

- Toronto, Ontario, Canada boasts the world's longest urban waterfront, which means they have tremendous revitalization potential in that area. But that potential has long been stymied by the Gardiner Expressway, another badly-planned urban highway that severed downtown neighborhoods from the water. Unwilling to demolish what was—mile for mile—the world's most expensive highway, the city has created a new linear park called the Bentway. It's an urban trail and series of pocket parks that repurposes and renews the ugly concrete dead spaces under the Gardiner, in order to reconnect the city to Lake Ontario and revitalize the neighborhoods. It seems to be achieving that goal nicely.
- The 278 hectare (695-acre) Green Square redevelopment in Sydney, New South Wales is Australia's largest urban revitalization project. Sydney's oldest industrial area, it's projected to house some 61,000 residents and 21,000 workers when revitalization is complete in 2030. The property is being repurposed and renewed in a green manner. Strategically located within one of the most important economic corridors in Australia—3.5 kilometers south of Sydney's Central Business District (CBD) and 4 kilometers from both Sydney Airport and Port Botany—its new transit connections mean the entire corridor will be reconnected to further the revitalization of adjacent neighborhoods.
- Atlanta, Georgia has long been a sad joke in urban planning circles, as badly-planned and unplanned sprawl over decades made the metro area increasingly unlivable and unmanageable. The ambitious Atlanta Beltline is their best-known large-scale revitalization effort. It's repurposing and renewing derelict rail lines to reconnect and revitalize neighborhoods on a grand scale. But they're also doing fascinating things with green infrastructure. To reduce flooding, they are repurposing and renewing vacant properties in to green infrastructure that doubles as urban parks.

These beautiful parks help reconnect and revitalize neighborhoods while adding resilience. They also reduce the strain on water treatment systems by pre-treating stormwater. Current projects consist of bioretention basins in parks and rights-of-way, constructed wetlands, and stream and floodplain restoration. Good examples are Rodney Cook Sr. Park in Historic Vine City, and the Historic Fourth Ward Park.

- Downtown Los Angeles, California was little more than a sleepy office district not long ago. Tens of thousands of suburbanites would clear out at the end of each workday, leaving scores of classic Beaux-Arts and Art Deco buildings vacant or underutilized. Today, cranes dot the skyline and construction routinely diverts traffic as Downtown Los Angeles—a neighborhood now known as DTLA—undergoes its largest redevelopment boom since the Roaring Twenties, when it was the center of the entertainment industry. As the city prepares for the 2028 Summer Olympics, a spate of new apartments, hotel rooms and retail and office space steadily comes online throughout the 5.84-square-mile downtown area. Existing structures are being repurposed and renewed, and the city's public transit system is being expanded and improved to reconnect the area.
- Back in London, England again. On February 15, 2019, one of the largest regeneration projects in Europe moved a step closer to fruition. That was when the city's oldest housing charity selected Sydney, Australia-based real estate developer Lendlease as the Preferred Bidder for the £8 billion, 11,500 home, 30-year Thamesmead Waterfront redevelopment in southeast London. The 250-acre site is currently in desperate need of revitalization, which will happen by repurposing, renewing and reconnecting the underutilized property.
- In Seattle, Washington, Mayor Jenny A. Durkan has been championing the revitalization of Fort Lawton, a defunct U.S. Army post overlooking Puget Sound. In 1973, the majority of the property, 534 acres, was given to the city, and was dedicated as Discovery Park. Now, in 2019, Ft. Lawton is becoming a significant part of solving both Seattle's housing shortage and housing affordability crises. The city plans to repurpose, renew and reconnect 34 acres of Ft. Lawton into a new affordable, livable community.
- Rotterdam-based design firm MVRDV has made a specialty of repurposing, renewing and reconnecting dead or dying urban commercial complexes into green, walkable, transit-oriented residential neighborhoods. Their most recent project is the grey, isolated, former

ING office complex location in Amsterdam-West. It will soon be revitalized as a green, lively neighborhood of approximately 750 homes.
- Urban sprawl has expanded Cambridge, England into what used to be a remote area, where a sewage plant currently exists. Now, people want to live there. In December of 2018, plans were published that showed how this major brownfield site on the northern edge of Cambridge could be repurposed, renewed and reconnected to transform it into a new low-carbon community with thousands of new homes, jobs and high-quality facilities near newly-created public transit.
- Long-term readers of REVITALIZATION are well-aware of the many failed attempts to revitalize a neighborhood—or an entire city—by building a new sports stadium. Even when a stadium is being redeveloped—rather than built from scratch—they pose tremendous reuse challenges. Unlike an industrial building that's easily converted to apartments, a sports arena's design doesn't readily lend itself to being repurposed. Shanghai's Hongkou soccer stadium is currently isolated and little-used. It sits empty on non-game days, and has few connections to the vibrant cultural and commercial areas surrounding it. But Boston-based design firm Sasaki—in December of 2018—unveiled a design to repurpose, renew and reconnect the stadium as a sustainable health and wellness hub. Rethinking China's first professional soccer stadium, the project aims to bring new life to this single-purpose 1990s structure. The design extends the park's landscape to reconnect the site to the Hongkou District's major north-south green corridor. The revitalized site will enjoy a wealth of public transit connections, including an elevated light rail and a subway.
- On a similar theme, many poorly-planned Olympic Games—such as in Brazil and Greece—leave useless facilities, vacant land, massive debt and public disappointment in their wake. Not so China's Nanjing International Youth Cultural Centre, which harnessed the energy of their 2014 Youth Olympic Games to create a revitalizing project that should have a lasting legacy. They have now repurposed, renewed and reconnected the site of the Youth Olympic Games. With a design by Zaha Hadid Architects, the property is now acting as both an anchor and a catalyst for future investment in Nanjing's Hexi New Town. It comprises two hotel towers that include the new Jumeirah Nanjing, a cultural centre with conference facilities, an urban plaza, offices and mixed-use areas.
- In Stockholm, Sweden, the Old Lidingo Bridge is one of the city's most beautiful bridges. Built between 1917 and 1925, its lattice structure resembles the Eiffel Tower, and features an arched steel truss that begins

the connection between Stockholm and the island of Lidingo. But the bridge has long been in a state of disrepair, and the local council decided recently to demolish it, citing the high costs of repair. Now, architects at local redevelopment firm Urban Nouveau have proposed repurposing and renewing the antiquated elevated transportation infrastructure into a linear park, similar in spirit to New York City's High Line. They have brilliantly proposed financing it by incorporating 50 high-end apartments into the bridge...what might be called "mixed-use infrastructure".

- The previously-mentioned design firm Sasaki has a mantra: "Great cities have a great park." That's a good thing, since one of their clients is Lakeland, Florida. The city intends to create a grand "Central Park" by repurposing, renewing and reconnecting a large brownfield near the downtown. The toxic, 180-acre former CSX railyards will soon become an ecological paradise called Bonnet Springs Park.
- On October 17, 2018, Boston, Massachusetts Mayor Martin J. Walsh introduced a grand vision of urban resilience for the city's future. It will adaptively renew all of Boston's many waterfronts to protect local residents, homes, businesses, and infrastructure from the impacts of rising sea level and the climate crisis. The strategies include repurposing and renewing waterfront properties to create elevated landscapes, enhanced waterfront parks, flood resilient buildings, and revitalized and increased connections and access to the waterfront.

I could literally fill this book with such brief descriptions of the 3Re Strategy at work. The examples I've offered here come just from the 9 months prior to this July 2019 writing. REVITALIZATION: *The Journal of Economic & Environmental Resilience* has over 7000 articles in its archives, and hundreds of them demonstrate revitalization efforts based on repurposing, renewing and reconnecting natural, built and socioeconomic assets.

SOCIOECONOMIC REVITALIZATION FACTORS

"It is not the man who has too little, but the man who craves more, that is poor."
– Seneca (c. 4 BC – A.D. 65), Roman philosopher

Most of the above examples deal with natural and built assets. Let's talk a bit about the human aspect: socioeconomic assets. Virtually every place needs some sort of revitalization. Even the wealthiest cities have distressed neighborhoods, and even the wealthiest nations have distressed regions and cities.

And many places that consider themselves wealthy actually have appalling pockets of poverty, pollution and/or infrastructure deterioration that they choose not to acknowledge. One way they stick their head in the sand is by focusing on misleading statistics.

For instance, most Americans assume that if someone is employed full-time, they aren't in poverty. But 8.9 million Americans who have full-time jobs are in poverty. The (usually giant) companies that employ them rely on government programs to help their employees keep food on the table. This is obviously a form of corporate welfare, since taxpayers are enabling them to earn huge profits by paying workers less. Another way poverty is masked is by focusing on GDP growth. But in America, 90% of our GDP growth goes to the wealthiest 1%—where's it's mostly sequestered rather than spent—so there's little benefit to the economy or the people.

Worse, GDP is based on faulty accounting procedures. Unlike the double-entry bookkeeping used by business, the federal government measures income—such as from natural resources—but doesn't measure expenses, such as the depletion of those resources. Even worse, it counts disasters as assets: adding the reconstruction income without deducting the destruction expenses. And, as first documented in The Restoration Economy back in 2002, government accounting doesn't differentiate between new development and restorative development. As a result, we're blind both to the bad news of sprawl and depletion, and to the good news of redevelopment and regeneration.

Thanks to incompetent (or purposely misleading) statistical analysis, most Americans don't realize that the poverty rate in the U.S. is higher than in Mexico. That doesn't surprise me much. About a decade ago, I counted the number of beggars per block in downtown Washington, DC, and then did the same in the center of Mexico City. DC had about 30% more. If Americans find that surprising, it because we turn a blind eye to our social problems by relabeling them. Thus, we don't have beggars; we have panhandlers. The thought of Americans begging is just too uncomfortable. Not so uncomfortable as to make us want to eliminate it, mind you, but uncomfortable enough to make us not want to acknowledge it.

Despite having by far the world's highest rates of both incarceration and drug addiction, few Americans have the courage to face up to how sick our society really is. Social health is a prime factor in both economic revitalization and community resilience, but how can we address a challenge we won't even admit exists?

One measure I use for quickly determining the social health of a place is to see how far children can wander before their parents panic. The further they can go, the healthier the society. In the U.S, that distance is measured in meters, usually not more than 2 or 3, except then they are in school or at a playground. In some countries, it's measured in kilometers.

Driving around Dominica in my rental car, I frequently picked-up children under 10 who were hitchhiking to school. Growing up in England, my parents thought nothing of sending me down to the corner grocery story by myself when I was 6 years old. My wife and I spend about two months annually in Mexico, where we still see very young children doing the shopping by themselves, many blocks from home.

Here in the U.S., parents are arrested for doing that. Debra Harrell worked at McDonalds, and thus couldn't afford a babysitter. In the summer of 2014, when she allowed her 9-year-old daughter to play unsupervised (but with a cell phone) in a nearby public park in North Augusta, South Carolina, she was arrested and her child was put into public custody. In that town, it's apparently against the law to trust your children or your neighbors. McDonald's then fired her, which means they—in effect—fired her because they weren't paying her enough to afford day care.

Similarly, in Montgomery County, Maryland, a 10-year-old boy and his 6-year-old sister were walking one mile home from a park when someone called the police, who picked them up and took them the rest of the way home. Their parents weren't charged, but the Montgomery County Children's Protective Services (CPS) threatened to take their kids if they did it again.

It gets worse. In 2013, a Tennessee father of two was arrested because he tried to pick up his children from school on foot (there was a mile-long backup of vehicles picking up other kids). Apparently, crime is so bad in Tennessee that even adults are only safe when locked in a motorized metal box.

In the U.S., the neighborhood is the threat. In Mexico, Dominica and many other healthier societies, the neighborhood is the protector. Any revitalization strategy that doesn't make people feel safer in their own neighborhoods is going to be of limited use in retaining residents, or in attracting new residents (and employers).

"Three grand essentials to happiness in this life are something to do, something to love, and something to hope for."
– Joseph Addison, British poet and politician.

Too many depressed communities think their revitalization will make them happy. In fact, the opposite is true: the residents, employers and investors they desire are attracted to happy places.

If the concept of happiness as a catalyst of revitalization sounds hippie-dippie or just plain weird, consider this: In 2018, a review of 225 studies in the respected journal, Psychological Bulletin, found that happiness in individuals doesn't necessarily follow success. In fact, research showed exactly the opposite: Happiness leads to success. [If you would like to explore this dynamic in more detail, read the 2018 book, *The Happiness Advantage: How a Positive Brain Fuels Success in Work and Life* by Shawn Achor.]

Conversely, pervasive fear and anger in a community drives away new residents, employers and investors. Even worse, those emotions—especially when pervasive and long-standing—do long-term damage by crippling our minds.

Here's an excerpt from Achor's book: "*Instead of narrowing our actions down to fight or flight the way negative emotions do, positive ones broaden the amount of possibilities we process, making us more thoughtful, creative, and open to new ideas. For instance, individuals who are 'primed'—meaning scientists help evoke a certain mindset or emotion before doing an experiment—to feel either amusement or contentment can think of a larger and wider array of thoughts and ideas than individuals who have been primed to feel either anxiety or anger. And when positive emotions broaden our scope of cognition in this way, they not only make us more creative, they help us build more intellectual social, and physical resources we can rely on in the future.*"

So, "don't worry, be happy" is a probably good starting place for any community revitalization program, and might be the best first step towards building a renewal culture, which seems to also be reliable path to happiness.

TRANSITION MANAGEMENT: A KEY TO RESILIENCE.

Whatever the motivations—and whatever the goals—of your renewal effort, two crucial challenges remain constant: your transition strategy, and your transition management. The key to successful transition management is having an effective process, but we'll save that for the next chapter. For now, let's just try to better-understand transition management itself.

This book could be seen as a "Transition Success Guide". Why? Because how we handle transitions determines the success of both our revitalization and our resilience efforts.

Restoration ecologists know that the value of a certain plant species might only be to help transition an ecologically-damaged property from one state to another, so that the ultimately-desired species can then be established. This same concept of what might be called "transitional value" needs to be adopted in revitalization and resilience initiatives.

Too often, planners try to force the desired end state into existence in one fell swoop, rather that taking a more oblique route. They (or, more likely, the elected leaders) want quick, visible results , and that comes at the cost of lasting results.

Many critics of urban farming point out that urban farms can never compete with rural farms in terms of economic efficiency. That's true enough, but highly misleading. Urban farms only make economic sense when you factor-in ALL of their health, educational and social services to the community, not just revenue from food production. And even then, they only make sense when done in the right place at the right time.

Sometimes, their economic value is transitory: they activate a dead space, which revitalizes the neighborhood, which leads to the land's becoming so valuable that it no longer makes sense as a garden or farm. This is why many urban farms are using portable modules; so they can move on to the next space that needs to be activated. If the goal is resilient prosperity, we shouldn't get too attached to the often-transitional tactics that help get us there.

An individual transitioning from one career to another wants a resilient profession or business: one that remains relevant and lucrative. A city or nation transitioning from one economic base to another (such as from fishing to tourism) has the same goal.

For almost two decades, communities and regions worldwide have brought me in to help them revitalize, or to help them enhance their resilience. While they all had unique cultures, assets, challenges, and aspirations, they could all be put into two basic categories: 1) those who had failed to perceive and prepare for a transition (or who had failed to adapt to it), and thus needed revitalization; and 2) those who see a transition on the horizon, and wish to boost their resilience in preparation for it.

Transitions can thus be either internally (proactively) or externally (reactively) triggered. And they can be either incremental or sudden. The former often chip away at a community for years (sometimes called "creeping crud"), but never create enough pain to trigger a response. The latter pounce on a community, such as the loss of the major employer or a natural disaster. But the result is the same: one day folks wake up and realize that their future looks bleak.

The key lesson is that transitions are constant: only the speed varies. Thus, the trend towards an ongoing process of repurposing, renewing, and reconnecting our existing assets, and away from the old model of economic growth via the frantic acquisition of new assets (which often creates three new problems from every one it solves).

In other words, there are two basic kinds of transition management: preventive and curative. The former happens when a place prepares for an impending or likely disruption. The latter happen when they fail to prepare for an inevitable transition (such as from dependence on fossil fuels or unsustainable resource extraction), or when they are hit by an unpredictable disruption, such as civil war or an earthquake.

There are many "soft" characteristics that can contribute to a community's resilience, such as harmony and tenaciousness. But these are relatively unmanageable traits. The essential resilience-enhancing behavior that we can control (to a degree) is transition management.

Other than process, the most crucial element of transition management is (no surprise here) the strategy. Major transitions are fluid and unpredictable. Thus, even the best transition plan is rapidly rendered obsolete (unless it's an adaptive, "living" document). That fate seldom befalls a good transition strategy.

Here are some of today's more common transitions that typically trigger revitalization and/or resilience efforts:

- From extraction of virgin natural resources to resource restoration;
- From a socially/politically unstable rich/poor economy to one with a strong middle class;
- From a raw resource export economy to a value-added manufacturing economy;
- From a heavy industry economy to a high/clean-tech or information-based economy;
- From a locally-focused economy to a globally-connected economy;
- From automobile-centric planning to mobility orientation;
- From situations of high crime, racial strife, and disease to justice-based with equal opportunity for all;
- From disaster and/or climate vulnerability to reconstruction, redesign, or relocation.

Revitalization and resilience can only be measured over time, not as a snapshot of conditions at any given time. One can say "I'm going north", but there's no actual place called north. Trying to define a static place called "revitalized" is the same as defining north as "the North Pole": as soon as one arrives at the North Pole, all directions are south. Thus, if there were a state called "revitalized", then the only direction one could go upon reaching it would be devitalization.

Revitalization is self-referential: it's not determined by comparing oneself (or a place) to any other entity or place, but to oneself over time.

It's like regenerative agriculture: there's no particular farming technique (no-till, organic, permaculture, biodynamic, etc.) that is intrinsically regenerative: we need to take context into account. If we are starting with an exhausted farm that's been depleted by industrial agriculture, then any one of those techniques will be regenerative. If we chop down old-growth forest to create a new farm, none of those techniques would be regenerative.

Revitalization can also be determined both subjectively and objectively. The subjective measure can be either a snapshot or a trend. Subjectively, one can say "I feel I'm on an upward trajectory", or one can say "I feel better than I did last year."

Objectively, one can measure the qualities that comprise revitalization (health, wealth, happiness). Add a baseline, et voila: metrics appear. In other words, revitalization and resilience are transitional dynamics: there's no actual state of resilience, only increased resilience.

As in our previous discussion of measuring confidence, revitalization an resilience analysis software should therefore be possible. It would give places a choice of objective and subjective factors that can be measured via surveys or data, connect those metrics to relevant sources of data (property value, tax revenues, etc.), periodically get new data, and do trend / progression analysis to determine whether a place is revitalizing or devitalizing.

City managers and real estate investors would, I imagine, love to see such an analysis. It would be far more valuable than the usual, data-deficient "Top 10 Cities for _____" articles that constantly appear in magazines, usually based on little more than a writer's impressions. Such software might be a great project for a group of graduate students somewhere.

For a real estate investor, being able to perceive that a neighborhood has ceased its downward trajectory and has entered a revitalizing phase before anyone else perceives it would be like a stock market investor getting a hot, accurate tip about an impending rise in a company's share price.

STRATEGIC RECAP

> *"The best CEOs I know are teachers, and at the core of what they teach is strategy."*
> *– Michael Porter, Harvard University.*

Before we dive into the ideal process for implementing a resilient prosperity (in the final section of this book), let's do one last recap to make sure the message about strategy's vital importance sinks in. Knowing the process will accomplish little if it hasn't.

Strategy is the key overlooked factor in most failures. A strategy is a small thing, and costs virtually nothing; like an automobile ignition key. But—like a key—if you forget it, you're going nowhere. So why are the military and business worlds almost alone in teaching strategy?

Again: a strategy is a technique or method for achieving a goal. A strategy isn't something we actually do: it guides actions and decisions. The right strategy maximizes chances of success, while minimizing time and resource needs. You see strategic thinking in the news daily. Here are some examples of what it looks like.

Both Apple and Google have explored the possibility of building their own cars. When that news first hit, most folks were bemused. Neither company is likely to actually do it, but it's a good example of strategic thinking. At both firms, a new business opportunity must address two strategic issues: scale and connectivity.

Both are huge, publicly-traded companies, so new markets must be vast to satisfy Wall Street's insatiable demand for growth. Personal transportation has the requisite scale. New markets should also connect with existing offerings, for synergy's sake. As accident rates show, automobiles are where we increasingly use Apple's and Google's products and services. Thus, an Apple or Google self-driving car is a concept worthy of considering.

Speaking of automobiles: back on August 2, 2006, Elon Musk published his so-called "secret" strategy (labelled a "master plan"), which he has successfully implemented: 1) Build sports car; 2) Use that money to build an affordable car; 3) Use that money to build an even more affordable car; 4) While doing above, also provide zero emission electric power generation options; 5) Don't tell anyone.

One of Musk's biggest challenges has been distribution. In bypassing traditional automobile dealerships, he made enemies of them (and of the politicians they fund). Product manufacturers often fail by focusing so heavily on the product that the distribution or marketing strategies are taken for granted (the "Better Mousetrap" trap). Your product might save consumers tons of money. But if it does so in a way that threatens the income of existing players—such as reducing service revenue or sales of more profitable items—expect pushback.

As Charlie Peters of Emerson (a 125-year-old manufacturer) says: *"The barriers to adoption are much more severe than the barriers to develop the technology."* He found that Emerson's design and production expertise is wasted without the right strategy for co-opting or bypassing the *status quo*.

The right strategy can emerge from identifying your chief threat. The rise of Netflix—and streaming video in general—convinced HBO to expand from content production into distribution.

HBO's strategy convinced Netflix to expand from distribution into content production (such as House of Cards). In 2013, Gus Sarandos, the chief content officer of Netflix described their succinct strategy: "to become HBO faster than HBO can become us". It worked.

So again: why do we mostly think of strategies in a military or business context? Aren't all of us trying to achieve goals? Why do we have so much economic, social, and environmental planning, but so little "pre-planning" (strategy) and "post-planning" (process)?

The tide might finally be turning on the urban front: Memphis, Tennessee recently embedded a blight- elimination strategy in their city charter, not just in policy. That's a major step forward. It would have been better, of course, if they had embedded a revitalization process into their charter, rather than just the initial step of removing blight.

Once in a while, I run across an organization that really understands what a strategy and a vision should look like. Heron Foundation is one of them.

Here's Heron's vision statement: *"Our vision is to help people in the United States to escape poverty, thrive and enjoy the benefits of full livelihood, opportunity and community."* And here's their strategy: *"Our strategy is to invest capital in ways that expand reliable employment and economic opportunity."*

No 90-page "strategies" or 500-word "visions" for them. Each gets just one sentence. Not surprisingly, Heron is one of the most respected foundations, despite their relatively small size. We featured one of their more-important initiatives in REVITALIZATION.

The Spring 2017 issue of *Strategy + Business* had an article titled "10 Principles of Strategy through Execution" by Ivan de Souza, Richard Kauffeld, and David van Oss. It said *"Quality, innovation, profitability, and growth all depend on having strategy and execution fit together seamlessly. ...Your execution occurs in the thousands of decisions made each day by people at every level of your company."*

Here's an expanded version of that previously-mentioned "elevator test": the next time you're talking to a mayor, planner, or developer who says they are going to revitalize a place, ask what their strategy is. If they're still talking a minute later, they might have a strategy, but not a good one. If they hand you a 50-page document, they don't have a strategy, but might not know it. If they say "*Go to hell*", they don't have a strategy, and they know it.

Strategists can be divided into two categories: formal and informal. The former devise stated strategies and build plans and/or processes around them. The latter are those blessed with what might be called "strategic intuition". It's similar to the way some cooks follow recipes (AKA "processes"), while others just throw stuff together. Both can produce wonderful meals, but the latter are far more likely to produce occasional disasters. Which style of strategist do you want in charge of your community's future? Either one is better than none.

Informal strategists (the good ones, anyway) are those folks who always seem to be in the right place at the right time with the right offering. They intuit effective solutions to problems, often without ever using the word "strategy". If your life has been marked by one "natural" success after another, you're probably one of these intuitive strategists. If not, keep reading, so you can become a formal strategist, with a formal process. You'd be amazed at how many major community renewal projects get launched without a strategic process just because someone (often the mayor) had a "good idea."

Just because a revitalization initiative is based on a good idea, doesn't mean it won't have a plethora of unintended negative consequences... economically, socially and/or environmentally. For instance, readers of REVITALIZATION know that I'm a big fan of repurposing and renewing old transportation infrastructure into linear parks that reconnect and revitalize neighborhoods.

But such projects are often planned by organizations with great expertise related to that central idea, but little if any expertise in revitalization strategies or processes. In Chicago, for instance, former Mayor Rahm Emmanuel pushed a number of large-scale regeneration projects that had the potential to bring large swaths of derelict land back to life. But he was been rather notorious for his aristocratic tendencies, which displayed little regard for the welfare of lower-income residents.

His most famous accomplishment might be the Bloomingdale Trail. The Bloomington Line was a 2.7-mile (4.3 km) elevated railroad running east-west on the northwest side of Chicago. In 2015, the city converted it into a High Line-style elevated greenway called The Bloomingdale Trail. It forms the backbone of a larger park and trail network called "The 606," and is reportedly the longest linear park in the Western Hemisphere. The trail reconnects and has helped revitalize the neighborhoods of Logan Square, Humboldt Park, and West Town.

The design and planning was put largely in the hands of the Trust For Public Land (TPL), one of my favorite non-profits. But an excellent December 7, 2018 article titled "The 606 Shows the Downside of Having Parks Nonprofits Lead Infra

Projects" by Lynda Lopez in StreetsBlog Chicago does a good job of illustrating the crucial gaps that emerge when there's lots of money and political support behind a revitalization effort, but no one with a deep knowledge of the comprehensive revitalization process in charge of it.

In this case, the failure was a common one: excessive and/or unnecessary displacement of traditional, usually lower-income residents.

Here's an excerpt from that article: "*...staff from TPL's Chicago office acknowledged that when they led the project, their focus wasn't on preserving affordability. "We are not in the business of housing," one unnamed staffer said. 'We are in the business of conservation and building parks. Housing is not what we do; that's not our mission.' An affordable housing advocate...argued that responding to gentrification and displacement threats is difficult, because different community groups are operating in silos. 'There is no overarching coalition to deal with these issues; even our organizing is segregated.'*"

Some say that the responsibility for the overall revitalization process should have been shouldered by Chicago's planning office. But this illustrates the yawning chasm between the public perception of what planners do, and what they actually do (mostly zoning and approving or denying development permits). Planners aren't taught the dynamics of revitalization, just as AMA-style doctors are taught almost nothing about creating health (the money is in treating sickness and delaying death).

And so it is with the traditional elements of planning profession. As long as cities are locked into the never-ending cycle of planning without an ongoing regeneration process, they will likely remain in an unhealthy, crisis-ridden condition. They'll constantly be driven into the arms of planners, just as people with degenerative diets and sedentary lifestyles are constantly driven into the arms of doctors.

MEASURING PROGRESS TOWARD RESILIENT PROSPERITY FOR ALL

Creating a strategic process to pursue resilient prosperity is one thing: managing it is another. And achieving specific goals based on often-fuzzy concepts is yet another.

For example, one "soft" attribute that is known to make places more resilient is inclusiveness, which leads to more-equitable economies. But how exactly does one make a local economy more inclusive, going beyond the usual lip-service charrettes and "stakeholder engagement" exercises?

There are many possible approaches, but the central factor—as with reducing displacement—is desire. Socioeconomic equity must be overtly stated as a community goal: it must be in the vision that underlies your strategy and plan.

Assuming you do have inclusiveness embedded in your vision/strategy, here are some tactics that can help you achieve that goal:

- Transportation: The lower a family's income, the greater the percentage of that income is devoted to their car: auto payments, insurance, fuel, parking, etc. If your affordable (or free) public transit does a good job of connecting the places that lower-income people live with the places they work, many will ditch their car. They can then spend that money on food, rent, healthcare, education, etc. But it's not just about money: given the obesity epidemic, making cities enjoyable and safe for pedestrians and cyclists is also important to health.
- Housing: Having affordable housing in sufficient quantity and of good quality in locations with effective public transit is a given. But the leading edge of economic inclusion strategies is mixed-age, mixed-income development. An example is Detroit's $28 million public-private partnership that's renovating the historic 1924 Strathmore Hotel into 129 affordable and market-rate apartments, plus 2000 sq. ft. of ground-floor commercial space. Resilient cities rid themselves of zoning and planning practices that isolate residents from each other according to income.
- Education: High-quality schools provide the most reliable path out of poverty. But too many cities take an elitist approach of focusing on preparing students for college and white-collar jobs, neglecting the needs of blue-collar workers. Boosting local trade schools, apprenticeship programs, and internships connects high school graduation with realistic local career opportunities.
- Entrepreneurial support: The path out of poverty isn't always employment. Many prefer to create their own career by starting a business. Downtown business incubators—often in repurposed industrial buildings—are increasingly revitalizing individual lives and entire communities simultaneously.
- Health, safety, and food: It should go without saying that people are less likely to take full advantage of transportation, housing, education, or entrepreneurial opportunities if they're in poor health, or in a threatening environment. But low-income neighborhoods—especially in the U.S.—are still typified by food deserts, with convenience stores supplying the "food" for meal preparation. And by poor policing. And by

a paucity of green space. And by contaminated soil from earlier industrial use. And by toxic air and water from current industrial or infrastructure use. Solutions include brownfield remediation, ecological restoration, affordable healthcare, publicly-engaged police, urban agriculture, and local food systems (which connect regional family farms to urban cores via farmers' markets, Community Supported Agriculture (CSA), and central food warehouses).

We must not be satisfied with merely stating socioeconomic equity as an objective: metrics must be established to ensure that the vision is translated into action. Researchers at McGill University, in a January 2015 report published in the Transport Policy journal, suggest the following four metrics to track progress on transportation-related social equity objectives:

1. Changes in accessibility to desired destinations, especially for disadvantaged groups;
2. Difference in travel times, to work and essential services, between car and public transit;
3. Difference between top and bottom income residents in the proportion of household expenditures spent on transportation; and
4. Difference between car users and pedestrians/cyclists in traffic injuries/deaths (per-trip basis).

If we don't quantify our results, adaptive management systems have nothing on which to base adjustments. We can't manage what we don't measure. The good news is that the cafeteria-style approach to revitalization described earlier lends itself to a simple, powerful management tool: checklists. As a former pilot, former military medic, and present-day SCUBA diver, I can attest to the life-saving power of checklists when fast decisions must be made in chaotic, stress-filled environments.

Again, the key is "performance" as opposed to "prescriptive" rules. Focus on the desired outcome: not the method. London famously got cars out of its city center via congestion pricing. But on February 9, 2015, then-London mayor Boris Johnson (now PM, but probably on his way out) announced a way to get cars out of the way of progress, without getting them out of the city.

He said they had identified 70 stretches of roads that could be buried. This would free-up the land for people, for business, and for reconnecting neighborhoods long-severed by those roads. In other words, repurposing land to higher and better uses for growth without sprawl.

"People are not lazy—they simply have impotent goals that do not inspire them." – Tony Robbins

What non-obvious factors should be measured? Here's one: immigrants and other newcomers are a major revitalizing factor in many places.

Many small towns renew themselves thanks to the work of public and private leaders who are lifelong residents. Such people are intimately familiar with the community: its assets, problems, and personalities. But long-time residents are also the ones most like to suffer from a defeatist attitude, thanks to decades of strategy-free failures.

Newcomers—immigrants or not—don't know that history, so they are often the ones who see possibilities that the native-born are blind to. Thus, adding "engage newcomers" to your checklist can make a huge difference.

On March 13, 2015, I posted the following advice in response to a discussion on the LinkedIn "Downtown Revitalization" group about overcoming local negativity: *"Newcomers are often the folks who see the potential of the place (after all: they just selected it to live in). The long-time residents are often the ones saying "we tried that already: nothing works". You can use newcomers kind of like product manufacturers use 'early adopters': Once newcomers get the ball rolling, and a project or program gains some momentum and credibility, long-time residents will start coming aboard."*

Six days later, Debra Felske, a community volunteer in Osceola, Arkansas posted this reply: *"Storm: I think you hit the nail on the head when you mentioned contacting the newcomers. I am a newcomer to my community and all I see is potential. It was very easy to get me to volunteer in the Downtown area because I wasn't living in 'remember when' like the majority of the residents."*

Most citizens say they want more prosperity, so politicians promise it, but they don't measure progress towards it. Few even issue quarterly reports on completed renewal projects. While helpful, that would be like accepting a list of our surgeries as an analysis of our health.

The medical analogy is apt: Classical Chinese medicine differs from allopathic (Western) medicine by enhancing the body's resilience and ability to repair itself. Western doctors merely react to illness, usually in ways that weaken the body. Likewise, most communities rely on "surgeries" (projects) and "drugs" (incentives) instead of boosting resilience and regeneration. Just as the AMA dismisses acupuncture successes with labels like "placebo effect" (which doesn't explain anything), so too do ineffective public leaders consider revitalization essentially unmanageable.

A May 30, 2014 article titled "When is civil society a force for social transformation?" by Michael Edwards said: *"There are more civil society organizations in the world today than at any other time in history, so why isn't their impact growing? ...the growth of civil society has been remarkable: 3.3 million charities in India and 1.5 million across the United States; ...81,000 international NGOs and networks, 90 per cent of them launched since 1975. But there's no sign that the underlying structures of social, political and economic violence and oppression are being shaken to their roots. (because) civil society groups are increasingly divorced from the forces that drive deeper social change."*

Michael Edward's question above might be at least partially answered by the fact that few civil society organizations are effectively connected to the community redevelopment process (if, in fact, a process even exists.) A well-designed strategic renewal process provides entry points for any kind of organization. It can effectively connect your government leaders, departments, and agencies, as well as your non-profits, redevelopers, schools, and foundations...all without introducing unmanageable complicatedness. It would make them all an intrinsic part of producing resilient prosperity, not just stakeholders to be engaged when convenient or politically expedient.

An important benefit of having a complete process is the ability to be aware of—and respond appropriately to—the many essential details that top-down initiatives tend to ignore. For instance, after ten years of impressive post-tsunami reconstruction in the devastated Indonesian province of Aceh, economic and social recovery has been elusive. 140,000 homes, 4000 kilometers of roads, a 242-kilometer coastal highway, 2000 schools, 1000 health facilities, 23 seaports, and 13 airports/landing strips have been built.

> *"Perfection has to do with the end product,*
> *but excellence has to do with the process."*
> *– Jerry Moran.*

But many of those houses are now empty and rotting. The occupants had no way to earn a living, and were forced to migrate elsewhere. Economic, social, and environmental "details" were overlooked in the rush to construct buildings and infrastructure. This insensitive, "engineered" recovery could have been far more revitalizing if they had used a strategic renewal process. Adaptive management would have altered the Aceh reconstruction effort years ago, back when the first signs of failed socioeconomic recovery became evident.

The irony is that none of this systemic work is capital-intensive: just the opposite, in fact. It wasn't a lack of money that caused Aceh's $7.7 billion recovery effort to fail: it was process ignorance. They knew how to spend money, and how to build "hard" structures. But they were clueless about "soft" factors, and about the dynamics of regeneration (such as creating confidence in the future of the place).

How could a massive, multifaceted effort like Indonesia's post-tsunami recovery be coordinated in an adaptive manner, especially with information infrastructure devastated? Again: checklists are the simplest way to ensure that changes to a program aren't taking it off course, and your RECONOMICS Process you'll learn in the next chapter is a great basis for a post-disaster reconstruction checklist.

The following list of insights relate to common strategic mistakes and successes I've observed when places try to create revitalization and/or resilience. Every place and time is different, so treat these as generalities, not universal rules.

60 INSIGHTS FOR CREATING PROSPEROUS, GREEN, EQUITABLE, RESILIENT PLACES

1. 80% of the revitalizing work done by urban planners and civil engineers in the 21st century will undo 80% of the work their predecessors did to cities and nature in the 20th century.
2. Good stakeholders create equitable visions. Good leaders create efficient strategies. Good partnerships create effective action.
3. Resilient places prepare for the exception. Vulnerable places prepare for the average.
4. Most places have either plans with no money, or money with no plans. Some places have plans and money, but no success.
5. Those with a strategic renewal process can generate what they need, or succeed with what they have.
6. Most plans seem to be commissioned as a substitute for action. Buying a plan doesn't revitalize a community, any more than merely owning a book enlightens a person.
7. The primary purpose of planning should be to facilitate action, not to create a plan.
8. The sole purpose of strategizing is to help actions succeed. Thus, a plan without a strategy is a plan to fail.
9. Strategies must be based on verbs. Adjectives and nouns are for visions. Beware of strategies containing words like "sustainable", "inclusive", "creative", "resilient", "innovation", etc.

10. A good regional strategy can revitalize a community faster than a local strategy, thanks to shared natural resources, infrastructure connectivity, and critical mass.
11. Just as green infrastructure helps cities absorb stormwater to reduce destructive flooding, regenerative strategies help cities absorb population growth to reduce destructive sprawl.
12. Community economic resilience is more likely to derive from strategies that grow local employers, rather than those that steal employers from other communities.
13. Economic development should be the process of creating a place where employers want to be. It should not be the process of bribing (incentivizing) them to move to your otherwise-undesirable place.
14. Places that value jobs over quality of life usually end up with neither. Places that enhance their quality of life attract jobs as a fringe benefit.
15. 3 ways to boost local tax revenues: 1) Raise rates; 2) Sprawl; 3) Revitalize. #1 angers everyone; #2 angers intelligent people; #3 makes almost everyone happy.
16. Badly-planned sprawl kills downtowns, while enabling leaders to boast of population and tax revenue growth. Such communities are like a bodybuilder with massive muscles, but a diseased heart.
17. Program, vision, strategy, policies and partnerships should come before design: Don't engage architects or engineers too early. A specific design for your project—no matter how good—stifles creativity, and closes-off paths to alternatives if it's created too soon.
18. A general who is winning the battles but losing the war changes the strategy. So should a city that's winning at redevelopment, but losing at revitalization.
19. Revitalization and resilience success stories usually feature:
    a) A shared vision of the desired future;
    b) A strategy to achieve that vision; and
    c) An understanding of process, and of how similar places achieved similar goals.
20. Mayors often copy the physical product of successful revitalization in other cities, rather than learning from the innovative, inclusive, adaptive process that created it.
21. Strategic public-private partnerships flow opportunity and risk to private partners, while flowing resources and influence to public partners.
22. Most cities that want revitalization or resilience have no one qualified to—and empowered to—deliver it. Their goals thus become wishes, dialogues or plans, not actual projects or programs.

23. Planners often say they want a downtown that's a good place to be, not just a good place to drive through. But their plans often say otherwise.
24. Retail is a sign of downtown revitalization; seldom a cause. Boost residential density via affordable housing + public transit, and retail follows. Count pedestrians annually to measure revitalization progress.
25. Tax Increment Financing: An excellent revitalization tool, but it's often a) misused [for sprawl], b) abused [developer subsidies], and c) overused [revenue depletion].
26. To build a tourism economy, design places that delight residents in your region: Locals provide year-round revenue, and most tourists prefer authentic, working places.
27. Immigrant families revitalize neighborhoods far more frequently and reliably than do the mostly-white males of the "creative class";
28. A vision or strategy that can't be recited in 30 seconds is probably too hazy or too complicated to succeed. If it can't be remembered, it won't affect daily decision-making.
29. A good vision without a strategy is a pleasant daydream. A good strategy without a vision is often the right route to the wrong place. A plan without a strategy is merely an activity catalog. And to implement a plan without adaptive management is to be guided by a relic.
30. Strategies are essential, fluid, and live in minds. Plans are optional, rigid, and (too often) rot on shelves.
31. For a resilient future, climate adaptation strategies must: a) restore green infrastructure to reconnect watersheds; b) repurpose energy infrastructure to renewables, c) revitalize today's economy to boost resources for resilience projects.
32. Devastated places should leverage their recovery process via research to build a restoration economy that becomes a regional, national or global nexus (cluster) of regenerative education, workforce development, and restorative technology.
33. Size often imbues a logarithmic dynamic in transit and trail networks: Each new node can double the value of the entire system.
34. Bilateral renewal strategies (and policies) reward what you desire and repel what you detest: Make downtown redevelopment easier and cheaper while making sprawl harder and more expensive.
35. Bilateral renewal strategies also reduce or remove the cause of the problem while undoing the damage already inflicted. E.g., industrial-style agriculture fuels the climate crisis. Regenerative agriculture sequesters vast amounts of carbon, thus removing carbon already

dumped into the atmosphere by previous farming, while ceasing to add new carbon.
36. Schizophrenic strategies self-destruct, such as redevelopment that exacerbates economic inequity, or policy frameworks that encourage sprawl and downtown revitalization simultaneously.
37. Economic development incentives have become commodities; Quality of life and confidence in the local future are usually the key differentiators when recruiting employers.
38. Your downtown revitalization effort shouldn't try to include affordable housing, public transit, walkability or heritage restoration. In most cases, it should be BASED on them.
39. You don't revitalize a downtown by bringing in more businesses. You revitalize it by bringing in more customers. Retail businesses follow opportunity: they seldom create it.
40. Economic Collapse Disorder (ECD): Unlike honeybees' Colony Collapse Disorder, the ECD pathogen is known...loss of confidence in the local future. Many factors can destroy confidence, but knowing the pathogen aids creation of the cure.
41. Revitalization Feedback Loop: Confidence in the local future attracts resources for revitalization; revitalization builds confidence in the local future.
42. Places that renew the natural, built, social, and economic assets they have today, tend to attract the resources they need to renew more of them tomorrow.
43. "Start with the petunias." This adage reminds us that there's always some action we can take right now. Action breeds more action. More action breeds momentum. Momentum breeds confidence in the future.
44. The more that people exercise, the more they CAN exercise.
The more that communities revitalize, the more they CAN revitalize.
The more that ecosystems are restored,
the more they CAN continue to restore themselves.
45. Don't wait until you're in trouble: Adaptive strategies constantly repurpose, renew, and reconnect your socioeconomic strengths and your physical assets (natural, historic, agricultural, infrastructure, etc.) to produce ongoing regeneration.
46. Revitalization strategies require thought. "Magic bullets" like stadiums, casinos, street banners, aquariums, or convention centers require only money.

47. Streetscaping is to community revitalization what nice clothing is to dating: It might get things started, but provides no foundation for the long term.
48. Moderate displacement is a natural result of revitalization: change begets change. Excessive displacement is revitalization done badly. Mixed-income neighborhoods are healthier.
49. Revitalization should pull residents up, not push them out.
50. A good revitalization strategy is simple; a good revitalization vision is holistic: Beware of simplistic redevelopment fads focused on a single attribute or asset type.
51. Optimize, Don't Maximize: Many revitalizing factors are devitalizing to both cities and nature when in excess, such as density, flows, connectivity, nutrients, change, and stability.
52. Good strategies solve underlying problems, tactics mostly deal with signs and symptoms. For example: Armoring streams to fix watersheds is a tactic: it's like armoring police to fix society.
53. Policies, partnerships, programs and projects implement strategies. Strategies implement visions. A vision is a cohesive set of aspirational goals.
54. If a lumber or mining town (or region) is devitalized due to resource depletion, a logical strategy for economic revitalization will be based on resource restoration.
55. Communities that renew what they have tend to revitalize. Communities that lament what they lack tend to devitalize.
56. Money alone CAN revitalize a place, but seldom does. Money, plus a strategic renewal process, seldom fails.
57. Affordable physical mobility boosts economic mobility. Public transit and bicycle/pedestrian trails revitalize: automobiles tend to devitalize.
58. As was the destruction and depletion of our world, our revitalized future—the global restoration economy—will be based primarily on business and government activity, not on philanthropy.
59. Unlike people, cities and nations don't die of old age. Like people, they die early from ignorance, fear, and neglect. Constant regeneration produces knowledge, optimism and care…thus yielding the "eternal" city or nation.
60. On our depleted, fragmented, contaminated planet, the heart of a sustainable development strategy is actually restorative development: After all, who wants to sustain this mess?

Let's wrap-up this chapter by pointing out that the two most important roles of a leader are:
- Make it easier for your team to do their jobs. That's the organizational management portion of a leader's job; and
- Help your team stay focused on the vision and strategy. That's the performance management portion of a leader's job.

The vision is where the purpose of your strategic renewal process is determined, whether that purpose is climate resilience, environmental justice, equitable economic renewal, more jobs, cleaner air, or simply a higher quality of life.

Since the strategy derives from the vision (and from the obstacles to achieving that vision)—and since the process' purpose is to deliver that vision—the vision thus guides everything. A regenerative vision and a regenerative strategy go hand in hand. Like male and female, their union regenerates life.

PART C - PROCESS: MASTERING THE OTHER MISSING KEY TO SUCCESS.

"What makes founders so great as entrepreneurs only rarely makes them the best person to run a business once it gets into the tens of millions of dollars. Their experience is not around process."
– John Kenney, TSG Consumer Partners.

John Kenney's insight about business startups (above) applies to many communities. While some new cities are still being created—primarily in China and Africa—most are at least a century old. But, with the exception of those cities that are locked-in by geography—like San Francisco, Hong Kong and New York City—most mayors are still treating their community as if it were just founded...as if it were a startup. They have a romantic image of their role as a pioneer, still pushing into new territory.

This pioneer psychology is just one driver of unnecessary sprawl, which is well-documented to undermine both the economy and the quality of life in the long term (though it sometimes generates short-term political or financial benefits). The vast majority of the communities that are desperately seeking to revitalize their downtowns need to do so because sprawl killed their city center. If that sprawl involved the city's planners (it often doesn't), then one could say that the death of their downtown was planned. Either way, the skills it took to create and grow the community are very different from those needed to heal its wounds and make it a better community.

"Better" is relative to current conditions, of course. If a place is boring—indistinguishable from most other places—then "better" means transforming it into a unique, genuine, attractive, stimulating place to live and work. If it's emptying-out due to a paucity of jobs and a perception that things will only get worse, "better" means growing the economy—not the geographic size, and not even necessarily the population—and reinstilling confidence in its future. If it is constantly damaged by natural, societal or economic disasters, "better" means healthier, more harmonious and more resilient.

The key to all of those transformations is process. Those mayors and city managers with pioneer mindsets will likely be as clueless about the process of regenerating their community as a kid with a lemonade stand would be if asked to revive a dying national franchise of a thousand lemonade stands. Most mayors promise revitalization on the campaign trail, but don't have the slightest clue as to how to deliver it.

Worse than being ill-suited, their pioneer mindset is the exact opposite of what is needed to revitalize. Making a place is very, very different from remaking a place. The world is awash with place makers, when what we desperately need is more place remakers. And what those remakers desperately need is a process for doing so.

Too many places delay creating a revitalization or resilience program or strategy after a crisis, as they want things to "settle down" first. To them I say "*Wake up, folks: this is as settled as things are likely to get. The time to strategize about your future is now.*" Properly applied, what you're learning in this book will boost your local future. But it will only improve your chances for resilient prosperity, not guarantee it. Extraneous, uncontrollable factors are always lying in wait.

For instance, numerous aid and government agencies worked heroically to rebuild confidence in the future of Liberia and Sierra Leone after both were ravaged by civil war. Great advances were made in health, education, agriculture, and assistance to war victims. Then, Ebola struck in 2014, wiping out that confidence. Once again, businesses were terrified of investing in either country.

But most places we can't afford wait for the bad things to stop before doing good things. While economic progress has certainly been undone in those long-suffering nations, they are both arguably more resilient than a decade ago.

Earlier, we saw how corporate culture consultants—and people who don't understand strategy—say silly things like "*culture eats strategy for breakfast*"; as if having a great culture could substitute for knowing how to succeed. Interestingly, one never hears "*culture eats process for breakfast*": most people seem to understand intuitively that nothing useful gets reliably and repeatedly produced without a process.

An organization with a great culture but no process merely results in a group of happy-but-unproductive people. Addressing the vital importance of having both a healthy culture and an effective process, Jan Bednar, founder of the super-successful young company ShipMonk (#29 on the 2018 INC 5000 list) says *"Process without people is as bad as people without process."*

Communities are constantly rolling-out initiatives based on the latest revitalization fad, and make the same mistake every time: lack of an effective process to make it reality.

"Makers districts" is one of the more recent of these trends, and it's based on a fairly sound concept: home-grown manufacturing. Manufacturing creates far more spin-off jobs than any other business sector, making this a solid foundation for revitalization;

"Ecodistricts" also have a very solid foundation in reality, and are well-timed to address the growing need for green infrastructure to make places more climate-resilient. Some cities have done great things with the idea, but it doesn't seem to be gaining much momentum (probably due to there being too much focus on design, and not enough on strategy and process);

"Innovation districts" (or "zones") can work, but present a chicken-or-egg problem: it's a build-on-strength strategy that usually requires an existing powerhouse institution. But "innovation" sounds great and is popular with voters, so politicians often push them, even when inappropriate. They also fit the "smart cities" trend (not to be confused with the fading "smart growth" movement).

Some old fads, like the "creative class", have mostly resulted in expensive failures. There's nothing wrong with the observation that creative types tend to pioneer the revitalization of derelict neighborhoods. The problem is twofold: 1) that dynamic is largely unmanageable, so it's fun to read about—and politicians love its simplicity—but it's difficult to make happen; and 2) that dynamic comprises maybe 1% of what it takes to bring a place make to life, so it's too superficial to rely on.

Bottom line? Choose whatever focus you think is best for your community at this point in time. But be sure to have a strategic renewal process to plug it into. Otherwise, it's likely to go nowhere fast, and suffer the fate of so many "new and exciting" consultant-driven redevelopment themes before it.

Are strategic renewal processes going to be the next revitalization fad? Hardly. Every depressed community or region on Earth has been trying to create one...usually without knowing it, which is why they always have gaps in their process. Calling process a fad for community revitalization would be like calling assembly lines a fad in manufacturing. So, process is what we'll dive into next.

CHAPTER 9 - PROJECTS VS. PROGRAMS: FROM SPORADIC RENEWAL TO REAL MOMENTUM.

"Incredible things are happening here. We're seeing validation from VCs & investment banks, and there is momentum around revitalization."
– Irma Olguin, Jr., CEO of Bitwise Industries, describing Bakersfield, California in 2019.

A ll around the world, cities have millions---even billions---of dollars worth of local redevelopment projects planned or underway. But few have a program tying them together in a way that could double or triple the ROI of those projects. The irony is that---while projects are capital-intensive---programs are cheap. Are those cities stupid? Nope. Just unaware of their options. Let's fix that.

First, let's start with a statement that will sound like heresy: redevelopment projects and planning exercises shouldn't have to engage local stakeholders. They also shouldn't have to explore ways in which to more-efficiently integrate the renewal of your natural, built, and socioeconomic environments. Why?

Because that stakeholder engagement and asset integration should already be in place, via an ongoing revitalization program. Effectively engaging all of your resident, non-profit, academic, business, and government stakeholders is a labor-intensive process that takes a significant amount of time. It's wasteful and counter-productive for each new project or comprehensive plan update to have to start that process from scratch. The broader the stakeholder engagement, the less vulnerable your program will be to changes in political administration.

If you've read this far, you now know how to create a revitalization strategy. Let's start filling in the other missing pieces of this jigsaw puzzle. In Chapter 10, you're going to learn what might be the ideal, universal process for creating resilient prosperity. I've encountered many places that had most of the elements of that process, but none that had all. The two elements of that are usually missing are strategy and program.

Until now, we've mostly focused on strategy, and on the fact that few places even have a partial process. Let's now dive into the other commonly-overlooked—but crucially-important—part of the process: the ongoing program.

Again, it's ironic then that programs are so cheap, while projects are so capital-intensive. Nothing adds more value per dollar invested than the tiny amounts required by an ongoing revitalization or resilience program.

An ongoing program is a community's "flywheel", capturing the momentum of each successful project, and using it to make subsequent projects easier to fund and launch. A well-designed program also captures the community's learning, and embeds those lessons in both policy and practice. Such enhancements of the community's "renewal capacity" reduce bureaucratic roadblocks for redevelopers, increase the kinds of incentives that attract what the community really needs, and enhance the community's partnering skills. Maybe more importantly, they restore hope and optimism concerning the future.

The general public often assumes that planning, economic development or redevelopment agencies are providing a systemic revitalization program. This is very seldom the case. For the most part, they are siloed activities with grand-sounding mandates, but surprisingly-limited footprints. Real estate investors and redevelopers put a lot of stock in their market analyses.

But the best market analysis in the world won't save them if the community goes downhill after they've made their investment. And they have no criteria on which to determine the likelihood of devitalization or revitalization. In the absence of a reliable strategic renewal process, all they have to guide them are snapshots of the recent past, and the hope that the past is prelude. It often isn't. As with the stock market, a streak of good numbers might only mean that the community has peaked.

Without a comprehensive, collaborative, ongoing revitalization program, even well-founded, well-intentioned redevelopment agencies often deteriorate into wasteful—often corrupt—playgrounds for the politically connected. That was the major motivation behind California Governor Jerry Brown's wholesale elimination of that state's 400+ urban redevelopment agencies—which together controlled over $5 billion in tax revenue—in 2011. Revitalization should be done by communities, not just to them.

Regionalism is important, too: most large, national real estate developers select sites based on their confidence in the future of a region first. If your community isn't in one of their selected regions, it doesn't matter what kinds of incentives you offer: they won't even talk to you. But if well-organized revitalization programs are hard to find at the community level, they're vanishingly rare at the regional level. The fact is that almost all redevelopment is done by local people and companies, which makes economic developers' mad scramble to attract outsiders even sillier. Again: far better to spend that time and money on efforts that inspire local investors with more confidence in the local future.

Over the past 18 years (24, if you include the 6 years spent researching and writing my first book, The Restoration Economy), some of the saddest places I've encountered in my professional travels are those that have worked long and hard on revitalizing their city, experiencing emotional highs when the initiatives are launched, followed by crushing disappointments when they fail. This can be devastating to the community psyche. I call it "bipolar redevelopment". Widespread negativity and pessimism—amongst residents and leaders alike—are the usual result. In fact, lifting communities out of such funks is one of the more common reasons I'm invited to do talks and workshops.

> *"Success and failure. We think of them as opposites, but they're really not. They're companions — the hero and the sidekick." – Laurence Shames, American writer.*

These disappointments usually derive the combination of three factors: 1) wanting to revitalize, 2) trying to revitalize, and 3) not knowing how to revitalize.

One source of such repeated failures is the previously-mentioned "schizophrenic" redevelopment: implementing polar-opposite development policies simultaneously. I already mentioned the most common form: working on downtown revitalization while allowing (even subsidizing) sprawl. But another common manifestation is when communities have a "blight removal" program that's demolishing reusable vacant homes (and commercial buildings that could be repurposed as housing) while another program is trying to boost affordable housing.

Another example concerns trees. Many enlightened cities—Melbourne, Victoria, Australia being a prime example—have realized that restoring and expanding their urban tree canopy is a crucial factor in creating a revitalized, resilient future. But announcements like this one are still common, even in places that are working to boost their green infrastructure: "*More than 150 trees have been cut down along one street in Kaduna (Nigeria) to make way for the state government's urban renewal project...*"

Granted, just as with old grey infrastructure, old green infrastructure is sometimes in the way of needed changes. But planners and developers are often too quick with the chain saws. One would think that creating a local policy to increase the planting new trees would be accompanied by a policy to decrease the cutting of old trees, but it's shocking how seldom that's the case.

What's even more frustrating is that the same places keep making the same mistakes. That's because they have no learning mechanism regarding revitalization, and no storehouse for what they do learn. This is one of the great values of having an ongoing program.

Three key factors differentiate revitalization programs from renewal projects:
- DURATION: A program is ongoing, or very long term, whereas projects normally have end-dates measured in months, or a few years. (Note: Duration isn't enough: having a 30-year plan or 30-year project doesn't mean you have a program);
- SCOPE: A program addresses the entire community or region, whereas a project normally focuses on a specific property or asset; and
- PURPOSE: A program includes some softer, harder-to-measure goals, such as inspiring confidence in the community's future, reversing a decline, raising quality of life, enhancing overall environmental health, etc. A project's goals are usually more tangible, such as attracting a particular employer to a particular site, widening sidewalks to make a downtown more pedestrian-friendly, adding green roofs to reduce the urban heat island effect, etc.

The primary source of those depressing scenarios mentioned above is a focus on projects, rather than programs. Communities throw everything they have into a project that revitalizes a specific property or area, and then take a few years off. By the time the next renewal project comes along, the previous one is often dead or dying. The same dynamic applies to landscape-scale environmental restoration efforts, where an ecologically-viable critical mass of restored habitats and connections isn't achieved.

Without an ongoing program, you have a stop-start situation that creates no revitalizing flow. Without a flow, no momentum is produced. Momentum is what inspires confidence in the local future. And increasing confidence in the local future—as you'll discover a bit later in this chapter—is the "universal goal" that few seem to be aware of.

And so it is with communities. A community that has hit bottom probably has poor schools, potholed roads, high crime, derelict parks, and vacant buildings galore. But if their revitalization program inspires confidence that they're on the way back up, many of those downsides can be perceived as positives, or at least opportunities: buy-low, sell-high real estate investments; lower-wage employees for your startup; affordable housing for the employees you hope to attract from elsewhere; etc. But most devitalized places are cheap, so that's not enough to attract investors: it's the combination of cheap and "on the way up" that brings them in.

And we shouldn't ignore the "cool" factor: neighborhoods on the rise are the place to be. Young people in particular tend find them much more attractive than a place that's already nice, but going nowhere. Rags-to-riches stories never go out of style: people love to tell them, and that's a free source of media attention for your community or neighborhood.

The flows created by a program are crucial: flows of money, people, opportunities, information and, of course, water. Cities don't build next to ephemeral wetlands: they build next to flowing rivers, flowing estuaries, and flowing tides. Inland communities without major water assets build at the intersections of different flows, such as highways or railroads, where flows of people and commerce are high.

Good redevelopment designers are always looking to restore or improve flows, and the opportunities to do so are endless. But don't make the mistake of assuming that "improve" means "accelerate". The ubiquitous traffic-calming measures and "complete streets" programs—both designed to boost pedestrian and cyclist safety —work to slow car traffic.

I was at a planning meeting in St. Louis, Missouri many years ago, during the discussion about building a new stadium in their devitalized downtown. A highway engineer bragged that his department could design the roads in a way that would get the sports fans out of the city center in less than 15 minutes.

One of the downtown revitalization leaders intelligently asked "is that what we want?" The downtown was lifeless enough at that point, and stadiums have little revitalizing impact by the very nature of their sporadic usage: why try to reduce it further by encouraging people to leave immediately after a game?

That's the kind of dysfunctional thinking one gets when highway planners aren't an integral part of a local revitalization program, where multiple agendas can be shared, and linked to a common vision.

As mentioned earlier, most of the urban planning work for revitalization efforts here in the 21st century is based on undoing the urban planning work of the 20th century. The earlier planning mode was largely based on fragmentation: single-use zoning, single-economic-class neighborhoods, severing neighborhoods with urban highways, etc. While many planners still suffer from that antiquated mindset, the best are oriented towards flows, which means reconnecting what their predecessors separated.

Look at the best regeneration initiatives going on around the planet, and you'll see that the restoration of healthful flows is their basis, and reconnecting is their modality. Some are removing those badly-planned urban highways to restore flows between neighborhoods, or between downtowns and waterfronts. Others are removing obsolete dams to restore fish migrations, thus revitalizing economically-important commercial and recreational fishing economies.

These are all long-term projects, so an ongoing initiative is the only way to ensure cohesive results. All such flow-based projects are naturally strategic. But to achieve the maximum revitalizing effect, they should cease being isolated, limited-term, restoration projects, and become comprehensive, ongoing revitalization programs.

Ongoing programs are especially important due to a universal behavior psychologists refer to as "recency bias". Humans tend to extrapolate the past into the future, but we put extra emphasis on recent events. Investors flock to a stock (or a stock market) that's been rising steadily, even though looking further into the past reveals the likelihood of a downturn.

Applied to community economic growth, this means that the $10 million redevelopment of a historic building into a new hotel—and which opened last week—will inspire more confidence in the future of a community than the $200 million convention center that opened 3 years ago. Thus, an ongoing program that spawns a constant flow of small and medium-sized renewal projects will likely attract more investment to your city than will large projects that occur once every 5 or 10 years.

I've seen many dedicated professionals throw time and money into creating innovative community revitalization and/or resilience apps and other tools that die on the vine due to lack of programmatic support. Without a program, there was no ongoing training to help leaders and citizens understand the need for the tool and how to use it, and the effort wasn't perpetuated long enough to reach a critical mass of adoption.

For instance, in April of 2017, a county in Virginia abandoned their Revitalization Map, a smart 2016 effort on the part of their Revitalization Manager. Why? Because a few city council members didn't want restrictions on which projects they could or couldn't incentivize (that is: financially reward their buddies). They could only see what the map prevented them from doing; not its strategic value. An ongoing program helps avoid the wasted efforts resulting from decisions by people who have taken their eyes off the prize.

PROJECT MANAGEMENT VS. PROGRAM MANAGEMENT

The Project Management Institute (PMI) is an organization of almost 500,000 members worldwide. The "bible" of professional project managers, PMI's *A Guide to the Project Management Body of Knowledge (PMBOK), Third Edition* defines a program thus: "*A program is a group of related projects managed in a coordinated way to obtain benefits and control not available from managing them individually.*"

In other words, the whole is greater than the sum of the parts, which is another way of describing emergent phenomena. [My thanks to PMI for having me keynote their Global Congress (along with former President Bill Clinton), where I first encountered this definition.] So, if the hundreds of thousands of project managers worldwide are aware of this simple (and rather obvious) insight regarding the value of programs, why don't communities put it into practice?

An alternate (and more mission-specific) definition of "program" is offered by the Gulf Coast Ecosystem Restoration Council: "*a suite of intrinsically-linked restoration and/or conservation activities that must be implemented together in order to achieve the desired outcome.*"

Just as the world has a surfeit of planners and too few strategists, so too does it have plenty of project managers and too few program managers. As previously mentioned, revitalization is an emergent quality of a complex adaptive system. It's the tipping point, where a system hits a critical mass of renewal and transitions to a different state.

At that point, revitalization becomes self-perpetuating—revitalization begets more revitalization—and public leaders no longer need to keep pushing so hard for it. Due to that emergent nature, revitalization can't be engineered on a schedule. Reliably reaching the revitalization tipping point means doing the right things until you arrive at the right time. That requires an ongoing, strategic, regenerative program, which requires a competent program manager.

Too many of today's resilience initiatives are not resilient themselves (as we saw with Rockefeller's defunct 100 Resilient Cities program). At the city and regional level, these initiatives tend to have a relatively fixed agenda, and poor responsiveness to a changing environment. They are trying to engineer something (resilience) that can't be produced by an engineering mindset. Like the revitalization of cities—and the resilience of our bodies' immune systems—urban and regional resilience too is an emergent characteristic of a complex adaptive system.

Also as with revitalization, the only way to have a chance of achieving resilience is via a strategic, ongoing program. Managers of such programs need to be comfortable operating somewhat "in the dark." Unlike a simple project with an engineered outcome, a revitalization or resilience manager never knows when s/he will bump into the goal.

As novelist William Kent Krueger says in Manitou Canyon, "*Sometimes a man walks into the night and does not understand why he cannot see. He blames himself for the darkness.*" And so it can be for the revitalization director who is asked by a frustrated mayor looking to blame someone "*Where are we in the process? When will our city be reborn?*"

It's not just cities that need ongoing regeneration: we thrive on it as individuals, and corporations can't survive without it. For instance, after decades of reportedly psychologically-abusive management by Bill Gates and Steve Ballmer, Microsoft had developed a toxic, fear-based culture.

Internal groups were at war with each other, and everyone was so terrified of making a mistake that innovation dried up. Then, Satya Nadella took over as CEO in 2014, and Microsoft has rapidly been reborn. The key was creating a risk-friendly environment where people felt free to fail, and where the company's products and services were regenerated on an ongoing, programmatic basis. "*We needed needed a culture that allowed us to constantly refresh and renew,*" he says.

He's talking about creating a "renewal culture," which emerges naturally when an organization or community has an ongoing regeneration program. In my experience, such renewal cultures tend to comprise happier-than-normal people.

THE UNIVERSAL GOAL OF RECOVERY, REVITALIZATION AND RESILIENCE EFFORTS: INCREASING CONFIDENCE IN THE FUTURE

"Optimism is the faith that leads to achievement. Nothing can be done without hope and confidence." – Helen Keller

Resilient prosperity is a universal strategic outcome, but the universal strategic goal of good revitalization or resilience efforts is increasing confidence in the local future. The relationship between confidence in the future and revitalization is obvious enough: who wants to stay in, invest in, or come to a place whose future is bleak? But the connection to resilience is just as direct.

Access to external resilience funding is highly competive, so agencies and foundations will put their money where successful outcomes are more likely. Internal resilience funding, on the other hand, is only available if the economy is vibrant. This makes resilience dependent on revitalization, which is dependent on confidence in the local future.

As several recent real estate analyses have revealed---most notably from First Street Foundation---the relationship between confidence in the future of a place and the value of the property in that place is dramatically and causally linked. Revitalization efforts that have failed to bring a distressed place back to life tend to have one thing in common: they didn't convince enough people that the local economy and/or quality of life would improve.

The reasons such initiatives fail to boost confidence vary widely—lack of vision, poor strategy, dysfunctional design, insufficient funding, bad implementation, etc.—but that one strategic outcome failure is fairly universal. I say "fairly" because some otherwise-excellent initiatives are rendered moot by disasters beyond their control: war, earthquake, etc.

The title of a Reuters article by Kathy Finn (August 18, 2015) connects investment and confidence in the future nicely: "Rebuilt confidence in New Orleans flood controls fuels rebuilding." As mentioned earlier, investors care little about the condition of an asset when they buy it. What they do care about is whether it will be worth more in the future.

They'd rather invest in a rusted-out hulk of a 1957 Chevy, knowing it will appreciate dramatically after restoration, than buy a brand-new automobile, whose value will only go down.

Likewise, when real estate investors' prime criterion is maximizing their return on investment, they'd rather buy property in a depressed, pathetic town that they're confident is on its way up, than in a beautiful city that has peaked.

Avinash Persaud, chairman, Intelligence Capital Limited (London, UK) once said *"Money, in the end, is confidence."* Without confidence in the future value of a $20 bill or a €20 note, they are quite literally just worthless pieces of fabric. Confidence in rising value props up economies. When the U.S. severed its last ties to the gold standard in 1971, the dollar became an abstraction. It has zero value when shorn of confidence in its future value.

When that confidence is lost, hyperinflation—as we've tragically seen recently in Venezuela—and devitalization are the inevitable results. And so it is with local economies: no confidence in the future = no improvement in the present. Confidence in the future can be easily measured in polls. For instance, 83% of Chinese citizens say their country is heading in the right direction. Only 23% of

Americans feel the same about their nation. Such lack of confidence in the future does not bode well for the U.S. economy.

Look at the world of business. Talented employees are often wooed to startup companies that offer poor pay and almost no benefits. How? Stock options. But stock options can only offset those downsides if recruits have confidence that the company has a great future.

If attracting private investors necessitates inspiring them with confidence in the local future, that means boosting that confidence must be one of your priorities. Achieving it requires an ongoing program, with a qualified program manager.

Here's an example of how powerful this dynamic can be. The long-depressed Canal District of Worcester, Massachusetts is now revitalized, based almost solely on confidence that their historic canal—buried for over a century—will someday be daylighted, thereby providing a revitalizing water feature.

But they have neither the money to unearth it, nor an official plan for doing so. What provided the confidence that created their revitalization? A clear, credible vision of how the area would be changed for the better, plus a trusted organization (the Canal District Alliance) to devise and follow-through on a strategy.

Fifteen years ago, few people had much confidence in the future of Los Angeles. Its downtown was dead, it was dependent on water piped from far away states, and it was a transportation basket case.

But in 2008, voters approved Measure R, raising $40 billion to re-do their transportation infrastructure. It will create 12 transit lines, 43 transit stations, and some 210,000 jobs. Combined with their 50-mile restoration of the LA River, this investment has already spawning dramatic downtown revitalization. It's also triggered widespread transit-oriented redevelopment projects around the metro area that are better-connecting residents to business opportunities, jobs, and housing. By renewing their future, the city that long epitomized sprawl is becoming a present-day model of resilient prosperity.

Confidence is a nebulous product of the human mind, so having the future of a place pivot on such an intangible, uncontrollable quality is anathema to those who enjoy the illusion of being in control. The ways people try to control—or at least spark—revitalization are legion. Many communities try to revitalize their downtown or historic neighborhood simply by declaring it a "revitalization district", or "innovation district", or some such vernacular, but don't do much else. In most cases, such superficial "efforts" come to nothing. But in a few situations that fly in the face of reason, revitalization really does occur, despite the complete lack of process. Why?

The two most common reasons for this "something from nothing" magic are:

- Fortuitous timing (the area was on the verge of rebirth anyway, and the formal declaration simply helped it along); and
- Confidence in those making the pronouncement. This second cause often arises when a public-private partnership of credible players makes the "revitalization district" declaration. But it can also derive from a single trusted and/or charismatic mayor.

In other words, confidence in the people behind the revitalization effort creates confidence in a better future, which—in turn—attracts the investment that makes that revitalization actually happen.

Confidence in an area's future can also be boosted by merely announcing certain kinds of initiatives, and that news can be enough to spark redevelopment. Transit projects are the most reliable in this regard, since reconnecting places is well known to be a powerful revitalizer, and transit-oriented affordable housing is the wave of the future.

In cities all around the world, the promise of a new streetcar or rail initiative has been enough to trigger redevelopment, even though the first shovelful of dirt hadn't yet been dug. In Kansas City, Washington, DC, and many other cities, announcing future streetcars immediately triggered redevelopment along their routes. Why? Because the announcement created new confidence in the future of the properties and neighborhoods along those routes. We saw the same dynamic in the 19th century, when speculators gobbled-up land in towns along the intended path of the transcontinental railroad.

On the other hand, DC's streetcar is poorly designed, poorly-scaled and poorly implemented, so confidence in the future might diminish, but it has already had its revitalizing effect. In Arlington, Virginia (where I live) voters killed our poorly-planned and badly-communicated streetcar proposal—due to a well-deserved loss of confidence in the county government—but revitalization along its route had already started, and continues to this day, years after the streetcar idea died.

Now, that "instant confidence" dynamic is happening again in the metro DC area with the forthcoming Purple Line light rail.

When well-designed in the right place at the right time, such transit-oriented instant confidence is a reliable revitalizer. In 2010, Copenhagen, Denmark city leaders predicted that the mere announcement of their new City Circle metro line (in Danish: Cityringen)—completed in 2019—would cause land values to skyrocket. They were correct.

A July 31, 2015 *Washington Post* article documented how Detroit's Woodward Avenue started coming back to life after restoration of the old streetcar system was proposed. It quoted Matthew Cullen, president real estate developer Rock Ventures, as saying that the permanence of a streetcar will send a stronger signal of confidence in the city's future than merely buying a few more buses. He expects the streetcar project to generate $3.5 billion of economic activity with thousands more apartments being built.

This instant confidence in the future of a place doesn't usually happen with bus-based transit: only rail. That's because rail is a permanent, big-dollar commitment, whereas a bus line can be removed with the stroke of a pen. The exception is BRT (Bus Rapid Transit) which does require significant infrastructure investment, and which has helped revitalize several major corridors in Mexico City.

Again: this dynamic only occurs when the local government is credible. For instance, South Africa's economy is deteriorating badly. Unemployment is now 5% higher than is was in 2008, and their level of economic inequality is among the world's worst.

Much of the problem can be traced to the dominant political party, the African National Congress (ANC). They propped-up President Jacob Zuma far past his sell-by date. Zuma's long string of corruption scandals eroded confidence in the economic and social future of the country. Here's what the July 24, 2017 issue of Bloomberg Businessweek had to say:

"To restore the ANC's credibility, party reformers need to defend the independence and integrity of South Africa's financial and judicial institutions. If they want to revitalize the economy, they need to expose floundering state enterprises to competition, and address the corruption and inefficiency that have caused the country to sink in global business rankings. If they really want to empower black South Africans, they should focus less on creating sweet deals for shareholders, and more on fixing a failing educational system and enabling first-time job seekers to join the workforce." This last part is key, since the country's population is growing faster than its economy.

Another confidence-sapping factor: If a government suffers from excessive partisanship—with each party blocking all initiatives of the other, regardless of merit and heedless of damage to public good—few will have confidence in its announced policies, programs, or projects. In that case, revitalization won't precede that wonderful, expensive infrastructure project. In fact, it will probably lag the project, with investors and redevelopers not trusting that it will be completed.

Is there such a thing as too much confidence? Absolutely. Hyman Minsky, the late American economist, said that economic stability creates its own instability by breeding over-confidence and investment bubbles. In 2017, Zhou Xiaochuan, Governor of the People's Bank of China, said *"If we're too optimistic when things go smoothly, tensions build up, which could lead to a sharp correction, what we call a 'Minsky Moment'."*

That said, if you're going to have an economic bubble, a regeneration-based bubble would best: it would tend to leave the positive effects of restorative projects in its wake.

When residents have confidence in a better local future, fewer move away, and more of them work on improving their community. When outsiders have it, more will move there. When a relocating employer has it, they're more likely to overlook a place's weaknesses, trusting that it will get improve. When developers have it, they see the place as having secure investment opportunities.

Earlier, I mentioned New York Governor Andrew Cuomo's 2012 "Buffalo Billion" program. The state is investing $1 billion over 10 years in revitalizing that long-beleaguered city's economy. Here's what the governor said in a February 5, 2015 Brookings interview, when asked how the program was doing:

"*To date, approximately $842.2 million of the Buffalo Billion has been announced, which is expected to generate a total investment of over $8 billion. Over 5 years, this is projected to add over $11.3 billion in direct and indirect value to the economy and almost 14,000 jobs. The secret of the Buffalo Billion, however, is that we actually haven't yet spent a billion dollars to see this change. We have only moved approximately $174 million out the door, and put just over $408 million under contract. What that shows is that this isn't just about an injection of capital. It is about our commitment to this region, which brought energy and excitement back to Buffalo, and an economic boom followed.*"

That experience demonstrates the revitalizing power of inspiring confidence in the future. Any evidence that a place's future will be more prosperous is a form of "currency". With it, a place can "buy" residents, investors, and employers. The first person to come up with a way to reliably measure confidence in the future will be in possession of a powerful community revitalization tool...and a very valuable investment guide.

Big numbers alone are a confidence-inspiring factor, but seldom sufficient. A strong "re" focus is essential, such as the $4.5 billion Restore Pennsylvania program recently launched by Governor Tom Wolf, which promises to renew the state's decrepit infrastructure. (I should mention the downside: it's funded by a tax on fracking, making the state even more economically dependent on that toxic, aquifer-destroying activity).

Confidence in the future creates revitalization, and revitalization creates confidence in the future. Lack of confidence in the future creates devitalization, and devitalization creates lack of confidence. This feedback loop can very rapidly propel places upward or downward, so governments must start measuring confidence, if only via polls. Without that data, they're flying blind, maybe into the wrong loop. As noted previously, governments mostly measure jobs, population, property values, and tax revenues, all of which fluctuate with transient internal or external factors. But none of these metrics reveal likely future prospects.

> *"Six years since the financial meltdown, a psychology of uncertainty has altered the homeownership calculations for young adults. It's more than the weight of student loans, an iffy job market, and tight credit. Even those who can buy are hesitant. The doubt is so pervasive that it's eroded entry-level sales."*
> – Bloomberg BusinessWeek, July 21, 2014.

A simple initial survey of residents could establish a baseline local confidence factor. A similar survey could be done nationwide to measure outside perception. Repeating the surveys annually would provide an early warning system for approaching economic "storms". It could be as simple as a phone app that asks one question: to rate their confidence in the local future on a scale of 1-10, or even single multiple choice: "*Do you feel this place is 1) getting better, 2) remaining the same or 3) getting worse?*" This would give leaders the opportunity to nip a negative shift in the bud with a confidence-building project or program, before a downward spiral spins out of control.

Measuring confidence could also alert leaders to hidden devitalizing influences. There's a lag between the time people start perceiving a place as being "on the way down", and the time they start moving away or stop investing locally. As governments increasingly strive for resilient prosperity and appoint people to deliver it, they'll be better able to "print" this currency by tracking and measuring confidence. In fact, simply having a qualified RE Facilitator is confidence-enhancing, as it provides evidence that the community has an effective process for delivering the desired results.

Some cities and regions with an urgent need to increase confidence in their future aren't presently distressed. Many are, in fact, presently wealthy. But some are overly-dependent on one industry, as Detroit once was.

Others are overly dependent on non-renewable natural resources, like oil and gas. Such fragile economies must take advantage of their current prosperity to make investments in a more-diversified economic foundation, and in more-efficient infrastructure. We'll explore such strategies in the next section, which uses Calgary as an example.

Inspiring confidence that a neighborhood is revitalizing—or is about to do so—is the key to many common community challenges: attracting a grocery store to a food desert; attracting a developer to clean up a brownfield; attracting an employer to an empty building; etc. One might thus be tempted to think that "inspiring confidence in the local future" is a perfect strategy for revitalization.

Nope. That's a goal, not a strategy. A strategy is how you overcome the obstacles to achieving that goal.

> *"(Tehran) has never been a place that was about to crumble,' Ghezelbash says. 'But the opportunity cost has been high.' What a (nuclear) deal will do most immediately is restore enough optimism so Iranians will invest in their own country again. 'That kind of psychology will take on a life of its own. If people are hopeful, they're likely to take more risks, get involved in entrepreneurship and new ventures.'"* – "Iran Is About to Open for Business", Bloomberg BusinessWeek, 2015.

It also doesn't count as a strategy because it doesn't provide moment-to-moment decision-making guidance. If one has adopted the 3Re Strategy, for instance, one knows at any given moment that a decision should help repurpose, renew and/or reconnect the place. That kind of clarity inspires confidence. It doesn't matter whether you're dealing with corporate stock, real estate, currency or an entire economy: when confidence evaporates, so does value. When confidence grows, value appreciates.

Climate resilience-boosting efforts are often billed as being done to protect properties and lives. But an overlooked value is the role resilience plays in building confidence that a place (or institution) is worth investing in. Resilience and revitalization aren't synonymous, but they are synergistic.

For instance, in June of 2019, the Bank of England asked UK insurers to assess how climate change might affect their bottom line. This was a new criterion, added to their biennial "stress test". In the same month, the governor of the Bank of France, François Villeroy de Galhau, called on central banks around the world to measure their bank's exposure to climate risk. This too, was a new criterion, meant to more-intelligently determine the amount of collateral needed when asking for central bank funding. He called for *"thoroughly integrating climate change into the monetary policy framework"*.

In other words, investors want to know which banks and insurers are likely to be wiped out by the next Hurricane Sandy. Their money will go elsewhere. This incorporation of climate resilience into insurance and banking is a big deal. On

September 20, 2019, the European Bank for Reconstruction and Development (EBRD) successfully launched the first-ever dedicated climate resilience bond, raising $700 million (USD). *"This is a major step forward in the development of capital market instruments that can crowd in private finance at scale for climate resilience,"* said Craig Davies, Head of Climate Resilience Investments at EBRD.

In the U.S.—where, for government officials, mentioning "climate change" is akin to mentioning "human rights" or "free Tibet" in China—the current head-in-the-sand approach could well become a major confidence-shaking factor in our financial institutions...and our economy in general. That would be a different form of climate-related national disaster.

I've mostly been referring to raising confidence in the "local" future, but the dynamic works at any scale. In fact, reduced confidence in our global future is fast becoming one of the largest economic impacts of the climate crisis, possibly exceeding the cost of storm damage. Some 44% of the world's population lives within 150 kilometers of an ocean. 123 million U.S. citizens (39%) lived in coastal counties in 2010. That's expected to increase to 47% by 2020. Rising sea levels, combined with the increasing frequency and severity of storms, is rapidly eroding confidence in the future of coastal cities worldwide.

Maybe the most dramatic example happened in August of 2019. That was when Indonesia officially lost faith in the future of their largest city, Jakarta, and decided to relocate their national capital from the Java coast to Borneo. This was due to a toxic combination of sea level rise, powerful climate-crisis storms and subsidence due to water extraction (the latter similar to what's been happening for decades in Mexico City).

Add to the climate crisis the rise of global terrorism, plus state-supported racism and anti-immigrant rhetoric, and it's not surprising that Andrew Young, former U.S. Ambassador and former 2-term Mayor of Atlanta, Georgia said (in April of 2014), *"The environment is so insecure and unstable right now that people are afraid to invest in the future."* The situation has only worsened since then.

The climate crisis isn't just undermining confidence via sea-level rise and storm damage: dying coral reefs (from ocean warming) and die-offs of other foundational species like shellfish (from ocean acidification) are undermining commercial and recreational fishing economies, which together account for over 10% of the global economy.

What's more, it's not just coastal areas whose "confidence factor" is vulnerable to climate change. Inland agricultural economies are being hugely disrupted as traditional crops no longer thrive there, and when hit by unusually-severe droughts and heat waves. Paper and lumber-based economies are disrupted when pests and diseases move into new territories as a result of warmer weather and rage out of control (as we've seen with the pine bark beetle).

Those folks in industries not related to natural resources might feel protected. They're not. What happens when those dependent on farming, fishing, or timber can no longer afford to buy a new iPhone? Or a new car? The trickle-down devitalization could easily trigger an unstoppable feedback loop.

As noted earlier, most cities have multiple agencies and organizations charged with renewing jobs, housing, infrastructure, brownfields, waterways, heritage, etc. But they are usually in dysfunctional isolation from each other. So too does the United Nations have many fragmented programs working to renew various aspects of our world, usually in crisis-response mode. Maybe it's time to recognize that regeneration is the essence of resilience and sustainability on a planetary level, and embed that mission in our institutions before it's too late.

Our national and international institutions can often learn about embracing appropriate priorities from even the smallest of communities. Stonington, Maine, a coastal community with a struggling economy and a commercially-important waterfront, has created a Working Waterfront Adaptation Committee. A pair of October 2014 articles in The Ellsworth American described citizens' efforts to prepare the waterfront and community for the future. They're not prosperous, but they see a clear and present danger to what prosperity they have. Here are a few relevant quotes from the articles:

- "facing multiple challenges...They include preparing docks and other facilities for more severe storms, changes in fisheries resources, and fewer job opportunities."
- "higher sea levels will stress Stonington's infrastructure...3-6 feet by the end of century."
- "Gulf of Maine is warming faster than 99.85 percent of the world's ocean; storms are likely to become both more frequent and more violent."
- "Stonington rarely conveys the impression of a progressive community," but [thanks to this adaptive renewal work] is now seen as being "on the cutting edge".

Stonington's focus is on protecting the future (resilience), not revitalizing it. But if other area communities don't do likewise, Stonington could have the only working waterfront in the region, which would likely revitalize it. That "sole survivor" scenario isn't a confidence-inspiring strategy, though.

An article titled"What Makes An Economist?" in the October 2007 issue of The Economist said: *"The years of graduate-school seminars and rigorous mathematical training empowers PhD economists to converse with each other in a language all our own [often having no practical value, predictive power, or relevance to reality]. This allows us...to believe that our years of education were worthwhile because we can recognize each other and sneer at the impostors. In the meantime, the rest of the world takes thoughtful* advice and opinions from people who sometimes, while not having our illustrious pedigree, have...better ideas."

Climate change is a global phenomenon with many local causes...and many great local ideas. Our global economy is an aggregation of local economies. As long as we rely on professional economists to decise solutions, we're lost.

What happens when investors' diminishing confidence in local and national economies hits a tipping point, and they lose confidence in the global economy? If it makes sense for cities, states, and nations to have resilient prosperity programs, might it also be time for the UN to create a global regeneration system, facilitating and supporting national systems?

The UN has already announced a "Decade on Ecosystem Restoration" (2021 – 2030), similar to the "Century of Restoration" I proposed in *The Restoration Economy*. Maybe it's time for them to take on the mission of restoring confidence in our global future.

INSPIRING CONFIDENCE IN YOUR LOCAL FUTURE: THE CALGARY EXAMPLE

> *"There was a lot of economic damage. But the greater damage is to the future.*
> *How many retailers will want to come to Baltimore? How many conventions will stay away? How many hotel rooms will stay empty?"*
> *– Anirban Basu, on the riots following the April 27, 2015 funeral of Freddie Gray.*

We've discussed the essential role of quality of life in attracting new employers to an area. But even quality of life is insufficient if confidence in the future is shaky. For example: if a city is perceived as an oil and gas town, or a lumber town, or a mining town, a boom-and-bust economy will be assumed. The boom years attracts workers looking for jobs, but not employers or investors looking for a growing—or at least stable—economic climate. In good times, such places might not need to fix their present, but they desperately need to fix their future.

How? It's better to make people want to move to your city or nation, rather than relying on expensive financial incentives. If their perception is that you're a one-trick economy, they'll not only worry about your stability: they'll doubt that your place is an interesting place to live. Most of our beautiful historic cities were based on manufacturing, not resource extraction (even though the former is usually based on the latter).

Cities based on resource extraction itself usually build in a way that reflects their economic transience. They build as if they don't intend to stick around. They create the bare necessities; eschewing major arts investments, failing to create inspiring public spaces or world-class higher education, etc. Fixing their future (strategic renewal) means rebuilding in a way that makes people rethink how they perceive the place.

Calgary, Alberta has been called "Canada's powerhouse". So, one wouldn't expect a focus on revitalization, right? For the past decade, Calgary has had one of the strongest-performing urban economies in the country, thanks to exploitation of local oil and gas, plus the notorious "tar sands" to their north. Of the six largest cities in Canada, Calgary has the lowest unemployment rate. Their population of 1.25 million grew by 120,000 people in the five years prior to 2018.

But what happens when the oil industry crashes, as it always has periodically in the past, and as it obviously will permanently in the long term? They aren't waiting to find out. The province of Alberta is known as the "Texas" of Canada: primarily beef and oil. Calgary's leaders are working to change that perception for their city. They don't want Calgary to be perceived as having a fragile economy; resilient prosperity is their goal.

Calgary needs more housing, but they're rightly worried about ruining their quality of life and sabotaging their future via too much sprawl. Unlike physically-constrained places like San Francisco (which focuses growth exclusively on redevelopment), Calgary is cursed with unlimited room for devitalizing developments that congest traffic, reduce greenspace, and fragment community cohesiveness.

Here are four recent and current local projects that fix their future, and that are creating a more-resilient form of prosperity:

- East Village: Until very recently, this area—immediately adjacent to Calgary's downtown—comprised 49 acres of blight and crime, and little else. As you read this, the first new homes and condos are being sold in an area that has been thoroughly redeveloped in a delightful manner;
- ENMAX Park: Restoring green space is essential to revitalizing most cities. Many Calgarians complain that they have few places locally to take out of town visitors. Most tourists fly into Calgary, and then leave immediately for Banff, maybe after a trip to the excellent Calgary Zoo. This ecological restoration of an industrial park to a waterfront park will help change that.

- Public Library: The East Village features an iconic new public library building that might be the world's first truly transit-oriented library. It has a metro station literally beneath it. In addition to the pride and joy this brings local citizens, the national and international attention this gorgeous building is attracting helps outsiders start seeing Calgary as a place that values knowledge and learning, not just oil and beef; and
- National Music Center: Calgary's most outrageous project (in the eyes of many Canadians) is building the first national center for Canadian music. As a relatively new, heritage-deficient city, Calgary is the last major city in Canada most would expect to boast such an asset. It's precisely this sort of bold, head-scratching move that can do wonders for the city's image. It too will be in the redeveloped East Village.

Calgary takes a strategic approach to public services, as well. Their highly-popular former police chief, Rick Hanson, didn't just focus on fighting crime (tactical) but on preventing it (strategic). He created programs that brilliantly helped fix the futures of both at-risk youth and entire at-risk neighborhoods.

Calgary is thus fixing its present and future together, with tactics (present) based on strategies (future):

- Tactical: Does Calgary need to redevelop the East Village? Absolutely. Vital downtowns need residents, not just businesses. Strengthening their downtown is crucial to Calgary's ongoing viability. You can't be a suburb of nothing: downtown is the heart of a city, and healthy bodies need healthy hearts. Research shows that people love living in "cool" places that are reviving.
- Tactical: Does Calgary need a downtown waterfront park? Absolutely: if they want the East Village full of residents, they need a truly livable downtown. That means greenspace and connectivity to water. A 3-year poll by the Knight Foundation and Gallup found 3 factors that attach people to their place more than all others: social offerings, aesthetics, and open spaces.
- Strategic: Does Calgary need a spectacular new public library? No: from a functional perspective, the old library system works well enough. But they need a knowledge-economy image.
- Strategic: Does Calgary need a national music center? No. From a functional standpoint, a more modest venue would suffice. But they need a more-cultured, interesting image.

The East Village and the waterfront park projects thus primarily serve existing needs. Both also have strategic value, so we shouldn't get too pedantic or arbitrary about separating tactics from strategy. But the library and the music center projects reposition the city's image, so they are primarily strategic, while also providing immediate value for residents. Both create the impression of a city with a diverse economy and an interesting quality of life, so as to attract more of both. (Fake it 'til you make it).

In other words, the new library and National Music Center provide the appearance of having the kind of diverse economy that spawns a rich arts and learning-based culture. It's a way of breaking out of the "chicken or egg syndrome": a greater diversity of employers creates a richer culture, and a richer culture attracts a greater diversity of employers. Which comes first?

Calgary's smart moves aren't limited to future projects. Maybe their most important strategic success has been the 1981 launch of their well-used C-Train light rail, connecting the suburbs to downtown. Together with buses, Transit Calgary's system has gone a long way towards mitigating the traffic congestion and other quality of life damage typically inflicted by sprawl.

In June of 2013, Calgary was hit by a catastrophic flood, the worst in Alberta's history. Five people were killed, and over 100,000 displaced. Economic damage exceeded C$5 billion: the costliest disaster in Canadian history. Calgary's well-managed recovery from the flood deserves a book of its own. A Flood Recovery Task Force was created, and—now that their work is basically complete—they wisely transitioned this group into an ongoing Resilience Team.

The most important element in boosting Calgary's resilience—economic diversification—got a huge boost in the provincial election of May 2015. The fossil fuel industry's political party was (shockingly) ousted, and replaced with the social-democratic New Democratic Party (NDP). This leftist party only held four seats in the 87-seat provincial legislature at the time of the vote, and defeated the 44-year dynasty of the Progressive Conservative (PC). This is akin to Texas electing Bernie Sanders or Elizabeth Warren as governor.

The political upset was triggered by the drop in oil prices, which undermined the government's ability to follow-through on many plans. [I had warned the city about exactly this scenario in my conference keynote, radio interviews, and meetings with local leaders just a few months earlier.] This political situation is unlikely to last long, so this is Calgary's golden opportunity to shake their economic dependence on fossil fuels and create a more stable, broader-based economy.

Their hard work seems to be paying dividends: in September of 2019, the Economist's Intelligence Unit ranked Calgary as the fifth most-livable city in the world.

During a speech in October of 2019, Calgary Economic Development (CED) chief executive Mary Moran said that their economy is diversifying, especially in technology, agriculture, and transportation. Some 80% of new businesses in

Calgary are technology firms, and the city is attracting significant venture capital to start or expand local companies.

WE CAN'T CREATE AN EFFECTIVE REVITALIZATION PROGRAM IF WE DON'T UNDERSTAND REVITALIZATION

Designing your local renewal program requires that we dive a little deeper into some of the dynamics of revitalization that we've only touched on earlier. For instance, we briefly mentioned various approaches, such as top-down, middle-out, bottom-up, etc. Which is best? It depends on your circumstances.

Sometimes the top-down approach is best. Hamburg, Germany recently launched HafenCity. It's a $14 billion ($3.25 billion of which was public money) waterfront redevelopment that's creating 100 buildings to house some 12,000 residents. This is exactly what Hamburg needs, and there's no way this could happen as a bottom-up, grassroots effort.

Bottom-up efforts—such as Héroes sin Fronteras in Medellín, Colombia, site of the UN's 7th World Urban Forum—are highly underrated by governments and large NGOs, getting only token attention at development conferences. Beirut endured decades of conflict that left public spaces dirty and dangerous. The city was unwilling or unable to revitalize its parks, so a young lady, Dima Boulad, created a grassroots program called Beirut Green Project. Their first project, restoring Sanayeh Garden, was a great success. A teenager said *"You can feel the air quality change as you enter the park."*

Impromptu (middle-out) efforts are often small, incremental improvements to a place, but can sometimes be transformative. Retired New York City police detective Greg O'Connell is a fixer: he's not a public leader, so his work isn't top-down. But he's not just s resident or neighborhood group leader, so it can't be considered bottom-up, either. He almost single-handedly revitalized his current home, the Red Hook area of Brooklyn, and his home town of Mt. Morris (pop. 3000) in upstate New York. Impromptu efforts are lovely when they happen, but can't be relied on, unless you create an effective local renewal culture. That's best accomplished by first creating a strategic renewal process.

Places that have great difficulty initiating or maintain their revitalization momentum are usually over-dependent on just one of these modes. In places that achieve resilient prosperity, all three of these modes are usually evident;

sometimes sequentially, other times simultaneously and (ideally) harmoniously. In fact, this is crucial to creating a constant flow of regenerative activities that builds momentum, and supportive optimism about what's coming next.

Of course, there's a flip side to everything. The town of Puolanka is the most remote municipality in Finland's most remote province. Of its 2600 residents, over 37% are over 64. Its population dropped by 50% since the 1980s as young people have pursued opportunity in the cities. The town is now basing its revitalization on pessimism. Puolanka received so much national press about being a dying town that was losing population that they embraced their bleak future, and made it a tourist attraction.

Tommi Rajala, head of the Puolanka Pessimist Association, describes their strategy: *"Alright, we're the worst, but we'll be the best worst in Finland."*

A November 14, 2019 BBC article said: *"Puolanka has turned pessimism into a brand, hosting a pessimism festival, a musical, and even an online shop – all served with a wickedly humorous twist. Videos depicting Puolanka in all its pessimistic glory have hundreds of thousands of views online."* As you drive towards the town, cheerful roadside signs say things like *"Soon, Puolanka. You've still got time to turn around."* Residents have embraced the humor, and greet each other with lines like *"I see you're still alive."* Referring to the town's marketing campaign, Rajala explains, "Usually, advertising is all about making things seem better than they are. The absolute best thing about pessimism is that I don't have to lie."

Have you ever felt really great, decided to go for a walk in the park or along a river, and come back announcing *"Wow: I feel revitalized!"*? If so, you know that you don't need to feel bad in order to feel better. And so it is with places: no matter how good things are, they can always be better. All places need revitalization and resilience. If one defines "revitalization" as "equitable economic growth that simultaneously increases both quality of life and environmental health", then that's something all places need, no matter how good or bad their current situation.

A central challenge to approaching community revitalization in a more systemic, holistic manner is rooted in our perception of how the world works. There are two fundamental approaches to understanding our physical reality: reductionism and emergence. The former says that we can understand the whole if we understand the parts. The latter says that the whole is greater than the sum of its parts.

The argument goes way back. Here's an excerpt from an article titled "Big Questions Come In Bundles, Hence They Should Be Tackled Systemically" (in *Systema*, Vol. 2, Issue 2, 2014) by Dr. Mario Bunge in the Department of Philosophy at McGill University:

"...Ancient Greek philosophy produced two great ontologies or worldviews: Democritus' atomism and Aristotle's holism. The corresponding methodologies were the bottom-up (elements > whole) and the top-down (whole > elements) strategies. ...radical atomists stress composition at the expense of structure, whereas structuralists pretend that there can be structures without components. For example, it is often said that Water = H2O, whereas in fact this is the formula for the composition of a water molecule. To account for a body of liquid water, even as small as a droplet, we must include the hydrogen bonds that hold the molecules together and explain the global properties of a watery body, such as fluidity and surface tension. As for the structuralists, they emphasize structure to the point of disregarding the stuff the system is made of – for instance, humans in the case of social systems. ...systemism should not be mistaken for holism, because the former recommends combining the bottom-up with the top-down strategies... [these] are mutually complementary rather than mutually exclusive."

In 2000, Marquette, Michigan created a program to transform their waterfront using modern form-based codes. Here's how their mission was later stated: "*The goal of Marquette's waterfront redevelopment was to transform the former industrial waterfront into a walkable, mixed use waterfront zone that was physically connected to the downtown and supported a host of water depended uses.*"

I submit that their goal was actually revitalization, and what they stated as the goal was the strategy. After all, if Marquette had ended up revitalizing their waterfront—but not in the way described above—would they be happy? Probably. If they transformed their waterfront in the above manner, and didn't achieve revitalization, would they be happy? Probably not. Thus, revitalization was the goal.

As with all complex systems, cities and nations experience tipping points, both on the way up, and on the way down. With revitalization (and devitalization), that tipping point usually occurs when the general perception of the place's future changes. It's at that point where the free market (especially home-grown businesses) either stops or starts investing in the place, which either puts the burden of revitalization on the public sector, or relieves government of that responsibility (to a degree).

Many places try to change that perception quickly, via marketing and rebranding efforts. These are seldom successful. Perceiving on-the-ground progress over time is far more convincing to investors, entrepreneurs, and redevelopers.

An article by Eileen Zimmerman in *The Atlantic CityLab* (Dec. 30, 2014) about the town of Vista, California illustrates the point: "*Craft beer has had a profound economic impact on Vista...the industry provides $272 million in annual revenue and supports 850 jobs in North County, an area that includes Vista. Kevin Ham, Vista's economic development director, says those beer dollars circulate through the local* *economy and support the creation of additional, indirect jobs and more business activity, like new restaurants and boutiques. 'It's helped to revitalize the downtown,' Ham says. 'We used to have to reach out to businesses to get them to locate here. Now they are coming to us.'"*

Vista's beer-powered revitalization was organic: no public agency or foundation can take credit for it. Of course, one of the "benefits" of not having a rigorous revitalization program is that anyone can take credit for such successes, and no one can prove them a liar. The cities are grateful these "miracles" happen, but are at a loss to accurately explain why they happened. But there's always a "why".

As described earlier, most of our modern problems in the Anthropocene can be categorized as assets that are 1) damaged/depleted (thus needing to be renewed); 2) outdated/obsolete (thus needed to be repurposed/replaced); or 3) fragmented / isolated (thus needing to be reconnected). The $115 million 2015 bond package for Albuquerque, New Mexico epitomizes the priorities of the 21st century. It's almost 100% focused on renewing (e.g., zoo renovation) and repurposing (e.g., rail yard redevelopment) existing assets. One of their few new projects is a park-like trail that reconnects the downtown to the rail yards.

The December 29, 2014 *Albuquerque Journal* quotes Gilbert Montano, the mayor's chief of staff as saying, "*We're going to try to invest some money into that path and corridor to better revitalize and connect the rail yards and the Downtown area.*" It says the budget "*focuses overwhelmingly on rehabilitation and shoring up deficiencies, rather than building new projects that are costly to operate.*"

New forms of threats now drive most planning. The Center for American Progress recently issued a report on "State Future Funds", expected to harness at least $200 billion for climate change-related water infrastructure renewal. In January 2015, the USEPA launched their new Water Infrastructure and Resiliency Finance Center to support such investment in renewing our future. Renewing, repurposing, and reconnecting is becoming the predominant public spending formula for achieving resilient prosperity.

Let's end this discussion of transition management with a perfect example of an institution in desperate need of it: the U.S. Army Corps of Engineers. Over the past century, they've built literally tens of thousands of dams. A few created human benefits that could honestly be said to outweigh their ecological damage.

But most were unneeded. Many were tiny, just 3 – 6 feet of head. But a 3-foot dam is more than enough to stop fish from migrating to critical upstream spawning habitat. The U.S. has added a dam a day since Thomas Jefferson was President (75,000 of them over 3 feet). Many of were built privately because the Corps of Engineers' told landowners that more dams are better, and all water flows should be controlled.

Why would the Corps of Engineers build a single unneeded dam, much less thousands of them? To justify and retain their peacetime budgets. Back when I was in the Army at Ft. Bragg, North Carolina in the early 70's, something strange would happen once a year. Our team would be driven out to a firing range, along with a 2 ½-ton truck loaded with dozens of different kinds of handguns, rifles, sub-machine guns and machine guns...plus an ungodly amount of ammunition.

We were told to fire these weapons as fast as possible into an earth berm, usually with few—if any—targets. The stated purpose was to familiarize us with the broad variety of weapons we were likely to encounter—and possibly appropriate for our own use—during typical covert, behind-enemy-lines SF operations.

That was valid enough, but the primary purpose was actually to maintain our battalion's budget. In the Army, as in many government agencies and even some poorly-managed corporations, there's a "use it or lose it" rule in place. If your department doesn't use its entire annual budget, the budget is in danger of being cut the following year. Rather than being lauded for your efficiency, you'll be labeled "overfunded."

This is why our A-Team developed blisters on our hands, spending hours firing overheated weapons once a year. And this is why the Corps of Engineers built dams no one needed. Are civil engineers stupid? Are they unable to grasp the concept of fish migration? Not at all.

But their institutions can be stupid, forcing employees to behave as if they, too, are stupid. The real problem isn't just wastefulness, though. In case of the Corps of Engineers, this mindless behavior gave our nation a massive case of arterial thrombosis. Our streams and rivers nationwide have tens of thousands of fatal clots, which have reduced the value of our natural resources by many trillions (yes: trillions) of dollars over the past two centuries.

No one would expect a human to remain healthy—or even alive—if the pulsing of their hearts were stopped. Yet civil engineers—with almost religious fervor—have stopped the hearts of just about every ecosystem they've touched. Whether it's the pulsing of floodwaters in rivers and streams, or the pulsing of tides in coastal marshes and estuaries, civil engineers seem to feel it's their duty to stop the pulse for the sake of being "in control".

So we see how transition management in an institution or discipline isn't just a matter of weeding-out dumb policies and bureaucratic practices like "spend it or lose it." We must also have the courage to address deep-seated failings in the psychology and assumptions of a profession, and that is far, far more difficult.

To recap this projects vs. programs chapter: Redevelopment projects are like delivering a load of firewood: they usually provide immediate benefits, and can provide a short-term blaze of renewed confidence in a community's future. But a revitalization program is like planting a forest: it will provide firewood ad infinitum if properly managed. But it's not projects or programs: a program that doesn't lead to projects is useless. If your community has a great opportunity now, by all means dive into a project. But don't expect it to deliver maximum long-term benefits without the support of an ongoing revitalization program.

So, why don't more communities have a revitalization program? Two reasons:

1. They lack an agency whose mission is to create a holistic program that renews all of their restorable assets: natural, built, and socioeconomic. Public agencies (and funding) are locked in silos: they can only approve and fund projects (such as transit, brownfields, heritage, watershed, planning, economic development, etc.). They can't create a program that addresses the community as what it is: a complex, living, evolving system; and
2. They lack the framework and tools to manage the complexity of effectively engaging all the stakeholders, facilitating partnerships, cataloging assets, managing policy changes, creating a shared vision, integrating and regionalizing efforts, etc. Without an appropriate framework and tools, the best of intentions are doomed.

Some communities already have a programmatic approach. But...

- Few have created a comprehensive process based on a shared vision;
- Few understand that a comprehensive plan is not a comprehensive program (or process);
- Few do the needed work on policies, regulations, building codes, and zoning. The right policies can create a renewal culture that makes restorative development easier and more profitable (for private developers) than sprawl;
- Few learn how to create effective public-public, public-private, and private-private partnerships (to ensure progress in the face of tight local budgets);
- Few understand the intimate link between social equity and sustained economic growth. They allow redevelopment to be the domain of a privileged few. The widening gap between rich and poor (not to mention property rights abuses) results in social tensions and decreased levels of trust, both of undermine progress and confidence in the future; and,
- Few create a comprehensive GIS database of renewable assets to facilitate projects. A few have mapped their historic assets, or their brownfields, or their vacant properties, or their buried streams, etc. But I've never encountered a place that had a handle on all its renewable natural, built and socioeconomic assets. Ideally, such a database would be crowdsourced to a degree—and would harness the 3Re Strategy—so that

each asset would catalog opportunities to repurpose, renew and reconnect it as people thought of them. Much of this data actually exists in many communities' GIS databases, but isn't being tagged in ways that facilitate regeneration. Sometimes, it only needs to be "re-filtered."

Revitalization programs that are primarily political initiatives are fragile. It's quite common for incoming political leaders to kill programs launched by previous administrations so the opposition party can't claim credit for successes that occur during their tenure. Political leaders should definitely be engaged, and should be given the opportunity to take credit for a program's successes, but a sustainable revitalization or resilience program is one that's owned and supported by all local stakeholders, not just the government.

The solution? An ongoing program is how a place gets a handle on assets, engagement, timing and all of the other critical factors. Revitalization is an intangible quality that emerges, seemingly on its own. Like pornography, few can define it, but everyone knows it when they see it. It can't be engineered on a timetable, but a process can be put in place that will make it far more likely that the revitalization "tipping point" will kick in at some point. This is the moment I call "critical renewal"; where revitalization starts feeding on itself, gaining its own momentum so you don't have to keep pushing.

As stated here many times, the most important factor in creating a good strategy is creating a clear vision for it to serve. And the key to a clear vision is focus: winnowing it down to a few distinct goals that reinforce each other.

The Federation of Canadian Municipalities (FCM) came up with four key strategic elements for their revitalization work: 1) better public transit, 2) affordable housing, 3) greener communities plus 4) jobs and growth. Their strategic assumption is that strengthening their communities is the best way to strengthen the nation. Since over 80% of Canada's population is urban, this makes a lot of sense as the foundation of a national resilience program, and of the federal policies needed to support it.

As important as it is, even the best affordable downtown housing projects won't reliably create revitalization without the support of a strategic process. Housing is just a project type: don't forget the other five essential elements: regenerative program, regenerative vision, regenerative strategy, regenerative policies and regenerative partners.

Too many communities operate their affordable housing and their public transit programs in separate silos. Low-income folks are far more dependent on public transit, yet many cities focus bus service on middle-income neighborhoods.

It's also common to see affordable housing developments lacking effective public transit. Cheap homes aren't affordable if the residents have to spend a large portion of their income on cars, gas, car insurance, etc...not to mention wasting their precious time in commuter traffic. With affordable housing and transit reinforcing each other, they create a real solution. The process element that contributes most to that is the program.

DESIGNING RESILIENT PROSPERITY

In case you're wondering, designing isn't listed separately in this process, because it's integral to most of the elements, such as visioning, planning, and projects. So, while planners and designers are important professionals to have involved in the process, neither activity has its own part of the process.

We shouldn't ignore the power of design, of course, since certain design-related needs appear to be in our genes. For instance, architects and urban planners discuss a concept known as "prospect-refuge theory." It attempts to explain why some buildings and urban layouts make us feel secure and enriched, while others don't.

First proposed in 1975, the premise is that we have a hard-wired need to observe (prospect) without being seen (refuge). Our "observation" component apparently prefers complex places that offer the ability to explore and discover opportunities. That's just one example of the subtle complexities involved in good urban design for activating and revitalizing places.

What about designing for resilience? At a symposium called "Resilient Design: State of the Art and Emerging Issues for the Built Environment" (February 22 and 23, 2018) sponsored by Cal Poly State University – San Luis Obispo's College of Architecture and Environmental Design (CAED), the following definition of "resilient design" emerged: "*Resilient Design is an intentional action that enables a system, in whole or part, to meet the challenges posed by changing, or unstable, conditions, to absorb a shock or stress while maintaining its identity and functionality through adaptive recovery.*" (My thanks to William Siembieda, Professor of City and Regional Planning at Cal Poly for these insights from the symposium.)

Nine "domains of resilience"* were also identified at the symposium:
1. Engineering resilience: System's speed of return to equilibrium following a shock;
2. Ecological resilience: Ability of a system to withstand shock and maintain critical relationships and functions;
3. Social-ecological resilience: (i) Amount of disturbance a system can absorb and remain within a domain of attraction; (ii) capacity for

learning and adaptation (iii) degree to which the system is capable of self- organizing;

4. Social resilience: Ability of groups or communities to cope with external stresses and disturbances as a result of social, political and environmental change;
5. Development resilience: Capacity of a person, household or other aggregate unit to avoid poverty in the face of various stressors and in the wake of myriad shocks over time;
6. Socioeconomic resilience: Socioeconomic resilience refers to the policy-induced ability of an economy to recover from or adjust to the negative impacts of adverse exogenous shocks and to benefit from positive shocks;
7. Community resilience: A process linking a set of adaptive capacities to a positive trajectory of functioning and adaptation after a disturbance;
8. Psychological resilience: An individual's ability to adapt to stress and adversity. Resilience is a process and can be learned by anyone using positive emotions;
9. Resilient Design:** An intentional action that enables a system, in whole or part, to meet the challenges posed by changing, or unstable, conditions, to absorb a shock or disturbance while maintaining its identity and functionality through adaptive recovery.

*#1-8 Quilan,
**#9 Resilient Design Symposium. 2018.

So, good design is obviously essential, but design activities are mostly confined to the "projects" portion of the RECONOMICS Process, so we won't focus much more attention on them in this book.

CHAPTER 10 - THE COMPLETE SOLUTION: CREATING A STRATEGIC RENEWAL PROCESS.

"When you do an organizational redesign... the most important aspect is always the process by which the work gets done."
— Rex Tillerson, former CEO of ExxonMobil, former U.S. Secretary of State.

By now, you're tired of hearing this, but it's essential that this message sinks in if you want your community or region to get out of whatever rut(s) it might be in: all competent organizational leaders know that reliably producing ANYTHING (goods, services, institutional change, etc.) requires the right process. So, why don't communities, regions and countries have a proven process for producing what they all want: resilient economic growth and higher quality of life?

Public and private leaders tend to treat regeneration as if it has no essential underlying principles, frameworks, or components. When opportunity arises, they reactively take whatever path seems to be dictated by their available human, organizational, physical, and capital resources. In other words, they're just winging it and hoping for the best. That's not exactly a responsible approach to creating a community's future. But it's the norm.

The funny thing is that these same local leaders are surrounded by process...their communities are a sea of processes. Local storekeepers have a process for renovating their stores and keeping their shelves full. Teachers have a process for educating local children. Redevelopers have a process for repurposing and renewing local buildings or infill sites that includes myriad details like arranging financing and permits. Architects have a process for designing, restoring or retrofitting buildings. Planners have a process for creating plans. Chemical and civil engineers have processes for remediating brownfields.

But there's seldom any process of renewal at the level of community or regional level. In this chapter, you'll be introduced to the RECONOMICS Process, which is what virtually every place has been intuitively striving towards, but never quite completing. But before we dive into that particular process, let's ensure that you have a firm grasp of the concept of process. Like "strategy", "process" is a word everyone uses constantly, often without any real grasp of its essence.

The reliable production of any desired result (tangible and intangible) requires a process:

- Farmers turning land into income have a process for planting, harvesting and selling their crops.
- The seeds those farmers plant have a growth and reproduction process of their own.
- Every company the farmers' output reaches has a process for creating, distributing and marketing value-added products.
- All of those companies are served by professionals and firms that have processes for delivering services.
- Each of the above steps is taxed and regulated by government processes that provide essential public infrastructure and safety.

Information is turned into knowledge via process. For instance, when disaster recovery and reconstruction agencies set up their IT (information technology) and GIS (geographic information system) in a post-catastrophe situation, they use a 3-step process: 1) gather existing data to better-understand the situation; 2) collect new data to stay on top of the situation; and 3) use mapping to allocate resources for an effective response.

As we've seen, virtually every community on the planet wants to boost their quality of life, their economy, their health, and their resilience. In other words, virtually every community wants to revitalize in some manner, even if they're in good economic shape. They all have myriad sub-processes that achieve isolated aspects of resilient prosperity—green infrastructure, renewal energy, job growth, etc.—but lack a good process for achieving the goal itself.

I emphasized "good" because bad processes abound. For example, most cities use the RFP (Request For Proposals) process when redeveloping their derelict properties. While that process certainly has value, many places sabotage it by being overly-specific as to what they want to see on a redeveloped site. They assume that no one could imagine anything better, and are often wrong in that assumption.

They'll have plenty of time to reject bad ideas later in the process: restricting creativity in the RFP itself is usually a mistake. One must not confuse vision with design. RFPs and RFQ (request for qualifications, often a precursor to an RFP) should usually be performance-based, not prescriptive. A well-written community vision is the basis of such a performance specification.

Some say that "RFP" stands for "Really Faulty Process". An example is an article by Nick Halter in the Nov. 30, 2017 Minneapolis/St. Paul Business Journal titled "RFP: Really Faulty Process. Why cities and counties struggle to develop their properties". In it, Halter says *"At least $600 million worth of development has been promised but not yet delivered, and that doesn't include the massive redevelopment of the Arden Hills ammunition plant, which also has been delayed and could eventually add hundreds of millions to the Ramsey County tax base."* He blames the RFP process for these delays and failures.

Projects not supported by partnerships (and policies) are more likely to fail. Partnerships not supported by ongoing programs are more likely to fail. Programs not based on a clear, concise strategy are more likely to fail. Strategies not based on a clear vision of the future that's shared by the community are more likely to fail. Using that as a guide, how many "points of potential failure" are present in your community?

> *"The process is the product."*
> *— Robert Cerwinski, on how manufacturers sometimes have more patents on the process by which a drug is made, than on the drug itself.*

Community leaders often throw up their hands in frustration when I ask them what tested, reliable solutions they are applying locally. It's not surprising, since even the experts tell them there is no better way. Here's what Alan Mallach says—in his excellent 2018 book, *The Divided City*—about how places can revitalize themselves: *"In the end, though, there is no magic bullet. It still comes down to figuring out what to do, and then digging in for the slow, difficult slog to make it happen, city by city or region by region."* That sounds wise on the surface, but it's some pretty bleak, hard-to-apply advice.

What's more, it's a red herring. The goal isn't to find a "magic bullet": it's simply to do what every intelligent, successful manager on the planet does: apply an efficient process. There's nothing magic about that: it's *de rigueur* for any producer of anything...except those who wish to produce revitalization or resilience.

To be fair, Mallach's book isn't about giving advice: it's an insightful analysis of what's actually happening—socially and economically—in about half a dozen (mostly Eastern) U.S. cities that are working to revitalize. That said, he does take a stab at a recipe for better renewal with the "four paths" he suggests on the book's final two pages (summarized here):

- Rethink municipal governance: It must be competent, trusted and transparent;
- Build human capital: all residents must have access to the education, skills training and opportunities needed to create economic mobility;
- Build the quality of life for the many, not the few; and
- Think long term: positive change requires a consistent, strategic use of time.

The excuse that most city leaders offer when asked why they haven't even searched for a reliable strategy or process is that they're convinced that their local aspirations and challenges are too unique for any standardized, cookie-cutter fixes to work. But that assumption comes from a misunderstanding of both strategy and process.

Strategy is like DNA: it adapts decisions to local conditions. Alligator eggs with identical DNA shift from producing male or female babies with changes of temperature. Some adult male fish shift to female if there aren't enough to keep the population strong.

Every place has its own revitalization challenges, and—since we know them intimately and feel the pain—ours often seem worse than the challenges faced by other places. But it's possible for all of us to adapt the same basic process to our unique situations (which are often far less unique than we think). In fact, there seem to be five common obstacles keep people from perceiving and applying replicable solutions:

- Most people focus on activities, rather than process;
- Most local leaders try to replicate the products of successful revitalization efforts elsewhere, rather than the process by which they were produced;
- Few people understand adaptive management (explained earlier);
- People tend to copy needs-based techniques that worked elsewhere, rather than asset-based approaches that can be customized to their unique situation; and
- Too many local leaders think in terms of prescriptive solutions, rather than performance-based solutions. (also explained earlier)

Overcome those five obstacles, and replicable solutions abound. This chapter will focus on obstacle #1: lack of process. Resilient prosperity derives from constantly repurposing, renewing, and reconnecting of your natural, built, and socioeconomic assets. How to build a process around that?

"Constant" was the key word. Creating a pulse requires an ongoing program, as discussed in the previous chapter, but that's only one of six elements of a complete process for producing resilient prosperity.

> *"Successful revitalization efforts are driven by leaders and residents who are tirelessly strategic about identifying their competitive advantages."*
> *– Patrice Frey, CEO, National Main Street Center.*

Many cities and organizations have several elements of a good process, but that still means they don't actually have a functional process. Nor are they aware of what's missing, making it hard to complete their process:

- Some places do visioning with residents, but forget to create a strategy to deliver the vision;
- Some places have a strategy, but forgot to facilitate a shared vision for the strategy to achieve;
- Some skip vision and strategy and go straight to creating a plan (which often isn't even a vital part of the process);
- Some forget to boost their capacity via public-private partnerships (or they don't create good ones);
- Some do almost everything right, but don't enact policies to allow, fund, or incentivize needed actions;
- Some don't bother preparing at all, and just start doing projects (the "throw stuff on the wall and see what sticks" approach);
- Some complete a project that yields a burst of hope, but it fades for want of an ongoing program to build on that momentum.

FROM STRATEGY TO STRATEGIC PROCESS

Earlier, we saw how the "critical mass" strategy was so successful at revitalizing Baltimore's Inner Harbor. In 2009, the Urban Land Institute called it *"the model for post-industrial waterfront redevelopment around the world"*. The other three keys to that success were 1) policy support from the city (such as massive rezoning) 2) a huge, innovative public-private partnership, and 3) an ongoing program that kept things moving until that critical mass was reached, and the revitalization became self-supporting.

The primary mover and shaker behind that effort was developer James Rouse, who was from the area. The heart of the Inner Harbor revitalization was the retail complex called Harborplace. It opened in 1980. That same year, Rouse—flush with success—decided to try his hand at revitalizing a poverty-stricken African-American neighborhood in West Baltimore. Partnering with the city, he created an initiative called the Sandtown-Winchester Neighborhood Transformation (NT).

Using a similar critical mass strategy, NT injected almost $250 million (in 2017 dollars) into housing, health care, schools and job training. It was a total failure, and many say the neighborhood is worse-off today than it was in 1980. What went wrong? Why didn't the critical mass strategy work again? At the risk of over-simplifying a hugely complex situation, it seems that the core failure was the lack of process.

A scholarly analysis was done by Stefanie DeLuca and Peter Rosenblatt in 2013, which showed that the neighborhood did indeed revitalize for about a decade, but then nosedived. It has continued devitalizing for the past two decades, and unemployment there is twice the Baltimore average.

The core of their analysis was that the investments failed to change the trajectory of the place. While many properties were improved, the neighborhood as a whole didn't gain the momentum needed to inspire confidence in its future.

That's the role of a strategic process. That renewed confidence makes the difference between a project that fosters spillover revitalization into surrounding areas (what I often call "restoration contagion") and one that doesn't move the needle.

As briefly mentioned in the Preface, since 1996—when I started researching and writing *The Restoration Economy*—I've been scanning the world for proven regeneration and resilience practices:

- As a writer, I'm constantly in research mode, exploring the latest happenings in urban, rural and natural resource renewal worldwide;
- As the publisher of REVITALIZATION, I scan the global news daily for projects, plans, successes and failures related to regeneration and resilience;
- As a consultant, I dive deeply into current practices as well as the causes of my clients' previous triumphs and disappointments; and,
- As a keynoter and workshop leader, I spend vast amounts of time at events in hundreds of cities across dozens of nations, all related to some form of urban, rural, economic or environmental regeneration. At each, I listened carefully to the talks and workshops of my fellow presenters, many of whom present case studies of success and failure.

I've likely been exposed and involved in more regeneration practices, in a broader variety of settings, than anyone else on the planet. Throughout these two decades, I've been analyzing what I've seen and heard, plumbing these thousands of regeneration stories for commonalities. What factors were usually present in the successes? What factors were usually absent in the failures?

The result? I've identified six factors whose presence reliably contributes to success, and whose absence reliably contributes to failure. It's now time for regeneration leaders to apply them as a whole, rather than in bits and pieces. So, I've assembled all six into what I call the RECONOMICS Process.

The good news is that your community probably has at least two of the elements in place already. This means you can create a local RECONOMICS Process in a plug-the-gaps manner that's minimally disruptive: no wholesale overhaul of your system is needed.

Even better: you can add the missing pieces at whatever speed and in whatever order works best for your situation. Each addition will accelerate your progress, but the real magic will happen when you've got the complete process working locally.

This process is the result of studying and/or being involved in over 300 community and regional revitalization efforts worldwide between 1996 and 2019, as well as being exposed to those aforementioned hundreds of case studies at conferences. Unfortunately, the complete RECONOMICS Process only recently became apparent to me, so I wasn't able to recommend it to my earlier clients. My work for them mostly focused on individual components of the process—primarily strategy, program and policies—as well as the integration of regenerative silos.

The primary purpose of three of the process elements—vision, strategy and policies—is to guide day-to-day decision making. Two of the elements—partnerships and projects—are where those decisions are made and action is taken. The purpose of the other element—program—is to enhance coordination, ensure continuity and build momentum.

Each of those elements has two aspects: structural and functional. If you have people or departments that facilitate visions, modify policies, form partnerships, etc., then that's the structural aspect. But to have a RECONOMICS Process that produces resilient prosperity means that each of these elements must be regenerative in their nature. That's the functional aspect.

The norm is a mix: the projects and partnerships might be functionally regenerative, but the policies might be functionally degenerative (such as incentives for sprawl or unsustainable resource extraction, or zoning that prevents mixed-agenda redevelopment).

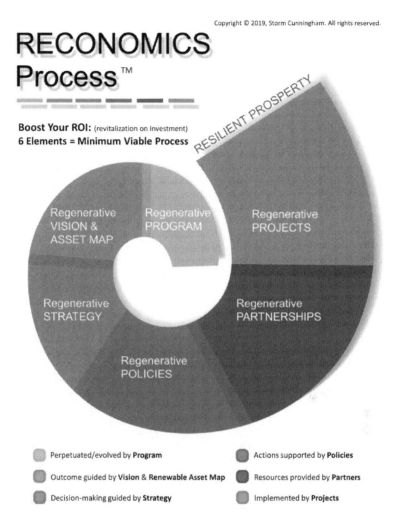

As a result, creating your local RECONOMICS Process will likely comprise two activities: plugging the structural gaps and repurposing the existing elements to be regenerative. Interestingly, I sometimes find places that have had all six elements, but not at the same time. The most common scenario is that they'll launch a major new project or partnership, and discontinue their program, thinking that the new entity serves the same purpose. This is what comes from understanding the bits and pieces, but not the overall process.

> *"We enjoy the process far more than the proceeds."* – Warren Buffett.

On October 29, 2019, New Jersey Governor Phil Murphy signed Executive Order No. 89 to establish a Statewide Climate Change Resilience Strategy. So far, so good: a strategy! The Executive Order establishes a Climate and Flood Resilience Program within the New Jersey Department of Environmental Protection to be led by a Chief Resilience Officer. Even better: a program, a strategy, and someone in charge! The Executive Order creates an Interagency Council on Climate Resilience, comprising 16 state agencies. Better still: a mechanism for public-public partnerships!

And now the bad news: the stated function of all this activity is to develop short- and long-term action plans. Let's hope that the effort isn't declared successful when those plans are written (the norm in most places). Let's hope that the program, strategy and partnerships produce some projects that actually accomplish their stated goal: "long-term mitigation, adaptation, and resilience of New Jersey's economy, communities, infrastructure, and natural resources."

Revitalization is a living process; a flow of ideas, images, relationships, and energy. "Stuff" is essential, but designing urban or regional resilience without a regenerative process is like basing personal wellness on buying exercise equipment, without actually using it in an ongoing exercise program.

The six elements of the RECONOMICS Process aren't just activities or checklist items: each is actually its own unique path to success. Some communities have revived themselves by focusing really good efforts on just one of them. But when combined, they create a broad, solid, safer highway to success.

Effective regeneration moves the community out of the "red ocean" of thousands of communities doing exactly the same official activities, and moves it into the "blue ocean" of places using a reliable regeneration process to create their own unique form of resilient prosperity.

There are myriad regenerative tactics that will help grow a local economy. All places have far more options and resources than they usually realize, such as:

- Reconnect to / daylight your water;
- Create a local food system;
- Create a comprehensive renewal process / confidence;
- Repurpose / remediate an old industrial area;
- Repurpose a major piece of infrastructure;
- Repurpose the community's economic base/purpose;
- Renew your historic inventory;
- Renew your natural resources;
- Grow local businesses (rebuild entrepreneurial capacity);

- Recruit new businesses;
- Reconnect severed neighborhoods/downtown; and,
- Reconnect urban/suburban/rural or connect to another economic engine.

So, the opportunities are almost endless. The problem is that community development is a hopeless mess in most places. It's actually devitalizing. One might even call it "DEconomics."

Most places revitalize in a hit-or-miss manner, having to remember and coordinate a grab-bag of miscellaneous tools and tactics such as the above list. The RECONOMICS Process attempts the make this crucially important activity more scientific.

The scientific method is based on two "re" words: reproducibility and replicability. The former refers to using the same data in the hope of getting the same results. It requires the original data from the earlier experiment, and the original experimental process. The latter uses new data, but uses the original process in the hope of getting similar results.

Since no two places have the same data and dynamics, the purpose of having a universal process for revitalization and resilience obviously isn't to reproduce the same results of one community or region in a new place. It's to replicate a similar level of success, in whatever form is locally appropriate.

Without a strategic renewal process, disappointment is—sadly—the norm after most resilience and revitalization efforts. This is true of rural towns, metropolitan areas, regions and nations alike. But, don't let all this talk of process obscure a simple truth: if your vision (mission) isn't worthy—or if you aren't committed to it—the most perfect of processes won't save you.

Today, the majority of my keynotes, workshops and consulting work focuses on helping public and private leaders better understand: 1) the community / regional revitalization process, and 2) how to strategically position their career, or their organization, within that process.

Many of the folks in my audiences are redevelopers. While sprawl developers are usually the "black hats", even redevelopers can be seen as the bad guys when what they create—or how they go about creating it—is out of tune with the community. It's easy to blame the redevelopers, but it's usually the community's fault. If they had a vision-driven strategic process for the redevelopers to work within, misaligned projects would be far fewer.

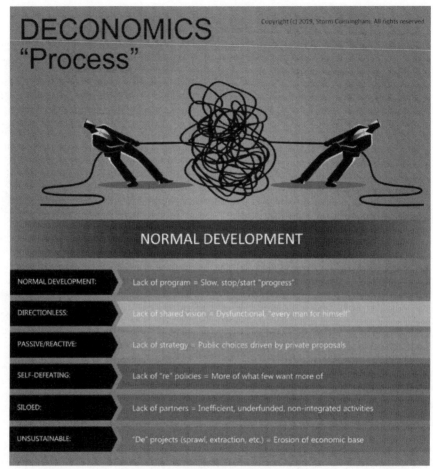

It would make life much easier for redevelopers, too. They are working on borrowed money, so delays can be fatal. One redeveloper told me "*I can handle good news. I can handle bad news. What I can't handle are surprises.*"

Delays don't just add bank interest to their costs. Permits, zoning variances, and approvals of all sorts usually expire. They are easy to renew before they expire, but often near-impossible to renew after expiration. The redeveloper's life is thus incredibly complicated and stressful. Some of that is unavoidable, but some is plainly unnecessarily. For example, properties advertised for sale as "fully entitled" are often nowhere near that status; not necessarily because the seller is dishonest, but because the entire collection of relevant agencies and stakeholders is so incredibly fragmented.

Many places start creating a revitalization process, such as with a public visioning session, but skip crucial steps after that because they don't understand the overall process. As we've discussed in great detail already, the two most common gaps in these partial processes are strategy and ongoing program. We'll now fill in the other gaps.

Let's start by clarifying the role of each element in the RECONOMICS Process:
1. Regenerative Programs initiate, perpetuate, evaluate, and adjust actions. Ongoing programs create synergies, capture momentum (to grease the wheels for more projects), and inspire confidence in the local future;
2. Regenerative Visions guide actions to researched, desired outcomes;
3. Regenerative Strategies drive actions to success;
4. Regenerative Partners fund or support actions;
5. Regenerative Policies enable and encourage strategic actions;
6. Regenerative Projects are actions.

Programs, policies, partnerships and projects are how we implement strategies. Strategies are how we implement visions. Embed a desired outcome in your shared local vision, and that quality will start manifesting everywhere. A vision is where the community embeds its values into its future.

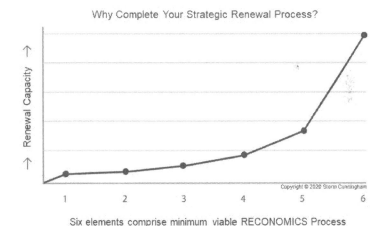

Six elements comprise minimum viable RECONOMICS Process

The power of the RECONOMICS Process increases nonlinearly when it's complete.

The RECONOMICS Process is the Minimum Viable Process (MVP). You can add other elements to it (such as a plan), as may be needed (or legally required) in your situation, but keep in mind that each additional elements adds "friction" that slow it down, and delays can be fatal to redevelopment projects. Crafting a formal plan is probably the most friction-creating element one could add.

So, add if you must, but don't subtract: if you don't have at least those six elements, you'll be missing crucially important functions, and will likely underachieve, or fail outright. If you do add a plan, be careful not to insert it too early in the process. The ideal would be after the first five elements are established, and you're ready to start launching projects. In other words, make creating a plan one of your projects.

Ironically, many places only have a plan. The common result is a plan without the necessary partners or funding to implement it. Such plans might be pretty—and even pretty impressive—but they lack credibility. Deep down, no one believes a document will alter their economic trajectory, and they're right. Unfunded plans are so common that many folks consider them normal. In reality, they are often just for show, and shouldn't be allowed. Spending taxpayer money on a plan, without a strategic process to fund and implement it, should probably be prohibited (or at least documented as bad practice).

The fact that the strategy and the program are usually missing from most attempts to create a local process explains why most urban or regional revitalization—and multi-jurisdictional environmental restoration (such as watershed, river, or estuary)—initiatives are outright failures, or only marginally successful at best.

It's important to note that the entity that hosts your local ongoing program does not own your overall process. The program is a flywheel that gathers momentum while coordinating and perpetuating your efforts. But the process itself is a distributed, intangible dynamic that exists primarily in the minds of those who participate in it. The process is needed by everyone, but owned by no one. It's thus highly inclusive, because those who support, or take leadership of, its component activities are often self-selected.

For example, a local policy expert might perceive that a key element of policy support is missing as regards achieving the vision. They could then propose a new or amended policy to the city council, or maybe they're already on the council. Ideally, they would run it by the managers of your local resilient prosperity program first. The key is that everyone involved must be guided by the vision and strategy. Public presentations to boost local awareness of the process is important to attract these "emergent leaders": the more who understand it, the more who can contribute productively to it.

Sometimes, places are working to boost their resilience without knowing it. For instance, many communities are (finally) undergrounding their power and telecommunications infrastructure. There's probably no single action that will do more to increase their resilience in the face of wind, ice and snow storms.

But in many cases, they are doing it as a beautification project: removing ugly wires and telephone poles. That's revitalization-related. Not recognizing such crossover benefits between resilience and revitalization efforts often results in missed funding and political support opportunities. If these efforts were part on an overall process, those synergies are far less likely to be overlooked, and more funding would likely be available for them as a result.

The turning point in the regeneration of our world will come when an influential national government creates a policy, training and funding program to catalyze such efforts in communities and regions throughout their country. Its success will inspire other nations to go forth and do likewise. Using a similar approach makes it easier for nations to coordinate their efforts with each other. At that point, global regeneration of economies and natural resources would likely kick into high gear.

Such a national initiative would likely start at the local or state level, of course: that's certainly where the U.S. federal government gets most of its good ideas. For instance, there are hundreds of foundations and state governments currently dispensing vast amounts of money for revitalization and resilience efforts.

The problem is that they assume the recipients will know how to spend it wisely, which is seldom the case. The local communities might well know what projects are most important, but they lack a process to turn those projects into a catalyst for larger-scale revitalization or resilience. Otherwise, communities can be like lottery winners, frittering away their windfall, and being left with little to show for it a few years later.

Such charities and agencies should require their recipients to get some training in creating a strategic renewal process. Or, better yet, provide such training as part of their funding package. Once they've operated such a program for a few years and worked most of the kinks out of it, it could serve as a model for a national initiative.

Such grand initiatives often have their genesis in a more-limited agenda...one that has strong public buy-in at the moment. The catalyst might be a socially-noble cause, such as the current global movement towards demanding increased economic, social and environmental justice.

The more-likely starting point would be a life-threatening emergency, such as the climate crisis. Or, the birth could be as mundane as simply wanting a better ROI from existing revitalization, redevelopment and resilience expenditures.

UNDERSTANDING POLICYMAKING

> *"The gentrification of District neighborhoods — forcing existing residents, mostly people of color, out and creating new, amenity-rich areas for generally white and wealthy newcomers — is not a force of its own. It is not the natural order of things. It is the result of conscious policy decisions." – Jonathan M. Smith.*

In the above quote from an article in the October 25, 2019 *Washington Post*, Jonathan M. Smith---Executive Director of the Washington Lawyers' Committee for Civil Rights and Urban Affairs---went on to document that the policies which instigated DC's severe displacement problem (maybe the worst in the nation) was the result of very recent policy changes, not leftovers from earlier, more-segregated centuries. He said that mixed-race and mixed-income neighborhoods were actually more common at the turn of the millennium.

But in April of 2003, then-Mayor Anthony A. Williams (who is black) announced his strategy to revitalize the District by bringing in 100,000 new residents. His administration set their sites on redeveloping the neighborhoods of Shaw, Petworth, Fairlawn, Takoma, H Street NE, Near Southeast, Congress Heights, Bellevue and Minnesota/Benning. They were all rich in "untapped potential" and "identifiable opportunity sites," and were all primarily African American.

District government agencies were instructed to "coordinate commercial, housing and capital investments," which they did with a vengeance. The ensuing economic growth and alterations to land use policy—designed to appeal to wealthier residents, such as eliminating multi-familiy housing from neighborhoods—attracted a flood of private real estate investors. These new policies contained nothing to protect families that had lived in these neighborhoods for generations: they were considered to be in the way of progress. As stated elsewhere in this book, while some displacement is a natural byproduct of change, excessive displacement if a byproduct of uncaring or incompetent governance.

Like "strategy", "policy" and "policymaking" are two words that folks use frequently, but usually have trouble defining concisely when pressed to do so. Part of the confusion arises from the afact that there are several different kinds of policymaking—statutory, regulatory and budgetary—and they can happen at all levels of government. The non-profit Prosperity Now has an excellent synopsis on their website, which I'll summarize here. The examples here are U.S.-based, but most democracies have a somewhat-similar general process, though the details differ hugely.

- Statutory (or Legislative): Legislative policymaking refers to the process by which elected officials (e.g., members of Congress, state legislators, school board officials, etc.) introduce and pass legislation that becomes law. For example, the Patient Protection and Affordable Care Act ("ACA" or "Obamacare") gave states the flexibility to expand their Medicaid programs. The Act specified eligibility requirements, but it was up to states to determine how they might expand eligibility and to decide which other strategies they might employ to lower uninsured rates among low-income residents.
- Regulatory (or Administrative): Once a law is passed, the responsible agency, or agencies, develop the rules and regulations to implement and enforce the underlying law. Advocating to inform or influence this process is known as regulatory or administrative advocacy.
  - For example, The Dodd-Frank Wall Street Reform Act created the Consumer Financial Protection Bureau and tasked it with writing rules to reform the mortgage-lending market and protect mortgage borrowers against the deceitful banking practices that led to the financial collapse of 2008-2009. Advocates who educated Bureau staff and shared stories about the importance of mortgage lending reform were engaged in administrative advocacy because they informed the rulemaking process without ever advocating for a piece of legislation to be introduced or passed. This process happens at the state and local levels, too: rulemaking at these levels of government often leads to the creation of new state programs.
- Budgetary Advocacy: Budgetary advocacy refers to the process of informing or influencing decisions about how public money will be allocated. This is an especially important process because in addition to passing broad legislation (legislative policy) and tasking agencies with transforming legislation into applicable rules (regulatory policy), elected officials also make decisions about how much money will be spent on the various programs that are funded by the government.

These funding decisions have huge impact. Citizens often get excited when a revolutionary policy they've fought hard for get's enacted, only wonder a decade later why nothing much changed: it was often because the policy wasn't funded, or received only token mounts. At the federal level, budgetary decisions get made by appropriations committees, and need to be voted on by Members of Congress. At the state level, budgets are often introduced by the Governor and approved or voted upon by the state legislature. In these contexts, budgets are frequently used as a means for introducing or enacting new state policies.

How does one go about introducing a new law? Most U.S. states use a variation of the following five-step process. As with the federal government, all states have two chambers, a House of Representatives and a Senate. Both chambers must approve the bill and the Governor must sign it, for it to become law. Bills can be amended, stalled, blocked, or voted down at many points in the process. In most states, fewer than 20% of bills introduced become law.

- Step 1: Introduce Bill
    - Members of the two houses put their ideas into writing in the form of a bill. Most bills result from an idea or concern from a single constituent. Once a bill is drafted, it's submitted to the clerk's office and assigned a number.
- Step 2: Committee Process
    - Members of both houses are appointed to various standing committees for considering bills, based on broad topics like environment or education. Experts, lobbyists and concerned citizens testify before standing committees. Many bills die in committee and never reach a floor vote.
- Step 3: Floor Vote
    - All members of both houses can debate and amend a bill when it goes on the floor. If a bill receives a majority of votes, it passes and moves on to the other house to repeat the process.
- Step 4: Concurrence of Both Houses
    - If the House of Representatives alters the bill, the Senate votes on whether they concur with the changes, or vice versa. Once both chambers approve the bill, it becomes an "act" and goes to the governor.
- Step 5: Governor's Signature
    - The governor can sign the act into law or reject it via veto. Typically, a 3/5 vote in both chambers can override a governor's veto.

In 2017, a non-partisan Ohio advocacy group, the Greater Ohio Policy Center (GOPC), started the process of improving the state's brownfields redevelopment laws. At the time, Ohio was behind other states in terms of protecting redevelopers from liability when unexpected contamination is found during or after their good-faith effort to remediate a property they purchased (but which they didn't contaminate). That potential liability scared away many redevelopers, leaving thousands of toxic, unproductive eyesores blighting communities.

Over a two-year period, GOPC crafted House Bill 168, which sailed through the Ohio House of Representatives in the Spring of 2019 with a unanimous vote. Why were they so successful? By following the process carefully. They researched and drafted the bill, found state legislators who would champion it, educated organizations that might object to it, and lubricated its progress at every step.

"We crossed every T and dotted every I" in drafting the legislation and made sure *"we had conversations with committee members and all the people (in the General Assembly) it will be in front of,"* said Aaron Clapper, project manager of GOPC in an article by Jim Debrosse on the Soapbox Cincinnati website. In this way does one use policy to accelerate a local restoration economy.

THE REVITALIZING (AND DEVITALIZING) POWER OF POLICIES

> *"In many cities, ordinances are still in place that prohibit or severely restrict a variety of sustainable land use practices. ...cities may prohibit downspout disconnections from the sewer or stormwater system, placing an unnecessary burden on gray infrastructure while restricting the effectiveness of green infrastructure. Or cities may require overflow drains that connect to the sewer system on even the smallest of green infrastructure."*
> — Vacant to Vibrant (Island Press, 2019)

Whenever I've mentioned "policies" in this book, I've meant that to include the cloud of laws, ordinances, regulations, incentives / disincentives, and codes that derive from policymaking. But changing policies requires significant time and effort, so it's often more expedient to amend their manifestations, such as zoning and building codes. I'm including such tinkering when I refer to policy work.

Policy changes are a key element of revitalization and resilience work that many communities overlook. When done well, creating regenerative policies are the most powerful way to support your resilient prosperity strategy. But every bit as important is eliminating old policies that undermine resilient prosperity. In other cases, creating regional policies to support community policies is what's needed.

Regional policies are especially powerful, but quite rare. Downtowns can't reach their full potential in isolation. A heart needs the body as much as a body needs the heart. But even if you heal body and heart together, city center revitalization will likely be far more effective. For instance, many developers complain that repurposing and renewing existing downtown buildings is too expensive, so they focus on sprawl. Most communities that say they want to revitalize their downtown actually sabotage their dream by directly or indirectly subsidizing sprawl (what's known as a "perverse subsidy"). This schizophrenic policy structure is depressingly common.

Downtown revitalization is best achieved when the downtown becomes the easiest and most profitable place for real estate developers to operate. So eliminating indirect sprawl subsidies—such as by charging developers the full cost of providing public infrastructure—is essential. Since the infrastructure is already in place downtown, that single policy change can shift the focus of investment to the urban core.

> *"Every time there's new strategy, you have to get rid of old dogma. I love doing that."*
> *– Ben Chestnut, CEO and co-founder, Mailchimp.*

What if the sprawl zone is outside your city's jurisdiction? Create a regional revitalization strategy in partnership with your county, and even neighboring counties. If they're smart—meaning they don't see downtown revitalization as a zero-sum game—then they won't want your downtown to be dead any more than you do.

You can use both incentives and disincentives to put your greenfields "off limits" to developers in other communities, and get those communities to put their greenfields off limits to yours. Strategies can be cooperative: they don't have to be competitive. In fact, real community resilience is probably impossible without regional cooperation. Good regional policymaking lays the groundwork for such cooperative strategies.

REGENERATIVE POLICIES

> *"...evidence suggests that central cities have an opportunity, through policies of resilience, to help steer entire metropolitan areas toward greater sustainability. To maximize this impact, cities need to understand that resilience may not necessarily contribute to sustainability, and use that understanding to frame their policies appropriately."* – Edward J. Jepson, Jr., AICP.

Creating regenerative policies often goes hand-in-hand with eliminating degenerative policies (along with related laws, codes and regulations). Witness the massive explosion of inner city investment that was unleashed by New Jersey's "Smart Codes" some 25 years ago. Other states later adopted similar programs, often calling them "rehabilitation codes".

The strategic disconnect is most damaging in policymaking, where local, state/provincial, and national policies affect so much of what happens. Policies should support strategies, and should be an integral part of your renewal process. Instead, most policies are tactical BAND-AIDs®. But the reverse is also true: the creation of policies should be guided by strategies.

On December 7, 2018, the Integrated Planners Network (IPN) of Zimbabwe came up with a potentially disastrous "solution" to the problem of planners' lack of training in the revitalization process. They proposed that the government stop funding urban renewal initiatives (which planners tend to do poorly), and start focusing exclusively on building new cities (a process some planners understand quite well). Policy changes at the national level tend to have huge consequences, so we can only hope that wisdom prevails.

Policymaking without a vision and strategy as a guide—and without a process to activate them—is wasteful at best, and deadly at worst. In 2008, the U.S. Army Corps of Engineers and the U.S. Environmental Protection Agency overhauled federal policy governing how impacts to wetlands, streams, and other aquatic resources authorized under §404 of the Clean Water Act are offset; an action known as compensatory mitigation.

Ten years later, a 2019 report by the Environmental Law Institute found significant progress had been made in the nation's approach to compensatory mitigation, but that much work remains to ensure an efficient process for wetland, stream, and other aquatic resource compensatory mitigation decision-making, and to ensure that compensatory mitigation is providing effective ecological restoration outcomes. This is what happens when policymaking is done in a strategic process vacuum.

New, regenerative policies support what you want, as does the removal of old degenerative policies. What does a regenerative policy look like? It can be simplicity itself. An example of a good regenerative policy can be found in Vermont, which automatically designates all brownfields as prime renewable energy sites, thus turning them into "brightfields".

This puts them back into economic use, and—if the contamination isn't migrating by air or water—they don't even have to remediate it first. This policy thus 1) paves the way for eliminating fallow properties from the tax roles, 2) reduces dependence of expensive fossil fuels, and 3) helps restore the global climate. Not bad for a few paragraphs of text.

Similarly, a March 2019 report by the Campaign to Protect Rural England (CPRE) found that England could greatly alleviate their national housing shortage—and protect their beautiful countrysides (their primary mission)—via a simple policy change that prioritizes brownfields for new residential development. CPRE estimates that over one million homes could be built on brownfields, and that two thirds of these opportunities are "shovel ready."

With or without such policy support, regenerative partnerships are often the best mechanism for funding ambitious programs, and for expanding them to the proper scale. A shared regenerative vision facilitates such partnerships, and a strategic renewal process holds them together.

One caution: a policy that isn't consistently enforced isn't a policy, and a process that isn't consistently used isn't a process. I mention this in the immediate wake of the Amazon HQ2 political disaster in New York City.

In the hope of accelerating approvals for the giant new Amazon headquarters, New York Governor Andrew M. Cuomo and New York City Mayor Bill de Blasio cut the City Council out of the normal review and approval process. That tactic backfired spectacularly, as local citizens protested how the world's richest man had apparently undermined local democracy.

Instead of accelerating project approvals, bypassing their long-established process virtually guaranteed a bitter fight with local stakeholders. That's what they got.

Amazon took the hint that they weren't wanted, and left town. If the city and state had used their process, local concerns would have been heard, the plans could have been adjusted to serve everyone's needs, and the governor and mayor wouldn't have egg on their faces.

Possibly as a result of that fiasco, Amazon held a public webcast (it was invitation-only for the physical event) of a forum with the Metropolitan Washington Council of Governments (COG) on February 21, 2019. It took place here in Arlington, Virginia, where I live, and where Amazon's new headquarters will be located. That's partly because it's a revitalizing location for HQ2, and partly because local officials used their established approval process.

In contrast to New York City, the crowd in Arlington mostly "protested" in favor of Amazon. That's not to say there are no concerns, of course.

For instance, Arlington County supposedly has a policy commitment to increase its supply of affordable housing. Yet weak-kneed county officials made no such demands of Amazon, even after Amazon was thrown out of New York City and they were in good position to do so.

On the plus side, much better dialog and coordination between Arlington County and the City of Alexandria has arisen, since the Amazon site sits on their shared border, making housing a shared concern.

Again: unenforced policies and processes are neither: they're just political eyewash. But the tide is turning, and many cities are now progressing towards a complete RECONOMICS Process.

WHERE SHOULD YOUR LOCAL RECONOMICS PROCESS BE BASED?

The choice of host for the program portion of your local resilient prosperity process might be the most important decision you make. It needs to be a trusted, transparent, permanent entity.

I specify "permanent" to exclude dependence on entities that are tied to a specific political administration. The norm is for new administrations to kill the initiatives of the previous administration, especially if it was a competing party.

Having local political support is important, but your revitalization or resilience initiative shouldn't depend on it. The better approach is to work fairly autonomously from elected leaders, but give them credit for your successes.

Not all RECONOMICS Process activities would necessarily be run by this hosting organization. At minimum, you could limit its role to the first three elements of the process: program, vision and strategy. As long as the ensuing Policies, Partnerships and Projects derive from the vision and strategy, they can—and probably should—by created and implemented by other entities.

But if it has the resources to devote more time, having them at least review proposed policy changes, partnerships and projects would be wise. It should be kept in mind, of course, that some partnerships and projects must be kept under wraps in the early stages, in order to avoid losing opportunities to real estate speculators.

In British Columbia, Canada, a public entity called Metro Vancouver is a federation of 21 municipalities, one Electoral Area and one Treaty First Nation that collaboratively plans for and delivers regional-scale services, such as drinking water, wastewater treatment and solid waste management. Metro Vancouver also regulates air quality, plans for urban growth, manages a regional parks system and provides affordable housing.

Now, Metro Vancouver is in the process of establishing a new economic prosperity service that will focus on regional collaboration to advance shared economic, livability and sustainability goals in Canada's Pacific Gateway. Metro Vancouver's Board of Directors endorsed a business plan for a new service that will establish a regional brand to attract strategic investment; the kind that contributes positively to livability and sustainability. It will work closely with public and private sector stakeholders to identify investment priorities and to collect and analyze relevant data, while leveraging the regional district's considerable resources and positive reputation.

Metro Vancouver's Chair, Sav Dhaliwal says *"Our aim is to enhance the region's economic prosperity by helping our member jurisdictions attract the right kind of large scale investments, so that we may more fully realize our region's vast potential as a great place to live and do business."*

The new service seeks to promote foreign investment that will increase the number of well-paying, high-quality jobs in the region, which will in turn contribute tax revenues to support public infrastructure and service upgrades for the benefit of all residents. *"World-renowned for its natural beauty, Metro Vancouver is home to diverse, innovative, and creative industries, public authorities, universities, and local government agencies. What's needed is a mechanism to coordinate the efforts of these sectors to enhance the region's shared prosperity, livability and sustainability,"* said Linda Buchanan, Vice-Chair of Metro Vancouver.

It will engage the private sector, member jurisdictions, and First Nations as well as agencies of the federal and provincial governments through two Advisory Groups, which will help set priorities and provide insights into broad national and international trends. The annual operating budget will start at $0.4 million for 2019 and is expected to increase to $2.5 million by 2023. I include all of this detail because this sounds like an ideal potential host for a resilient prosperity program.

Besides being trusted, transparent, permanent and of the right geographic scope, your host should be as holistic as possible in its reach, rather than confided in a narrow silo. For instance, I've always felt that community foundations had tremendous untapped potential as community revitalizers.

The function of most community foundations is to provide infrastructure in support of local efforts that benefit the community. That could be administrative (shared offices), fundraising (shared events) or capacity building (shared training). As such, they tend to be connected to a broad spectrum of revitalizing efforts, and tend to reach throughout the community or region.

Given the approximately 1700 community foundations worldwide, if one were to become the successful host for their local RECONOMICS Process, it could become a template for many other communities.

Your program host needn't be a community foundation, of course: I simply offer that example to illustrate the sorts of qualities you might look for in a host. All that being said, we shouldn't get so attached to the institutional model that we forget the importance of the personal factor. I just got off the phone with a local leader in a town that's trying desperately to revitalize, and he made it clear that partnering with the local community foundation was not an option for them. "The Executive Director of our community foundation thinks about nothing but raising money, and guards her power like a snake," he said.

As noted earlier, there's a vast amount of "wheel reinvention" going on. Each redevelopment project has to investigate the various funding sources and tax credit programs available to them. Each new project must engage stakeholders, often facilitating a resident-derived vision to drive their strategy. Someone (like a local RE Facilitator) using the RECONOMICS Process would, ideally, have all of this information at their fingertips. Thus, stakeholder engagement already would be in place—as would the shared vision—each time a new project was launched.

A RECONOMICS Process thus becomes your local "immune system", repelling "pathogens" like unnecessary sprawl, heritage demolition, unsustainable resource use, and inequitable redevelopment schemes. It would systemically encourage repurposing or replacing decrepit assets, reconnecting isolated healthy assets, and reorienting all activities towards the common goal of Resilient Prosperity.

You could also perceive the RECONOMICS Process as the regenerative "nervous system" connecting your area. As noted earlier, healthy cities and nations are complex adaptive systems. But disconnected government agencies tend to make them complicated, not complex.

A well-executed RECONOMICS Process would itself be resilient. Even if your resilient prosperity program were birthed by a mayor or city council, it would be difficult—maybe even political suicide—for a new administration to kill it simply because "the other party" created it. Once a community has a well-communicated resilient prosperity process in place, losing it becomes unthinkable.

The need for a RECONOMICS Process is, in some ways, greater in rural regions. Their small communities generally have a paucity of regenerative experts. Revitalizing a rural area—or a multi-jurisdictional metro area—demands integration of the natural, built, and socioeconomic environments. When most communities in a given area have renewal processes with shared principles and characteristics, regional efforts become far easier.

> *"A man watches his pear tree day after day, impatient for the ripening of the fruit. Let him attempt to force the process, and he may spoil both fruit and tree. But let him patiently wait, and the ripe pear at length falls into his lap."*
> *– Abraham Lincoln*

Some might read the above Lincoln quote as a rehash of the "all good things come to those who wait" aphorism. But the key word was "process." If that pear-production process weren't in place, all the waiting and non-interference in the world wouldn't produce a pear.

And so it is with community regeneration: put the RECONOMICS Process in place, and let it do its thing. That's not to say you won't be busy: devitalization is what generally comes to those who just sit around and wait. The point is that—with a process in place—you'll actually have a valid reason to expect good results to appear.

A STARTING POINT FOR CREATING YOUR RECONOMICS PROCESS

Just as the 3Re Strategy is an ideal basis for almost any revitalization/resilience strategy, so too do the other five elements of the RECONOMICS Process have ideal starting points. You can ignore or modify these as you see fit of course, but here's my take on specifying some characteristics for each element of an ideal process:
- Program: Inclusive; transparent; adaptive.
- Vision: Resilient health, security and prosperity for all.
- Strategy: Repurpose; Renew; Reconnect.

- Policies: Encourage redevelopment/discourage sprawl; integrated asset management; full-cost accounting.
- Partnerships: Begin each as think-do team; transfer risk from public to private; reward successful risk-taking.
- Projects: Planning guided by Program; designing guided by Vision; decision-making guided by Strategy.

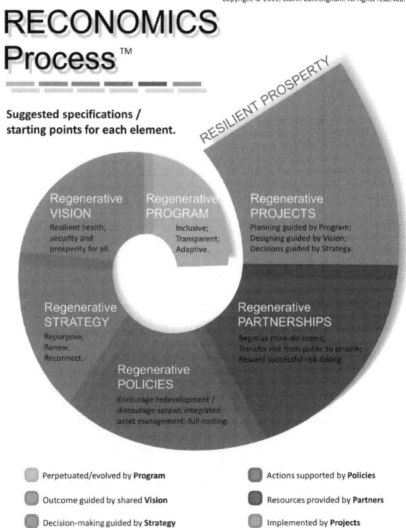

A widespread obstacle to addressing multiple agendas simultaneously is the aforementioned conflicting constraints, whereby being in accordance with one set of instructions puts one in violation of others. The budget, scope, and schedule of a project are conflicting constraints. Reduce the time for delivery, and you'll need to hire more people (increase the budget), or reduce the scope.

In urban redevelopment, the fact that public agencies operate in silos—infrastructure, environment, economic development, planning, heritage, arts, etc.—impedes the resolution of conflicting constraints, demanding even more of your plans and strategies. In "Why Strategy Execution Unravels" by Sull, Homkes, & Sull (Harvard Business Review, March 2015) the authors state *"No plan can anticipate every event that might help or hinder a company trying to achieve its strategic objectives. Managers and employees at every level need to adapt to facts on the ground, surmount unexpected obstacles, and take advantage of fleeting opportunities. Strategy execution, as we define the term, consists of seizing opportunities that support the strategy while coordinating with other parts of the organization on an ongoing basis. When managers come up with creative solutions to unforeseen problems or run with unexpected opportunities, they are not undermining systematic implementation; they are demonstrating execution at its best. Such real-time adjustments require firms to be agile."*

Even if they understand the RECONOMICS Process, many folks within well-established institutions will find themselves constrained from implementing it. And it's not just individuals who are frustrated. Most communities and regions encounter one or more of the following constraints when trying to revitalize:

- TIME CONSTRAINT: Achieving resilient prosperity requires an ongoing (or at least long-term) process, but elected leaders are usually around only for a few years;
- SCOPE CONSTRAINT: Achieving resilient prosperity requires a critical mass of human and physical assets, and often works best on a regional scale. But that defined region often lacks a legal jurisdiction, and thus lacks an official leader. It's a rare city or county mayor who can lead an entire region;
- ASSET CONSTRAINT: Achieving resilient prosperity requires repurposing, renewing, and/or reconnecting ALL of your local assets—natural, built, and socioeconomic—but architects tend to think it's all about vertical infrastructure (buildings), and civil engineers tend to think it's all about horizontal infrastructure (water, dirt, pipes, roads, bridges, cables, etc.);
- PROCESS CONSTRAINT: As we've seen, achieving resilient prosperity requires a comprehensive process comprising a shared vision, a strategy for success, an ongoing program to keep implementing until the vision is achieved, supportive policymaking, effective partnerships, and adaptive management. But planners and designers are taught little or none of that.

And even if they understand the process, they lack the authority to dictate the actions of the agencies responsible for the needed actions and assets. And economic developers only recruit employers, which is just a project; and

- EXPERIENCE CONSTRAINT: Achieving resilient prosperity requires inclusive, equitable stakeholder engagement, so "people-oriented" professionals—such as executives from universities, foundations, non-profits, or businesses—are sometimes assigned the role of leader, but they suffer from ALL of the previous challenges. And even if they had all the right knowledge and skills, they would lack experience in running such an initiative: they would be learning on the job...a scary proposition when the future of the place and its people are at stake.

The RECONOMICS Process can go a long way towards avoiding conflicting constraints, or speeding their resolution. It does this both by bringing them to light, and by "forcing" agencies to take a more holistic approach to community management. If you can't change the goals, change the constraints. And that is usually best done via regenerative policy changes.

New Jersey did this brilliantly with their Smart Codes program (documented in *The Restoration Economy*). In 1996, New Jersey overhauled their rigid, antiquated fire codes. Designed for new construction, the old codes made reusing old buildings cost-prohibitive, which constrained urban revitalization.

The Smart Codes program gave redevelopers the flexibility they needed to adapt and renovate old industrial buildings in ways that complied with modern building codes for fire and safety, without busting the budget. The program cost New Jersey virtually nothing to implement, and triggered an instant explosion of reuse projects statewide. Renewal of existing buildings in New Jersey's 16 largest cities rose 62.5%, from $363.3 million in 1997 to $590.4 million in 1999.

The research possibilities are endless, since so few revitalization tools or initiatives are ever studied, either while active or forensically. For instance, there's a global trend towards restoring rivers by removing outdated dams. Once removed, migratory fish—whose spawning grounds have sometimes been blocked for over a century—return, revitalizing economies and ecosystems. A 2014 study by Oregon State University revealed that undammed "rivers can return surprisingly fast to a condition close to their natural state." Most folks assumed that might be the case, but now we know it, thanks to what might be called "regenerative research".

Dam removal can be used as a metaphor in urban revitalization. Many places have significant private money ready to flow into regenerative activities. But antiquated policies, incentives, zoning, and building codes block their "migration". Unblocked, revitalization can be surprisingly fast. New Jersey's policy revisions were "bureaucratic dam removal". Yyon Chouinard, CEO of

Patagonia, says "Time and again, I've witnessed the celebration that comes with the removal of an unnecessary dam. After a river is restored and the fish have returned you never hear a single person say, 'Gee, I wish we had our dam back'." Neither does New Jersey mourn the loss of their old fire codes.

To put more power into your RECONOMICS Process, each element (especially the projects) should have both a project and a program goal. In other words, the work should have goals for its own sake, and goals that advance the resilient prosperity initiative. So, converting a historic downtown building into a microbrewery has the goal of being a successful business. But it should also have the goal of advances the downtown revitalization process. Doing so doesn't usually require any change to the project itself: it's usually just a matter of timing.

Bad timing can completely eradicate something's value. For instance, the ancient "why did the chicken cross the road?" joke completely loses any humorous value if you don't wait after asking the question. Giving the listener time to try figure out the answer is what gives the no-brainer "to get the the other side" answer its element of surprise. And so it is with revitalization: the most wonderful "3Re" project in the world might have little or no revitalizing value to a place if done at the wrong time.

A BETTER WAY TO CREATE LOCAL PARTNERSHIPS

> *"Urban Partnership Operations (UPO) are a Brazilian creation, established by federal legislation that provides general guidelines for land value capture, redistributive land use planning and zoning, and public–private partnerships in urban development. The instrument aims to stimulate area-based revitalization and renewal through concentrated public and private investments that are allocated within a predetermined perimeter."*
> *– "Steering the Metropolis".*

Before going any further, let's explore that word "partner", to make sure we're on the same page as to its definition. For at least two decades, the largest trend in public financing of infrastructure and redevelopment projects in the Americas has been public-private partnerships (P3). I specify "the Americas" because P3s are nothing new in Europe, especially for infrastructure.

P3s are a major reason that Europe's rail system makes U.S. rail look like that of a third-world country. Canada is generally better at P3s than the U.S., because they share learning among provinces. In the U.S., the situation is more uneven: Virginia, Texas, California, Arizona, and Puerto Rico are up to speed, but most other states are far behind the curve.

As with all tools, P3s have been abused. "Bought" politicians have used them to disguise an outright privatization of public infrastructure that robs the public blind. My 2008 book, *Rewealth*, had two chapters on public-private partnering. It told the story of a water infrastructure "P3" (really just privatization) that was so out of control, it charged citizens for the rainwater falling in their yards. But when used properly, P3s can be an ideal solution to the massive challenge of funding the renewal of our outdated power, transportation, sewer, drinking water, and green infrastructure.

Here's a quick and easy way to determine whether a proposed P3 is a true partnership: the private entity should be taking a risk that the public entity can't (or shouldn't) take.

While P3s are often used for large urban redevelopment projects, I haven't encountered any for ongoing revitalization. But even if a city or county wanted to create a P3-based revitalization program, what AEC firm understands the revitalization process well enough to be a good partner?

We've already seen many examples of revitalization and resilience projects based on partnerships: public-public, public-private or private-private. As with all other elements of the RECONOMICS Process, partnering can be done well or poorly; efficiently or inefficiently.

For instance, in most communities that have active recovery, revitalization or resilience efforts, task teams are a part of the process. Volunteers—too often people with too much time on their hands and few other qualifications—are assigned to a group to stuck a particular problem and recommend solutions. That can work, but there's a much better way; one that enables you to move from research to action far more quickly.

We've previously talked about how research and learning should be an integral part of the visioning element of your process. But it should be integral to all elements of your renewal process. There's an efficient way to accomplish both learning and partnering.

When you identify a challenge or opportunity, and wish to create a task team to study it and devise an approach create the team with the people who own the assets (financial, property, etc.)—and who have the relevant decision-making authority—so the team can move straight from report-writing into partnering. In other words, devise your task teams as if they were already the ideal partnership for the project.

HARD PROJECTS VS. SOFT SERVICES

> *"I'm really passionate about making things work. Creating systems and processes is a big part of my skill set."*
> *– Michael Lenard, founder & CEO of the successful regional restaurant chain TaKorean.*

Let's end this chapter by clarifying the nature of your potential projects, since that's the part of the process where what's perceived as the "real" work takes place, and where 99% of the expenditures will be made.

A project doesn't necessarily involve a hard asset, like a building or tract of land. It could be a capacity-building service, such as training, mentoring or start-up funding assistance for local entrepreneurs that you hope will bring new activity to your downtown.

A mentioned earlier, the key differentiator between a project and a program is the completion date: if it has one, it's a project. But that's not the only difference: something that's ongoing might be considered a project simply because it has a very small scope.

For instance, some endeavors—like the above-mentioned services for entrepreneurs—might be intended to be ongoing, in which case it would be a program. That doesn't mean it would be THE program that houses your RECONOMICS Process, however.

The ongoing nature of services like that those is often dependent on continued funding from a local sponsor—or from outside sources like a foundation or state agency—so the plug could be pulled at any time. A revolving loan fund for entrepreneur assistance would be a good example of a self-sustaining, ongoing service program. So, don't get too rigid about the project/program divide: you will probably have some ongoing services in the "projects" portion of your RECONOMICS Process.

People don't have as much time to get involved in community issues as they used to. So, they should love having a local renewal process: it gives them something they can influence over time, rather than just reacting to the latest developer's proposal. In other words, whatever time they can put into it becomes a long-term investment, rather than a one-time expenditure.

As noted earlier, all healthy living systems—ecological, economic, immunological, etc.—renew themselves constantly via a regenerative process. Without such a process, they suffer from what might be dubbed a "degenerative disorder." Devitalization is inevitable, likely leading to death.

> *"Kindness is not enough: Australia needs a strategic national response to the bushfires. We've seen deeds of great courage and charity... Now we need an effective, coordinated process to help the nation rebuild."*
> *- Title and subtitle of Op-Ed by Audette Exel in the January 26, 2020 issue of The Guardian.*

Many communities and regions suffer from what I call "civic degeneration disorder". You can identify them via the most common signs: increasing levels of economic devitalization, social disharmony, environmental degradation, crime, homelessness and drug abuse. While those factors are increasing, other factors are usually on the wane: confidence in the local future, cultural uniqueness, economic and social equity, etc.

Most places try to revitalize by tackling those outcomes individually. The more intelligent places tackle the cause: the lack of an ongoing regenerative process. The strategic regeneration process presented in this book can be applied at the local, regional and national levels.

If that happens, a new age of resilient prosperity will likely follow. In other words, the RECONOMICS Process is the cure for civic degeneration disorder.

CHAPTER 11 - RECONOMICS: FUSING RECOVERY, REVITALIZATION & RESILIENCE.

"I am no longer accepting the things I cannot change. I am changing the things I cannot accept." – Angela Davis.

Now that you've learned the RECONOMICS Process (in the previous chapter), let's dive into some of the dynamics you'll encounter in your efforts to effectively apply it. There are four advantages to achieving your community's crisis recovery, economic revitalization and clmate resilience aspirations by creating a RECONOMICS Process:

- It gives you an ideal to shoot for: You are no longer in a directionless, stop-start, "let's try it and see if it works" mode of renewing your local future;
- Each element that you create advances local revitalization: You don't have to wait until it's complete to see results. That said, the vast majority of the value comes from the complete process, as you saw in the earlier chart;
- Getting started is easy: You probably have several of the elements already, so you can start with whichever missing element is easiest, or makes sense for your situation; and
- Getting started is cheap: With the exception of the physical projects, none of the elements require any significant monetary expenditure.

If you're a consultant, rather than a local leader, let me first prepare you for the reactions you're likely to encounter when proposing that a community should achieve revitalization and resilience via a strategic renewal process.

Go to the leaders of any of the tens of thousands of communities that are attempting to revitalize or boost resilience and ask what their process is, and you'll get a blank look. They will probably start listing their activities, such as recruiting employers, or restoring green infrastructure, or redeveloping brownfields.

But they won't have a process that ensures these things are being done in a productive sequence. They are like farmers who don't know that crops have to be planted before they can be harvested. Their more-likely reaction to your question would be to explode: *"I don't have time for that ivory tower nonsense! I've got things to do!"*

SEQUENCING AND PUBLIC ENGAGEMENT

The sequence of the RECONOMICS Process described in the previous chapter can be adapted to local needs, but the program, vision and strategy should usually be #1, #2 and #3, respectively. The program hosts the visioning process, the resulting vision drives the strategy, and together they drive the rest of the activities. If you're using the 3Re Strategy, you're automatically advancing both revitalization and resilience---since both are largely based on regenerating natural, built and socioeconomic assets---so that's the perfect starting point.

It's not just sequence that's important, of course. Not understanding the process means that key steps in that process will likely be missing. In that case, these community leaders are more like farmers who don't know that crops must be watered after planting. Skip that step and they can forget about the harvest.

Witness the number of places whose wonderful public visioning session isn't followed by the development of a strategy. Or strategies that lack supporting policies. Or projects withering in the absence of an ongoing program. They are unlikely to harvest any resilient prosperity.

A mistake made by many well-meaning communities is engaging the public in every element of the RECONOMICS Process. Trying to constantly involve the public in every phase of revitalization or resilience-enhancement is a recipe for disaster.

If the average leader doesn't understand strategy, you can imagine what a mess it would be trying to create one with a crowd of enthusiastic, opinionated residents. Ill-timed public engagement can slow the process to the point where private partners flee (time is money), and where changes of political administration either disrupt the process, or kill it entirely. Project delays are especially dangerous, since redevelopers are—as described earlier—usually working on borrowed money, and their entitlements have expiration dates.

Counter-intuitively, excessive engagement can actually increase disharmony, as unqualified people try to influence decisions requiring deep knowledge. In the study of complex adaptive systems, it's well known that there can be both too little and too much connectivity.

Visioning is the portion of the RECONOMICS Process where most of your community engagement should take place. In fact, visioning is the only element that requires deep public input...assuming that subsequent steps rigorously reference that vision.

If you do a good job of creating a shared vision, and if the citizens trust that your subsequent work will adhere to that vision (a big "if", granted), then relatively little further public engagement should be needed. One aspect of public engagement that many communities fail to do is to identify the emergent leaders. We aren't going to get far if we don't know WHO is going to help get us there. We can also get into trouble if we become rigid about the sequencing of the process. Any one of the six elements can actually be the starting point, as we'll see next.

WHO REALLY REVITALIZES DOWNTOWNS?

Many people believe that it's the presence of a sufficient number of residents that revitalizes a downtown. You might be under the impression that I believe that also, based on what you've read so far. I do, but those residents are an outcome, not a cause. People can't move downtown if there's no residential capacity for them to move into, so it's the people who understand the need for those residents—and who create that capacity—who are actually behind the revitalization, not the residents themselves.

That makes it sound as if I'm saying it's residential and mixed-use redevelopers who trigger revitalization, but that's not true either. Often, it's the local leaders (public and private) who make policy and regulatory changes that open the doors to that real estate investment who are the actual catalysts.

For instance, Lower Manhattan had just 800 residents in 1950: the place was lifeless when the office workers (mostly financial services) went home. By 2017, some 61,000 folks lived there, and it's a real, living neighborhood.

In 1998, there were just 11,600 residential units in downtown Los Angeles. By 2017, there were some 65,000. In both cases, the vast majority of those new residential units were created by repurposing older Class B office buildings into condos and apartments. Over a 16-year period starting in 2001, 96 office buildings were repurposed into 10,675 apartments in Lower Manhattan.

The usual reason those Class B buildings were vacant was because they lacked the electrical and electronic infrastructure needed by today's internet-dependent businesses. Adding that wiring in the course of converting them to residential added the "reconnecting" aspect to repurposing and renewing the structures, so one could say the 3Re Strategy was at work, however unknowingly.

In New York City's case, another revitalization trigger was that they greatly improved the quality of life via their Green Streets Program, which started in 1996. By 2007, vast expanses of lifeless concrete and asphalt had been repurposed and renewed into 2468 lovely green pocket parks citywide, which helped reconnect thousands of blocks and revitalize dozens—if not hundreds—of neighborhoods.

So, yes: those "3Re" redevelopers could be said to have triggered downtown revitalization, but wait: what about the policymakers who facilitated their doing so?

In the 1960s, the Soho district of Lower Manhattan was in steep decline, with many of its historic buildings occupied by illegal residents. They were illegal because these buildings—mostly office and manufacturing—didn't meet residential safety codes.

In 1971, the city's policymakers granted property owners a 12-year tax abatement if they brought those buildings up to code for residential use. Policymakers at the state level helped in 1976 when they amended the New York State Multiple Dwelling Law to allow "residential occupancy of loft, commercial, or manufacturing buildings" that met residential use requirements.

As a direct result, that vast inventory of dilapidated buildings was renovated en masse, and Soho began a long period of revitalization that continues to this day. So, it could be said that—at least in such situations—it's the policymakers who generate downtown revitalization.

But policies aren't just a starting point for revitalization and resilience efforts: they can also be used to accelerate or scale-up successful initiatives. Maybe the most impressive community "fixer" in late 20th century America was Dana Crawford. She moved to Denver, Colorado in 1954 when she was 23 years old. While everyone else was focusing on new construction, she fell in love with the historic, vacant buildings of the Lower Downtown (LoDo) area.

Three years later, she had repurposed and renewed eight of those buildings as retail and restaurants, all of them on Larimer Street. She created a new identity for the area by calling it Larimer Square, but couldn't expand it and reconnect it to the rest of the area due to zoning restrictions.

Ideally, zoning reflects policy, and local policymakers liked the revitalization they saw her creating. So they granted her request to rezone 20 blocks of old industrial and warehouse areas around Larimer Square to allow residential redevelopment. Formerly-decrepit Lodo was reborn as one of the most popular live-work-play areas of the city as a result. [statistics in this section courtesy of *The Heart of the City* by Alexander Garvin, Island Press, 2019]

FROM ECONOMIC DEVELOPMENT TO RESILIENT PROSPERITY

> *"We are delighted to welcome Lance Forest Products to New Mexico. This company will revitalize the forest restoration economy in Cimarron, restoring confidence in the community, bringing needed jobs & improving forest resilience to climate change. It's a win-win for all." – Governor Michelle Lujan Grisham.*

The above quote refers to a $350,000 investment by the New Mexico Economic Development Department to bring a sawmill operator to the town of Cimarron in December of 2019. I can't vouch for whether her use of the term "restoration economy" meets the definition in my book, *The Restoration Economy*, but the governor's statement addresses most of what's to revitalize the area: jobs, natural resource restoration, confidence in the local future and climate resilience.

If they truly are accomplishing all this in a way that restores the forests, it would be a welcome change from the usual practices of economic development agencies. Most of them don't perceive any agenda beyond jobs, nor any way of boosting employment beyond attracting companies from outside the community via tax incentives.

As noted earlier, communities should improve their quality of life and restore their resource base first. That's a reliable attractor of good employers. It's also safer: the community gets a better quality of life even if the jobs don't come...a "can't lose" strategy. Many places instead do things backwards. This is usually as a result of the antiquated "economic development" model. We've mentioned the problems with this earlier, but overcoming resistance—or, better-yet, getting buy-in—from this well-entrenched profession is often key to establishing your strategic renewal process. That said, many more-enlightened economic developers are well aware of the problems with that old model, and might welcome a better alternative, so don't assume they are the enemy.

The old model is based on attracting employers by giving away future tax revenues, assuming that more jobs translates to revitalization and better livability. It seldom does. Such incentives often attract low-quality jobs from firms that disappear when the freebies run out. Meanwhile, the city struggles with insufficient tax revenues to fund maintenance and improvements, so quality of life declines.

The over-use of tax incentives by economic developers often leads to municipal devitalization and even bankruptcy. General revenues dry up because companies are paying no taxes, thus degrading public services (such as infrastructure maintenance) and quality of life. Further devitalization then ensues, since high-quality employers are primarily attracted by high quality of life and efficient infrastructure. Having a reliable process is thus prudent...simply a matter of fiduciary responsibility.

A perfect example was the Foxconn deal in Wisconsin. Desperate for a political "win", Donald Trump—teamed with former Wisconsin governor Scott Walker—offered some $4.5 billion in freebies to Foxconn, a Taiwan-based conglomerate whose manufacturing facilities are mostly in mainland China.

Anticipating a $10 billion investment to build a 20 million sq. ft. facility, Governor Walker stopped at nothing to please Foxconn. Numbers like "22,000 indirect jobs" and "10,000 construction jobs" were paraded around.

Foxconn promised 13,000 high-paying jobs, at an average of $23/hour. Each of these jobs would thus cost the state $219,000, putting the state in the red on the deal until at least the year 2042 (not including the cost of public infrastructure needed to support that growth.)

Then it turned out that Foxconn has no intention of bringing in 13,000 jobs. They had previously made similar deals with gullible politicians in Brazil, India and Pennsylvania, none of which came to fruition. They apparently just wanted the handouts.

And it's not as if Foxconn is a dream employer: nightmare is more like it. Their Chinese factories are infamously surrounded with nets. These are to help save the lives of the desperately-unhappy employees who tend to jump off the factory roofs in suicide attempts.

According to a February 11, 2019 article by Justin Carr in *Bloomberg Businessweek*, Foxconn currently has a grand total of 178 employees at the

Wisconsin facility, and was only advertising for an additional 122 at that time. At that point, they were hinting that it might only become a small R&D facility, rather than a huge manufacturing plant.

But, in a private October 22, 2019 communication with me, Rob Richardson, Chair of the Mt. Pleasant Community Development Authority and Tourism Commission in Racine, gave me this more-positive update on the project: *"One building is done, and the first million square foot building is getting its roof now. Bids are out for the starting work on buildings 3 and 4. Building 5 goes to planning commission soon. There is a long list of other developments going on because of the impact of Foxconn on the Village, County and SE Wisconsin."*

In other words, as with the transit projects discussed previously, revitalization is occurring because the Foxconn announcement has inspired greater confidence in the future of the region. Let's hope that this confidence isn't misplaced, and that there's a happy ending here for the good folks of Wisconsin.

Even if Foxconn does fulfill its employment promises, the entire project was an example of horrendously-bad urban, regional and environmental planning. Rather than making use of a renovated, existing manufacturing facility—of which Wisconsin has plenty—they are building everything from scratch. That wouldn't be so bad if they put it on a brownfield site, which Wisconsin also has in plenty. But no: they are paving-over 3000 acres of prime farmland, thus undermining the state's vital agricultural economy.

Wisconsin "won" Foxconn from other states not only with that ludicrously generous package of tax incentives, but also with infrastructure commitments and environmental regulation waivers. Foxconn was told they could discharge dredged materials into waterways, fill wetlands, change the course of streams, build artificial bodies of water that would connect with (and likely pollute) natural waterways, and could build on riverbeds or lakebeds without permits. Foxconn was even exempted from having to file state environmental impact statements.

Wisconsin basically spread its legs and told the Chinese, *"do whatever you want to us."* Governor Walker called it a *"once-in-a-century opportunity"* for Wisconsin. It was more like a once-in-a-century abdication of responsibility by a state government. Donald Trump heralded it as a great victory for America. We can do better.

This is the kind of antiquated, self-destructive activity that passes for "economic development" all across America. Professionals who understand the strategic process of economic regeneration are in very short supply. Instead, we have "professionals" whose sole "strategy" is to generate ephemeral political wins at the cost of long-term health, wealth and resilience.

What's needed are planners, politicians, architects, engineers, managers, non-profit leaders and citizen activists who have been certified in facilitating the creation of a strategic renewal process. That's exactly what's happening now, as you'll learn in the following chapter.

The "can't lose" strategy mentioned above was how Chattanooga became a poster-child of revitalization. As described in Chapter 6, they first cleaned-up their god-awful air quality. Then they focused on repurposing their waterfront from industrial to residential and recreational use, renewing their brownfields and greenspaces, and reconnecting downtown to the waterfront. Then they landed a $4 billion VW plant on the largest of those remediated brownfields.

Granted, they used economic development incentives, but VW executives ignored the other cities offering similar incentives because Chattanooga offered that magic feature: extending their riverfront trail to the site, so employees would have a lovely walk to the revitalized downtown for lunch...or to return home to one of the many new waterfront condos. That trail enhanced the executives' quality of life and their employees' well-being: the tax incentives didn't. It was a corporate decision, but a personal decision as well.

The assumption of most economic developers is that attracting a large employer is virtually synonymous with revitalization. How then, does one explain the situation described in the following excerpt from an article in the June 15, 2016 issue of *Fortune* magazine?

"For the past 10 years, Hormel Foods (whose best-known product is Spam®) has been on a tear. Revenue has increased from $5.4 billion to $9.3 billion...Earnings have more than doubled, the dividend has almost quadrupled, and the stock has returned roughly 400%. Austin, Minnesota...is the hometown of Hormel Foods... Nearly everything in Austin owes its existence to Hormel. (but there's) no Starbucks and no Toyota dealer. The Target closed last year. Staples the year before. The only Airbnb option is a fifth-wheel trailer." Sounds like there's not much spillover of wealth from Hormel to the community.

Mayors love "economic development" because successes are visible and failures are largely invisible. And because the strategy is simplistic (not to be confused with simple): "bribe employers to come here with tax savings and/or free land." But a concise strategy isn't automatically a good strategy. And every professional marketer knows that competing on price is a sign of desperation.

Mayors also love economic development because it uses the magic phrase: "job creation." But stealing jobs from another city or state is a zero-sum game, as described in Chapter 3: one place's gain is another's loss. There's certainly no net gain for the region or nation. In fact, it's a net loss in terms of aggregate public revenue, since each move involves a tax holiday.

An ad for the city of Atlanta, Georgia in the March 1, 2017 issue of FORTUNE magazine brags that they succeeded in getting Mercedes-Benz to relocate their North American headquarters from Montvale, New Jersey, saying the move created "800 new jobs." Really? If the headquarters had moved 900 feet to another block in Montvale, would that also have created 800 new jobs? How does moving 900 miles change that? This insanity was most recently documented in a March 16, 2017 article in the *Wall Street Journal*.

New York City, Columbus, Boston, and Seattle have some of the highest tax rates in the nation, and are all economically robust. Hundreds of other cities have spent decades enticing relocating employers with massive tax breaks, and are in worse shape than ever. "*Abandoning local economic development policies is almost politically impossible for local leaders. But it is the right thing to do,*" says Richard Schragger, University of Virginia law professor in his new book, *City Power* (2016).

Employers are just one of the ingredients of revitalization. The RECONOMICS Process is the recipe. Again, three key dynamics of revitalization are confidence, momentum, and alignment. One common area of non-alignment is between a community's revitalization or resilience efforts and their job-creation efforts.

A BETTER WAY TO PRODUCE BETTER JOBS

Economic developers focus on attracting employers for a very good reason: without a sufficient quantity and quality of jobs, any revitalization progress your community makes will likely be superficial and transitory. But economic developers seldom attract quality jobs. And when they do, the norm is that the community grossly overpays for them, and the employer leaves when the tax holiday is over.

Another fairly universal problem is that local schools aren't generating enough young people who are employable. Either their high school graduation rate is too low, or the graduates they do produce don't have useful knowledge or skills. Fixing the school system is vitally important, of course, but it tends to take forever and be fraught with failure. Basing your job growth efforts on fixing a system that's so resistant to change is probably not your most effective path forward.

We've already talked about how the best way to attract jobs is to make your community attractive to employers...in ways other than "we're cheap" or "we'll pay you to come here". But here's a way you can align quality job production with the revitalization of your community: integrate workforce development and skills training to the process of regenerating your community or region.

It's not just a matter of requiring the real estate redevelopers and engineering firms to mostly hire locally: that's a given. You need to create apprenticeship and other programs that ensure that your unemployed and underemployed are repurposing, renewing and reconnecting their lives in the process of repurposing, renewing and reconnecting your natural, built and socioeconomic environments.

Far too many places see the revitalization of their place as a purely business transaction: write a check and get it done. In fact, the process of making your community healthier, wealthier and more resilient is a tremendous research and training opportunity.

Virtually every other community and region on the planet has needs similar to yours, so your people will be learning highly-portable skills. And since the global restoration economy—and the demand for increased resilience—is growing explosively, they will be learning skills that will be increasing in demand for decades to come.

The presence of a workforce with such skills would then attract employers needing such skills. This can feed on itself in a virtuous circle, as each new such employer attracts more of the same: your community or region thus becomes a cluster of similarly-focused businesses, academic offerings and supportive non-profits. Given the multi-trillion-dollar size of the burgeoning global restoration economy, your cluster could be fairly tightly-focused, most likely on skills specific to your local challenges.

For instance, if you're a rural region, you might develop a cluster focused on regenerative ranching, or regenerative farming, or watershed restoration. Or, if you're a metropolitan area, you might develop a cluster focused on restoring green infrastructure, transportation infrastructure renovation, brightfields, brownfields redevelopment, historic restoration, etc.

Another advantage of this "restoration economy" approach to growing local employment is that it doesn't produce "garbage jobs": the kind that won't support a family with full-time hours. Your residents would be learning solid, well-paid skills, not just how to clean a toilet, how to flip a burger, how to say *"have a nice day"*, or other such service industry "skills".

Still another advantage is that few of these jobs require a college degree. Hundreds of thousands of young people are discovering that the degrees that put them so far in debt really don't add that much to their employability. Others are realizing that they don't really want a management or office job: they want to do satisfying "real" work that produces visible improvements in the real world.

To make all this happen, insert something like *"the revitalization of our community will be a job skills learning opportunity"* into your vision. Then create whatever policies are needed to support it, along with public-private partnerships to make it happen.

Private companies will likely want some public funding to support the apprentice programs, but that's fine: whatever monies the government needs to inject will likely be far smaller—and far more productive—than what they currently waste on economic development incentives, stealing crappy jobs from their neighbors.

A FEEDBACK LOOP TO CREATE THE REVITALIZATION TIPPING POINT

The RECONOMICS Process—when properly implemented—should yield increased confidence, more momentum and greater alignment of diverse agendas. With the right strategy, a single regenerative project can trigger a "restoration contagion" that ripples out, raising property values and neighborhood health as it expands.

Revitalization usually takes longer to gain momentum than anyone expects. But once it does, it often transforms a place far faster than anyone expected was possible.

This tipping point-style behavior results from the confidence-based revitalization feedback loop: Regenerative projects ("renewal" on the chart) boost confidence, and increased confidence in the future of a place attracts more regenerative projects. While confidence and optimism aren't synonymous, they can produce similar results.

Sergio DellaPergola, an Italian demographer who emigrated to Israel and now teaches at Hebrew University (which kindly let me use their faculty guest quarters while I was keynoting a conference of the Israel Planners Association), was struck by his adopted country's higher level of optimism, and the effect it has on economic growth. *"In Israel, people start families even without resources,"* he said in the June 11, 2018 issue of *Bloomberg Businessweek*. *"Babies bring optimism, and optimism brings babies. So the economy works."*

But optimism and confidence in the future will only take us so far. Too many places succumb to the temptation to use only those modes they find familiar, comfortable, and convenient. We need a complete process for revitalization, since an incomplete process isn't a process at all: it's just activity.

Why? Let's review:

- Without an ongoing regenerative program, you might not get started at all. And if you do, you probably won't gather the momentum and confidence needed to reverse a downward trajectory.
- Without a regenerative vision and asset map, you won't know what you have to work with, and probably won't achieve the desired outcome;
- Without a regenerative strategy, you might not achieve anything at all;
- Without regenerative policies, stakeholders might not be allowed to do what's needed, or it might be more difficult than necessary;
- Without regenerative partners, you might not have the necessary resources or political support;
- Without regenerative projects, nothing real actually happens.

Leaving out one element of the RECONOMICS Process might not seem to be a big thing, especially in those places that are currently missing almost all of the elements.

A city manager might be tempted to say *"We've already got some great redevelopment projects underway: do we really need supportive policies?"*

To use the automobile manufacturing process metaphor once again, this would be like a Ford executive saying *"We've already got wheels on the cars: do we really need tires?"*

TRANSIENT CHAOS, PULSING, AND FALSE ALARMS

In September of 2014, Henry Kissinger—one of the 20th Century's masters of creating chaos and devitalization—was asked by TV host Charlie Rose, "*Is there an absence of order in the world right now?*" Kissinger's answer: "*This is one of the most chaotic periods that I know about. Every part of the world is redefining itself.*"

As mentioned in the Introduction, we are now in the Anthropocene Epoch: a time when humans are the dominant planetary influence. We spent the 12,000 years of the previous Holocene epoch adapting the world to our needs (adaptive conquest), breaking much of it in the process. We must now adapt to the consequences of those adaptations—climate change, lifeless oceans, loss of topsoil and crop diversity, etc.—and that's driving the current rise in resilience efforts.

The resulting barrage of economic, political, social, and environmental disruption pretty much dictates that only an ongoing RECONOMICS Process (or something very similar) is likely to yield resilient prosperity. Chaos can actually help: One of the central tenets of complexity science is that healthy complex adaptive systems tend to thrive at the edge of chaos: enough order to hold them together, but enough disorder to catalyze evolution. Too much order, and there will be too much resistance to adopting a strategic renewal process.

Likewise, a central tenet of Jane Jacobs' view of dense, well-designed urban environments was the value of chance (chaotic) encounters. For more on these subjects, read *Complexity: The Emerging Science at the Edge of Order* and *Chaos* by M. Mitchell Waldrop (1993); *The Death and Life of Great American Cities* by Jane Jacobs (1992); and chapter 12 of *The Restoration Economy* by this author (2002).

Modern military professionals refer to operating in a "VUCA" world: volatility, uncertainty, complexity, and ambiguity. In such a world, stability is an illusion, causes are effects, allies are enemies, and supply chains are made entirely of weak links. The VUCA world is now the environment in which community revitalization, natural resource restoration and economic resilience efforts take place. In such an environment, "change of plans" is now a constant, and it's downright aberrant for a project to come off as planned. So, being a successful director of resilient prosperity (or RE Facilitator) means assuming your renewal plan (if you were required to write one) will probably fail, but not the renewal itself, thanks to adaptive management.

There's a story (possibly apocryphal) about a smug English journalist who asked Mahatma Gandhi "*What do you think of Western civilization?*" Gandhi replied "*I think it would be a good idea.*"

That acerbic insight could be applied here. If someone asked me what I think of resilient prosperity, I'd reply "*Sounds like a good idea: someone should try it.*" Remember that I pointed out earlier that I've never encountered a place that enjoyed an entire RECONOMICS Process: they are always missing at least one element. And when they finally add the missing element, they've often lost one of the earlier elements, as we saw in Chattanooga and Bilbao. Again: this is because they weren't working from a process template, so they never really knew what they were missing, or why the elements they already had should be preserved.

The 2000 movie, *The Perfect Storm* (based on the 1997 book of the same title), documented the collision of three violent weather systems in 1991. One story (inaccurately told in both the book and the movie) described a private sailboat heading to Bermuda, manned by a captain and two paying passengers.

When the storm hit, the captain did exactly what he was supposed to do: heave-to and go below to ride out the storm. His two panicked, inexperienced passengers mistook his inaction as giving up, and radioed the Coast Guard for help. A brave man lost his life unnecessarily "rescuing" the three off the boat. (The boat was later found, safe and sound.)

Citizens in places undergoing revitalization are sometimes like those two panicky passengers, demanding that leaders abandon their plans when things go wrong, or when things stop happening.

This is often because they don't understand two key dynamics of living systems that are undergoing change: transient chaos and pulsing.

TRANSIENT CHAOS: When a complex adaptive system moves from one state to another—such as from a devitalized state to a revitalized state—it often goes through a zone scientists refer to as "transient chaos".

That "perfect storm" was a period of transient chaos: one that could not be controlled or managed, but merely experienced and survived. Just hunker-down, have faith in the process, and don't waste energy fighting the sometimes-disruptive symptoms of progress. Your goal will often be found on the other side of the disruption. Pain is information: don't fear knowledge.

PULSING: No matter how prosperous a place is, it needs an ongoing pulse of regeneration in order to keep the Good Times going. A place that isn't regenerating is degenerating, because Mother Nature abhors stasis as much as she does a vacuum.

This is one of the dangers of the word "sustainable": it implies a static situation in many folks' minds. We have few cells in our bodies now that we had a decade ago: true sustainability derives from the ongoing replacement, repurposing, renewing and reconnecting of our components.

Revitalization doesn't come in a constant flow, but rather a pulsing flow. This is important to know, so leaders and citizens don't mistake the resting stage between pulses as a loss of momentum, and thus become discouraged.

All living flows are actually within cycles and have pulses within pulses: our blood pulses; rivers pulse with floods; the ocean pulses with tides; the planet pulses with seasons. The entire universe pulses, according to the latest theories of creation: rather than a single, nonsensical "Big Bang", there's a pulse of Big Bangs, with billions of years between the cosmic heartbeats.

In economics, trends are normally longer than economic cycles, and comprise cycles. Despite everyone's being aware of cycles, decline usually takes places by surprise. Someone asked me *"Why don't more communities take action when they're on the verge of decline. Why do they wait until the situation is desperate?"*

The reason is that—in the absence of some major natural, social, or economic cataclysm—the "verge of decline" is only visible in retrospect. If places could actually perceive that they were on the verge of decline, more would probably take action. Only the decline itself is perceivable, not the verge.

An ongoing "pulse of renewal" (or "pulse of regeneration", if you prefer) helps prevent such delayed-reaction revitalization initiatives. It might even prevent decline. The goal of the pulse of renewal you create locally should ideally be resilient prosperity for all, wildlife and humans alike.

A personal comment: I've been advocating ecological restoration for over two decades. During this time, I've frequently encountered push-back from despairing folks who say *"Why bother? Our climate is in crisis, and the fossil fuel industry owns our politicians, so what difference is it going to make if we restore a wetland today?"*

I certainly agree that shucking fossil fuels is Job #1. But that doesn't mean there aren't other jobs. I try not to let the big picture blind me to the present-day suffering we are causing wildlife. I tell such folks that they should personally participate in an ecological restoration project.

The joy of seeing frogs, fish, and other wildlife flourishing in a previously degraded area is without compare. It might not mean a lot in the greater scheme of things, but it sure means a lot to those particular frogs.

Hands-on restoration work is good therapy for those many environmentalists who are too wrapped up in the cold, sterile, soulless world of long-term policymaking and management.

We must not lose touch with the day-to-day reality of existence on the part of those creatures—and far away people—who are forced to co-habit the Anthropocene with us.

WHERE CAN THE RECONOMICS PROCESS BE APPLIED?

> *"Invite people on the journey
> so they'll embrace the destination."*
> – Chris Grams, President, New Kind.

The RECONOMICS Process described in this book is completely generic: it's designed to be used by any individual, organization, community or country. Thus, it contains no regeneration components that vary from place to place, such as legal, financial, political, etc. It can be applied no matter what the nature of your primary agenda may be: ecological, social, economic, etc.

Any competent cook knows that reliably recreating a favorite dish requires more than just throwing ingredients together: a recipe is needed to ensure the proper combining and timing of those ingredients. The recipe is the process. Some recipes must be followed to the letter. Others allow a tremendous amount of freedom to improvise and be creative. The RECONOMICS Process is the latter type of recipe.

If hundreds of millions of amateur cooks and professional chefs around the world know the value of process, why don't city and national leaders? Why are they so focused on the ingredients (like plans and projects) and so oblivious to the recipe?

The RECONOMICS Process requires constant lubrication to work well, and that lubricant is trust. Trust is one component of resilient prosperity that's truly universal.

Where people can't trust the players—politicians, private developers, etc.—to create a better future, they should at least be able to trust the process.

So, each step should be executed in a way that builds trust in the people and institutions behind the process. Building trust in each other is integral to building confidence in the local future.

The path to revitalization can be as important as the destination. In Chattanooga, it was the process of working together successfully to rid their city of horrific air pollution that made them realize that they could work together. Previously, the community had been torn by racial strife. That new cohesion led to the creation of a revitalization process, and an entity to house the ongoing program and vision.

When I first visited, there was a delegation of community leaders from Vietnam who were in town to view the Chattanooga's miraculous recovery first-hand. Such is the inspirational power of seeing a place heal its society, environment, and economy simultaneously.

MIXED-AGENDA REDEVELOPMENT

Places with large populations and fixed geographic boundaries, like Manhattan, have long been forced into the mixed-use redevelopment that sprawl-based cities have only recently begun to appreciate.

Mixed-use development is how the world's cities developed for thousands of years, until very recently. The current revitalizing trend back towards mixed-use development is thus nothing revolutionary: just a return to sanity on the part of urban planners.

But, as with many good things, some allow their enthusiasm to deteriorate into fundamentalism. They force mixed-use into every situation, with no attempt to determine if it's appropriate. The result is that some places already possessing sufficient retail space have more crammed down their throats, when all they really need is residential space. Empty storefronts then appear, which make the area appear distressed, sometimes leading to devitalization.

The segregation of urban society by class and income has been with us for millennia, but never to the extent we see in the U.S. and many other places today. A very healthy trend towards mixed-income development is gaining some steam, usually led by affordable housing and downtown revitalization advocates. In the U.S., our aversion to seeing decrepitude leads us to warehouse the elderly, so we've further fragmented society with retirement communities. The current trend towards mixed-age redevelopment is reconnecting society on that front.

But most planning is still done in silos, so the next big trend is likely to be mixed-agenda development, a holistic approach to renewing our built, natural, and socioeconomic (including heritage) environments together.

So, one fix for places that are having trouble getting their revitalization ball rolling might be to replace that mysterious word "revitalization" and that intimidating word "integration" with friendlier terminology that's more in keeping with industry standards. The word "mixed" seems to be acceptable to practitioners and voters alike. "Mixed-use" is very well established, with "mixed-income" and "mixed age" well on the way to becoming so. "Redevelopment" is also a word that everyone seems to grasp.

Mixed-use redevelopment combines residential, commercial, and cultural functions into a given property, in order to recreate vibrant places. That's one agenda. Mixed income and mixed-age redevelopment are ways of reducing racial, income and age segregation, which also helps recreate vibrant places. Mixed-mobility strategies are reducing car dependence while enhancing affordable connectivity and public health. That's four more agendas.

But what about agendas like heritage restoration? What about brownfields remediation/reuse? What about infrastructure renewal/removal/reuse (such as urban highway removal, "High Line" parks, etc.)? What about watershed restoration (such as with green roofs and bioswales)? What about local food system restoration (such as with urban farms and farmers' markets)? What about ecological restoration (such as replacing invasive species with natives)?

Combining one or more of these revitalizing, restorative goals with mixed-income, mixed-use, mixed-age, mixed-mobility redevelopment gives us a great formula for the future of our cities, but it's far too wordy, so places that aren't getting any traction with normal terminology might want to try mixed-agenda redevelopment. That pretty much opens to door to any "re" activity, renewing our natural, built, and socioeconomic environments together to trigger revitalization.

As logic would suggest, there's often a fairly direct correlation between the size of a project and the number of agendas it can effectively address. Think, for instance, of the 50-mile Buffalo Bayou revitalization project in Houston, or the 38-mile Los Angeles River revitalization project. Or, the green infrastructure strategy that's revitalizing so much of Philadelphia's waterfront neighborhoods. One can fit any number of revitalizing agendas under those huge umbrellas.

A large scope doesn't guarantee that more agendas will be integrated, nor does small size dictate fewer agendas: size only makes mixed-agenda redevelopment easier. Among other advantages, mixed-agenda redevelopment becomes easier to justify financially as the project scale expands geographically, and as the project expands chronologically to become a program.

Many large redevelopment projects already repurpose historic buildings, remediate brownfields, renew infrastructure, and restore greenspace. Integrating the renewal of our built and natural environments comes easily to professions like landscape architects. And their clients will usually on the economic renewal, since they want property values to rise. It's the social aspect that usually gets ignored; partly because it's complex, and partly because there's no clear-cut profit mechanism. The clients know that harmonious, low-crime neighborhoods help underpin economic stability, but they shy away the minefield of addressing it directly. Again: if the visioning element is done properly—and the rest of your RECONOMICS Process hews to it—all of these agendas can be addressed in a holistic, ongoing manner, avoiding the disastrous quick-fixes that are so common.

Mixed-income, mixed-age and mixed-use have been around for millennia, but they were all consciously abandoned for about 60 or 70 years during the 20th century. That was when professional planners (a relatively new profession) came onto the scene, and their control-hungry engineering mindset started dictating single-use, single-class, single-agenda development. The mixed-agenda redevelopment trend has arisen in large part to correct those dysfunctional, devitalizing practices.

The mixed-agenda trend has another salubrious effect: it generally leads communities to shift from one-time projects to ongoing programs. Leaders are realizing that these larger agendas—watershed restoration, ecological restoration, urban resilience, rural revitalization, reconnecting local food systems, etc.—simply can't be effectively addressed at the project level.

Only an ongoing, coordinated effort—underpinned by an actual process—will produce the desired result. So, the biggest difference between mixed-use, mixed-age and mixed-income redevelopment and mixed-agenda redevelopment is that the latter is primarily strategic and programmatic, whereas the first three are primarily tactical and project-based.

Today, mixed-agenda redevelopment is accelerating—though not by that name—driven in large part by the resilience and adaptation agendas spawned from the climate crisis, and by a rebellion against gross economic inequity.

What stands in the way of wider adoption of mixed-agenda redevelopment? Three things:
1. Fear that multiple agendas will complicate projects to the point of becoming unmanageable;
2. Lack of dedicated, disciplined focus on revitalization and resilience; and
3. Lack of a comprehensive, proven process driving redevelopment activity.

All three of these barriers can be overcome with the same solution: an ongoing mixed-agenda redevelopment program led by people who are trained and certified in the RECONOMICS Process.

The global crisis of rising sea levels offers myriad opportunities to create such resilient, multi-agenda projects and programs. In fact, addressing multiple agendas will likely be the only way these huge resilience efforts will get financed.

For coastal areas, another obvious agenda that will drive the ability of projects to get financed is vulnerability to sea level rise. I've noticed that many of the huge private equity firms—like BlackRock, which owns about $24 billion worth of real estate—tend to fund the same climate-crisis-denying political candidates as the fossil fuel companies.

This makes me wonder: maybe they see the sea level rise handwriting on the wall, and want to forestall general acceptance of that reality long enough for them to unload their most-vulnerable holdings....shifting their portfolio to higher ground, so to speak. Keeping a large portion of the public in ignorance makes the awareness of sea level rise a form of "insider information" from an investment perspective.

But back to resilient, mixed-agenda redevelopment: Venice, Italy provides a good case in point. Its low elevation makes it a canary in the coal mine for sea level rise, and its status as a global heritage treasure ensured that large sums of money would be thrown at protecting it.

So they built the kind of project environmentalists often categorize as "dumb engineers' tricks" (simplistic projects that only alleviate symptoms, but that make design and construction firms rich): the €5.4 billion Mose flood barrier.

The Mose barrier only protects against a 3-meter flood, so it's virtually guaranteed to fail eventually, as seas rise and storms get more powerful.

A far more resilient approach would have been a "living shoreline" (multi-purpose levee): a 12-meter earthen wall designed in a way that creates both a beautiful linear park for the public, and restores wildlife habitat, such as for oysters, which would also clean the water. This would boost Venice's tourism industry, adding a nature experience to the historical architecture attractions. It would help revive Adriatic Sea fisheries, giving local economies another boost.

And, it would be a far more resilient protective barrier than failure-prone machines needing constant maintenance and replacement. Like the Mose barrier, this approach is also expensive. But it provides far more public and economic benefit, which opens up additional sources of funding.

These days, leading-edge urban redevelopment strategies are multi-agenda: mixed-use, mixed-income, mixed-ethnicity (such as immigrant-friendly communities) and mixed-age (this last one applies to both buildings and people). And the most resilient ones renew the built, natural and socioeconomic environments together as a well-connected system.

Houston's aforementioned Buffalo Bayou effort has been managed as an ongoing program by the Buffalo Bayou Partnership since 1995, and was master-planned in 2002 (updated 2012). A public outlay of $800 million over 20 years is projected to catalyze $56 billion in private investment.

The $58 million, 160-acre Buffalo Bayou Park recently opened, which—besides providing a healthful recreational space—serves as green infrastructure to bolster flood resilience. This is mixed-agenda redevelopment in the flesh (though the city needs to extend their flood resilience to a much larger footprint if they hope to avoid repeats of recent disasters). What's more, it's a strategic, programmatic, partnered approach to repurposing, renewing and reconnecting their built and natural assets. That sounds suspiciously similar to the RECONOMICS Process.

CREATING RESILIENT PROSPERITY IS A NATURAL PROCESS

As noted earlier, processes are always based on flows, and are usually based on cycles. Flow is universal, extending into—and defining—the human-made construct we call time. Time comprises cycles. Everything constantly transforms as it leaves one cycle and begins a new one.

Carbon and water molecules keep getting "reincarnated" in new life forms: your coffee today contains yesterday's brontosaurus piss. Every human on the planet has molecules in their body that were once in the bodies of Buddha, Quetzalcoatl, Mohammed and Jesus.

Ideas, memes, and genes adapt and express themselves differently according to their environment. They likewise die and are reborn as better—or sometimes worse—ideas/memes/genes in never-ending cycles, and cycles of embedded cycles.

Every sub-atomic particle, atom, molecule, organism, place, and planet has its own electromagnetic fields, nested like Russian dolls. This allows flows of everything that can be transmitted as energy. This connectivity and flow extends into the sub-atomic (quantum) realm, where time, space, and matter don't exist. This, in turn, adds mysterious and paradoxical elements to our existence, from which both science and religion earn their livings trying to explain. And since cycles are replaced by new cycles, they too can be said to be renewed and reborn. Indeed, rebirth and renewal can be seen as the most basic universal life function and cycle.

But we tend to behave as if everything begins and ends with our current generations. Getting a handle of creating better personal, organizational, local and planetary futures means getting a handle on regenerative processes, and getting beyond our narrow temporal perspectives.

At any given time in the lifecycle flows of a city (or nation), the vision, leadership, and resources needed to renew, repurpose, or reconnect a building, neighborhood, downtown, or natural resource can bloom at unexpected times, and from unexpected sources: a real estate developer, a mayor, a government agency, a citizens' group, a foundation, an elementary school project, or a local business.

Therein lies the challenge. This sort of disorderly, itinerant power is anathema to most institutions. Ordinary mayors stand ready with weed killer when renewal sprouts outside their control. Mayors with a resilient prosperity program would stand ready with compost to help them grow, because a RECONOMICS Process provides emergent leaders myriad opportunities to connect and serve.

The goal of most ecological restoration is to take an ecosystem back to health and resilience, not back to the way it was before it died. While some ecosystems will, no doubt, respond well to the efforts of restoration ecologists to restore them in accordance to a historical reference ecosystem that simulates what it once was, most won't. Climate change and a host of other anthropogenic influences mean that their only hope of returning to a state of health will be in the restoration of resilience so they can adapt to current conditions. It's not just human communities that need resilience programs.

The same can be said of businesses, governments, communities, and other human inventions: leaders attempting to return to an organization's glory days will likely need to describe an entirely new form of glory, and an entirely new way of achieving it. It's likely that the glorious old organization thrived in a governmental, economic, social, and natural resource situation very different from the one they're living in today. Granted, all of these have always been in a state of flux, but it's the frequency of perturbations—and the amplitude of the oscillations—that is so different now.

To someone with a vivid sense of the past, most of the world is now blighted. Sometimes, blight simply needs to be removed, so something new can take its place. But increasingly, it needs adaptive renewal.

Medellín, Colombia, for instance, brilliantly used transit-based connectivity to resolve many of their safety, crime, economic, and environmental problems. Infamous for drug crime and human trafficking in the 80s and 90s, Medellín was structurally and economically polarized: Wealthy and poverty-stricken neighborhoods were completely disconnected from each other.

> *"The income of the rich should not exceed the income of the poor by more than five times. Any more would create economic inefficiency and generate the greatest social risk: civil war."*
>
> *– Plato*

At the beginning of the 21st Century, public and private leaders worked together to create a world-class public transit system, including the Medellín Metro commuter rail. It connected the slums to economic opportunity, thus reducing residents' need to be involved in the drug trade. Along with improvements to their policing and educational system, this renewed connectivity changed everything. By 2013, Medellín was winning global awards as "most innovative city", "most livable city", "best business location", etc.

In Europe, researcher Sonja Braaker at the Institute of Terrestrial Ecosystems recently mapped the movements of hedgehogs in Zurich. She was studying urban habitat connectivity; specifically, how hedgehogs use corridors to commute among suitable environments. Such biomimetic research can lead to better city planning. Connectivity enables urban hedgehogs to find mates and maintain genetic diversity. So too does it facilitate human cultural and economic diversity, while enabling enterprises to find customers, employees, and partners. Reconnecting our fragmented places is a core contributor to resilient prosperity.

As mention in Chapter 8, Boston's new resilience plain is based on repurposing, renewing and reconnecting all of the city's waterfront properties. But they've got a recent history of taking on grand, politically-risky renewal efforts.

In the 70s, Boston, Massachusetts was a wealthy (if troubled) city that few would have called a candidate for revitalization. Revitalization was for places like Buffalo (which was once larger than Boston: the #10 city in the U.S. in 1850, but only #73 today). But some very smart Bostonians realized that their city had structural problems that would forever keep them from becoming all they could be. Those problems derived from auto-centric urban planning mistakes made as far back as the 1930s.

The program that became known as "The Big Dig" was born. It was officially completed in 2005 at a cost of $14.8 billion (not including interest on loans). The Big Dig was a brilliant strategy for revitalizing Boston's future. Unfortunately, its implementation wasn't brilliant; often described as monumentally inept, and rife with corruption.

The Big Dig had little value in its immediate present, other than job creation and enhancing confidence in a better future. It severely disrupted local traffic flows, making a lot of people very unhappy for years on end.

If Bostonians aren't already saying that the Big Dig—along with their heroic clean up and restoration of their massively-polluted Boston Harbor—weren't worth the pain and expense, they will soon. Vast swaths of formerly-isolated waterfronts became available for new, green public space (enhancing quality of life) and for redevelopment (enhancing economic growth). It's hard to justify expensive long-term investments if we can't quantify their future value.

ENHANCING PUBLIC & PRIVATE RESOURCES FOR PUBLIC GAIN

At its heart, the RECONOMICS Process could be seen as a system for harnessing a broader spectrum of private and public resources for public gain. When private investment is inspired and rigorously influenced by a shared public vision, everyone benefits, and resilient prosperity is a likely result.

Here's my current working definition of resilient prosperity: "Resilient prosperity is a feedback loop, whereby rising levels of equitable wealth, quality of life, security, environmental health and confidence in the local future derive from—and accelerate—an ongoing, adaptive process of regeneration."

"Equitable" and "rising" are key words:

- "Equitable" because a society with growing economic disparity and a shrinking middle class is increasingly unstable, usually leading to disharmony, dysfunction, and even violent revolution; and
- "Rising" because—given today's global degradation of air, watersheds, fisheries, topsoil, infrastructure, climate, etc.—the only way to increase both quality of life and ecological health (especially with a still-growing population) is by revitalizing the urban environments we've already developed, and by restoring the natural environments we damaged along the way.

A humane, knowledge-based revolution in revitalization practices—renewing the natural, built, and socioeconomic environments together—won't be fomented by planning, development, policy, or design professionals who are comfortable in their silos. Ideally, it should come from the top, since that's the whole purpose of having leaders. But it can also come from lower in the management structure, such as those who hire the managers of public agencies, and those who write the RFPs that lead to on-the-ground redevelopment.

For instance, smart cities are becoming less car-centric, with pedestrian malls being a positive urban trend. Yet many pedestrian malls fail. In almost all cases, failures derive from unattractive designs, bad locations, or poor timing.

Get the timing wrong—such as creating the mall before you have sufficient downtown residents or enough transit connections—and the mall won't serve any valid purpose after office hours. It will instead attract excessive panhandlers and loiterers who repel the desired clientele (just ask the folks in Winchester, Virginia).

Failing to lead communities from the top often means leadership arises from the bottom. But citizen advocacy shouldn't be necessary to promote strategic, adaptive renewal. Government is supposed to be about the whole, not just the pieces. In today's increasingly broken world, voters shouldn't have to push their leaders so hard for what everyone—progressive and conservative—wants: resilient prosperity.

In their November 2014 report, "Climate Change and Poverty" (on how poor populations can adapt to climate change), the World Bank Group identified four channels through which people either escape or fall into poverty: prices, assets, productivity, and opportunities. Local governments don't have much control over prices, but they can certainly renew assets, boost productivity, and foster opportunities.

Resilience is toothless without revitalization, which more a journey than a destination. Human regenerative processes start in the womb. They define aging when they slow down; death when they stop. Communities are no different in this respect: regenerative processes are the root of their resilience and sustainability.

> *"Broad prosperity lubricates the machinery of government and is the glue that binds our society together. ...If the West fails to address economic stagnation, other domestic and foreign policy issues will prove intractable."*
> *– William Galston, Brookings Institution (2014)*

Most resilience efforts focus on restoring green infrastructure, and on connecting siloed government agencies so they can respond in a quicker and more-coordinated manner to emergencies (as they've done in Boston). This is all well and good, but many communities are already distressed, with their budgets under severe pressure. Their primary concern is economic renewal. Unless a flood or other disaster is impending, resilience is seen as a luxury: to be attended to when there's a budget surplus (which is always just around the corner).

The answer is to fix both problems simultaneously: to wed what people care about now (boosting their economy and quality of life) with what they should care about for the future (boosting their security).

The holistic nature of resilience programs is exactly the integrated approach that's desperately needed by local revitalization efforts. And attracting new residents, employers, and redevelopers is what resilience programs desperately need to secure funding and support from public and private leaders alike.

Resilience programs must therefore be integrated with a revitalization process. Managing resilience and revitalization efforts in an adaptive manner is the surest path to a secure, inclusive, green economy.

THE SUBJECTIVE ECONOMICS OF RESILIENT PROSPERITY

> *"Democracy is a process, not a static condition. It is becoming rather than being. It can easily be lost, but never is fully won. Its essence is eternal struggle." – Justice William H. Hastie (first black U.S. federal judge).*

As with Justice Hastie's view of democracy (above), both resilience and confidence in the local future are qualities that are easily lost, but never fully won. They both require an ongoing process of regeneration.

In communities torn apart by internal strife—or where the citizens don't trust the government—an ongoing process of shared visioning, partnering and regenerative action is exactly what's needed to heal and build trust.

People and companies who move to a community—and those who decide to stay there—are investing their time, work, money, and future in that place. Revitalization strategies must recognize that such decisions—which powerfully affecting communities' futures–are investment decisions. The decision-makers are investing the development and well-being of their families and firms in the development and well-being of the community. In other words, they are primarily buying confidence in the future, as opposed to "stuff" like real estate.

So, those planning the regeneration and redevelopment of a place need to understand how investment decisions are really made. It's important to distinguish between real value and perceived value. A company might have excellent fundamentals, but its stock price could still be depressed if that value isn't perceived by the market. Thus, the expensive corporate ads one sees in FORTUNE and Forbes that don't sell products or services: they're trying to inspire confidence in the company's future.

Cities also embark on positioning campaigns, using advertising to sell themselves, primarily to employers. These usually turn out to be a waste of money, unless they convey solid evidence that inspires confidence that things are good and will soon get even better .

When a city doesn't yet have numbers to brag about, the most confidence-inspiring (and non-capital-intensive) assets they can bring to bear on their future are a credible, easily-communicated strategy and a comprehensive renewal process, backed by credible partners.

Michael D. Bauer and Glenn D. Rudebusch of the Federal Reserve Bank of San Francisco) refer to two basic types of decision-making approaches by investors: "real-world" and "market-based".

Real-world expectations are based on external evidence, such as forecasts by experts, surveys, company analyses, or weather predictions (such as for commodity prices). Such analyses are based on hard data, but their conclusions are often based on personal opinions, statistical models, and inferences. So, despite the "real world" moniker, they usually include a substantial degree of uncertainty.

Market-based expectations skip evidence and analysis, and draw conclusions directly from prices and their own perceived risk. An economist might tell you that "the market" has already processed all the relevant data to derive the present price. In actuality, the price is based more on investors' expectations of other investors' likely behavior than on data. In other words, investors are basing decisions on prices, which are based on assumptions about future price-based decisions of other investors.

Since no information beyond price is necessary, and since timing is everything, most trades are executed by computer algorithms. In general, the shorter the time horizon, the more decisions and forecasts tend to be based on market-based, rather than real-world, expectations. Some might call real-word expectations "rational" or "real investing", and market-based expectations "irrational" or "gambling". But "rational" to an investor is whatever works: whatever makes money.

What does this have to do with community revitalization? Everything.

That decision to "invest" in a community by moving to it, or staying in it, is based on a combination of objective and subjective factors, even at the corporate level. A CEO looking to relocate a plant—or to expand with a new plant—doesn't just base her/his decision on economic development incentives. Those are commodities. They base it, maybe primarily, on whether the community is where they want their children to grow up, and on whether its image and quality of life will attract top talent to their ranks.

When deciding between City A and City B, they can and do observe the quality of life and the economic indicators to derive real-world expectations. But the final decision is almost always based to a tremendous degree on two subjective factors: 1) how the place makes them feel, and 2) how they perceive its trajectory: up, down, or stasis.

If they perceive a place's incipient revitalization sooner than others, they get to buy low and sell high, like any successful investor. Unlike most other investments, however, the more they invest in the community, the more it revitalizes: revitalization (and devitalization) are dynamics that are highly subject to feedback loops, as we've seen. Also unlike most other investors, they will be applauded as heroes for contributing to the public welfare.

ONE LAST NOTE ON DESIGN

Most people—tourists and residents—prefer being in genuine, highly-diverse, functioning places over artificial, engineered, over-planned places. I'm on the Education Committee of the National Working Waterfronts Network, and can say from experience that visitors and locals alike are drawn more powerfully to waterfronts with real activities (such as fishing boats and cargo ports) than they are to the hyper-retail, New Urbanist, Disney-ish waterfronts that are proliferating. They also enjoy encountering surprises, like a century-old, family-owned fountain pen and stationery store.

Here in Washington, DC, an ugly old convention center and vast expanse of surface parking lots has been replaced with the mixed-use CityCenterDC redevelopment project. CityCenterDC lacks both diversity and surprises. When people talk about "mixed income" development, they're usually discussing residential areas. But urban planners need to realize that it's essential to purely retail areas, as well.

The wealthy like to be "seen" by their fellows, but they delight in showing off to their economic inferiors even more. So, designers shouldn't fear mixing the economic classes. On the flip side, window shopping is a legitimate form of entertainment, so expensive stores aren't totally useless to the working class. A good mix helps the place derive income from all.

CityCenterDC is certainly an improvement on the lifeless area it replaced, but its major value is in the residents it brings to the area, not the ground-level retail. The design isn't unpleasant: it's just bland and predictable. It's all about money, it lacks vision, and enhancing the public good doesn't seem to have been a major objective.

People have a tendency to assume that, if a person is an expert in one area, they'll have intelligent things to say about a totally different subject. Thus, they ask business moguls their opinions on society; brain surgeons their opinions on diet, and actors their opinions on everything.

Likewise, we tend to think that urban planners, architects and civil engineers have more understanding of community revitalization and devitalization dynamics than the person on the street. The opposite is often true. For instance, America's greatest public space designer, Frederick Law Olmsted, Jr. is considered the "father" of the landscape architecture profession. He deeply understood the dynamics of buildings and natural features alike, and their effect of people. But in 1910, he predicted that New Haven, Connecticut would grow from its population of 134,000 to 400,000 within 40 years.

Instead, 1910 turned out to be the very year that the city entered a half-century of stagnation and devitalization. By the turn of the millennium 90 years later, New Haven still had 10,000 fewer folks than in 1910. That's finally starting to turn around, as Yale University—which dominates the city, its staff and faculty alone accounting for 11% of the city's population—is finally taking the revitalization of their host city seriously.

Architects and planners often say that the key to revitalizing a downtown is design, called "placemaking" when that design is developed with public input. Design is a core skill of any urban regeneration team, of course.

But when architects and placemakers are leading the revitalization effort, they often start with a charrette or other design exercise. Even when those up-front exercises are themselves wildly successful, the effect they have on the community's revitalization is sometimes disastrous. Not because of what they did, but because of when they did it. Design should never come first, unless it's part of a visioning exercise where the resulting vision statement is kept, and the design is thrown away.

None of the projects in their design are going to happen without money. Unless the public coffers are overflowing, it will mostly be private money. And private money will usually want to do their own designing. Trying to shove the charrette's design (which might be several years old) down their throat will likely scare real estate investors away.

CAN PLACES WITH CORRUPT GOVERNMENTS REVITALIZE?

You might be wondering why the RECONOMICS Process has no element that guarantees transparency. The simple answer is because I want it to be adopted widely, not just in the tiny portion of cities, regions and nations that have open, honest governments.

If I inject transparency into the process, I'm basically asking the city to do two things 1) adopt the RECONOMICS Process (that's hard enough already) and 2) rid their government of corruption. Demanding that only honest governments use the

RECONOMICS Process would exclude literally billions of people from enjoying its benefits. It would be like a public health advocate proselytizing about eating a good diet and getting more exercise...but saying that only morally-upstanding citizens should do so.

So, if your place suffers from "pay to play" and other common governance maladies that reduce its ability to attract investment, by all means put "greater transparency" in your vision. Every change you want in your local future needs to be concisely captured in the vision, because—as you've heard repeatedly—the vision drives everything. Do you want to improve racial relations? Boost opportunities, pay and safety for women? Reduce litter and graffiti? If it's not captured in your vision, it probably won't manifest in your program, strategy, policies, partnerships or projects.

But be careful not to load your vision down with politically-correct agendas that no one will take seriously. The vision isn't there to make you feel good about yourselves: it's there to drive your RECONOMICS Process. When you inject feel-good, wishful thinking garbage into it, you're undermining the entire process, which means you're undermining your future. If people don't take your vision seriously, nothing that ensues from it will be taken seriously.

So, to answer the above question: yes, places with corrupt governments can revitalize. In fact, they do it all the time, as we saw with the Big Dig in Boston. But places with honest governments are far more likely to create resilient prosperity, and that's different from simply revitalizing.

CHAPTER 12 - THE RISE OF REVITALIZATION & RESILIENCE FACILITATORS

"Your present circumstances don't determine where you can go; they merely determine where you start." – Nido Qubein

It's time for our crisis-ridden world to get serious about creating resilient prosperity. We need to better-define recovery, revitalization and resilience, measure them better, better understand how to trigger them, and figure out who to put in charge of facilitating such efforts. Let's make the creation of resilient prosperity a real discipline, with the requisite research, education, funding, and qualifications of a profession. Otherwise, it's snake oil.

Redevelopment projects are readily funded and professionally managed. Revitalization and resilience programs? Not so much. It's almost as if local leaders don't believe they are real, because they don't involve bricks and mortar.

But saying that redevelopment is real, but not revitalization, is like saying surgery is real, but not regaining health. Doctors will promise to fix your broken leg, or to relieve your pain with a drug. But when do they promise to restore your health? How can they promise something they've never been taught, and don't understand?

Saying that redevelopment is real, but not revitalization is like saying working is real, but being a success isn't, and that one can't learn how to become more successful. It's like saying individual brushstrokes are real, but creating a beautiful painting isn't, and that one can't learn how to paint more artistically.

Health, success, beauty, and revitalization are all real, but they are all emergent qualities deriving from a whole, not from any specific individual action. To use a tired-but-apt analogy, revitalization and resilience are like great art: we can't define it, but we know it when we see it. In today's increasingly-broken and devitalized world, that's not good enough. Treating a process that's so crucial to our future in such a cavalier manner is simply irresponsible. We have to stop assuming that individual, isolated projects can foster the emergent quality we desire: resilient prosperity.

STASIS IS NOT AN OPTION: IF A PLACE ISN'T REVITALIZING, IT'S DEVITALIZING.

Why is it important to define revitalization, as being different from regeneration and redevelopment? Because revitalization is the goal of regenerative activities and redevelopment projects, and too many places are so focused on activities and projects that they lose track of the goal.

Achieving progress towards that goal creates confidence in the future, which attracts more regeneration and redevelopment, which creates more revitalization.

When folks do try to define revitalization, they tend to do so according to their own occupation, needs, and passions.

To a historic preservationist, it's about saving, restoring, and/or repurposing heritage structures. To an economic developer, it's about recruiting jobs. To an environmentalist, it's about restoring ecosystem health. To residents, it's about adding whatever's missing from their neighborhood: safety, greenspace, business opportunities, social justice, clean air, affordable housing, etc. To a developer, it's about boosting real estate values. To a mayor, it's about voter happiness and optimism.

Can we achieve what we can't define? Separating the goal of revitalization from the process of revitalization in our dialogues would be a good first step.

We've mentioned several times throughout this book that places seldom have anyone in charge of revitalization or resilience. Some places do have such a person, but tracking them down is hard, because they are often found in positions and agencies that aren't normally in charge of such things. These can include "capital improvement officers," "public works directors," "regional planning director," "community development director," "economic development departments," "housing and redevelopment authorities," etc.

> *"Now and then it's good to pause in our pursuit of happiness and just be happy."*
> *– Robert Brault.*

Based on their names, some of those disciplines and organization sound as if revitalization would be a natural part of their mission, such as "community development director." But here are two common definitions of that position:
- The director of community development is responsible for planning and organizing the implementation of projects, administering community development activities, and coordinating the implementation of public facility improvements, public services and other related programs.
- A community development director is responsible for overseeing the planning and zoning activities of a community. The job entails deciding how best to zone areas of the city, making recommendations to a zoning board regarding requests for changes to ensure businesses and residences are in compliance. If they aren't, the community development director may be responsible for levying fines.

Two definitions, neither of which mentions any kind of goal or mission, much less anything grand like revitalization or resilience.

So, when we do find people in such positions who are undertaking truly programmatic renewal work, it's because they have seen the need for a revitalization or resilience director, and have personally taken on the responsibility.

But they usually find this very difficult, due to the official limitations imposed by their job description. What they need is some kind of certification that shows others that they are qualified to lead such initiatives. Just such a certification is now in existence.

BUT FIRST, ONE LAST REVIEW OF THE CHALLENGES

Most cities and regions—including those that are otherwise well-managed—grope in the dark when it comes to revitalization, largely because no qualified person is in charge of it. Other places suffer from the illusion that they don't need revitalization, so they are also in the dark. Or they know how to create a flash of renewal with a big project, but don't know how to build on that momentum and make their prosperity last...how to make it resilient.

Here are four reasons governments seldom put anyone in charge of revitalization...even those that have been smart enough to put someone in charge of resilience (which can't happen without ongoing regeneration):

1. It isn't controllable. As described earlier, revitalization is what scientists who study living (complex adaptive) systems refer to as an "emergent phenomenon". It's a surprising quality or behavior that appears spontaneously, untraceable to a specific cause. This means that, unlike projects, revitalization can't be done on deadline, or on budget. This terrifies bureaucrats and politicians alike.

2. It's too aspirational. Many places are already stretching the limits of their self-confidence when they do a large redevelopment or restoration project. Shooting for overall revitalization—especially if the area has been "down" for an extended period—sounds too ambitious. They dream about it, but are too timid to go for it. It's understandable, but a problem nonetheless.

3. It's not a goal with an endpoint. Regeneration is a constant process of all healthy systems. Regeneration is the basis of desirable qualities like sustainability and resilience. But most places only think of revitalizing when they're in pain. This crisis mentality prevents healthy places from having a revitalization program: they think it's only for sick places. That misguided assumption creates sick places. Ongoing programs ameliorate the scariness: Without a project-style deadline, there's no point at which we've failed or finished. We're free to continue improving.

4. It isn't a recognized discipline. Human Resource directors protect themselves by requiring degrees or certifications of their new hires. They don't want to be solely responsible for determining if a candidate is qualified. It's like the "nobody ever got fired for buying IBM" syndrome in the 20th century: IT directors bought IBM equipment—even when outdated or overpriced—because it was a safe career move. Why would

they hire someone to create revitalization or resilience if they can't distinguish between qualified and unqualified applicants? Now they can, as you'll discover in a moment.

As mentioned earlier, national and state government agencies have limited funding, and prefer to put it in places they are confident will spend it wisely. The same can be said of private foundations. Having someone in charge of revitalization is a confidence-booster—and thus a grant-attractor—but only if they have relevant credentials, sufficient authority and an appropriate budget.

Most renewal projects have managers with relevant training and certification: planners, architects, watershed managers, civil engineers, etc. Revitalization and resilience efforts also have professionals at the helm—often those same designers and planners—but they lack revitalization or resilience training and credentials. At best, they specialize in one small aspect of renewal; such as a certain kind of redevelopment project. They are usually completely clueless about the dynamics of revitalization itself, and how to facilitate its emergence.

> *"Smarter Government is also about the process, the data, the map, and the method for achieving dramatic public sector progress. And, as the author rightfully claims, '... about making complex problems visible and understandable for everyone who has a stake in seeing better outcomes and results.'" – Stephen Goldsmith, reviewing Smarter Government, by former Maryland governor Martin O'Malley.*

It's like being put in charge of renovating a region's electrical grid, simply because you know how to change a light bulb. Many public and private leaders work heroically to renew their cities, regions, and nations. But their efforts are undermined by revitalization process ignorance. So again, if everyone wants resilient prosperity, why don't more places have a process to create it? Usually it's because it never occurs to them that such a process might exist.

Typically, they understand one small part of it and think that's sufficient because they simply lack awareness of the missing parts. Traditionally, especially in the United States, the job of revitalizing a community has been assumed by:

MAYORS. There are two problems with the mayor-led approach:

Resilient prosperity is an ongoing, long-term process, but most mayors are in office for a very limited term. Worse, mayors often terminate the policies and programs of previous administrations, so their predecessors can't take credit for good news; and

Few mayors have any awareness of a process for producing resilient prosperity. That said, there are a few multi-term mayors—such as Bill Peduto in Pittsburgh and Mike Duggan in Detroit—who are supporting some remarkable turnarounds.

ECONOMICS DEVELOPERS. Yes, I know we've covered this subject several times before, but getting your community out of this mode is central to your ability to create resilient prosperity, so we're going to hit it one last time. Besides the fact that few economic developers have any knowledge of processes for producing resilient prosperity, the big problem here is that "economic development", as it's normally practiced, is based on two deceptions:

- Economic developers woo employers to their communities with incentives, the most common of which are "tax holidays" that undermine the community's finances and economic health. Mayors support this deception, because they get to brag about bringing jobs to the community in the short run, and subsequent administrations will have to deal with the long-term budget problems. The only winners are corporations, which end up paying no local taxes: they generally just move when the freebies run out. Many observers, such as Good Jobs First, consider this fraudulent; and,
- Jobs that move from one place to another are counted as "job growth". It's like thinking that rearranging one's living room creates more furniture. Again, politicians support this practice because it creates the illusion of accomplishing something. Let's be clear: a job that moves from Newark to Trenton is NOT job growth for New Jersey. A job that moves from New Jersey to Pennsylvania is NOT job growth for the United States. But they are reported as such, which is obviously dishonest.

That said, there are a few economic development agencies that actually focus on regenerating the community, such as the New York City Economic Development Corporation. Many of these revitalizing agencies have changed their names to "Redevelopment Agency" to better reflect their mission. (Unfortunately for them, the widespread abuse of redevelopment agency power and funds is leading some to abandon the use of "redevelopment" in their name.)

PLANNERS. There are two problems with the planner-led approach:

Few plans are actually implemented, and most of those that are implemented fail to achieve the goal of community regeneration. Planners and mayors know this, but both keep on producing plans: planners because it keeps them employed, and mayors because it creates the risk-free illusion of doing something.

Planners receive little or no training in creating revitalization or resilience. Any expertise they in these areas results from personal study, or is picked up on the job.

The result is that the politicians, economic developers and planners usually come away the winners, and communities usually come away the losers. Where revitalizing funding and policymaking is often best implemented—at least in theory—is at the state level. Such initiatives could encourage more regional cooperation among communities, more local food networks, and more-effective watershed restoration.

There are a few revitalizing state governors, such as Andrew M. Cuomo in New York. As mentioned earlier, one of his revitalization programs awards $10 million to communities that seem ready to revitalize their historic downtowns. This Downtown Revitalization Initiative (DRI) is great, but would likely be far more successful if the state provided revitalization process training with the award: most of these winning communities simply spend the money on isolated projects.

Dropping $10 million for downtown revitalization in someone's lap without educating them as to the best process for turning that money into revitalization can be a recipe for trouble. That's what's happening in late 2019 in Plattsburgh, New York, one of the DRI winners in 2017.

City officials want to turn Plattsburgh's largest public parking lot, known as Durkee Street, into a retail and housing complex. So far, so good. But, rather than using a strategic renewal process, they went straight to an RFP (request for proposals, AKA "really faulty process"). For some reason, they only allowed developers three weeks to respond, which is a bad idea for two reasons: 1) it doesn't allow sufficient time to some up with a really good proposal; and 2) any proposals that do come in will be suspected of having been forewarned.

Sure enough, the city received only one proposal, and the Plattsburgh Citizens Coalition—a newly-formed citizens' group led by a former city employee—alleged corruption. They also complained that the proposed redevelopment wasn't sufficiently visionary, thus wasting opportunities, and doesn't fit the local historic character.

North Country Public Radio reported *"The Durkee Street project is controversial. A lot of people—it's hard to say how many—think it's not the best way to revitalize downtown, that it doesn't serve the community."* In December of 2019, the public radio station also investigated the accusations of self-dealing on the part of local officials, and said they found no evidence of corruption.

But it's a shame that what should have been an exciting, positive moment in the city's history was tarnished so quickly from lack of a good process.

In Queensland, Australia, after the Brisbane City Council (BCC) released their new master plan for the redevelopment and revitalization of the city's central business district waterfront, one anonymous user on the Brisbane Development website commented *"Why should we trust BCC after they butchered the HSW? They have essentially allowed the privatization of that whole section of river frontage which went against their previous masterplans and river edge strategies."* (HSW refers to the historic Howard Smith Wharves, another of the city's redeveloped waterfronts)

Too many "comprehensive plans" resemble rearranging the Titanic's deck chairs, rather than a strategy for avoiding the iceberg. Land use planning is land use planning: it's essential, but it's not revitalization.

As noted earlier, creating a vision and strategy is not the planners' job. Asking them to create a plan for your community without supplying them with a vision and strategy is like asking a travel agent to plan your vacation, without telling them where you want to go. We must stop such planner abuse.

Smaller communities that successfully revitalize often have a core group of trusted, visionary "doers" who are always at the table. In the best situations, these folks keep the revitalization process going, due to their awareness of continuing local needs. They're motivated to "do the right things" by their deep familiarity with—and passion for—the future of their community. For those on the private side, a profit motive is often involved, but everyone at the table understands this. When such groups work to benefit all, they can be wonderful. But if they are bigoted, misogynous old men who are insensitive to the needs of youth, women, and minorities, the place is in trouble. A lot of places are in trouble.

GLIMMERS OF BRILLIANCE IN THE DARKNESS OF REVITALIZATION IGNORANCE

Revitalization ignorance results in waste, distress, and pessimism...and in community devitalization. This ignorance is seen in the constant waves of revitalization fads that sweep through cities. It's similar to how management fads continually wash through the corporate sector, as CEOs desperately try to convince employees, investors, and themselves that they have some control over the future.

We saw revitalization ignorance at work in earlier kneejerk attempts to become the next "Silicon Whatever", and in "strategies" based on positive-but-generic characteristics like innovation, creativity, smart, green, etc. We see it at work when cities copy the physical manifestations of revitalization, rather than the processes that led to them.

Witness the explosion of public aquariums aping the successes of Baltimore and Chattanooga. Witness the global frenzy of "starchitecture" museums and arts venues aping Bilbao's Guggenheim Museum (which was only one of many contributors to that city's heroic 30-year regeneration effort).

All three of those successful urban rebirths had their own unique and locally-appropriate revitalization process and strategy. Baltimore's was primarily a developer-led partnership ("impromptu"). Chattanooga's was primarily grassroots and foundation-led ("bottom-up").

None were perfect, but all worked very well. Baltimore didn't do a good job of integrating the revitalization of its Inner Harbor with the rest of the city. Chattanooga made the mistake of disbanding their excellent citizen-led visioning organization, which had served as their ongoing revitalization program.

Bilbao's was primarily government-led ("top-down") in the beginning, but it quickly became partnership-driven: public-public, public-private and private-private. Thanks to the provincial government of Viscaya's fiscal independence from Spain, they are able to do a much better job of multi-jurisdictional revitalization efforts, such as public transit. Early on, Bilbao could have done a better job of engaging the citizens of revitalization-affected neighborhoods—such as the one around the Guggenheim Museum—but it's still one of the most successful long-term urban regeneration efforts on the planet.

In fact, Bilbao recently launched a huge new regeneration project that will repurpose, renew and reconnect the post-industrial peninsula of Zorrotzaurre into a live-work-play destination. It boasts a sustainable redesign by Zaha Hadid, and will feature significant amounts of both affordable housing and public green spaces. But they have also—rather counter-intuitively—transformed it into an island by opening the Deusto Canal. New bridges will boost connectivity over the canal, but being able to call it an island should increase its marketability.

On the negative side, the Zorrotzaurre plan seems to have insufficient residential density. It also has too much office space, which will cannibalize other areas of the city. Even worse, the city has effectively killed Bilbao Ria 2000, the agency that has long served as their ongoing program and partnership creation entity of their regeneration efforts.

Their revitalized future now seems to be almost entirely in the hands of politicians, which is usually the kiss of death. Viscaya would seem to me in a good position to host the ongoing program for the greater metropolitan area, but they don't seem to have any interest in doing so. Long-term revitalization initiatives usually get the point where they themselves need to be revitalized. Bilbao's seems to have reached that point.

In each of the above cases, spectacular results were preceded by many years of thought, planning, alliance-building, and public engagement. But their imitators didn't want to learn, or change their behavior. They weren't interested in processes. They just wanted to buy products, like casinos, aquariums, stadiums, and convention centers. And it's not just cities: Nations also jump on one-size-fits-all economic fads, like fiscal austerity, no matter how poor their track record. They could instead fix fundamentals, such as restoring natural resources, or reducing economic "friction" via infrastructure renewal, but don't.

Another outcome of revitalization ignorance is when public leaders confuse cause with effect. Mayors tour revitalized cities, and witness the plethora of retail and restaurants. They then return home and artificially stimulate retail and dining in their devitalized downtown via subsidies and other incentives. A year or two later, that downtown—formerly full of long-dead stores—is now full of recently-dead stores. The psychological impact can be devastating, as citizens start thinking of themselves as losers.

Appointing a RE Facilitator with a grasp of regenerative principles helps avoid painful mistakes, and helps reduce institutional memory loss deriving from turnover of elected leaders. If you've watched the "American Restorations" TV show, you've seen the difference between restoring something old to its original appearance, restoring its original functionality, and restoring better-than-original functionality (due to modern materials). Whether restoring an iron lung or a motorcycle, conflicting constraints—such as aesthetics, performance, time, and cost—must be dealt with at every step.

I would avoid riding a motorcycle that had been restored with aesthetics taking precedence over functionality. So too would I be nervous about investing in a city whose revitalization was only skin deep. In the absence of trained revitalization professionals, we often get a focus on form over function.

The painful, expensive ways in which revitalization ignorance manifests are endless. The few mentioned here could all have been avoided with common sense. But that's the point. Even with good intentions, the same mistakes keep getting made and the revitalization "wheel" keeps getting reinvented—community-by-community, nation-by-nation—without qualified people focused on revitalization.

> "I decided to study architecture to help improve the conditions of my city and country. However, after arriving at university, I quickly realized that humanity was far from the focus of my studies." – Miguel Córdova Ramírez (Peru).

There's a trend towards greater innovation in cities (such as "Innovation Districts"), but innovation can either improve or damage a place. Tying innovation to a resilient prosperity program ensures the former.

As described earlier, the most tragic display of revitalization ignorance took place in the U.S. during the 50s and 60s. No enemy could have hoped to inflict the physical and economic devastation we did to ourselves. The federal government provided "urban renewal" funding to cities for tearing down old buildings. The premise was "destroy it, and they will come." "They" never came, and—over 60 years later—many cities still suffer from massive downtown dead spaces, and from the lack of restorable, beautiful old buildings.

Most local redevelopment agencies in the U.S. arose during this "urban renewal" fad. As mentioned in Chapter 9, California Governor Jerry Brown killed every one of them in that state in 2011, claiming they had become wasteful, corrupt, and autocratic. But in 2014, he introduced a smaller, more transparent form of redevelopment agency, and a reformed TIF model. Governor Brown was making a bold attempt at redeveloping the practice of redevelopment, and revitalizing the practice of revitalization. But the process was traumatic, as major surgery tends to be, and more than a few great projects died as a result.

The urban renewal debacle of the 20th century—although created by a badly-designed federal funding program—caused citizens to lose faith in their local mayors and planners. Local government power was greatly curtailed, and U.S. cities became overly dependent on private developers to "do the right thing".

A few rose to that challenge, but most didn't, and U.S. cities have missed many opportunities to develop responsibly as a result. Most improvements in national policy derive from local innovations, so it's time for the pendulum to swing back, giving cities more control over their future.

The national economy doesn't matter as much as most local leaders think it does. There's always money looking for opportunity...lots of it. We have to beware of the mental trap of basing our confidence in the future on averages: just because your national economy is projected to grow at only 1% next year doesn't mean your metropolitan economy can't grow at 10%.

How bad is investors' current level of confidence in the global economy, and most national economies? As of September of 2019, some $12 trillion (USD) of European and Asian money alone was parked in negative-interest-rate accounts. They're purposely losing money because they are too scared to invest it in ways that offer more upside.

On the bright side, some communities are waking up, and are starting to take their future more seriously. They might not yet have a full RECONOMICS Process, but they have 1) combined the complementary goals of revitalization (regeneration in the UK) and resilience; 2) created an ongoing program to deliver those goals; and 3) put someone in charge of it.

Witness the town of Calderdale in West Yorkshire, England. In November of 2019, the Calderdale Metropolitan Borough Council created the new position of "Programme Manager – Town Regeneration & Resilience" and started a search to hire someone for that role. I congratulate them on their enlightened approach, and look forward to monitoring their progress!

SO, WHO SHOULD LEAD A RESILIENT PROSPERITY INITIATIVE?

> *"The most deep-seated, universal anxiety in all of us is the fear that our life is being wasted."*
> *– Fred Kofman, The Meaning Revolution.*

By now, you've encountered many references to the role of architects, civil engineers and urban planners that probably sounded like criticism. But in most cases, the problem wasn't with those disciplines, so much as reliance on them to do things for which they weren't trained. Like producing resilient prosperity.

When we try to generate revitalization purely through design or planning, we get situations where a street or a downtown is much prettier, much more pedestrian-friendly, and where the historic buildings have been restored. In other words, where they seemed to do everything right, yet the desired economic vitality didn't manifest.

So, if resilient prosperity is your goal—not just the appearance of it—the ideal is to employ certified architects, engineers and planners who are ALSO qualified to facilitate revitalization and resilience. Only then will you move beyond tactical projects to strategic programs.

Throughout this book, I've been going on *ad nauseum* about the importance of having an ongoing program. But a serious challenge awaits those pioneering places that actually create a revitalization program: they will be hiring a "pig in a poke" when they choose someone to run it.

Until now, there's been no professional certification they can look for that will indicate to them that a candidate actually understands the process of bringing a place back to life. As a result, they will probably get someone who's an expert in a related discipline—like planning, or transit, or brownfields, or economic development—each of comprises maybe 1% or 2% of a comprehensive revitalization initiative.

Like most people who work at the strategy level, I specialize in being a generalist. That said, specialists are certainly needed. I was one of the original 200 members of the Society for Ecological Restoration, which has been working to advance that field since 1987.

While I'm not a restoration ecologist, I've been reading their professional journals and have attended and addressed some of their conferences over the past two decades. I can thus attest to the overwhelming complexity and requisite expertise of just the ecological component of a resilient prosperity effort.

So, if a multitude of specialists is needed, how do we put all that multifaceted expertise together, to create a resilient prosperity program? This book has already documented a few of the paths to advancing such a practice. Academic leadership will be needed to advance research and curricula. Private leadership will be needed to make elected leaders aware of both the problems and the solutions. Public leadership will be needed to create positions, budgets, agencies, systems, and partnerships to make it happen.

I've been hired by hundreds of non-profits, foundations, universities, companies, and government agencies (local, state, and national) worldwide over the past two decades, usually in a behind-the-scenes role. I've seen places fail to revitalize. I've seen them moving towards an uncertain outcome. And I've seen some achieve miraculous, back-from-the-dead rebirths. I've met people who would be wonderful RE Facilitators. I've seen conscientious organizations and agencies that could be highly effective leaders of a local RECONOMICS Process.

> *"The good life is a process, not a state of being.*
> *It is a direction, not a destination."*
> *– Carl Rogers*

But I've never met a well-funded, high-level Director of Revitalization, or anything similar. The first city-level Chief Resilience Officers have only need in place for a few years (and many of those are no longer in place), and none that I know of have significant budgets or influence: as described earlier, most seem to be wrapped-up in endless plan-writing.

And I've yet to encounter a complete RECONOMICS Process, though many places have come close, missing only one element. But plugging that gap makes all the difference. A car with all four wheels doesn't just go 25% faster than one that's missing a wheel.

In December of 2014, the American Planning Association (APA) issued a report titled "Planning for Post-Disaster Recovery: New Generation". It concluded with this message *"...opportunity to combine aspects of community economic revitalization with environmental restoration and serious considerations of social equity, particularly in the context of adapting communities for a future of greater climate resilience and adaptation, draws upon some of the most powerful, creative, and visionary skill sets that planners can offer to a community."*

I was very happy to see all those elements finally combined in an APA document (it's probably just coincidence that this appeared just a few months after a draft of this book was circulated at APA headquarters).

When hiring a resilient prosperity director or RE Facilitator, you'll likely have to choose someone whose experience is in one or more of the component silos. At that point, the personal characteristics of the candidate—positive, integrative, inclusive, adaptive, etc.—are likely to be more important than whether they are an engineer, planner, ecologist, sociologist, economist or architect.

> *"A maestro cannot play all the instruments.*
> *What he does is create a collaborative effort."*
> *– Merck Orchestra conductor Wolfgang Heinzel.*

An obvious starting point would be if you already have someone heading-up a resilience or revitalization effort. Resilience is the crucial missing ingredient of most revitalization efforts, and revitalization is the crucial missing ingredient of most resilience efforts. Effectively combining them, and managing them adaptively, gives us resilient prosperity.

But resilience efforts often fall into project mentality: a one-time redesign of the physical environment (e.g. - grey and green infrastructure) to cope with disasters or climate change. A programmatic approach would enable ongoing redesign, reconnection, and repurposing of all at-risk natural, built, socioeconomic, and human assets. A Resilient Prosperity program connects the goal of resilience to the public desire for equitable prosperity, better quality of life, and more natural resources. This focus on what more people really care about facilitates funding.

Experience in running a Main Street program is also a great background. Many of the National Trust for Historic Preservation's Main Street initiatives are successful specifically because they're ongoing programs, rather than one-time fixes. Revitalization is based on the simple assumption that things could be better. That applies to every community and nation on Earth, and downtowns / main streets ("high streets" in the UK) are often the best place to start.

Main Street programs are also good because they document in hard numbers the economic benefits of restoring and reusing existing assets. But they mostly operate within the silos of "downtown" and "heritage". There are so many other natural, built, and socioeconomic assets that contribute to revitalization that a Main Street background is only a decent starting point for a RE Facilitator.

Relevant experience could come from a community foundation, EcoDistricts, Innovation Districts, BIDs, CDCs, and planning for sustainability/climate change adaptation. Also excellent would be experience with a Smart Growth program. The "smart growth" concept emerged in 1992 at the UN Conference on Environment and Development held in Rio de Janeiro. It's been championed in the U.S. by the American Planning Association, the Environmental Protection Agency, and by the non-profit Smart Growth America. Smart Growth is neither revitalization nor resilience, but it embraces many relevant component activities.

A Certified Project Manager (CPM) with program management and/or adaptive management experience might also be excellent. Program management is managing multiple projects in way that derives more benefits than would come from those projects in isolation. Creating a whole that's greater than the sum of the parts, in other words.

You want a systems thinker who embraces complexity, rather than trying to engineer-out surprises (the ability to display surprising behavior is a defining characteristic of complex systems). Familiarity with adaptive management would be perfect, of course: it's the technique for complex, ongoing challenges. You want a networker who connects diverse players. Experience working with minority, poverty, or homelessness issues would be useful. Skills are learnable: sensitivity and empathy for under-represented stakeholders? Not so much.

A RE Facilitator might best report to an appointed city or county manager (CAO in Canada), rather than an elected mayor. This enhances continuity: few mayors are public-spirited enough to launch efforts that primarily benefit the next administration.

That said, a long-lived, revitalization-focused "strong mayor" like Joe Riley of Charleston (in office since 1975) could work. A state-level RE Facilitator should report to the governor, a national-level to the president or Prime Minister, etc.

YOU CAN BE PART OF THE SOLUTION TO ALL OF THOSE CHALLENGES

> *"If you work for a living,*
> *why do you kill yourself working?"*
> *— from "The Good, The Bad, and The Ugly".*

A solution to all of the above obstacles to resilient prosperity is now emerging, and you can be part of it. Deciding to revitalize places for a living might well be the most personally revitalizing decision of your life.

Since many well-established professions already provide the majority of technical, legal, political and financial aspects of creating resilient prosperity, you would only need to focus on plugging the gaps in the process.

Who would be unhappy to see an RECONOMICS Process created, and/or a RE Facilitator appointed? Any existing agency that misinterprets it as a threat to their influence or funding. In fact, the RECONOMICS Process should create a community tide that raises all agencies' boats.

While you need a organization home for your resilient prosperity program, the overall RECONOMICS Process isn't owned by anyone. It thus provides numerous entry points for anyone wishing to improve the local situation., but it doesn't (or shouldn't, anyway) threaten anyone's "turf."

Who should be happy to see revitalization pursued in a disciplined way, rather than as wishful thinking?

- Real Estate Developers: Revitalization helps prevent projects from being undermined by overall decline;
- Business Owners: Revitalization means more customers, with more money to spend;
- Politicians: Nothing contributes to re-election or higher office like revitalization success; and
- Local Residents: Living in a revitalized place revitalizes us.

For resilient prosperity in general—and the RECONOMICS Process in particular—to take off as a more-rigorous practice requires only a few pioneers. Cities are me-tooish: they like to copy what works elsewhere, and nations learn from cities. This copycat tendency also has a downside: it results in sameness of places, which is deadly if you want tourists. The single most important factor in attracting visitors is uniqueness.

A very positive example of me-tooishness is how the New York City borough of Queens is planning to turn an abandoned railway into a linear park (dubbed "The Queensway), a la the famous High Line in neighboring Manhattan. These sorts of projects hit on all three cylinders: they renew, repurpose, and reconnect assets, often inducing dramatic local revitalization.

A December 26, 2014 article in the *New York Times* said: "...the QueensWay would be a boon to the borough, transforming a humdrum stretch of residential-commercial-industrial-whatever with the sylvan graciousness that the High Line brought to the West Side of Manhattan, but on a far bigger scale. It would open a walk-and-bike gateway to another big park, Forest Park, that is now dangerously hemmed in by roadways. The study tallied other benefits: fewer traffic fatalities, better flood control, cleaner air, fitter New Yorkers and new commercial and cultural amenities. As new parks go, it would be relatively cheap — about $120 million."

A network can grow and evolve forever, but there will only be one opportunity to be the creator of your local RECONOMICS Process. Many elected leaders will fail to rise to this challenge of taking resilience and revitalization seriously. This will be a great opportunity for local non-profit, foundation, or grassroots leaders to grow the size, influence, and relevance of their organizations.

CERTIFIED REVITALIZATION & RESILIENCE FACILITATORS ("RE FACILITATORS")

"If your actions inspire others to dream more, learn more, do more and become more, you are a leader." – John Quincy Adams.

Let's start taking our future seriously. Governments shouldn't have to rely on geriatric autodidacts such as myself. They need young leaders with rigorous, relevant training. This can be a great career path.

A growing number of institutions—from governments to non-profits to development banks—would benefit greatly from adding revitalization to their mission. It could key to their growth and survival.

In today's hyper-broken world, the first obligation of new mayors, governors, or presidents/PMs should be: 1) appointing a RE Facilitator, and 2) launching an RECONOMICS Process.

So again, who should lead an resilient prosperity program? Someone who understand the RECONOMICS Process is essential. For that reason, on March 1, 2020, **RECONOMICS Institute** (reconomics.org) launched their online training program to produce Certified Revitalization & Resilience Facilitators™ (RE Facilitators™ for conversational purposes).

These facilitators will put "RE" after their name (like a professional engineer puts "PE" after their name), to make them easy to spot. Many will be folks practicing another core profession: planners, lawyers, mayors, real estate developers, architects, etc. But that's certainly not necessary.

They will remain in their current position, but get certified so they will be the person at the table who knows how to create revitalization and resilience. Such knowledge can enhance careers, positioning them at the heart of local renewal.

Others will get certified because they want to work full-time directing their community's or region's revitalization or resilience efforts. Still others seek self-employment as a consultant, facilitating resilient prosperity in multiple places.

In addition to achieving RE certification, local resilient prosperity leaders should be people who "get" adaptive management. They should be people who dream of creating secure, inclusive, green economies. They should be someone who can recruit and lead a team.

RE Facilitators would ideally be positive, results-oriented folks in this world of angry, frustrated, ineffectual people. What else would define an appropriate leader of resilient prosperity? First we should distinguish two basic species of leaders:
- Formal leaders lead by dint of their title: they may or may not actually exert any leadership abilities beyond that.

- Informal (or emergent) leaders lack an official role, but lead anyway as a result of their knowledge, intelligence, passion, vision, strategy, charisma and/or trustworthiness.

Many communities and organizations go into decline because their formal leaders aren't leading. Those same leaders are often so insecure that they ignore or actively suppress emergent leaders. Conversely, many communities and organizations revitalize because their formal leaders are smart and confident enough to actively scan for emergent (informal) leaders, and give them the resources and/or power they need to accomplish their goals.

An resilient prosperity program should harness "emergent leadership". Just as strategies and projects must adapt to the current situation, so should leadership. The leader your community needs at any given moment could come from anywhere inside—or outside—the community.

If official leaders aren't fixing local problems, "fixers" ignore them and get the job done. Officials will support the efforts of fixers when it's politically safe to do so: when a project has so much momentum and public support that it's safer to say "yes" than "no". When followers lead, leaders follow.

> *"Being rich is having money;*
> *being wealthy is having time."*
> *– Margaret Bonanno, American writer.*

I would amend Margaret Bonanno's insight to say "*being wealthy is having time, and something worthwhile to do with it.*" Facilitating resilient prosperity for all would seem to qualify as worthwhile.

This author's reSWOT Workshops use his variation on the SWOT Analysis to help clients customize the RECONOMICS Process to local assets, needs, challenges and dreams. RE Facilitators will also perform reSWOT Workshops, if they wish.

Revitalization and resilience are the largest and most important "industries" for which a corresponding profession has not emerged. There are plenty of professionals in charge of the component activities, but (until now) no one to facilitate the overall process.

This lack of rigor wastes hundreds of billions of dollars of public and private investment worldwide annually. In our rapidly-urbanizing world, the human and environmental consequences are severe and worsening. Does the presence of credentialed professionals guarantee success? No, but it certainly reduces the likelihood of failure.

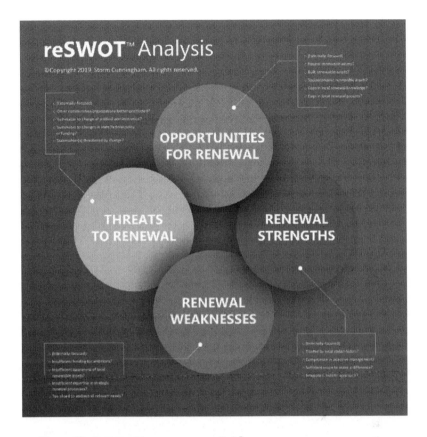

What could certified RE Facilitators accomplish?

Could they make recovery, revitalization or resilience occur on a timetable? No.

Could they guarantee recovery, revitalization or resilience will occur at all? No.

Could they increase the chances of recovery, revitalization or resilience success? Yes.

Could they make the process faster, more efficient and more harmonious, boosting your ROI (Revitalization On Investment)? Probably.

If more places had RE Facilitators using shared principles, models, and missions, our ability to solve multi-jurisdictional challenges—like restoring estuaries and revitalizing bioregions—would be greatly enhanced. In virtually every long-term revitalization success I've encountered, one shared characteristic rises above all others: the presence of an informal network of political, business, non-profit, and citizen leaders.

They all have a similar complaint *"This shouldn't be so hard: we shouldn't have to keep reinventing the process—and remaking connections—with each new initiative. We need a system or process.*" Places need a resilient prosperity leader, facilitating the RECONOMICS Process.

Since revitalization is an emergent quality of the whole, a RE Facilitator would focus on the whole. This means they usually wouldn't do physical projects, so they wouldn't need a large budget. But they would need "teeth": the ability to say "yay" or "nay" to inappropriate projects and policies (or at least flag them). They would be evangelists with leverage.

Would a RE Facilitator add another layer of project-delaying bureaucracy? The opposite is true: They would likely speed decisions and entitlements. Currently, every new project and program in a community must reinvent multiple wheels, such as public engagement, visioning, etc. As the facilitator of the shared vision of the community's future (and strategy to achieve it), and as the connection to all renewal activities, your RE Facilitator would help governments eliminate duplication of effort.

Your local RE Facilitator would also help developers avoid wasted time and effort. Currently, the public doesn't get a chance to voice concerns about most projects until they are well into the design process. In many cases, projects are virtually "done deals" by the time the public notices are issued, with the funding already in place. A delay due to citizen protests over heritage, social justice, or environmental issues is then hugely expensive, as the interest accumulates on construction loans. Having a RE Facilitator would give developers someone to consult at the earliest stages, helping them avoid snags.

The six elements of the RECONOMICS Process aren't just activities or checklist items: each is its own unique path to success. When combined, they create broad, solid highway to success. There's no rigid process by which this process should be created. As long as you start with the three core elements—program, vision and strategy—the policies, partnerships and projects can be implemented in whatever manner, and on whatever schedule, is appropriate for your situation.

Each place has its own challenges, resources, and aspirations, so each RE Facilitator would have uniquely place-based responsibilities and priorities. Here are a few obvious ones:

- Facilitate the creation of a vision/map, strategy, program, reporting system, etc. Ongoing programs create a flywheel effect: capturing momentum from each success to make the next step easier. Momentum creates confidence. By tracking and communicating successes, citizens perceive recovery. Coming back to life often makes a place "cool", and always makes it joyful. Measuring each project's benefits (and taking "before" photos) enables your PD to issue reports with numbers and "after" photos as proof of progress.

- Training: It's difficult to initiate or manage a process if leaders have no idea what that process is. Few understand the dynamics, practices, tools, and models common to revitalization successes worldwide. Your RE Facilitator could provide such training, staying on top of the latest research. An example of such research is the recent study revealing that development impact fees do slow sprawl, but often don't—by themselves—increase investment in the downtown.
- Policy advice: Your RE Facilitator could help policymakers embed a few basic rules into policies, plans, regulations, incentives, projects, and decision-making. Provide policy advice to make a place regeneration-friendly. For instance, a downtown in need of revitalization should be made an easier and more profitable place for developers to operate in than sprawl areas. Regenerative policies help keep everyone moving in the same direction: towards a more secure, inclusive, green economy. Here are three key rules that should guide such policies:
    o Renewal: Economic growth is sustainable if based primarily on renovating, reconnecting, and repurposing existing assets. Sprawl might occasionally be needed, but asset renewal (redevelopment) should be the default, and sprawl (new development) the exception. We live in the Age of Re. "Re" words are non-partisan. Everyone loves acts of renewal. "Re" words are powerful: Transit-oriented development is good: transit-oriented redevelopment is better; transit-oriented revitalization is best.
    o Integration: Much revitalization potential is wasted when renewal projects are done in silos. Watershed restoration here. Brownfields remediation there. Historic building reuse here. Infrastructure renewal there. Integrating the renewal of natural, built, and socioeconomic assets produces efficiency and synergy. For example: An island nation trying to revitalize its fisheries must restore damaged reefs. This requires restoring mangroves (which filter reef-killing sediments from terrestrial runoff), restoring watersheds, restorative farming practices, upgrading sewage systems, etc. Sounds like a job for a RE Facilitator.
    o Equity: Increased community harmony is common in revitalized locales. But many places expend copious amounts of money redeveloping blighted areas in a way that's unfair to a portion of the populace (usually low-income families and ethnic minorities). Advances made economically are thus offset by loss of trust in government, which can retard revitalization by

making the entitlement process for redevelopers too long and difficult. Citizen anger can also scare away residents or employers who prefer places with a better sense of community.
- Supporting economic development efforts: Economic developers mostly attract employers via tax holidays. Such incentives are now a commodity, no longer making any place stand out. The feature that firms most desire in a place is a great quality of life, which helps them attract and retain top-quality talent. When CEOs make the final decision on a location, they're seldom thinking about incentives. They're thinking about their families, and the families of their workers. Are the schools good? Is the place safe? Is it beautiful? Is it unique? Is it on the way up? Your PD can help your Economic Development Director go into these pitch sessions fully armed.
- Create and run an ongoing resilient prosperity program.

In our focus on program, process, policies, etc., we must never forget that these systems comprise people, all of whom must be valued. As Dr. Robert Bullard says, "*Addressing equity is a prerequisite to achieving sustainable and livable communities.*"

Also as noted earlier, prosperity isn't just money. Even if it were, there's no natural limit to economic growth, even on a finite planet. But there are definitely limits to population growth, virgin resource extraction, and sprawl. Some new cities and suburbs need to be built, and there is a resilient prosperity approach for this (the "restorative sprawl" mentioned in Chapter 1). But our existing cities have much untapped capacity. The single most important function of government might be to tap that potential. This will require renewing, repurposing, and reconnecting damn near everything.

Order emerges naturally in a just society. So the first responsibility of a political leader in a dysfunctional, distrustful community should be to impose justice, not order. This is just one of the myriad goals that can be embedded into the vision the drives your RECONOMICS Process.

I say "your" to remind you once again that the RECONOMICS Process described here is the Minimum Viable Process: You can massage it and add to it as needed, but don't subtract from it. The ideal, of course, would be for someone to turn the RECONOMICS Process into an app. Anyone want to partner with RECONOMICS Institute on that project?

HOW COULD A REVITALIZATION & RESILIENCE FACILITATOR EARN A LIVING?

Thousands of "help wanted" ads are placed annually by organizations seeking a coordinator, manager or director of neighborhood, downtown or community revitalization. They are placed by a wide variety of public agencies (such as a CDC, BID, Chamber of Commerce, or a mayor hiring a Deputy Mayor for Neighborhood Revitalization), non-profits (such as the Main Street program and Habitat for Humanity in the U.S.), foundations (focused on poverty, environmental justice, etc.) and for-profit firms (such as architects, planners and consultants). This is generally same group of entities who also hire coordinators, managers or directors of resilience.

The revitalization positions can be hard to track down, because they don't necessarily use the word "revitalization" in the title. It might be regeneration, redevelopment, recovery, economic development, renewal, growth, rejuvenation, rehabilitation, etc. As we've already seen, this vitally-important function has so far failed to coalesce as a profession. The certification program for Revitalization & Resilience Facilitators (RE Facilitators, for short) is the first significant step towards filling the need for recognizable expertise in this field.

So, help-wanted ads for existing positions aside, how else might you put such a certification to use? Here's an overview of the possibilities, as relates to standard employment paths:

- For many folks, this is an add-on certification, not a profession unto itself. So, if you are already a certified architect, civil engineer, planner, project manager, etc., the RE certification positions you to take on higher-level responsibilities that enhance your current career.
    o You could boost business development, showing communities that your employer is a better choice because it understands the community revitalization process better than do your competitors;
    o You could enhance the firm's proposals—again adding to your rainmaker status—by adding a resilient prosperity process option that lifts the firm far above the usual design or planning proposals of your competitors.
- Students looking to earn a living restoring nature, revitalizing communities or making places more resilient are often frustrated by the paucity of relevant degrees offered in institutions of higher education. Now, you can simply choose a degree based on your interests and

passions, and then add the RE certification to "re-orient" those skills, making yourself more marketable to an employer that enhances places in some way;
- Or you might already be employed, but lack a degree or certification in a specific discipline. You might, for instance, be working your way up the managerial ladder in a non-profit, company or government organization that's focused on cities, heritage, parks, infrastructure, the natural environment or serving the public. The RE certification would enable you to carve-out a unique career path in that organization, pretty much free of competition. You would become the staffer who can help make the organization more relevant to the myriad growth industries focused on improving our world.

As stated, those were all normal employment situations. For those with a more-entrepreneurial bent, you might start a consulting practice or a company offering an app, technology or service related to the built, natural or socioeconomic environments. In such cases, the RE certification would provide the credibility to market something related to renewal or resilience.

There are also possibilities that lie somewhere between employment and entrepreneurship. Many organizations might respond positively to your offer to help them become more of a player in the fields of community revitalization, regional resilience, or the like. But they don't have an existing staff opening to plug you into, nor do they have the budget to create a position for you. In this case, you need to be more creative and proactive, such as being their on-call trainer for all things "re".

> *"Revitalization doesn't have a color or a party; it starts in the heart." – Scott Turner, Exec. Director, White House Opportunity & Revitalization Council.*

The possibilities are endless, depending on the challenges, politics and aspirations of your particular city, state or nation, but here's one scenario at the community level that you might use as a starting point to get the ideas flowing. I'm going to use a community foundation as the specific example, so you'll have to modify it if your goal is to work for some other kind of not-for-profit group, or for a government agency.

Community foundations provide a central giving point for residents and companies to provide philanthropic support to their town, city, county or region. Sometimes, they pass donations along to neighborhood groups and non-profits in the form of cash. But they primarily support such entities by providing the infrastructure they need, but can't afford, such as shared staff, office space, event management, marketing, outreach, etc.

With that model in mind, you (with your RE certification) might approach them with a strategic growth opportunity for the community foundation. You could suggest that:
- The community foundation become the program host for the establishment of a local RECONOMICS Process. This means they would facilitate the creation of a shared vision / asset map and strategy, recommend needed policy changes, facilitate task teams to study challenges and recommend solutions, and facilitate the creation of partnerships to make projects happen. They would also host public presentations: the better stakeholders understand the RECONOMICS Process, the better it will work;
- Each of those functions has real value to someone...these are services that the local government, philanthropists, property owners and redevelopers will pay for;
    o For instance, a real estate investor investigating opportunities in your community would find it very valuable to have someone who could quickly orient them to the local vision and strategy, show them available properties, make them aware of community needs, introduce them to local partnerships, etc. No one would be better qualified to provide such services than someone who's at the heart of the local RECONOMICS Process.
    o Unless yours is a very small town, it's likely that there would eventually be an entire team of RE Facilitators locally. They might divide their duties geographically, such as downtown, suburbs and rural areas. Or they might be functionally divided, such as infrastructure, watershed, brownfields, agriculture, structures, etc. Since they would all be part of the same process, driven by the same vision, making decisions based on the same strategy, they are less likely to become the usual disconnected silos.
- With your RE certification, you would perform those functions. The fees would be paid to the community foundation, which would pay you a salary. Thus, your position is self-funded and you've helped the community foundation position itself as more of a central player in creating the local future. You've also created a new revenue stream for the foundation, which can only expand as the local RECONOMICS Process becomes better-established, and as the community grows economically.

(If you need help selling the foundation on the idea, or helping the foundation sell the idea to the city, you can bring me in to do a public talk and leadership workshop.)

The RECONOMICS Process comes to life locally via Certified Revitalization & Resilience Facilitators. Without at least one person who understands the process working on it full time, it's unlikely to manifest in any meaningful way.

At the most basic level, the RE Facilitator is simply 1) ensuring that each necessary element of the process exists (structure), 2) ensuring that each of those elements is regenerative (function); and 3) ensuring that they are implemented in the most productive order (process).

CREATING AN AGENCY AND/OR TEAM TO IMPLEMENT RESILIENT PROSPERITY

> "One of the biggest challenges facing cities today is that no single organisation has complete control over the solutions to increase our resilience to the broad range of challenges we face." – George Ferguson, mayor of Bristol (UK).

When looking for a home for the program portion of your resilient prosperity process, it's important to remember that they are only in charge of the program: the overall process belongs to the community.

Revitalization doesn't just happen to a community. It's self-inflicted healing. Three of the fundamental characteristics of resilience are redundancy, scalability, and integration. A system with redundant functionality can better-withstand damage while continuing to operate. A scalable system will be able to grow without losing its balance or structural integrity. An integrated system allows resources and information to flow efficiently to wherever they are needed.

New technologies are often the key. [For instance, cities are now switching to inexpensive, cloud-based disaster recovery solutions, such as CloudVelox. Until recently, redundant data systems were hosted locally. Besides being vulnerable, this was expensive; prohibitively-so for smaller communities.]

It's all well and good to know how to revitalize a place and/or make it more resilient. It's another thing to know how to actually implement a program that can cope with loss of resources or personnel (redundancy), that can reach into all corners of your community or region (scalability), and that represents the needs of—and taps the resources of—all stakeholders (integration).

A major challenge to achieving both revitalization and resilience is their holistic nature. A single person as RE Facilitator can't be expected to cope with the breadth and depth of knowledge required to manage all aspects of the natural, built, and socioeconomic environments, not to mention the legal, political, cultural, and financial components. That's why they focus on strategy and the overall process, leaving tactics (projects) up the partnerships and other stakeholders who contribute to the process. It's also why a team of RE Facilitators will usually be needed in larger cities, and especially in regions. Maybe even an entire agency, eventually.

CREATING A PROSPERITY AGENCY: For places with the necessary funding, the "normal" approach to addressing that multifaceted complexity is to create a new public agency with the mission of advancing resilient prosperity. Or, an existing public agency could be repurposed for that purpose, reconnecting it to other agencies to make it more effective, and likely renewing it as a result. This would mirror the same 3Re Strategy this agency might apply in the community.

But such a transformation of an existing agency would require a visionary leader with serious commitment, since there would be a powerful gravitational pull back to the institution's comfort zone. If an agency were troubled or underutilized, and already due for an overhaul, this could help. But the ideal would be an agency so influential, so trusted, and so well-funded that they could add resilient prosperity to their mission.

Repurposing or expanding an existing agency makes sense, since a budget and personnel would already be in place. What sort of agency might be repurposed in this manner? Almost any kind:

- Agencies already focused on redevelopment, regeneration, and/or economic development;
- A regional agency would be connected to a broad diversity of environments and stakeholders;
- Natural resource agency (such as watershed) are well-positioned because they affect everyone;
- A social service agency might have good public trust and outreach abilities;
- An infrastructure or public works agency would be well-positioned since they deal with the structure, flows, and vital functions of the community; or

- A planning agency might work, if they were willing to break their traditional habits and renovate their procedures to live up to the vast untapped potential of that profession.

CREATING A PROSPERITY TEAM: If launching a new agency or repurposing a public agency is too much of a stretch at present, then creating a multifaceted team might be more practical. But how could even the most competent team be effective across an entire city, region, or nation? Only via redundancy and scalability. Using the same template for each, you could have a leadership/advisory team, a training team (which could create more teams, if needed), and as many project teams as needed.

A shared template helps teams communicate with each other. It enables each team to the various elements of your resilient prosperity program. There will be a tendency to create specialized teams with reduced diversity. Avoid it. If a project team is formed to restore a historic theater, there's no problem with boosting architectural and heritage expertise on the team. But it would be a mistake to eliminate seemingly-irrelevant members, such as watershed, ecosystems, or agriculture.

For instance, a theater doesn't exist in isolation; its real estate and function is part of the natural and socioeconomic fabric of an entire region. Agricultural team members don't just represent corn or cattle: they represent farmers and ranchers. They could thus ensure that the theater's plan takes into account reaching out to rural audiences. They would think to use its parking lot as a farmers' market on weekend mornings, thus making the theater a connection between downtown and rural. Of course, you shouldn't feel forced to justify the presence of a fishery expert at a discussion of downtown parking. It's the holistic perspective of the group—and its ability to produce surprising ideas and insights—that counts, not the ability to draw direct lines among every aspect of the community.

Likewise, the watershed team member might think of putting a green roof on the theater, or bioswales around the parking lot. The ecosystem member might suggest native plant species for the green roof that might otherwise have been ignored, thus boosting native pollinators. A fishery expert might suggest including a seafood section in the farmers' market, thus connecting downtown to different rural stakeholders. And any of them might think about including adjacent properties in the project, whereas your historic preservation expert might tend to focus solely on the building envelope of the theater.

The central principle at work here is to avoid assuming that any aspect of your community is irrelevant to any other. One of the common factors I've encountered in stellar examples of revitalization is the presence of a visionary individual who "gets" it all: a Renaissance person who has a better-than-average understanding of how natural, built, socioeconomic, and human assets and dynamics all fit together.

Such visionaries—whether mayors, developers, social entrepreneurs, or non-profit leaders—are rare, but they can be fostered. The key is cross-training: assemble a team with all of the necessary component disciplines, and then have them constantly train each other. They won't all become experts in every field, of course, but they will gain a basic understanding of each. This gives them an ability to converse effectively with experts in each field. Some fields will likely require a sub-team. Your infrastructure specialist, for example, might rely on specialists in each of the many forms of infrastructure.

You aren't likely to get far in convincing your community they need your services as a RE Facilitator if they don't know they have a problem you can fix. Residents and leaders alike need to learn to recognize the signs and symptoms of bad local governance. One sign of poor governance is a tendency to manage the community or region on a project-by-project basis, rather than creating ongoing programs for ongoing challenges.

> *"Above all be of single aim; have a legitimate and useful purpose, and devote yourself unreservedly to it." – James Allen, British writer.*

In medicine, a sign is something that can be observed by a third party, whereas a symptom is something the patient perceives subjectively. Allow me a bit of a tangent here, in order to make an important point.

In cases of dehydration, a sign would be when you pinch the skin on the back of a person's hand, and the skin doesn't immediately flatten with no trace when you let go. Irritable behavior is another observable sign of dehydration. On the other hand, headaches, itchy eyes, constipation and dry throats are all symptoms (not signs) of dehydration. If you know all the signs of dehydration, and you tell someone who doesn't know them that they are dehydrated, they'll normally protest, saying *"no I'm not: I'm not thirsty"*. They think that thirst is the only symptom of dehydration. They might be constipated, irritable, and headachy, but they'll insist that they aren't dehydrated, because thirst is the only symptom they know.

So it is with communities. Tell them they are devitalizing, and the most common reaction will be *"no we're not: our unemployment rate is average, our crime rate is below average, and our quality of life is good."* Jobs, safety and health are the only signs that come to mind for most people. They don't recognize the myriad signs of decline; especially the early ones.

THE WORLD'S MOST RESILIENT ORGANIZATIONAL MODEL: THE GREEN BERET A-TEAM

> *"Climb mountains not so the world can see you,*
> *but so you can see the world."*
> *– David McCullough Jr.*

It doesn't make much sense to create a local organization for resilient prosperity if it isn't itself resilient. This is crucially important, so please allow me a much longer tangent here, so you fully understand the dynamics behing one potential solution. An ideal resilient prosperity team model comes from an unlikely source: U.S. Army Special Forces (SF), popularly known as Green Berets. They are probably the most efficient, effective and resilient military outfit ever created.

We discussed SF earlier in this book, as relates to strategy. Let's revisit them now as relates to team-building. After all, when someone refers to the best of a group of teams, they normally call them the "A-Team", right? That terminology came from SF, and not without reason.

The Special Forces A-Team's resilience comes primarily from: 1) careful selection of candidates; 2) an intensive initial qualification course; 3) structural redundancy; and 4) functional redundancy via ongoing cross-training of team members by team members (the best way to learn is to teach).

I served on a SCUBA A-Team as a medic in B Company, 2nd Battalion of the 7th Special Forces Group (1972-4). [I never saw combat: By the time I finished the one-and-a-half years of SF training, the Army wasn't sending new SF troops into Vietnam. Green Berets are normally first in and first out. As a peace-loving ex-hippie freshly back from 3 years of hitchhiking around the world in search of Truth, that didn't break my heart.]

Back then, Army SF was the only U.S. military unit referred to as "Special Forces". Today, the U.S. Special Operations Forces (SOF) comprise elite units from the Army, Navy (SEALs), Marines, and Air Force. As of 2013, SOF teams are operating in about 70 countries.

As mentioned earlier, Unconventional Warfare (UW) missions are what make Green Berets fundamentally different from Navy SEALS, Marine Corps Raiders, Army Rangers, Army Delta Force, or Air Force Special Operations Forces. All of those other units exclusively conduct Direct Action (DA) missions. These are the operations you see in the movies and news media: rescuing hostages, killing Osama bin Laden, etc. While DA accounts for 100% of the missions of the other Special Operations outfits, it traditionally comprises only about 20% of Green Beret missions.

The other 80% is Unconventional Warfare. UW derived from the CIA's Civilian Irregular Defense Group (CIDG) program in Vietnam. Some say it was best idea the CIA ever had. Other says it was the only good idea the CIA ever had. Green Berets were created primarily to serve as the combat arm of the CIA, and so have sometimes been used in nefarious ways. That's not their fault, of course: troops are seldom aware of the hidden agendas their sacrifices serve. The CIA now has its own combat unit, the Special Operations Group (SOG) of the Special Activities Division (SAD), but it still recruits from both active and former Army SF.

Unconventional warfare is a very different mode of winning a war. It's based on befriending, educating, and supporting local communities, so they can defend themselves and become more resilient. A Green Beret team is designed to train and equip a 4000-person guerrilla battalion. This is what they did with the indigenous Montagnard (Degar) tribes of South Vietnam, who were being persecuted by the North Vietnamese communists.

This mode involves working behind enemy lines for long periods of time. The Green Beret motto is de oppresso liber: to liberate the oppressed. They live with, work with, and teach local people (in their own language) to fight their own battles. So, Green Berets are primarily teachers. Unconventional warfare is thus a force-multiplier, which is exactly what most community revitalization efforts need.

Green Berets can turn the course of a war with very little financial expenditure. We saw this when rag-tag groups of guerrillas—aided by Army Special Forces teams—kicked the mighty Soviet military out of Afghanistan (triggering the collapse of the Soviet Union).

You might have heard stories of bearded U.S. soldiers in native garb joining a horseback cavalry charge by Northern Alliance mujahedeen fighters against a Soviet armored column in Afghanistan. Those were Green Berets in UW mode. A visiting Pentagon general at the scene said it was the most magnificent spectacle he'd ever witnessed. This was recently dramatized in the movie "12 Strong" (with Chris Hemsworth), a pretty good depiction of SF operations by Hollywood standards. The first such movie, "The Green Berets" (with John Wayne), was truly awful and totally inaccurate.

Back to the A-Team model: There might have been some changes in the 35 years since I left active duty, but during my time, a U.S. Army Special Forces A-Team (Operational Detachment) comprised 12 individuals, with built-in redundancy that allows it to split into two completely functional halves if needed.

This redundancy creates resilience, allowing the team to maintaining its ability to accomplish the mission despite serious casualties. Each team has two medics, two engineers (for building things or blowing them up), two communication specialists (radios, etc.), two weapons specialists, two operations/intel specialists, plus a commander and assistant commander.

> *"He who stops being better stops being good."*
> *– Oliver Cromwell (1599 – 1658), English leader.*

All team members go through the same Special Forces qualification course, plus their own specialized training. Structural redundancy is complemented by functional redundancy, via cross-training. Team members constantly teach each other. Teaching reinforces the teachers' knowledge, while learning other disciplines boosts the team's resilience to attrition.

How might you apply this model to create a local resilient prosperity team? Using an expanded version of the 8-sector taxonomy of restorative industries first documented in The Restoration Economy, your prosperity team could echo a Green Beret A-Team. With just 12 people, it wouldn't have structural redundancy, but cross-training would provide functional redundancy, and adding teams create structural redundancy, if desired.

An ideal 12-person Prosperity Team might have one each of the following specialties/functions, but your local assets and challenges will probably necessitate some modifications to this template:

- Infrastructure renewal (energy, telecommunications, transportation, water, sewage, etc.);
- Brownfields remediation & reuse;
- Heritage structure renovation & reuse;
- Catastrophe recovery (natural disaster, human-made disaster, etc.);
- Ecosystem restoration & reconnection (boosting biodiversity);
- Watershed restoration (improving water quality & availability);
- Fishery restoration (aquatic or marine, commercial or recreational);
- Agricultural regeneration (restoring native pollinators, increasing topsoil quality/quantity, creating local food system to improve rural economy, reducing nutrient/pesticide runoff, etc.);
- Social renewal (housing, education, health, support services, etc.);
- Finance/economics (TIF, bonds, equity, grants, tax credits, entrepreneurial support, relocation & retention incentives, etc.);
- Policy/legal (reducing obstructions/adding incentives for renewal, etc.); and,

- Team leader.

Resilient solutions are 1) redundant; 2) flexible / scalable; and 3) integrative / strategic. The above team model would embody all of these qualities. By "integrative", I mean that team members could be from both the public and private side, with the private sector comprising members from for-profit and non-profit organizations, as well as residents. This helps remedy silos and fragmentation.

For instance, the policy expert might come from government, the brownfields remediation expert from an engineering firm, the ecosystem restoration expert from a non-profit or university, the finance expert could be your economic development official, and so on. With such a team creating more such teams, your resilient prosperity program would model the very resilience it's intended to create.

RE Facilitators should be doers, not just teachers. One of the major roadblocks to effective revitalization work is that making revitalization a responsibility of government means politicians have to actually DO something. Most elected leaders prefer to just approve or reject the proposed actions of others, not risk taking meaningful action themselves.

So, your Prosperity Team need not be limited to training. Just as Green Beret teams often fight alongside the local folks—despite their official status as "military advisors"—so too could your teams help implement projects. The key is in your selection of team members. If you want a prosperity team to actually design and launch a project, choose team members who bring the necessary resources (money, property, authority, etc.) to the table. That way, the team can instantly form a funding and implementation partnership when the project is approved.

REVITALIZING "RETIREMENTS"

> *"Most people die at 20*
> *and live until they are 75."* – Les Brown

I've been talking primarily about creating resilient prosperity as a vocation, but there are vast opportunities to do it as an avocation. The American dream of retirement that I grew up with is dying fast, and good riddance.

The vision of endless days of useless card games and golf was created primarily by Sunbelt retirement community developers in the mid-to-late 20th-

Century concept. I lived in Pinellas County, Florida (home to "wrinkle city": St. Petersburg) for 15 years. What kind of life is based on waiting to die?

One of my favorite things to witness is when someone retires from the U.S., Canada, or Europe to Latin America, and makes restoration the basis of their retirement. Gorgeous old haciendas become B&Bs, providing income on top of the therapy of turning something historic and decrepit into something vital and productive. The lovely city of Merida (in the state of Yucatan) has been greatly revitalized by the adoption and rehabilitation of so many of their restorable assets by northern retirees.

Of course, the revitalizing effect of being an ex-pat in Mexico is based as much on the restorative influence of the local people and culture as it is on any restorative activities. Read the 2011 book *Magic Made in Mexico* by Canadian author Joanna van der Gracht de Rosado for some good insights into this dynamic. Some such stories of rebirth can be simply traced to the adventurous spirit of those who pull up roots to start a wholly-new life, no doubt.

Here's an excerpt from *Magic Made in Mexico* about the resilience of the local culture: "*But many others are rooted in the effect of moving from a society where most folks barely know their neighbors' names, to a place where community is everything. I remember when Hurricane Isadora hit Mérida...the destruction was unbelievable. ...I figured it would be weeks before we could get back to normal. But...In just 24 hours, the roads were mostly clear; there were basic services downtown, and every day afterwards the improvement continued...neighbors all pitched in to clean up the streets. ...when the Mexican Caribbean was hit very hard (again, in 2005) by Hurricane Wilma, almost 60,000 tourists were evacuate from Cancun to Mérida (which is) not equipped to handle anything of magnitude, but the citizens opened their arms wide (took) people in and offered what they could. Students patrolled the streets looking for 'refugees'.*"

I saw this dynamic at work first-hand in the Mexico City earthquake of 1985. My wife and I arrived there the day after the earthquake, and was amazed to see how spontaneous work brigades instantly emerged to dig victims out of the rubble, and how private vehicles were instantly transformed into ambulances. Despite living in their country's capital, the citizens of Mexico City knew better than to rely on their federal government for assistance, something the citizens of New Orleans tragically learned the hard way.

> *"The secret to having a rewarding work-life balance is to have no life. Then it's easy to keep things in balance by doing no work."*
> *– Wally, February 21, 2014 Dilbert cartoon strip.*

As the preceding Dilbert quote suggests, the pursuit of balance might actually be silly. Except at the highest levels of organization—and when viewed from the longest timescales—little in nature exists in balance. The natural state of a healthy ecosystem or immune system is at the edge of chaos: enough order to maintain function, and enough adaptation to surprises to maintain resilience.

I saw first-hand how a lifestyle based on consumption and uselessness to society transformed "aging in place" to "rotting in place". Healthy adults in their late 50's and early 60's would arrive in our neighborhood, fresh from their retirement, and would proceed to age at an incredible rate, often dying in just two or three years. Read about the role of the elderly in traditional Asian and Native American societies and you'll quickly see how diseased America's passive "Golden Years" concept was. (I say "was" because the massive transfer of wealth from the middle class to the top 1% has now made such retirements impossible for most.)

The lesson here, as mentioned earlier, is that restoring and revitalizing our world restores and revitalizes us. What better time to do that than in the final third of life, when many of us are blessed with both resources, time, knowledge and (hopefully) some wisdom? And what better way to prepare for such a revitalizing "retirement" than to get certified as a Revitalization & Resilience Facilitator (RE Facilitator)?

A FEW FINAL THOUGHTS

> *"I think a hero is any person really intent on making this a better place for all people."*
> *— Maya Angelou*

In 1994, Nelson Mandela quoted author Marianne Williamson in his inaugural speech: *"Our deepest fear is not that we are inadequate. Our deepest fear is that we are powerful beyond measure."* Most folks seek endless diversion to avoid thinking about what a waste of potential their life represents. What better way to unleash our untapped power than to focus on improving the future for all, and getting trained to become more effective in that revitalizing work?

In her response to reading an early draft of this book, Nina Dauban, CEO of the Nottinghamshire Community Foundation (UK) said, *"We shouldn't worry that we can't see the future. We should worry about whether the future can see us."* Becoming a

RE Facilitator at the local, state/province, or national level is the finest way I know of for us to become "visible" to the future.

We *homo sapiens* weren't so wise during the Holocene Epoch: we've created a planet of assets that are now obsolete, fragmented, depleted, toxic, and/or decrepit...our ecosystems, energy sources, infrastructure, heritage, water, soil. Coupled with the climate crisis, even the newest of institutional plans and strategies are obsolete if they don't reflect this reality.

In an article titled Industrial watershed management in the September/October 2014 issue of World Water, author Jim Lauria wrote, "*A 2013 poll...found that 79% of companies...faced current water challenges, and 86 percent expected to face water challenges within 5 years. 57%...reported that water issues affected their bottom line; the same number stated water would affect their growth in the next 5 years; and 80% expected water to impact where they will locate a facility in the next 5 years. Growth, supply, and siting – if those aren't strategic issues, I don't know what is.*"

The adaptive renewal megatrend (theoretically) enables us to reverse climate change while simultaneously adapting to its disruptions. This is the ultimate convergence of importance (long-term priority) and urgency (short-term priority), and only the RECONOMICS Process (or something very similar) has any chance of addressing it.

Economic growth in places all around the globe is now increasingly based on novel ways of restoring, repurposing, reusing, replenishing, remediating, or reconnecting natural, built, and/or socioeconomic assets:

- Restored local food systems: They were the norm until half a century ago) are revitalizing urban and rural economies by linking the two;
- Coastal cities and island nations face declining fisheries, rising / acidifying seas, and superstorms: Boosting coastal resilience is a fast-growing, multi-billion-dollar industry;
- Cites, regions and territories (such as Puerto Rico) are busy adapting to the climate crisis switching to resilient renewable energy microgrids to reduce dependence on oil, and by revitalizing the local economy to reduce dependence on national government assistance;
- Rural communities are switching to regenerative farming and ranching to deal with accelerating topsoil loss, droughts, floods, loss of pollinators, catastrophic fires, and more.

Whether you're trying to make a community or nation more revitalized, more sustainable, or more resilient, all three goals require the same thing: a strategic, integrated process of repurposing, renewing, and reconnecting your natural, built, cultural, and socioeconomic assets.

The central problem in most government agencies isn't the people, it's in the limited mission and focus of the department. Planning isn't revitalization.

Economic development isn't revitalization. Revitalization is revitalization. And revitalization is the process of increasing the strength and vibrance of a living system...in whatever way is appropriate to that system.

One place might revitalize by increasing social justice, another by adding jobs, and yet another by restoring natural resources. The possible types of revitalization visions/goals are as endless as the diversity of problems.

To reiterate the key point one last time: a factory producing air conditioners has a process. A school producing graduates has a process. All professional managers seem to know that they need a process...except public leaders who promise revitalization.

In the February 1, 2019 issue of FORTUNE magazine, there was an excellent article by Rick Tetzeli about a new approach to researching treatments for Alzheimer's disease. For some 20 years, drug companies and government agencies have thrown billions of dollars into the effort, but every one of them was working from the same flawed assumption about the cause. As a result, effectively zero progress was achieved, and many are abandoning the effort.

Working with a comparatively tiny budget, a non-scientist named Paul Cox has made far more progress. His model brings together a broad variety of disciplines, rather than the normal siloed approach that hasn't worked. Here's what Dr. Zaven Khachaturian, editor of *Alzheimer's & Dementia*, said about Cox's work: "*One doesn't have to judge whether Cox's idea is good or not. His process is important.*"

A community or region wishing to produce economic growth and enhanced livability should have a RECONOMICS Process if they want to reliably produce revitalization. But most just have activities: a plan here, a project there, and a lot of hope that this will magically result in revitalization or resilience at some point.

Rather than relying on magic, it would be better if they had state and federal resilient prosperity training programs to help them create local renewal processes.

But the crucial factor is not who does it, but what is done. Many communities and regions are too dysfunctional to create any kind of new team, agency or program. So, the ideal solution in such cases might simply be a phone app. In fact, an app to support strategic renewal processes would be valuable, especially in the places that create excellent real-world organizations for resilient prosperity.

> *"We feel as if our lives count when—and only when—we brush against our dreams, with the fingertips of our days. When we feel them; when we know them; when we become them."*
> *– Umair Haque.*

Someone (maybe a company like Esri, or one of their licensees) needs to create a tool that allows any organization to (1) inventory and map a place's natural, built, and socioeconomic assets; (2) identify their condition (reusable, replaceable, or already-productive); and (3) tag them with any needed actions (repurpose, renew, reconnect). Planetary renewal could be the result.

Literally trillions of public and private dollars are already being invested annually on the repurposing, renewing and reconnecting of our natural, built and socioeconomic assets, producing pockets of resilient prosperity. Why aren't there more such pockets? Why isn't resilient prosperity more equitably distributed within those pockets?

Yep, you guessed it: lack of a template...a replicable strategic process based on a vision of resilient prosperity for all. For those of your who have read Blue Ocean Strategy and/or Blue Ocean Shift (both highly recommended), you'll understand what I mean when I say that a complete RECONOMICS Process would move a community or region out of the "red ocean" of thousands of communities doing exactly the same official activities, and into the "blue ocean" of places creating their own unique form of resilient prosperity.

People without hope don't take action.
Regenerative visions and regenerative strategies inspire regenerative action.
Regenerative action restores confidence in the future
by revitalizing the present.
Restoring confidence in the future revitalizes the future.

The Society of Revitalization & Resilience Professionals
IMPROVING THE PROCESS OF IMPROVING PLACES™

INDEX

100 Resilient Cities, 50, 119, 120, 272
3Re Strategy, 137, 138, 139, 140, 141, 143, 220, 221, 222, 223, 224, 226, 228, 229, 231, 232, 235, 237, 242, 280, 292, 320, 331, 385
accounting, 61, 65, 66, 70, 76, 193, 221, 243, 321, 356
Adam Smith, 75, 93
adaptive conquest, 32, 33, 45, 340
Adaptive management, 35, 36, 37, 41, 44, 50, 51, 54, 213, 256
adaptive renewal, 12, 33, 34, 40, 44, 45, 54, 77, 90, 91, 92, 130, 213, 282, 349, 351, 394
adaptive reuse, 34, 43, 69, 133, 221
adaptive systems, 24, 36, 40, 65, 319, 330, 340
affordable housing, 142, 164, 252, 268, 294
African-American, 62, 200, 301
air quality, 144, 145, 149, 195, 204, 287, 318, 335
Alan Mallach, 266, 298
Alberta, 207, 284, 286
Alexander Garvin, 14, 77, 332
American Planning Association, 1, 108, 109, 371, 372, *See* APA
Anacostia, 87, 203
anaerobic, 29
Anthropocene, 33, 66, 129, 213, 235, 290, 340, 342
APA, 108, 109, 371
Apple, 249
Aquifer, 57
architect, 182, 371, 381
Architects, 21, 110, 241, 297, 356
Arizona, 136, 325
Arkansas, 255
Arlington, 178, 276, 317
Asian, 200, 368, 393
Atlanta, 132, 133, 224, 239, 281, 335

Australia, 18, 37, 81, 89, 202, 239, 240, 268, 364
automobiles, 58, 176, 249, 261
Avinash Persaud, 274
Ball State University, 164
Baltimore, 112, 132, 169, 170, 171, 233, 283, 300, 301, 366
Battle Creek, 139
Belize, 38
Berrett Koehler, 8
Berrett-Koehler, 59, 196
BID, 78, 381
Big Dig, 350, 357
Bilbao, 341, 366
Bill Peduto, 42, 363
biosolids, 29
blight, 46, 62, 82, 84, 85, 87, 121, 137, 138, 139, 140, 141, 182, 183, 250, 268, 284, 349
Bloomingdale Trail, 224, 251
Bob Corker, 200, 205
Boeing, 24, 193
Boston, 2, 20, 45, 102, 203, 241, 242, 336, 350, 352, 357
Brazil, 107, 117, 148, 185, 241, 333
Brent Toderian, 179, 196
Brian Arthur, 36, 75, 76
Brisbane, 364
Britain, 157
British Columbia, 2, 8, 9, 19, 101, 237, 318
Brookings, 127, 144, 278, 352
brownfields, 6, 8, 9, 12, 47, 56, 58, 66, 69, 78, 81, 84, 87, 90, 91, 97, 99, 100, 101, 116, 122, 141, 144, 151, 185, 209, 213, 222, 282, 292, 297, 312, 316, 329, 335, 337, 345, 369, 383, 391
Bruce Katz, 127
Brutalist, 117, 133
Buffalo Bayou, 345, 347

Building Owners and Managers Association, 109
Bus Rapid Transit, 277
Cal Poly, 294
Calgary, 111, 202, 207, 279, 283, 284, 285, 286
California, 1, 10, 64, 84, 112, 136, 160, 200, 240, 267, 289, 325, 368
Camden, 122, 123
Canada, 5, 72, 90, 117, 136, 198, 202, 207, 231, 237, 239, 284, 285, 293, 318, 325, 372, 392
capitalism, 93
carbon, 10, 25, 28, 29, 30, 31, 38, 57, 89, 105, 106, 194, 225, 241, 259
Cardiff University, 212
Catastrophe, 58, 390
CDC, 78, 381
Center for American Progress, 290
Center for Community Progress, 138, 141, 142
Chamber of Commerce, 179, 381
Charleston, 20, 116, 372
Charlotte, 168
Chattanooga, 149, 187, 200, 204, 205, 206, 335, 341, 343, 366
Chesapeake, 87, 88
Chicago, 37, 64, 115, 162, 186, 224, 251, 252
Chief Resilience Officer, 28, 370
China, 45, 87, 220, 241, 263, 277, 281, 333
Chinese medicine, 255
Christie, 97, 122, 123
CIA, 104, 389
Cincinnati, 52, 84, 184, 313
city managers, 161, 264
Civil Rights, 217, 310
Clearwater, 125, 126, 127, 186
Cleveland, 62, 184, 207
climate adaptation, 51, 57, 259
climate crisis, 5, 7, 14, 19, 28, 29, 30, 31, 43, 57, 58, 105, 143, 149, 161, 177, 209, 231, 235, 236, 242, 259, 281, 309, 346, 394
climate resilience, 20, 51, 97, 189, 262, 280, 332, 371
climate restoration, 10, 29, 30, 31, 57, 58, 106, 225
CLT, 142, 143

coal, 67, 104, 105, 347
coastal, 14, 51, 221, 231, 235, 256, 281, 282, 291, 346, 394
Colombia, 54, 287, 349
Colorado, 47, 99, 152, 166, 233, 331
Columbus, 184, 216, 217, 336
Commonland, 89
community foundation, 202, 207, 208, 382
Community Land Trusts, 142
complex systems, 36, 44, 65, 289, 372
comprehensive plan, 51, 95, 109, 115, 211, 266, 292
Conference of Mayors, 90, 223
Congress, 127, 134, 203, 223, 272, 277, 310, 311, 312
Construction Specifications Institute, 109
Copenhagen, 276
Corporate Social Responsibility, 215
Cory Booker, 97
crowdfunding, 52, 78, 216
CSR, 215
Cummins, 216, 217, 218
Cuomo, 179, 198, 278, 316, 364
Curitiba, 185
Dam removal, 323
dams, 271, 290, 291, 323
Dan Kildee, 137
Dana Crawford, 233, 331
Danish Architecture Centre, 29
David Allen, 139
David Brooks, 81
David Korten, 59
daylighting, 95
Decade on Ecosystem Restoration, 89, 283
Denmark, 276
dense, 22, 340
Denver, 113, 166, 203, 233, 234, 331
Desertification, 71
designers, 21, 109, 217, 223, 238, 270, 294, 322, 355, 362
Detroit, 52, 184, 188, 203, 218, 224, 253, 276, 279, 363
Developers, 21, 52, 198, 205, 373
displacement, 23, 47, 142, 162, 163, 164, 165, 166, 167, 168, 170, 252, 253, 261, 310

District of Columbia, 120
Dominica, 244
Downtown Revitalization Initiative, 199, 364
downtowns, 6, 46, 65, 77, 81, 117, 156, 186, 187, 227, 258, 263, 271, 285, 364, 371
drug enforcement, 104
ecological restoration, 20, 36, 72, 87, 100, 205, 254, 284, 316, 342, 345, 346, 349
ecologists, 9, 15, 35, 36, 38, 39, 246, 349
EcoMobility, 158
economic developers, 9, 114, 122, 123, 124, 131, 268, 323, 333, 335, 336, 363, 364
economic development, 122, 258, 260, 395
economists, 67, 73, 74, 75, 80, 126, 282, 283
ecosystem restoration, 390
education, 209, 253, 355
Eisenhower, 107, 172
Ellen MacArthur Foundation, 56
Elon Musk, 249
emergent, 22, 23, 49, 52, 54, 75, 98, 190, 212, 272, 308, 348, 359, 361, 376, 378
Engineers, 21, 45, 189, 222, 290, 291, 315
England, 2, 47, 56, 67, 136, 148, 160, 182, 237, 240, 241, 244, 280, 316, 369
entrepreneur, 102, 153, 326
Environmental Protection Agency, 56, 217, 315, 372
Environmentalists, 21
EPA, 79, 87, 147, 204, 210, 217, 218
equitable, 26, 46, 90, 92, 130, 131, 132, 134, 135, 142, 156, 182, 196, 202, 252, 257, 262, 288, 323, 351, 371
Erasmus University, 89
Estuary, 57
Europe, 64, 89, 240, 325, 350, 392
European Bank for Reconstruction and Development, 281

extraction, 7, 32, 59, 61, 66, 69, 70, 80, 81, 150, 223, 247, 281, 284, 302, 380
Facilitator, 319, 340, 371, 372, 373, 374, 378, 379, 381, 384, 385, 387, 394
farming, 57, 150, 188, 194, 220, 225, 235, 246, 248, 260, 282, 337, 379, 394
FBI, 62, 104
Federation of Canadian Municipalities, 293
feedback, 16, 30, 39, 40, 70, 74, 75, 82, 90, 109, 110, 144, 278, 282, 338, 351, 355
feedback loop, 30, 40, 70, 82, 90, 110, 144, 278, 282, 338, 351
FEMA, 48, 173, 223
feminine, 148
Finland, 288
fishery, 5, 49, 57, 91, 185, 386
fishing, 5, 150, 235, 246, 271, 281, 282, 355
fixers, 28, 51, 52, 53, 78, 146, 204, 207, 376
flood, 51, 119, 172, 189, 194, 207, 233, 242, 274, 286, 310, 347, 352, 374
Florida, 15, 50, 51, 125, 126, 127, 229, 242, 392
flywheel, 7, 267, 308, 378
forest, 67, 99, 101, 105, 198, 248, 292, 332
forestry, 95, 235
fossil, 58, 61, 66, 70, 71, 80, 81, 97, 104, 149, 150, 236, 247, 286, 316, 342, 346
Four Point Approach, 155, 156
Foxconn, 333, 334
full-cost, 61, 65, 70, 76, 193, 221, 321
Gandhi, 75, 340
GDP, 70, 172, 243
General Electric, 97
gentrification, 23, 162, 163, 252, 310
Georgia, 83, 133, 138, 233, 239, 281, 335
Germany, 149, 171, 182, 217, 287
ghettos, 164
GIS, 184, 185, 292, 297
Google, 76, 78, 249

Government Alliance on Race and Equity, 164
governor, 91, 97, 122, 123, 170, 173, 179, 198, 200, 267, 277, 278, 304, 312, 316, 332, 333, 334, 368
Grand Rapids, 139, 203
Greece, 241
Green Berets, 159, 388, 389
Green Bonds, 86
green roof, 79, 386
green space, 254, 284
GreenTIF, 86, 87, 88, 89
Greenway Foundation, 233, 234
Hamilton, 72
happiness, 18, 22, 60, 110, 148, 149, 157, 244, 245, 248, 359, 360
Harrisburg, 82, 83
Hartford, 116
Harvard, 18, 68, 76, 210, 249, 322
Hebrew University, 339
Helen Keller, 273
Helsinki, 177
heritage, 6, 7, 9, 10, 39, 79, 90, 91, 100, 126, 144, 157, 160, 167, 175, 185, 195, 207, 220, 232, 233, 260, 282, 285, 292, 319, 322, 344, 345, 347, 359, 372, 378, 382, 386, 394
Heritage, 58, 90, 95, 390
Heron Foundation, 250
High Line, 45, 168, 224, 225, 226, 242, 251, 345, 374
Hiroshima, 159, 210
historic, 8, 12, 20, 27, 59, 62, 63, 64, 69, 71, 77, 78, 79, 81, 111, 112, 117, 122, 145, 151, 155, 157, 176, 178, 195, 209, 221, 227, 232, 233, 234, 237, 238, 253, 260, 271, 275, 284, 292, 304, 324, 331, 337, 345, 359, 364, 365, 369, 386, 392
historic preservation, 20, 62, 151, 157, 209, 227, 386
Holocene, 33, 38, 220, 340, 394
homeless, 131, 189, 199, 215
Hong Kong, 263
housing, 9, 16, 18, 20, 21, 41, 47, 66, 79, 84, 99, 110, 112, 116, 120, 121, 125, 129, 139, 141, 142, 145, 155, 162, 163, 164, 166, 167, 170, 176, 196, 202, 221, 227, 234, 237, 238, 240, 252, 253, 259, 260, 268, 270, 275, 276, 282, 284, 293, 301, 310, 316, 317, 318, 344, 359, 360, 364, 366, 390
Houston, 345, 347
Hudson Yards, 226
Hungary, 148
ICLEI, 158, 222
ICMA, 15
incarceration, 104, 243
inclusive, 5, 10, 47, 90, 92, 99, 118, 130, 131, 132, 134, 135, 142, 148, 163, 253, 257, 258, 308, 323, 352, 371, 375, 379
incremental, 20, 28, 52, 61, 70, 87, 169, 246, 287
India, 46, 101, 256, 333
Indiana, 64, 216, 217
Indonesia, 148, 257, 281
industrial, 6, 31, 38, 39, 53, 57, 71, 82, 85, 87, 101, 110, 148, 150, 162, 172, 175, 188, 194, 205, 220, 221, 233, 238, 239, 241, 248, 253, 254, 259, 284, 289, 300, 304, 323, 332, 335, 366, 374
infill, 58, 69, 81, 125, 297
infrastructure, 6, 8, 9, 12, 20, 21, 24, 27, 29, 37, 39, 46, 51, 54, 58, 62, 74, 78, 80, 81, 84, 86, 87, 90, 91, 92, 97, 100, 101, 102, 113, 116, 119, 121, 122, 124, 126, 135, 139, 141, 151, 157, 160, 165, 175, 176, 185, 200, 207, 208, 209, 212, 213, 220, 221, 222, 223, 224, 232, 235, 236, 237, 238, 239, 242, 243, 251, 254, 256, 257, 258, 259, 260, 265, 269, 275, 277, 278, 279, 282, 290, 297, 304, 308, 313, 314, 318, 319, 322, 325, 331, 333, 334, 337, 345, 347, 351, 352, 367, 371, 382, 383, 385, 387, 394
Innovation districts, 265
International Economic Development Council, 123
invasive species, 8, 39, 345
InvestAtlanta, 123
Israel, 339
Italy, 347
Jakarta, 281
Jane Jacobs, 111, 206, 340
Japan, 63, 210

Jenny A. Durkan, 129, 240
Jerry Brown, 200, 267, 368
Jim Lauria, 394
Joe Riley, 372
John Hicks, 75
John Ruskin, 53, 148
Johns Hopkins, 233
Joseph Stiglitz, 93
Judith Rodin, 48, 49
justice, 21, 23, 92, 97, 100, 129, 132, 135, 157, 167, 168, 170, 179, 235, 247, 262, 309, 359, 378, 380, 381, 395
Kalamazoo, 139, 140, 141
Kent County Land Bank, 140
Kentucky, 156, 223
Knight Foundation, 64, 203, 285
Koch, 85
Kurt Lewin, 6
land bank, 78, 137, 138, 139, 140, 141, 142, 143
Land Bank, 62, 63, 120, 121, 138, 139, 140, 141, 184
land value tax, 81, 82, 83
landscape, 15, 89, 182, 209, 241, 269, 345, 356
Las Vegas, 97, 117, 164, 220
Latino, 200
Law enforcement, 21
LEED, 205
Lisbon, 48
local food systems, 157, 182, 254, 346, 394
London, 70, 111, 163, 237, 240, 254, 274
Los Angeles, 29, 77, 87, 120, 189, 240, 275, 331, 345
Louisiana, 14, 43, 91
lumber, 81, 215, 261, 281, 283
Main Street Program, 156, 227
Maine, 88, 136, 282
mangrove, 57, 105
Manhattan, 41, 45, 224, 226, 330, 331, 344, 374
mapping, 78, 185, 199, 297
Marjorie Kelly, 59
Mark Gerzon, 196
Mark Zuckerberg, 97
Marquette, 289
Martin Luther King, 75, 79

Maryland, 101, 169, 170, 244
Massachusetts, 2, 45, 72, 73, 91, 242, 275, 350
mayors, 6, 9, 19, 53, 62, 82, 96, 106, 107, 108, 121, 124, 161, 163, 165, 199, 211, 214, 263, 264, 348, 362, 363, 368, 372, 374, 375, 387
McGill University, 254, 288
Medellín, 54, 287, 349
Mediterranean, 34
Melbourne, 37, 268
Memphis, 250
Merida, 392
Mexico, 81, 135, 136, 148, 231, 243, 244, 277, 281, 290, 332, 392
Michigan, 37, 47, 137, 138, 139, 140, 203, 216, 289
Microsoft, 273
middle class, 163, 164, 247, 351, 393
Mike Duggan, 363
Mike Tyson, 42
military base, 130
Milton Friedman, 93
Milton Keynes, 47
Milwaukee, 86, 113
minimum viable process, 7, 16, 107, 115
minimum wage, 134
mining, 67, 81, 104, 150, 215, 223, 261, 283
Minnesota, 60, 84, 310, 335
Missouri, 138, 187, 270
mixed-age, 164, 253, 344, 345, 346, 347
Mixed-income, 164, 261, 345
mixed-race, 165, 310
mixed-use, 77, 164, 175, 187, 221, 226, 241, 242, 330, 344, 345, 346, 347, 355
mobility, 95
Monsanto, 214
Montgomery County, 244
Mumbai, 46
Namibia, 71
Nanjing, 241
Napoleon, 34, 161
National Trust for Historic Preservation, 155, 371
natural resource restoration, 13, 50, 80, 97, 130, 332, 340

natural resources, 27, 33, 44, 51, 56, 59, 60, 66, 67, 69, 74, 77, 86, 88, 92, 94, 105, 132, 157, 167, 173, 195, 202, 243, 247, 258, 279, 282, 291, 304, 309, 367, 371, 395
Nature Conservancy, 91
Nelson Mandela, 75, 393
Netflix, 65, 250
Netherlands, 89
New Jersey, 14, 97, 122, 123, 238, 304, 315, 323, 335, 363
New Orleans, 20, 52, 118, 119, 120, 274, 392
New Urbanism, 117
New York City, 20, 37, 170, 171, 225, 226, 237, 238, 242, 263, 287, 316, 317, 331, 336, 363, 374
Newark, 97, 363
Niagara Falls, 136
NIMBYism, 210
Nina Dauban, 393
North America, 64, 185
North Carolina, 91, 123, 168, 231, 291
Nova Scotia, 5
nuclear, 106, 159, 193, 221, 280
Oakland, 10, 200, 201
ocean, 88, 150, 235, 281, 282, 304, 342, 396
Ohio, 62, 138, 184, 207, 216, 312, 313
oil, 47, 85, 91, 192, 207, 215, 223, 279, 283, 284, 285, 286, 358, 394
Oklahoma, 85
Ontario, 72, 117, 136, 231, 233, 239
Oregon, 59, 112, 176, 323
Oscar Wilde, 42
Pam Warhurst, 160
Paris, 64, 66, 67, 177, 224
parking, 40, 41, 113, 116, 126, 176, 196, 253, 355, 364, 386
partnerships, 26, 27, 82, 96, 99, 108, 138, 142, 143, 147, 157, 168, 184, 200, 205, 208, 209, 223, 257, 258, 261, 292, 298, 300, 302, 304, 307, 316, 318, 322, 324, 325, 337, 357, 370, 378, 383, 385
pedestrianization, 158, 232
Pennsylvania, 81, 82, 83, 105, 120, 138, 225, 226, 233, 278, 333, 363
Pete Seeger, 54
Philadelphia, 120, 123, 124, 136, 141, 142, 199, 208, 213, 224, 226, 345
philanthropy, 202, 203, 204, 215, 261
photovoltaic, 193, 222
Pinellas County, 125, 392
Pittsburgh, 42, 52, 81, 82, 120, 123, 206, 233, 363
placemaking, 118, 356
planners, 9, 15, 21, 46, 62, 107, 108, 109, 110, 111, 112, 113, 114, 115, 116, 117, 131, 163, 188, 230, 246, 252, 257, 263, 269, 270, 271, 272, 294, 315, 322, 334, 344, 346, 355, 356, 362, 363, 364, 365, 368, 369, 371, 375, 381
planning mistakes, 48, 173, 176, 350
Plato, 123, 214, 349
policy, 25, 37, 38, 46, 66, 69, 73, 77, 80, 82, 112, 121, 128, 135, 151, 168, 172, 173, 198, 209, 213, 221, 231, 250, 260, 267, 269, 280, 292, 295, 300, 308, 309, 310, 311, 313, 314, 315, 316, 317, 318, 323, 330, 332, 351, 352, 368, 379, 383, 391
policymaking, 10, 40, 46, 65, 112, 212, 310, 311, 313, 314, 315, 316, 322, 342, 364
politicians, 10, 31, 35, 46, 47, 65, 69, 70, 106, 108, 134, 145, 149, 150, 172, 214, 230, 249, 255, 265, 325, 333, 334, 342, 343, 361, 363, 364, 366, 391
pollution, 8, 31, 38, 81, 88, 106, 121, 175, 204, 243, 343
population, 18, 22, 32, 33, 52, 55, 62, 66, 71, 78, 82, 85, 91, 110, 121, 126, 162, 163, 175, 178, 188, 211, 212, 216, 258, 264, 277, 278, 281, 284, 288, 293, 299, 351, 356, 380
Portland, 102, 112, 176
Portugal, 34, 48
poverty, 31, 80, 163, 164, 165, 182, 204, 229, 243, 250, 253, 295, 301, 349, 352, 372, 381
program managers, 272
Project Management Institute, 272
project managers, 21, 272
public transit, 40, 58, 80, 81, 85, 86, 116, 122, 158, 176, 177, 195, 196,

238, 240, 241, 253, 254, 259, 260, 293, 349, 366
public works, 209, 359, 385
Puolanka, 288
quality of life, 5, 8, 11, 13, 16, 17, 23, 26, 31, 41, 45, 46, 49, 59, 66, 69, 80, 81, 83, 90, 116, 122, 126, 129, 157, 160, 166, 167, 177, 179, 188, 194, 195, 207, 211, 219, 229, 234, 258, 262, 263, 269, 274, 283, 284, 286, 288, 296, 297, 299, 331, 332, 333, 350, 351, 352, 354, 371, 380, 387
Queensland, 37, 364
Rails To Trails, 227
Ralph Waldo Emerson, 151
RE Facilitators, 199, 370, 374, 375, 376, 377, 381, 383, 385, 391
real estate investor, 248, 383
RECONOMICS Institute, 4, 375, 380
reconstruction, 10, 58, 131, 243, 247, 256, 257, 297
recovery, 12, 15, 48, 97, 119, 122, 202, 256, 257, 259, 286, 294, 295, 297, 328, 343, 358, 377, 378, 381, 384, 390
redevelopment, 1, 2, 8, 12, 16, 17, 19, 20, 25, 26, 49, 51, 52, 53, 58, 61, 66, 69, 77, 82, 83, 84, 85, 86, 87, 88, 90, 93, 98, 99, 106, 110, 112, 115, 123, 124, 125, 126, 130, 132, 135, 144, 145, 164, 169, 170, 171, 173, 175, 181, 187, 196, 200, 216, 225, 226, 228, 229, 230, 239, 240, 242, 243, 256, 258, 259, 260, 261, 265, 267, 268, 270, 271, 275, 276, 284, 287, 289, 290, 292, 298, 300, 302, 307, 309, 312, 319, 321, 322, 325, 332, 337, 339, 344, 345, 346, 347, 350, 351, 353, 355, 358, 359, 360, 361, 362, 363, 364, 368, 379, 381, 385
reductionism, 99
redundant, 49, 384, 391
reef, 53, 57, 379
regenerative agriculture, 10, 20, 89, 105, 194, 220, 225, 248
remediation, 8, 12, 56, 58, 61, 79, 84, 90, 116, 123, 144, 209, 213, 254, 345, 379, 390, 391

renewable energy, 104
reSWOT, 376
retention, 98, 145, 390
Rewealth, 11, 59, 117, 168, 200, 206, 325
RFP, 297, 298, 364
Rick Rybeck, 170
Rio de Janeiro, 107, 372
River, 59, 87, 120, 136, 176, 177, 189, 208, 233, 234, 238, 275, 345
Robert Moses, 48
Roberta Brandes Gratz, 52
Rockefeller, 48, 49, 119, 120, 201, 203, 272
Rodale Institute, 225
ROI, 9, 16, 21, 90, 208, 226, 233, 309, 377
Roosevelt, 49, 56, 192
Rotterdam, 89, 224, 240
Russia, 148, 161, 238
Rust Belt, 65, 204
Ruth Glass, 163
Rwanda, 26
Ryerson University, 231, 232
salmon, 88
San Francisco, 112, 168, 200, 263, 284, 354
Santa Clara, 113
Sasaki, 241, 242
Savannah, 20, 52, 180, 233
schools, 12, 52, 84, 85, 133, 165, 170, 200, 203, 210, 212, 213, 217, 226, 233, 253, 256, 270, 301, 336, 380
Scientology, 126
sea level rise, 11, 14, 44, 50, 51, 54, 143, 221, 281, 346, 347
Seattle, 129, 240, 336
seaweed, 57
security, 135, 149, 166, 320, 351, 352
Seoul, 224
sequestration, 57, 105, 194
sewer, 37, 38, 126, 199, 313, 325
Shanghai, 220, 241
Silicon Valley, 113, 154
silos, 98, 100
Singapore, 92, 224
Sociologists, 21
solar, 105
South Africa, 89, 158, 277

South Carolina, 99, 116, 179, 193, 223, 244
South Korea, 148
Spanish, 34
Special Forces, 159, 388, 389, 390
sprawl, 22, 26, 32, 38, 40, 47, 52, 55, 58, 59, 65, 66, 69, 70, 71, 80, 81, 84, 85, 92, 99, 111, 124, 167, 180, 195, 198, 221, 233, 239, 241, 243, 254, 258, 259, 260, 263, 268, 275, 284, 286, 292, 302, 305, 314, 319, 321, 344, 379, 380
St. Louis, 270
stakeholder engagement, 98, 148, 253, 266, 319, 323
Stanford University, 228
steel, 25, 64, 196, 215, 241
Stephen R. Reed, 82
Stewart Brand, 43
Stockholm, 241
Stonington, 282
stormwater, 38, 240, 258, 313
strategic plan, 119, 120, 141, 178
Streamkeepers, 8, 10
Sustainable, 68, 71, 72, 79, 237
Sweden, 241
tactical urbanism, 160
Tampa, 125, 126, 127, 227, 229, 230, 231
tar sands, 61, 284
Tax increment financing, 83
taxes, 80, 81, 82, 83, 85, 86, 87, 88, 124, 126, 167, 168, 333, 363
Temple University, 82
Tennessee, 138, 149, 187, 204, 205, 244, 250
Texas, 135, 136, 156, 284, 286, 325
The Restoration Economy, 8, 10, 11, 30, 48, 56, 57, 58, 59, 65, 91, 94, 184, 197, 223, 225, 243, 268, 283, 301, 323, 332, 340, 390
TIF District, 83, 85
TIGER Grant, 41
tipping point, 8, 30, 39, 74, 272, 283, 289, 293, 338
TOD, 223
Todmorden, 160
Tony Hsieh, 97, 164
topsoil, 55, 71, 92, 150, 340, 351, 390, 394

Toronto, 43, 61, 136, 210, 224, 231, 232, 239
tourism, 95, 334
transition management, 245, 247, 290, 291
transit-oriented, 40, 116, 160, 196, 240, 275, 276, 285, 379
transportation, 27, 58, 101, 110, 176, 183, 228, 242, 249, 251, 253, 254, 275, 286, 325, 337, 390
Trust For Public Land, 251
Union of Concerned Scientists, 67
United Arab Emirates, 192
urban renewal, 46, 47, 111, 112, 113, 116, 117, 269, 315, 368
Vancouver, 8, 318
Venezuela, 274
Venice, 347
Vermont, 173, 316
Victoria, 232, 268
Vietnam, 13, 172, 205, 343, 388, 389
Virginia, 115, 133, 138, 178, 193, 271, 276, 317, 325, 336, 351
wabi-sabi, 63, 64
Wales, 67, 81, 239
Washington, 23, 26, 62, 87, 101, 116, 129, 146, 162, 178, 203, 207, 215, 240, 243, 276, 310, 317, 355
Washington, DC, 23, 26, 62, 87, 101, 146, 203, 207, 215, 243, 276, 355
Waterloo, 117, 118, 161
watershed, 8, 9, 10, 57, 79, 81, 90, 91, 100, 152, 185, 194, 195, 223, 292, 308, 337, 345, 346, 362, 364, 379, 383, 385, 386, 390, 394
wetlands, 6, 14, 78, 238, 240, 270, 315, 334
Whole Oceans, 88
William Siembieda, 294
Winston Churchill, 149
Wisconsin, 86, 162, 333, 334
Worcester, 275
workforce, 9, 98, 116, 129, 170, 217, 220, 259, 277, 336, 337
World Economic Forum, 144, 219
Yale University, 356
Yorkshire, 160, 369
Youngstown, 62
Yucatan, 392
zero-sum, 122

RECONOMICS

Made in the USA
Middletown, DE
21 March 2020